D1637120

BANNERS SOUTH

CIVIL WAR IN THE NORTH

Series Editor,
LESLEY J. GORDON,
University of Akron
Advisory Board

WILLIAM BLAIR,
Pennsylvania State University

PETER S. CARMICHAEL,
University of North Carolina Greensboro

STEPHEN D. ENGLE,
Florida Atlantic University

J. MATTHEW GALLMAN,
University of Florida

ELIZABETH LEONARD,
Colby College

ELIZABETH VARON,
Temple University

JOAN WAUGH,
University of California Los Angeles

BANNERS
South
A Northern Community at War

EDMUND J. RAUS JR.

The Kent State University Press
Kent, Ohio

© 2005 by The Kent State University Press, Kent, Ohio 44242
All rights reserved
Library of Congress Catalog Card Number 2005010935

ISBN-10: 0-87338-842-9
ISBN-13: 978-0-87338-842-9

Manufactured in the United States of America

09 08 07 06 05   5 4 3 2 1

Library of Congress Cataloging-in-Publication Data
Raus, Edmund J., 1945–
      Banners south : a northern community at war / Edmund J. Raus Jr.
          p. cm. — (Civil War in the North)   ∞
      Includes bibliographical references and index.
      ISBN-13: 978-0-87338-842-9 (alk. paper)
          1. United States. Army—Military life—History—19th century. 2. Soldiers—New
York (State)—Cortland—Biography. 3. Soldiers—New York (State)—Cortland—
Social conditions—19th century. 4. Cortland (N.Y.)—History, Military—19th cen-
tury. 5. Cortland (N.Y.)—Biography. 6. Cortland (N.Y.)—Social conditions—19th
century. 7. New York (State)—History—Civil War, 1861–1865—Social aspects. 8.
United States—History—Civil War, 1861–1865—Social aspects. 9. United States—
History—Civil War, 1861–1865—Campaigns. I. Title. II. Series.
F129.C83R38   2005
973.7′44772—dc22   2005010935

British Library Cataloging-in-Publication data are available.

IN MEMORY OF MY GRANDMOTHER

Sarah Augusta Bowker Curtis
(1885–1972)

Youth! Ah Youth!
The wellspring of Desire
Wrap me in thy Banner
Consume me by thy Fire

CONTENTS

Preface

Our lives pass in a series of circumstances, made meaningful by memory. We live in the world, take our sustenance from the days, but the lifeline of the spirit forever draws upon the people, places, and lost special moments of our past.

Some of my fondest memories are of Cortland, New York. Although I was born there, in November 1945, my family not long after moved to Syracuse, New York, leaving Cortland for me a place of special holidays, cool summers, and affectionate, doting grandparents. Children, of course, can readily appreciate the unhurried nature of a small town, where their bicycles can take them most everywhere worth going and the world moves to their pace rather than to the adult rush of larger cities. I remember summer evenings after supper when the quiet street in front of my grandparents' house would be given over to the neighborhood youngsters for games of kick-the-can or capture-the-flag. At dark a mother's shrill whistle for her children to return home officially ended the day.

My grandmother, Sarah Augusta "Gussie" Curtis, lived most of her life on Harrington Avenue. She was a tall woman, with her middle girth daily encased in a heavy, ribbed corset that felt like the trunk of a maple tree when I hugged her. She had many friends in the community: I can still recall those seemingly interminable conversations with Mss. Sanders, Gutches, Ames, and so many other of her acquaintances who stopped to chat during our walks down Main Street. She belonged to a number of local civic and church organizations, and she was particularly proud of her membership in the Daughters of the American Revolution.

One summer day while sitting in the sunporch overlooking the garden below, my grandmother imparted to me the family story. Now, I believe that most families have stories or traditions that are passed on from generation to generation and contribute to a person's identity. That particular day she told me of our relative Gilbert Edgcomb from Groton, Connecticut, who at age fifteen in 1777 joined the 1st Connecticut Regiment of Foot and served with George Washington at Valley Forge. Upon his discharge from service Gilbert returned to Groton, where, on the morning of September 6, 1781, while clearing brush with a scythe, he heard the alarm guns fire from nearby Fort Griswold. He arrived at the fort shortly before it came under British attack, led by the infamous Benedict Arnold. The fort fell after a brief but fierce struggle. Edgcomb and about thirty other survivors were bound and forced to remain prisoners, first in the hold of a British man-of-war in New York Harbor and then on land in a sugarhouse. Gilbert suffered a number of indignities at the hands of the British, including having to eat rats to survive. He was released to return home after the British surrender at Yorktown.

My grandmother told me the Edgcomb story with emphasis, especially the part about eating rats. At times she read from a yellowed piece of paper that documented the event in the words of Gilbert's grandson Isaac. Obviously she intended the story to serve as a source of family pride and inspiration. She then showed me the Civil War letters of Isaac's brother, George, and told me stories about George and his other brothers, the soldiers Martin and Clark, whom she had known personally. Viewing their photographs and listening to stories of Gilbert and the rest, I realized the fragility of time and the power of memory to compress the years. Dim shadows emerged for me as fully formed individuals who had once walked the streets of Cortland and led lives not dissimilar to our own despite the daily circumstances and trappings of their times. I came to see the study of history as a striving to understand the common life struggles of individuals whose collective actions shape the fate of families, towns, and nations.

My intent in writing this book is to illuminate the major themes and events of the first two years of the Civil War in the eastern theater from the perspective and experience of Cortland soldiers and civilians. My starting point will be the letters of drummer George Washington Edgcomb and those of his comrades in the "Cortland Volunteers"—Company H, 23d New York Volunteers. This two-year regiment of infantry belonged to the Army of the Potomac and fought in the major battles of Second Bull Run, Antietam, and Fredericksburg. I also suggest that the war experience of the central New York farm communities represented by the 23d was not unlike that of many other of the rural counties that made up much of the Civil War–era North. By the use of extensive and previously untapped primary source material, I present a profile of the Union soldier from up-state New York: why he enlisted; how he lived, marched, and fought; his attitudes toward slaves, African Americans in general, and Southerners; the homefront influences on his service; and his successful reintegration into civilian life. I will show that despite the shifting course of the war, the one sustaining surety for Cortland soldiers and civilians was their belief in and commitment to the cause of the Union and a reunited nation.

I have many people to thank for their assistance and support in my efforts: Edwin C. Bearss, historian emeritus, National Park Service; Bob Krick and John Hennessy, Fredericksburg and Spotsylvania National Military Park; Noel Harrison, Fredericksburg, Virginia; Brian C. Pohanka, Alexandria, Virginia; Ray Brown, Jim Burgess, and Becky Cumins, Manassas National Battlefield Park; Ted Alexander and Keith Snyder, Antietam National Battlefield Park; Mike Musick, National Archives, Washington, D.C.; Amy Wilson, Chemung County Historical Society, Elmira, New York; Daniel D. Lorello, Archivist, New York State Archives and Records Administration, Albany, New York; Dick Buchanan and Carl Morrell, Elmira, New York; David W. Hayt, Los Angeles, California; Seward Osborne, Olivebridge, New York; Ronald G. Matteson, Walworth, New York; Mary Ann Kane and Anita Wright, Cortland County Historical Society, Cortland, New York; and Bob Mudge, Groton, New York. The maps were drawn by John Heiser.

Prologue

A pril had come again, bringing with it the unmistakable proof that Cortland had shaken off another one of its nagging winters. That particular April day began like most others. Children with their lunch bags hurried down the center of Main, Court, and Port Watson streets in Cortland Village heading toward the district schoolhouses on Church Street. Along Main Street young store clerks, like the twenty-year-old George Edgcomb of the dry goods establishment of S. E. Welch, busied themselves getting ready to open for business. By all outward appearances it was the start of another uneventful day, except for the anticipated installation of a new telegraph office in Aaron Sager's drugstore near the corner of Court and Main. A mechanic down from Syracuse worked on the connection most of the day, much to the interest of the locals, who occasionally dropped by to note his progress. Come evening, his work completed, the operator strolled down Main Street to the Eagle Hotel for supper. Upon his return, however, he noticed that quite a crowd had gathered around the telegraph instrument, which was ticking as the first message came in. The man hushed the crowd as he studied the tape. "Is that so?" he muttered to himself in exclamation. Then, turning to the waiting onlookers he shouted, "Fort Sumter has been fired upon!" The crowd dispersed into the street to spread the alarm. The date was April 12, 1861.[1]

In the turbulent days that followed the fall of Fort Sumter, Cortland County struggled to do its part to put down the Southern rebellion. From a population of about 26,000, the county furnished more than 1,500 soldiers[2] and suffered about 310 service-related deaths. Today, the names of the county's 115 or so battle dead appear etched in polished granite on a monument placed on the grounds of the county courthouse. This study will assist the passerby to understand how many of the familiar Cortland surnames came to be there.

CHAPTER 1

The City
of the Seven Valleys

The early history of Cortland, New York, is told in the story of Moses Hopkins and Jonathan Hubbard, who in 1794 climbed a tall tree on the prominent gumdrop-shaped hill later named Court House Hill, or Monroe Heights, to survey the wooded countryside. Around them seven valleys seemed to converge like the spokes of a wheel. Thick stands of beech, elm, and hemlock concealed the dark valley floors where hunted the bear, wolf, panther, and occasional Indian party. Up the steep hillsides, two to five hundred feet high, large maple, oak, and chestnut trees spread their broad branches to the sunlight. Looking to the east about a mile and a half they could see through the trees the sparkling waters of the stream Tioughnioga, a name given by the Indians that meant "waters with flowers overhanging their banks." The stream flowed south to join eventually the Susquehanna River on its journey to the Chesapeake Bay.[1]

Here, surely, was a new land unspoiled and full of promise. Sheltered by nature on the back side of the Appalachian Mountains, the area had been set aside by the New York state legislature as part of the million-and-a-half-acre military tract for use by Revolutionary War veterans as bounty lands. Since few of the veterans chose to settle on their allotted six hundred-acre parcels, at the end of the eighteenth century the area opened for new settlers, speculators, and talented young entrepreneurs like Hopkins and Hubbard.

From 1808, when Cortland became a county—taking its name from New York's first lieutenant governor, Pierre Van Cortlandt—the progressive leaders of the community struggled mightily to fulfill the vision of the area's early pioneers. They settled in townships and gave them such classical and historical names as Preble, Truxton, Homer, Solon, Virgil, and Cincinnatus. For the principal villages of Homer and Cortland they laid out broad Main Streets, where wealthy and influential families like the Barbers and Randalls built pretentious and conspicuous houses and gardens. Cortland Village won a competition to be the site of the new county seat. In 1813 the village proudly opened the doors of the new frame courthouse perched on the brow of the hill that had first inspired Hopkins and Hubbard.[2]

Cortland's beginnings coincided with a time of general optimism in America based upon an abiding faith in the individual's ability to achieve his or her potential and, in the process, advance the interests of a democratic society. The 1812–43 religious revivals that overtook Cortland's evangelical Protestant churches encouraged the individualistic approach to the awakening of religious faith and personal salvation, which shook up the more authoritarian and moralistic Calvinist beliefs of their New England forbears. Education and knowledge were idealized as critical elements of self-improvement. District public schools and church Sunday schools proliferated, as well as institutions of higher learning, including Cortland Academy at Homer (1819–73), Cortlandville Academy at Cortland Village (1842–69), and the New York Central College of Mc-Grawville (1849–60). In its day, New York Central College represented a bold experiment in liberal education. Founded in 1848, it opened its doors to all, "regardless of sex, color or religious belief." In the early years of the college, about a third of the students were black, and half were women. Both blacks and women could and did serve on the faculty.[3]

But the inspired work of the county boosters faced many obstacles. Poor, gravelly soil, long winters, and short growing seasons limited the county's major agricultural crops to wheat, corn, oats, and potatoes. By 1845 two-thirds of the productive land had been developed, with most of it (75 percent), of necessity, devoted to raising livestock, dairy products, maple sugar, and hardy varieties of fruit trees.[4]

At the same time the surrounding hills isolated Cortland from the full benefits of the Erie Canal, which had been completed across the central part of the state in 1825. Without a supportive transportation system,

Cortland Village, New York, around 1870. View of Main Street
looking north from Port Watson Street. Squires Hall was located in this block.
(Author's collection)

commercial agriculture and manufacturing were slow to develop in Cortland. Adding to the county's economic woes, by 1840 the flow of water
in the Tioughnioga had diminished to the extent that the flat-bottomed
"arks" that had once carried gypsum, salt, oats, potatoes, pottery, whiskey, and other Cortland products to market could no longer float downriver on spring freshets from launch points near the community of Port
Watson. By 1860 the county lagged behind most other New York counties
in manufactured value per capita. With a sluggish economy and productive land no longer readily available, population growth slowed—only 0.3
percent per year from 1830 to the Civil War.[5]

In national politics the county marginally voted Whig from 1828 until 1856, then Republican for the presidential elections of 1856 and 1860 (favoring Abraham Lincoln 3,893 votes to 1,712). For the most part, the county supported Whig-Republican policies favoring "internal improvements," economic growth, the temperance movement, and opposition to the extension of slavery into the western territories. While most residents considered slavery a national curse and anathema to a democratic society, they did not go so far as to embrace the abolitionist cause of immediate slave emancipation in the South or the concept of social equality for free blacks. When John Thomas, a member of the state assembly and staunch abolitionist, joined forces with some church and community leaders to form Cortland's first antislavery society in 1837, he and his colleagues were labeled "fanatics." The prominent and influential Democrat Henry S. Randall led the attack against this group in the *Cortland Advocate*. He spoke against what he identified as Thomas's "scheme of agitation," which would result only in the "embroiling neighborhoods and families——setting friend against friend—overthrowing churches and institutions of learning—embittering one portion of the land against the other."[6]

Cortland's pro-abolitionist minority found political voice in the Liberty party, organized locally in 1841. Although the Liberty vote in Cortland showed some strength in the 1844 elections, by 1848 resident Samuel Ringgold Ward, a former slave and now a Presbyterian minister, could garner only 120 county votes in his bid for the state assembly on the Liberty ticket. Embittered over his defeat, Ward left the county for greener pastures, declaring that Cortland represented for him "more of the foolishness, wickedness, and at the same time the invincibility of American Negro–hate, than I ever saw elsewhere."[7]

In general, Cortland residents shunned the abolitionist demand for collective social action and change in the service of what they perceived to be the radical and unlawful political and social agenda of a few. When the Reverend John Keep in 1833 strayed from the gospel to preach abolition and social reform from his pulpit in the Homer Congregational Church, he was forced to resign. John Thomas eventually left Cortland for Syracuse, Onondaga County, where he thought he could more fruitfully promote Liberty party causes. The New York Central College, derisively referred to as a "nigger" college by some, closed its doors in 1860, not only because of the controversial racial issues of the day that embroiled it but also because of community indifference and lack of local financial support.[8]

Like many American communities in the 1850s, Cortland County staked its future on the coming of the railroad. The Syracuse, Binghamton, and New York Railroad, which ran across the county through Homer and Cortland Village, began operation in 1854 under its first president, Judge Henry Stephens of Cortland. Dignitaries and supporters celebrated the long-awaited completion of the road on October 9, 1854. On that day citizens gathered near the Tioughnioga just south of Cortland Village to drive the final spike. As two locomotives touched their cowcatchers, symbolizing the official opening of the road, cheers from the crowd competed with screeching train whistles and the thunderous sound of cannon fired from Court House Hill.[9]

The railroad opened on October 18, 1854, with an excursion train made up of three locomotives and twenty-eight cars, filled at one point with about two thousand "merry," albeit crowded, passengers. Throngs of people gathered beside the tracks along the route to salute the passing train with cheers, banners, music, the firing of cannon, bonfires, and the ringing of church bells. At an official Cortland stop the local ladies set out tables near the station laden with many good things to eat and drink for the passengers. A Cortland singing group, the "Melodeons," rode the train for a time, singing an ode to the people's faith in the ability of the iron rails to unite Cortland with the outside world in a wondrous future of mutual progress and growth. They sang:

> For lo we live in an iron-age,
> In the age of steam and fire.
> The world is too busy for dreaming,
> and has grown too wise for war,
> So, today, for the glory of science,
> Let us sing of the railway car.

Ironically, when conflict finally came, the railroads would serve as its indispensable agent, contributing to warfare's destructive power.[10]

On the eve of the Civil War, few could deny that Cortland County, despite its often difficult early history, had achieved a privileged maturity and was poised for a bright future. In 1855 the county boasted ninety-five merchants, twenty lawyers, fifty-six clergymen, forty-nine doctors, thirty-two inns, and 184 schoolhouses. In 1860 the population had reached 26,000, including sixteen African Americans and 1,300 foreign born (mostly Irish and English). There were fifty-five churches in the county (including nineteen Methodist and eleven Baptist), three newspapers, and three academies or secondary schools. The principal villages of Homer and Cortland had shown a 31 percent population growth over the previous three decades, to reach totals of about 1,600 and 2,000 residents, respectively. This ready and able workforce was to support the spurt in local manufacturing that would come in the 1870s.[11]

As sectional animosities intensified during the heated presidential election campaign of 1860, Cortland residents increasingly became drawn into national events. In the evenings, after dinner, those living in Cortland Village would often walk down Main Street to the dry goods stores of S. E. Welch or James S. Squires to discuss the issues of the day. Young George Edgcomb, who boarded with Welch and clerked in his store, recalled that the New York City papers, especially Horace Greeley's Republican *New York Tribune,* would be read out loud to the gathering by the store proprietor or his designee. The paper spoke out against the growing intransigence of the South concerning national economic and political matters, especially the volatile issue of extending slavery into the West. An often-told story indicates the temper of the times. It seems a young Cortlandville boy returning on the train from Syracuse with his mother brought smiles to the other passengers when, after the brakeman announced the town "Preble," he spoke up: "Mama, what made the man open the door and holler rebel?"[12]

However, before Fort Sumter, in Charleston Harbor, South Carolina, came under the fire of Southern forces on April 12, 1861, few in Cortland thought that the sectional differences between North and South would lead to war. William Saxton, a student at Cincinnatus Academy, expressed the common notion that there would be no fighting. "All we had to do," he thought, "would be to show those Southern fellows that we could not be browbeaten any longer; that if we put on a bold front . . . they would yield and all would be settled."

After Sumter fell on April 13 and President Lincoln called out the state militias, the enthusiasm for military action among the general population, if not their leaders, knew no bounds. The Cortland *Republican Banner* of May 1, 1861, reported that since April 12, "nothing else was talked of, and nothing thought of but punishment to the rebels." One Cortland soldier, John Lane, recalled from those days that "every time they went anywhere

George Edgcomb,
recruit. *(Author's collection)*

George Edgcomb,
veteran. *(Author's collection)*

or met anybody all they heard was War! War! War!" "What a picnic," Saxton and his schoolmates now thought, "to go down South for three months and clean up the whole business."[13]

As Cortland County braced for war, the initial opportunities for its young men to serve in the military were limited. Lincoln's April 15 call for 75,000 men obligated New York to a quota of 13,280 officers and men, or seventeen of its militia regiments. On the books of the state militia organization, Cortland County had two "active" companies of infantry and one of artillery, in the 42d Regiment, Nineteenth Brigade, Fifth Division. Actually, however, like most of the state militia regiments, the 42d was deficient in supplies and manpower and was in no condition to take the field.[14]

The situation changed on April 16, when the state legislature authorized Governor Edwin D. Morgan to enlist into state service about thirty thousand "Volunteer Militia" for two years' service. These men would be formed in companies and then organized into regiments by state authorities under state militia laws but "without regard to existing military districts." Thus, as the Federal government began accepting New York's available organized militia regiments (the famous 7th New York State Militia left the state on April 19, followed by ten others), the door opened for communities across the state to raise their own independent companies for active service. As a result, in about three months' time New York would accomplish the remarkable feat of organizing, equipping, and making available to the Federal government an additional forty-six infantry regiments, mustering about 38,000 officers and men.[15]

As the state prepared for war, Cortland citizens put pressure on their leaders to begin organizing county resources to respond to the national crisis. Notices went up in Cortland Village announcing a war meeting to be held at the courthouse on the evening of Saturday, April 20. That morning the Stars and Stripes, often homemade, suddenly appeared throughout the village, reflecting, as noted in the *Republican Banner,* the "patriotism of all, old and young." In the afternoon local militia member Alonzo Blodgett and Justice of the Peace P. Bacon Davis canvassed Main Street seeking the signatures of village elders in support of the evening program. The prominent local lawyer and Democrat Horatio Ballard at first refused to sign but later came around after negotiations placed him at the head of a slate of candidates to officiate over the meeting. Ballard won election as president and chairman of the meeting, serving with twenty-four vice presidents and six secretaries who represented Cortland's most respected and influential citizens.[16]

The stores on Main Street closed early Saturday afternoon so that all in the community could attend the evening event. The activities began with Major James C. Pomeroy leading a fife and drum corps and a procession of citizens through the streets of Cortland Village to the large, brick, Greek revival–style courthouse on the corner of Church and Court streets. The eager crowd pushed up the steps to fill the main hall, leaving hundreds more standing in the broad expanse of Court Street. Many of the women occupied the galleries and "vied with the male portion of the audience in giving response to the patriotic proceedings."[17]

The words of the venerable Judge Henry Stephens set the tone of the evening program. Described as a "lifelong Democrat," Stephens immediately drew the attention of the crowd as he rose to speak. His tall, bony figure stood beside his desk, which had been covered by an "immense" national flag. In his low, heavy voice he said that he had come not to lecture on the current crisis but to see "whether you would conclude to roll up this flag, this old flag, the Star Spangled Banner."[18]

Arthur Holmes, Cortland's former Republican representative in the state assembly, eloquently stated the case for war after the attack on Fort Sumter:

> Rebel hands have desecrated our national flag, insulted our national honor, and now threaten the overthrow of our seat of National Government. Our entreaties for peace they have answered with a declaration of war. Our confidence they have abused. — Our forbearance they have charged as cowardice. Our expressions of patriotism they have derided as hypocrisy. Aye, they have struck the fatal blow. As there is a God in heaven, and strength in the good right arm of freemen, they shall repent that insult in dust and in humiliation.[19]

It was time, said Chairman Ballard, for the community to rise as one to defend constitutional liberty. Cortland's Republican representative in the U.S. Congress, Rodolphus Holland Duell, echoed this theme, declaring, "We are all Democrats — we are all Republicans!" He urged that the county "as one man, go forth to meet the traitors who are striving to overthrow the best government that the world ever saw." Former assemblyman Holmes went further, urging Cortland citizens to shun any dissenters at home. He directed the people to use "the power of public sentiment" to make sure that "the soil of Cortland County, cannot and *shall not be the nursing ground of treason, or the abettors of treason.*"[20]

The spectators responded enthusiastically to the heated rhetoric of war. They cheered a resolution drawn up and approved that stated: "If war *must* come, . . . we are in favor of its vigorous prosecution." When the call came to form a company of volunteers from Cortlandville, a number of young men stepped up to sign their names to a list of recruits. County judge Hiram Crandall (D), although he declined to speak, offered the first fifty dollars toward a Volunteer Fund for the support of local families whose members entered military service. Twenty-five others quickly joined him in pledging a total of $465.[21]

When the singing group, "Melodeons," broke into the "Star Spangled Banner" the audience rose and joined in. Finally the band played "Yankee Doodle," causing the "wildest enthusiasm" to prevail. The ladies waved their handkerchiefs from the galleries "presenting a perfect sea of waving cambric," while thunderous cheers shook the building "from its foundation to the roof." The meeting ended with "cheers for the Union, cheers for Gen. [Winfield] Scott, cheers for the Stars and Stripes, and cheers for Major [Robert] Anderson [the 'hero of Fort Sumter'].["]22

The courthouse meeting of April 20 had a profound effect on the sentiment of the community. Abram P. Smith, the former district attorney of Cortland County (R), noted that the week before the meeting he had been "disgusted" by the antiwar church sermon given by his preacher. The Sunday after the war meeting he noted in his diary, "Good war sermon. . . . Tone of the preacher changed by the public demonstrations." George Edgcomb confirmed that after the Saturday meeting, "'America' was sung in all the churches and treason was denounced from the pulpits."23

In the weeks that followed, a tidal wave of patriotism swept over the county. Flags seemed to appear everywhere, including a "superb flag" purchased with ten-cent contributions from the citizens of Cortland Village and flown by the local fire company. People began stamping patriotic emblems and mottoes on their writing paper, and schoolgirls walked about the streets wearing red, white, and blue ribbons. "There was also 'music in the air,'" Edgcomb remembered, with the singing of the "Star Spangled Banner," "Colombia, the Gem of the Ocean," "The Sword of Bunker Hill," and "Our Flag Is There." One day an effigy of the Rebel president Jefferson Davis wearing a plaque around his neck stating "The Traitor's Doom" was suspended over the street near the center of town, later to be taken down and burned. A store advertised "New Union Badges" for sale, and doctor Theodore C. Pomeroy put a notice in the paper offering free medical services for the families of volunteers.24

Additional war meetings were held on April 22 at several locations in the county. At Wheadon Hall in Homer a gathering enrolled forty-two men for a proposed Homer company of cavalry. Virgil held a flag-raising ceremony punctuated by the firing of the village "anvil cannon" (wounding two of the crew in the process). In Cortland Village a meeting held in Squires Hall on Main Street enrolled additional members for the Cortlandville company, including George Edgcomb and his friend Samuel L. Palmer, a letter carrier. Young Willis Babcock of Homer wrote his brother after the Wheadon Hall meeting, "The whole town is very much excited." He asked his brother's advice on signing up in the Homer company, admitting, "I am almost crazy to join."25

On April 23 nearly a thousand people attended a meeting at the Congregational church in Homer to witness forty-seven men of the Homer company being mustered into state service. The company had been accepted as part of the "Onondaga Regiment" under Col. Ezra L. Walwrath; a regiment formed in Syracuse, New York, from many members of the old 51st Militia Regiment. Homer magistrate William Andrews administered the oath of allegiance to the men of the company and oversaw the election of officers (upon certification of the election results the state would issue commissions). The popular twenty-one-year-old student George Whitford Stone won election as captain by the almost unanimous vote of his men. On May 1 the company left Homer by train for Syracuse to become Company D in what became the 12th New York Infantry in two-year state service. They mustered into Federal service for three months and fought on July 18 at Blackburn's Ford in the first significant action of the Battle of Bull Run (Manassas).[26]

The same day that the Homer company left for Syracuse, the Cortlandville company mustered seventy-two men. The men elected Martin C. Clark captain, Alvah Waters first lieutenant, and Benjamin B. Andrews ensign (second lieutenant when in Federal service), along with four sergeants and four corporals. All three of the line officers were single, twenty-three years of age at enlistment, and residents of Cortland Village. None of the three had any discernable military or militia experience, nor did they own property; all had become lawyers through study in established law offices. Captain Clark had been born in Groton, Tompkins County, New York, on December 9, 1837. Having a "distaste for agricultural life," he had traveled some, teaching in Kentucky and pursuing business interests along the Mississippi River before returning to Cortland to become a lawyer in 1861. All three men participated in the early efforts to raise troops in the county by giving patriotic speeches to encourage enlistments.[27]

Using the various available service and pension records in the National Archives, newspaper rosters, and the state and national census records, we can profile the ninety-eight soldiers who joined the Cortlandville company from the time of muster into Federal service, June 20, 1861, to their mustering-out in May 1863. As best as can be determined, sixty of the ninety-eight lived in Cortland County, with the greatest number coming from Cortlandville (twenty-eight, including those from McGrawville and Cortland Village), and ten each from the townships of Truxton and Cuyler. The non–Cortland County men came mostly from the surrounding counties, including seventeen from the Groton area of Tompkins County. Ten of the ninety-eight were foreign born (England four, Ireland three, and Canada three). Sixty-four members of the company identified their occupations as farmer or farm laborer, with the remainder representing a diversity of occupations including blacksmith, cooper, carpenter, and tailor. Before entering service, forty-three of the men in the company had lived at home with their parents, and sixteen had "worked out" (the common practice of boarding with and working for other families). Only ten members of the company had wives, and six of the married men had children. All but a very few of the men could read and write, and according to the 1860 Federal census, fewer than ten of the Cortland County men owned real estate in the county.

Thus, the first volunteers from Cortland County represented similar life experiences. The typical county volunteer was twenty-two years old, five feet seven inches tall, and single; he either lived at home or had begun the process of establishing himself in the community by working out or attending one of the local secondary schools or academies. His world had revolved around his family, most likely living on one of the isolated farms clustered near small villages that usually supported a general store, harness shop, blacksmith shop, church, and a schoolhouse where pupils sat in one room on wooden benches. A Cortland farm boy's daily life normally consisted of time at school during the winter, sandwiched between farm chores that included milking the cows, cleaning the stables, feeding livestock, gathering eggs, and carrying firewood. Boys were expected to master a number of farm skills including caring for stock, harnessing and driving horses, repairing harness and farm equipment, and cutting hay and grain, binding it, and storing it in the loft. They also spent long hours working in the fields alongside the men hoeing corn and potatoes. One Cortland resident looked back on his boyhood days as bittersweet — "Those were days of toil, hardship and self-denial, borne with courage, patience and hope, fathers and mothers losing life to find it in their children."[28]

That is not to imply that a boy's life in Cortland County before the war was not without its adventures or amusements. Many a man fondly recalled fishing in the summer, sledding and skating in the winter, anticipating Christmas and Fourth of July celebrations, making "New Years Calls," marveling at the wonders of the traveling circus, and attending the annual county fair. Further, what boy's heart did not thrill at the toot of the horn that announced the daily stages drawn by four horses that galloped down Main Street in Cortland and Homer to swing around in front of one of the big hotels? Better yet was the shrill whistle of the black "iron horse" that panted great gusts of smoke as it pulled its long line of cars majestically through the Cortland countryside. Upon reaching adolescence, a young man's opportunities for socializing expanded beyond weekend trips to the village with his parents for market or church to participation in house and barn raisings, singing societies, candy pulls, spelling bees, corn husking, and church donation parties.[29]

The annual general training days of the local militia unit seemed especially suited to capture a boy's fancy. After the fall haying, hundreds—at times thousands—of people gathered at the Homer Village Green, on the fields west of South Main Street in Cortland Village, or in Virgil, Cincinnatus, or Truxton to watch the military pageant from the roadside or perched on fences. "Scores of farm-wagons, carrying barrels of new cider, golden fruit, pies and gingerbread" provided an open market for the refreshment of the many spectators. Awestruck boys watched with wooden swords at their sides and mouths full of gingerbread as the troops marched past in their fancy feathered hats and colorful uniforms. The fifes and drums played stirring patriotic tunes, and the cannon boomed. Some of the luckier boys got to hold the horses of the dismounted officers. One man chuckled to recall, "We could hardly contain ourselves when the regiment marched in review to the tunes of 'Bonaparte Crossing the Rhine,' and 'Yankee Doodle.'"[30]

The firing on Fort Sumter dramatically disrupted the routine of village life. Emotions of fear and dread for the future mingled with the thrilling excitement of impending action and change. The single young men responded first to the call, as if by nature, like the geese that rose from Little York Lake in the autumn to fly south. These men did not join for money. (The eleven-dollar-a-month pay of a private was less than the fifteen dollars they could expect to make working out during the summer.) For the most part they did not join to become professional soldiers, or to conquer the South, or to sanctify the nation by freeing the slaves at the point of their bayonets. Indeed, in early 1861 few of them thought beyond a brief military campaign and single battle to restore the Union. Some simply jumped at the opportunity for change and adventure. Daniel O. Clough, for example, used the occasion of his wife's absence on a business trip to walk from his home in Groton to Cortland to enlist in the Cortlandville company.[31] Many others joined up as a way to speed their difficult transition from youth to adulthood. They had reached an age when they were no longer content to loiter on the edge of life and simply count the years. Restive, unsure of the future, and emboldened by the strength and vitality of their youth, they sought to test themselves, gain the attention, respect, and admiration of the community, and strike out on their own.

A strong sense of family and community obligation also contributed to their initial motivation to serve. After George Edgcomb signed up at Squires Hall for the Cortlandville company, he walked across to Greenbush Street to see his mother Clarissa and receive her blessing on his decision. Because he was under twenty-one years of age, state militia law required the signed consent of a parent or guardian before he could enter service. At the time his mother lived with his brother Isaac, their father, Isaac Allyn Edgcomb, having died on July 5 the year before. George remembered the conversation with his mother that night as a "trying one for her and too sacred to put into words." She finally consented to his going, with the admonition "not to disgrace the names of my grandfathers," who had served in the Revolutionary War. No doubt she reminded George of his grandfather Gilbert's experience at Valley Forge, his subsequent capture at Fort Griswold, and his imprisonment. George believed that such "sacred" discussions occurred in families throughout the land and reflected what President Lincoln described in his first inaugural address as the "mystic cords of memory" that bound an individual to his family, to his community, and to the common historical experience of the nation. Lincoln put great faith in the ultimate power of those historical ties to assist one day in reuniting the divided nation.[32]

On May 7, after a busy week trying to expose his new recruits to the rudiments of military drill, Captain Clark received orders from the state capital at Albany to bring his company to the place of rendezvous established at Elmira. The day of departure, May 9, began with scenes of sad family partings. Friends and neighbors visited the soldiers' homes with gifts, and few of the men could forget how "our father's tightened grip . . . bade us 'God speed.' . . . Mother could not, for grief that choked her utterance, speak the good-bye that her tearful eyes looked; and sisters clung to us as if to shield us from the dangers that awaited."[33]

By three o'clock, eighty-six of the "Cortland Volunteers" stood in Main Street in front of Squires Hall behind Major Pomeroy and a small number of men playing fifes and drums. The volunteers looked self-conscious from all the attention showered on them by the hundreds of onlookers who lined the sidewalks or stood in the middle of the broad thoroughfare. The men wore civilian clothes, some sporting red, white, and blue neckties or other patriotic emblems. Some of the men carried the popular oilcloths, used as covers in case of rain. A number clutched satchels or grips filled with changes of clothes and assorted "little knick-nacks" slipped in by mothers or sisters, items that previously "we never before knew that we wore or needed." The musicians struck up a tune, and the column marched through the cheering, flag-waving crowds to turn on to Court Street and form a hollow square before the front steps of the courthouse.[34]

Professor Nathaniel Mighill from Cortlandville Academy had the honor of addressing the volunteers. The tall, twenty-one-year-old teacher, a recent graduate of Amherst College in Massachusetts, stood bareheaded under a bright cloudless sky on one of the raised platforms bordering the steps of the courthouse. He began by presenting to the company a silk national flag flying from a tasseled pole topped by a gilt eagle. Attached to the pole above the flag, a white silk banner caught the balmy spring breeze. It read, "Cortland Volunteers: Presented by the Ladies of Cortland." The crowd cheered as the flag came into view. Mighill then expounded on the symbolism that the flag evoked and the great issues at stake for the men charged with its ensign's defense. He concluded his talk with a poem that began with the commission "Take then thy Banner!" In one stanza he spoke directly to the friends and relatives of the soldiers who would remain behind:

> Take thy Banner! Many a heart
> Bids tears in heavy eyes upstart:
> But keep tears back, their cause is true,
> They fight, O grieving friends, for you.[35]

After Mighill's talk, Captain Clark stepped forward to accept the flag in the name of the company and to promise that the men would protect it with their lives if need be. Lieutenant Waters accepted swords donated by Gen. Roswell Randall for the use of the commissioned officers. The company then marched up Main Street for a farewell meal provided at the Cortland House Hotel. Afterward the column continued to the depot where the men were to board a waiting passenger train. The local newspaper noted the many touching final partings as the men entered the cars and took their seats: "More handshakings and farewells from the windows followed, and the cars soon moved off, amid the waving of handkerchiefs and the cheers of the multitude."[36]

As the train disappeared over the Tioughnioga, the cheering faded, and the reality that would be expressed by the stark words of the next day's paper, "the brave boys have gone!" gradually sank in. Ensign Andrews observed that when the departing soldiers got beyond the view of their loved ones, "a still and gloomy sadness seemed to fold every heart in its mist" and give vent to the "sympathies, passions, and weaknesses of our own contradictory nature." It was strange that their hearts did not rejoice in the fulfillment of boyhood dreams that one day they might board the outbound train to adventure and adulthood. Perhaps they realized, maybe for the first time, that the decisions they make in life are not theirs to make alone; they are tempered by the past, filtered by the values and influences of youth, hampered by obligations unfulfilled, and haunted by the pleasures and pain of remembrance. At the same time what were the thoughts of the soldiers' loved ones as they silently walked home from the depot? "The unfeeling haste of the iron horse," as Andrews described it, had torn families apart and left a vacuum in the community. Along with a pervasive sadness, perhaps too they felt a little guilt that the sons they had so willingly sent off to war were not prepared for the life-and-death challenges they would soon face. Mighill's words echoed in their ears—"they fight, O grieving friends, for you!" With anxious hearts they would wait for any news of their "Cortland Volunteers."[37]

Elmira was the site of one of three military depots established by the state to receive, train, and equip the new companies and organize them into regiments in preparation for muster into Federal service. To reach Elmira by train, the Cortland Volunteers had to take a circuitous route beginning not to the southwest toward Elmira but north to Syracuse. Arriving in the "City of Conventions" without notice on the evening of May 9, the company marched unescorted to the Voorhees House Hotel at the corner of North Salina and West Genesee streets, where they spent the night. The next morning they continued their journey on the New York Central Railroad to Geneva. When they pulled into Geneva, a military company welcomed them and escorted them from the train depot to the shores of Seneca Lake, where they boarded the steamer *Ben Lodore* along with three other "rough" looking companies. At the request of the officers, the boat's captain, E. C. Daniels, locked away all the liquor on board and would not sell a drop.[38]

After a three-hour ride down Seneca Lake, the men landed at Watkins, New York. Having just missed the regular train to Elmira, they waited in an unfinished hall for a special train that did not arrive for them and the other stranded troops until seven in the evening. Marching down to the train that night in the rain, six-foot one-inch color bearer John Traver, a forty-one-year-old Cortland carpenter, lovingly wrapped the flag in his oilcloth to protect it. On the last leg of their trip the men amused themselves by telling jokes and singing patriotic songs. "It would have done your soul good," wrote Sgt. Alvin F. Bailey, "to have heard the boys come in on the chorus to the 'Star Spangled Banner,' and the 'Red, White and Blue.'" They arrived in Elmira at nine o'clock on the night of May 10 to find temporary quarters with three other companies in the First Independent Congregational Church on West Gray Street. In the churchyard they helped themselves to the blankets, a cheese, and a barrel of crackers provided for their comfort.[39]

Elmira at this time bustled with the influx of new recruits, whose increasing numbers (five thousand by early May) soon approached the civilian population of 8,800. Gen. Robert Van Valkenburgh, the state official in charge of the depot, scrambled to find quarters for the incoming companies, utilizing every available church, public hall, or large "loft" while he pushed forward construction of three barracks complexes on the outskirts of the city.[40]

The Cortland Volunteers remained at the church of Reverend Thomas K. Beecher from May 11 to 29. The men proudly hung their flag from the gallery of the church and slept below it, two men to a pew. They washed and drilled in the churchyard and marched to their meals at the nearby Haight's Hotel, where the officers had their quarters. On Sunday, May 12, the minister spoke to the company in a sermon on Luke 3. Beecher, of the famous family that included Henry Ward Beecher and author Harriet Beecher Stowe, brought tears to many of the men by reminding them of their homes and leading them in singing "Greenville" and "Auld Lang Syne." "Every heart was strengthened, and every arm nerved with new vigor," Sergeant Bailey observed, "when he spoke of the justice of our cause, and implored the blessing of the God of Battles to rest upon us." On May 17 members of the Young Men's Christian Association of Elmira distributed free New Testaments to all in the company who would take them.[41]

The chaotic logistical situation in Elmira became even more so after state authorities found themselves with more troops than were needed under Lincoln's call of April 15. After much discussion, Federal authorities agreed that New York's two-year regiments then forming would count against a new call by Lincoln (dated May 3, 1861) for additional regiments of state troops for three years in Federal service. Van Valkenburgh then put added pressure on the military companies at Elmira to form regiments by May 17.[42]

The need to organize companies into regiments opened opportunities for ambitious individuals to secure the regimental field officer positions (as colonel, lieutenant colonel, and major). Those successful in forming a regiment would most likely be elected to command positions and thus acquire additional influence over the appointment of regimental staff, aide, sutler, and medical personnel. Captain Clark, who had been released from an earlier conditional understanding to join his company to the "Oswego Regiment" (24th New York), found the competition for his favor distressing. He wrote to a friend on May 18 that "'log rolling' and wire pulling are the order of the day. Men are not placed in [command] positions because of merit, but for favor to their 'constituents.'"[43]

Clark eventually joined his company to the Southern Tier Regiment, or what became the 23d New York Volunteers, in two-year state service. The nucleus of the regiment came from the "Southern Tier Rifles" militia company of Elmira. The regiment formed on May 15 with the company line officers electing the field officers. Henry Cane "Barney" Hoffman, a thirty-four-year-old farmer, Democratic officeholder, commander of the Southern Tier Rifles, and member of a prominent local landholding family, became colonel. Nirom M. Crane, a thirty-two-year-old militia officer and financial banker from Hornellsville in Steuben County, was elected lieutenant colonel, and William M. Gregg, a thirty-nine-year-old Elmira harness maker and ex-sheriff became major. All three were married (Hoffman in September 1860), two had children, and by most accounts, all proved to be excellent officers, rising to the rank of brevet brigadier general by the end of the war. Additional regimental appointments included the fifty-year-old Owego physician Seymour Churchill as surgeon, William A. Madill as surgeon's mate (assistant surgeon), and Ezra F. Crane, a fifty-two-year-old Baptist minister from Elmira, as chaplain.[44]

During the Civil War the ten companies of an infantry regiment usually took their letter designations within the regiment according to the ranks or dates of commission of their captains. The letter order for the organization of the Southern Tier Regiment and the principal places of

Col. Henry C. "Barney" Hoffman. *(National Archives)*

recruitment were as follows: A—Bath Company, Steuben County; B—Cuba Company, Allegheny County; C—Owego Company, Tioga County; D—Corning Company, Steuben County; E—Waverly Company, Tioga County; F—Elmira Company, Chemung County; G—Hornellsville Company, Steuben County; H—Cortlandville Company, Cortland County; I—Watkins Company, Schuyler County; and K (the former Southern Tier Rifles), Elmira Company, Chemung County.[45]

Once the companies were lettered, they would occupy a specific numbered position in regimental formations. In general, the initial organization for a regiment in a normal battle line would have the companies placed in the following order: 2/B, 7/G, 10/K, 5/E, 8/H, 3/C, 9/I, 4/D, 6/F, 1/A. The most important positions fell to the captains with the earliest dates of rank: in order of importance, 1/A (the post of honor on the right flank of the line), 2/B (the left flank guard company), and 3/C (the color company, which guarded the two regimental flags or "colors" and helped to focus the operation of the regiment). Although the letter assigned to the company would not change, the number position of the company in formation might change if the company received a new commander of lower rank or later date of rank. The significant issue of the commander's date of rank also determined the position and status of regiments in brigades and of brigades in divisions.[46]

On May 29 the Cortland Volunteers joined the other companies of the regiment in their new barracks located northeast of Elmira near the Chemung Canal at the northern extension of Lake Street. Within the complex, called Barracks Number 6 (later Post Barracks), each company occupied a separate one-story wooden building eighteen feet by eighty-eight feet, outfitted with two rows of bunk beds. A separate building housed the field and staff officers, and midway along the line of barracks stood a mess hall that could seat a thousand men at a time.[47]

Despite their twelve-hour-duty days while in barracks at Elmira, the men still found time for entertainment. They welcomed visitors from home, formed a glee club, and participated in recreational activities such as wrestling, leapfrog, boxing with gloves, football, and baseball. Other "sports" included "making pyramids" (six or eight men standing in a circle with four or five on their shoulders and three others on top) and "throwing up in a blanket," where forty soldiers tossed a man up in the air on a tent fly. Several Cortland Volunteers one evening found the inspiration to join together under their blankets to form the shape of an elephant. They then "tramped heavily around" the camp for the amusement of comrades.[48]

At the mess hall the Cortland Company gave feminine names to their fellow soldiers serving as waiters, prompting the waiters to take on mock airs "a la femme" that, attested Lieutenant Andrews, were "quite amusing." Outside of their barracks building they placed a large H on a pole.

Inside, Cortlandville Academy student James W. Manier decorated the walls with scenes of the flag ("long may they wave") and of Confederate president Jefferson Davis on the gallows ("Jeff Davis' fate"). The men added obscure sayings, such as "take pains with our brains," "auction every evening," and "pies wanted, not to eat, but to look at." The company also acquired a cat named "Union" as a mascot and outfitted the feline with a silk scarf imprinted with the company identification.[49]

As the days dragged on, the eager warriors at Elmira chafed over any perceived inaction, incompetence, or abuse among authorities. They apparently paid little heed to Reverend Beecher's advice in his sermon from the book of Luke: "Rob no one by violence or by false accusation, and be content with your wages." Instead, the men readily complained about most aspects of soldier life. They fussed about their lack of uniforms, weapons, and pay, and especially the quality of their rations, which included boiled beef, potatoes, bread, coffee, eggs, and milk. Negative reactions to the food ran the gamut from holding a mock funeral for a piece of beef they buried in the ground "with the honors of war" to two companies of the "Union Regiment" (27th New York) kicking over tables of soup.[50]

When the general "contagion" of dissatisfaction reached the ranks of the Southern Tiers, the situation rapidly deteriorated until only one captain of the regiment dared call his men to daily drill, the others fearing that their troops would refuse duty and return home en masse. At this juncture Captain Clark marched the Cortland Volunteers a mile out of camp and gave them a fatherly talk on their responsibilities as soldiers. He called attention to their beloved flag and invoked its symbolism to inspire their most worthy and honorable efforts. His words had the desired effect, for when he called for three cheers in honor of their banner "nearly every hat went up, and every throat responded." The crisis having passed, the company returned to barracks professing a renewed determination "to see the thing through." Lieutenant Andrews noted with pride that later when the men of another company attempted to "institute a row" in the mess hall, the Cortland Volunteers paid them no notice and continued with their meal "with the most stoical coolness and indifference."[51]

Such is not to report that the men in any way seriously modified their behavior during the remainder of their stay in Elmira. One Southern Tier man stated that there continued plenty of "quarrels, fights, running guard, burlesque, etc. [to] keep up the life and interest of the soldiery."

He related the story of a 23d man sprung from the guardhouse by comrades. When rearrested, the soldier "fought like a tiger," striking Major Gregg before being subdued.[52]

Many conflicts also sprang up between the soldiers and Elmira civilians. Members of the 23d found great delight in marching past the local female academy in order to catch the attention of the young ladies and at the same time torment their stern principal. Sergeant Bailey told of Lieutenant Andrews's poking fun at local blacks on the streets of Elmira by ordering his companions in a loud voice to "salute the *color-bearers.*" Andrews himself gave an account of a scuffle between some soldiers and the black owner of an Elmira saloon. The soldiers decided not to pay for their beer, claiming "this war is all on account of your people and we are soldiers!" Andrews described the ensuing brawl as a "dark day for the 'niggers,'" who apparently got the worst of it. He concluded from the incident, "the soldiers are not, apparently, over friendly toward Sambo." The local papers reported other serious crimes involving civilians and soldiers, including the "assassination" of two soldiers in the street and the attempted rape by a soldier of a ten-year-old girl.[53]

No doubt a contributing factor adding to the soldiers' dissatisfaction with army life was the sobering passage of time, which gave them the opportunity to reflect on their decision to enlist. After experiencing the crowded and coarse conditions of the camps, the debilitating effects of disease (the regiment suffered over a hundred cases of measles at Elmira), and homesickness, many of the men had second thoughts about becoming soldiers. Also, letters from loved ones expressed concerns for their welfare and a desire for their early return home. On May 30 George Edgcomb received a letter from his mother that must have affected him deeply, as apparently it was the only letter from her that he saved during the war. She began by describing the sewing needles, black thread, and bed quilt that she had sent him. She told him of the efforts of herself and other local women to gather donations of supplies for the soldiers, and of his sister-in-law Eva's going door to door in the community collecting cloth. Then, however, emotions directed her pen, and she revealed her true feelings at that moment:

> Oh my boy I miss you and wish you were with us as you were in months past. I am lonesome without thee. As my children scatter around this world wandering in this vale of tears it gives fresh tears to the avenue

Maj. William M. Gregg. *(National Archives)*

which mine are want to trace. . . . I never could put my signature to another consent for you to go for another term or for the extension of this so if it is a possible thing in any of these turnings or twistings for you to get released you must do it.[54]

Although Edgcomb and most of his fellow Cortland Volunteers remained in service to fulfill honorably their terms of enlistment, a number of men did leave the company before being mustered into Federal service. Three examples provide a range of reasons. Thomas Lee, a twenty-year-old Irish-born farm laborer from Truxton, deserted, returned home, and then apparently disappeared with his young wife, never to be seen around Truxton again. Philip J. Mosher left the company for, he claimed, health reasons. He returned to his home in Tompkins County and later enlisted in the 10th New York Cavalry, where he served honorably until being mustered out for physical disability in December 1861. The third case involved Shewman Wattles of Summer Hill, Cayuga County, who returned home to support his wife and children after learning that they had not received any of the promised local aid for soldiers' families. He was arrested on August 4, 1861, and sent back into service, only to die of disease that October. About twenty of the original eighty-six recruits that left Cortland did not appear on the list at joining Federal service. Most of them simply decided to enlist in other companies or were mustered out of service for medical reasons. Also, Sergeant Bailey reported one unnamed man driven from camp after he "shamefully disgraced himself and the company."[55]

To prevent further hemorrhaging of the strength of the company, Lieutenant Andrews attacked Mosher and the others who left the company, labeling them in the *Republican Banner* "cowardly and dishonorable" deserters who had "forgot their oaths, their honor and their manhood." The paper printed their names in lower-case letters and surrounded the list with a black border. Andrews singled out Mosher, who suffered, according to the lieutenant, with "a disease of the heart, which finally *settled* upon one of his ancles [sic], causing him to limp most *lamely*." Andrews shouted in the paper "For shame Mosher!" with the probable effect of contributing to Mosher's flight. Andrews assured his readers that he expected no more names to be added to the infamous list of cowards and that his Cortland readers could count on those remaining in the company to do their duty fully. With extravagant prose he declared, "If they go, they go to fight, if they fight they will fight to kill. If they fall they will die like men, brave and yet gentle."[56]

The fortunes of the Cortland Volunteers at Elmira took a welcome turn for the better on June 20 when they received their uniforms and were mustered into Federal service. Captain Clark wrote in a letter that night, "The boys are delighted. . . . They can hardly contain themselves." Their uniform consisted of a dark-blue wool forage cap and jacket. The distinctive cotton-lined jacket had a low standing collar, shoulder straps, eight brass "Excelsior" state militia buttons in a single row down the front, and trim of light blue. The trousers and overcoats were of light sky-blue wool and, like the jackets, usually came in only four sizes. State regulations also called for men to receive one pair of sturdy pegged cowhide shoes or "brogans," two canton flannel shirts, a blanket, long cotton under drawers, two pair of woolen socks, and a waterproof cap cover. [57]

Other issued uniform items soon followed. They included an oilcloth square haversack for rations and a round tin canteen covered with gray woolen cloth "for the double purpose of spoiling the glistening mark [target] it would otherwise make, and also of keeping the drink therein contained cool by dipping it in the water occasionally." A bulky, black oilcloth knapsack with the unit indicated in large white letters and numbers sat high on the soldier's back, held in place by broad leather straps. A black leather cartridge box for ammunition hung from the left shoulder to the right hip on a strap, and a leather waist belt fixed by a metal oval belt plate, embossed with the letters SNY (State of New York), held a cap box and bayonet scabbard. Just before the regiment left the state, the men received antiquated smoothbore .69 caliber converted muskets (model 1840) and bayonets.[58]

Lt. William Woods Averell of the regular U.S. forces arrived at Elmira on June 11 to assist in mustering state troops into national service. He described the official muster-in ceremony of a regiment as "impressive and solemn." First the colonel formed his men in line on the parade ground. "As the roll of each company was called the men answered to their names and stepped to the front and then altogether, with uncovered heads and uplifted right hands, repeated the words of the oath of allegiance and obedience, sentence by sentence, after the mustering officer." Then the officers and the adjutant advanced to the colors, removed their hats, and took the oath. Anyone who refused the oath was mustered out of state service. Apparently all seventy-two men on the roster of the Cortland Volunteers participated in the ceremony. The official mustering-in of the 23d into Federal service was backdated to May 16 to reflect the date of regimental organization.[59]

On Saturday evening, June 22, the Southern Tier Regiment formed for dress parade with everyone in uniform for the first time. Chaplain Crane read the War Department regulations on the duties and obligations of a soldier, followed by a few words of "kind and friendly admonition" by

Colonel Hoffman. The ceremony sparked a hectic two-week period of preparation for departure to the front. During this period Hoffman allowed brief furloughs for groups of his men to visit their homes and collected the sick from the loving care of local families. The state paymaster arrived to issue the soldiers the few dollars' pay due them for their time of state service before May 16. Many spent the money in Elmira to purchase the popular rubber blankets or have their photographs taken.[60]

On the Fourth of July the 23d joined in the gala parade through the streets of Elmira, an event that served as a dress rehearsal for their departure from the city the following day. The field officers, mounted on prancing horses, led the fully equipped column through the streets and under banners the citizens had stretched across the road displaying words of tribute for the Southern Tiers. At times officers forced the men to double-quick under the hot sun with their heavy packs, resulting in a few sunstroke victims. On Water Street, near the Brainard House, the men halted to take a welcome rest and watch a performer walk a rope stretched over the street above them. The men eventually returned to their barracks at about five o'clock, none the worse for wear, to discover to their surprise that the local ladies had prepared a farewell banquet. The long mess tables were covered with white linen cloths for the occasion and decorated with bouquets of flowers. The women who waited the meal wore distinctive badges representing the companies they were assigned to serve. The men enjoyed themselves immensely, with the companies vying with each other in cheers for their particular female waitresses.[61]

At nine o'clock the next morning Colonel Hoffman formed his men on their barracks parade ground for the last time. Many civilians and the local fire companies were on hand to participate in the event. After Hoffman gave a short patriotic address, the men offered three cheers each for the firemen, for the ladies, for their friends at home, and for their colonel. A fire company and the Elmira Cornet Band led the fully equipped regiment up Washington Street to Main. As the men turned down Main and marched to Second Street, they were "preceded, flanked and followed by a perfect sea of humanity." Entering Second Street the regiment had to push through the mass of eager spectators to reach the railroad tracks, which ran perpendicular to Second Street on Railroad Street. On the tracks waited a seventeen-car passenger train pulled by two locomotives.[62]

The regiment made its way alongside the train and stopped with the companies aligning on individual cars. As the men entered the cars the crowd pressed in to say their final good-byes. Seymour Dexter looked down the length of the train at the confused scene and observed, "As far as the eye could reach seemed like one ocean of people moving to and fro as some impulse stirred or some object attracted its attention." Lieutenant Andrews noticed many a mother holding and kissing her son perhaps for the last time. "Sisters rushed frantically along the line, and cried through their tears, 'where is Willie?' or 'Eddie?'" Stoically the fathers stood before their sons, seeing "the last prop of age slipping from under them, and with a faint 'be good, be true,' turned from the scene they could not witness." The emotional scenes were so distressing to Pvt. Henry C. Scott that he wrote in his diary, "Most glad I did not have any friends to say goodbye to."[63]

The loading of the cars continued amid "earnest prayers and fondest expressions of kind wishes." Even after the men had settled into their seats, well-wishers passed small bouquets of flowers, cakes, or other treats up through the windows. A shrill warning whistle soon sounded, leaving only Colonel Hoffman visible to all, standing on top one of the cars in the bright sunshine to speak final words of farewell to his Elmira friends and fellow citizens. Finally, around eleven, the train slowly pulled away, carrying the regiment and a host of local dignitaries who planned to ride as far as Williamsport, Pennsylvania. "As the wheels began their onward revolution," Private Dexter wrote in his journal, "cheer upon cheer rolled up from the vast throng for the Southern Tier Regiment which continued until we had passed the bounds of the city."[64]

CHAPTER 2

Banners South

The train rumbled south carrying the Southern Tier Regiment over a scenic route through the Allegheny Mountains toward Harrisburg, Pennsylvania. About three o'clock it made a two-hour stop at Williamsport, where the men left the cars to join in a local street parade and partake of a "sumptuous meal" laid out on tables under some shade trees. For a time they sat drinking lemonade and ice water as the town feted them with "speeches, toasts, music, laughter and cheers." Women held umbrellas over the heads of some to keep off any errant rays of the sun. Too soon the whistle of the train called them back to the cars to resume their journey. For the remainder of their trip through Pennsylvania at almost every village "crowds met us, cheering, waving flags and handkerchiefs, and the ladies throwing bouquets to us." Field hands along the route looked up from their work to smile and wave their hats at the passing train. Entering the border state of Maryland early on July 6, the men exchanged greetings with soldiers positioned along the tracks, especially at the bridges, to discourage any pro-Southern saboteurs.[1]

As the regiment neared Baltimore, its mood turned serious. To reach Washington all trains traveling south on the Northern Central track had to stop at Baltimore for the passengers to disembark, pass about a mile through the city, and then board Baltimore and Ohio Railroad cars for the last leg of the trip. Earlier, on April 19, a Baltimore mob had fired upon Union troops making this transfer between trains. Taking no chances,

Colonel Hoffman had his men march in close column of companies extending from curb to curb with muskets loaded and primed, and bayonets fixed. Itching for a confrontation, the regiment unfurled its flags and the drum corps played "Yankee Doodle." The men shouted taunts at bystanders along the sidewalks. In return they got back mostly blank stares and a few expressions of outright support or enthusiasm. At the Baltimore and Ohio depot they traded their relatively plush passenger coaches for freight cars, in which they had to sit on rough boards packed together like a "heap of livestock." This "tired old jade of a train" then rattled on toward Washington with its passengers still primed in spirit and "spoiling for a fight."[2]

The Southern Tier Regiment arrived in the nation's capital inauspiciously, at about one in the morning on July 7. Because of the great amount of baggage to be unloaded at the depot, the train stopped just outside the city to disembark the men, who marched the rest of the way. Stumbling about in the rainy black night, they first had to crawl beneath the cars of a cattle train and then slide down a muddy embankment, ending up in a very unmilitary-looking crowd beside the tracks. For the next two hours the men marched, seemingly back and forth, up and down the streets of Washington, until most found shelter in the public buildings on Louisiana Avenue near the capitol. No one complained. In fact, at one point during that dismal march, eight hundred voices spontaneously rose in singing the "Star Spangled Banner." The Cortland Volunteers and two other companies crowded into Trinity Congregationalist Church at Third and C Streets until, experiencing "two hundred and fifty different smells arising" from the damp rooms and their wet wool uniforms, many of the men opted to sleep out on the sidewalk in the rain. Lieutenant Andrews noted the similarities of this experience with the arrival of the Cortland Volunteers at Elmira on May 10 and their stay at Beecher's Congregational church.[3]

The next morning began with their further immersion into the "realities of war." The men awoke that Sunday to a breakfast of salt pork and hardtack. When not in a stationary camp, army regulations called for each man to receive a daily "marching ration" that included coffee beans; twelve ounces of fatty, raw, salted pork; and nine or ten biscuits, baked of flour and water, three by three and a half inches wide and a half inch thick, called "hard-tack." Lieutenant Waters disdainfully described the meal as consisting of "a few sea or flint crackers full as hard as pencil

Gen. Irvin McDowell. (*MOLLUS collection*, USAMHI)

stone and a quantity of the greasiest pork ever seen, the very sight of which was enough to sicken any one, and such would be the inevitable result of smelling it."[4]

That Sunday, except for attending the mandatory late afternoon regimental dress parade before an appreciative crowd of civilians along Pennsylvania Avenue, the men had the day to themselves. Many joined the crowds of uniformed soldiers who walked the streets of Washington to see the sites as tourists. In the days that followed they wrote many letters home describing the impressive national landmarks of Washington, which they had read about as schoolboys but had never thought they would have a chance to visit. The highlights of Seymour Dexter's trips to the city included listening to speeches in Congress, looking over models of inventions in the patent building, walking through the front door of the White House to visit the East and Green rooms, contemplating the unfinished marble obelisk monument being built in tribute to George Washington, and visiting the Smithsonian Institution to view the Egyptian mummy and other curiosities. After a similar excursion that included a glimpse of "Old Abe" and other statesmen and celebrities, Orderly Sergeant Duane Thompson concluded, "I am more than ever convinced that this is a great country."[5]

Notwithstanding the impressive national monuments, the soldiers found Washington an "abominably dirty and dingy looking city." Lieutenant Andrews thought the city a "stupendous humbug." "Imagine a place," he wrote in the *Cortland Banner*, "where all the streets lead anywhere you want to go, and every place is 'just around the corner'; where brick, stone, mortar and wood, are piled up in all conceivable shapes and called 'dwellings'; where niggers can be found from the shade of an envelope to, oh! *so* black . . . , where the water tastes of old boats and rusty nails . . . ; where they sell water and give away corn whisky—and it is Washington." Adjacent Georgetown he described similarly as having "tall, gaunt, dingy blocks [that] throw their shade upon squalid hovels, that seemed teeming with ebon hued humanity."[6]

On July 8 Hoffman led the 23d along Pennsylvania Avenue and then up Fourteenth Street to reach Camp Diven on Meridian Hill near Columbia College at the northern edge of the city. Because of the heat, some of the company captains hired carts to carry their men's heavy knapsacks up the hill. The regiment made one brief stop along the way, reverently standing silent with caps off as a hearse bearing the flag-draped coffin of a fellow soldier crossed their path. The funeral procession included a military escort and a drum corps marking a slow time by muffled drumbeats. The accidental encounter, according to Lieutenant Andrews, fell upon the cheerful spirits of the men like a "leaden incubus," reminding them of the seriousness of their undertaking.[7]

When the 23d arrived in Washington they joined more than sixty other regiments, most of them untrained state volunteer units under short enlistments, that had been rushed to the defense of the capital.[8] The regiments that remained in and around the city became part of Brig. Gen. Joseph K. F. Mansfield's Department of Washington. Those units identified as ready for active service crossed the Potomac into Virginia, where they

were organized in brigades and divisions as part of Brig. Gen. Irvin Mc-
Dowell's field army, the Army of Northeastern Virginia. Confederate Brig.
Gen. P. G. T. Beauregard, the hero of Fort Sumter, gathered his opposing
Army of the Potomac about twenty-five miles to the west at an obscure
Virginia railroad junction called Manassas Junction (see map p. 130).

Camp Diven occupied the "Mount Pleasant" property of William J.
Stone. A number of officers, including Captain Clark, took quarters in the
main house. The picturesque mansion house, with honeysuckle trailing up
its sides, sat on high ground surrounded by stately ivy-covered oak trees.
From the upstairs windows Union officers had a panoramic view of the
city and the Potomac River. Mr. Stone, being absent, had left the house in
the care of his black servant, "Uncle James," who served his new masters
in fine style as long as Stone's supply of Madeira wine lasted. The troops
camped on the grounds near an inexhaustible bubbling spring of cool
water; also nearby, in a wood, flowed a stream where they could bathe
and wash their clothes.[9]

At Camp Diven the Southern Tier men "commenced soldier life" in
earnest. A military camp, according to regulations, typically covered an
area of ground three hundred yards square. Each company lived in ten
"A" or wedge tents, five or six men to a tent, the men sleeping in the con-
fining eight-foot-square space "in the style of a set of tea spoons, packed
up for sale." The line of company tents ran back perpendicularly like
ten teeth of a comb from the color line, where the entire regiment would
form. The tents of each company were divided evenly into two rows facing each other across a twelve-to-fifteen-foot company street. At the end
of the company streets opposite from the color line were located the kitchens, officers' tents, and so on. At some distant point at the edge of the
camp the men dug trench latrines, or "sinks," and surrounded them with
bushes for privacy.[10]

Once in camp the men, many on their own for the first time in their
lives, faced the daunting task of cooking their own meals and washing
and mending their own clothes. Regimental quartermaster Myron H.
Mandeville issued bulk quantities of coffee beans, rice, bread, raw meat,
beans, and sugar to the companies for distribution in rations to the men.
Given the soldiers' inexperience in the culinary arts and the lack of cooking utensils (one man reported only one pail and one iron pan for eight
men), Lieutenant Andrews found it "real fun to witness the maiden attempts of the boys at cooking." He reported that "burnt food and fingers,

smokey coffee and any amount of hard words, are the natural consequences of such endeavors." Seymour Dexter related how he struggled to
grind his coffee beans with a stone in an iron dish and how his rice burned
upon the bottom of the kettle. Two of the luckier Southern Tier men had
their wives with them in camp who could help them with domestic chores.
Most of the men, however, quickly turned to the expedients of assigning
one or two of their more skilled comrades to act as cooks for their company or hiring servants to do the work. Former Cortlandville tailor Stephen Clearwood found a high demand for his professional services within
the company, enabling him to earn an extra two or three dollars a day.[11]

While at Meridian Hill the soldiers' inexperience and ignorance in
matters of camp hygiene brought down upon them the scourges of the
Civil War soldier—diarrhea and dysentery. Surgeon Seymour Churchill
treated two or three hundred cases of diarrhea in the regiment daily. Cpl.
Henry C. Scott of Company E noted in his diary for July 18 that his
"bowels moved 18 times in three hours. Friend sat up most of the night
with me." Samuel Palmer of the Cortland Volunteers recounted tent mate
George Edgcomb's affliction with the disease and his frequent nightly
"evacuations" that occurred at times even "before he could get out of the
tent." Palmer added that "on many occasion [he] had to get out in a very
great hurry."[12]

On the evening of July 17, 1861, the 23d experienced the rite of passage of most volunteer Civil War regiments, the presentation of the regimental flags, or colors. Most infantry regiments received a stand of two
large silk flags on long staffs, each flag made of heavy embroidered silk
about six feet square, normally sewn or purchased by the women of the
regiment's home district to a design in accordance with military regulations. The flags of the 23d cost three hundred dollars, raised by the ladies of Elmira through subscription. The national emblem, the Stars and
Stripes, displayed the added words, "Twenty-third Regiment New York
Volunteers." The state, or regimental, flag had a dark field fringed with
gold. One side displayed the national coat of arms, and on the reverse was
the state coat of arms, with the name of the regiment enclosed in a circle.
Each staff had a golden plate affixed with the inscription, "Presented by
the citizens of Elmira to the 23 Regiment, N.Y.S.V. [New York State Vol-
unteers]; Col. Hoffman commanding." Once presented to the regiment,
the flags would direct the life of the soldier—in camp, on the drill field,
or waving above the smoke-shrouded battlefield. The company flag of

the Cortland Volunteers, having no official regimental status, probably remained in the loving care of Lieutenant Andrews, to emerge from his camp trunk only on special occasions.[13]

The flag ceremony began about six in the evening on an open field near Columbia College. Colonel Hoffman formed his scrubbed and polished regiment of 770 men in ranks along three sides of a square. The speakers and numerous spectators, including President Lincoln and Secretary of State William H. Seward of New York, faced the troops from the open side of the square. The principal speaker was Republican congressman Alexander S. Diven of Elmira, for whom the regiment's camp was named.[14]

Diven spoke on what was expected of the men as soldiers. He told them, "You have not left your homes and come here in pursuit of conquest. You are here, not as soldiers of the State of New York, to make conquests upon the State of Maryland, Virginia, or any other state; you are here as soldiers of the Republic—called hither in defense of the Constitution of our common country. The Virginian is as much your countryman as I, or any other citizen of New York." Diven continued, "Your duty is not subjugation; your duty is not to impair the rights of any State in this confederacy; your duty is not to impair the property, liberty, or right of any American citizen: but your duty is to put down the rebellion at all hazards and at every sacrifice."[15]

Diven also attempted to imbue their new flags with additional meaning. He encouraged them to view the banners as a direct link to their dear homes, families, and friends, and thereby to gain strength for the trials that lay before them. He did not question their bravery or physical courage. But, he said, there were other equally important attributes of a soldier that they must acknowledge, including "justice, humanity, sobriety." Moral dissipation, he warned, posed a more dangerous threat to them than the Rebels. "If at any time you are tempted to yield to this enemy in any of its forms," he told them, "look at these colors, wrought by the care of loved mothers, sisters, and wives, and ask yourselves if you will disgrace them by yielding to the temptation." Then, after bringing not a few soldiers to tears by his invoking the scenes of tender partings from their families, Diven dramatically ended his address with the charge, "Never return to your homes with this flag disgraced. No, Never! A thousand times better that these banners be folded around your corpses, than that you return alive with these colors dishonored."[16]

34

The applause for Diven's words had died down when Lieutenant Colonel Crane and Major Gregg stepped forward leading the regimental color guard made up of one sergeant and eight corporals. The group approached Diven's carriage, received the flags from Diven and his daughters, and unfurled them to the breeze as the twenty-member regimental fife and drum corps struck up a lively tune. Colonel Hoffman then gave a short address in which he assured the crowd that when the regiment returned, the flags, so generously provided, might be tarnished from active service but would not be dishonored. Following the speeches the men formed in two ranks in open order with fixed bayonets for inspection by President Lincoln and Secretary Seward.[17]

The men watched with much interest and curiosity as Lincoln walked along the line, hat in hand, "pleasantly bowing to us all." Surgeon Churchill assured his hometown newspaper readers that "'Old Abe' is not half so homely as his pictures represent him to be." Another soldier remembered the tall, awkward president "striding up and down in front of our line without the slightest idea of keeping step to the music. Beside him, looking almost diminutive, the secretary of the state, taking two steps to his one." The regiment afterward passed in review by companies before the president, once in slow time, then again in quick time. Thus the ceremony came to an end, no doubt mercifully for many who continued a "quick step" to the sinks for relief from the rampant diarrhea that continued to ravage the camp.[18]

Diven's unbellicose speech reflected the thinking of most Northerners at this early stage in the war and no doubt struck a responsive chord among members of the regiment. This view held that the Constitution, for which their ancestors had fought and died, had been sullied and thrown aside by a conspiracy of powerful Southern slave interests. This oligarchy of slave holders had led astray their fellow Southerners and provoked acts of insurrection, most seriously the firing on Fort Sumter, that threatened the very foundation of their cherished republican form of government, based upon the principles of self-government, the rule of law, and the protection of individual rights from the tyranny of a few.

Once Fort Sumter fell, Northerners rose to excise this perceived malignant cancer of rebellion and restore the pre-Sumter health of the nation. The politically volatile questions concerning the status of slavery and the slave were not at issue for the majority of Northerners, as they focused their attention on the restoration of order in the rebellious Southern states.

Given superior Northern resources and available manpower, success seemed assured. The majority of the population believed that it would be a short war, of little cost to the nation. The general in chief, Winfield Scott, in a July 4 speech told his soldiers that they could look forward to eating Christmas dinner that year at home.[19] Once the traitorous Southern cabal had been broken, presumably as a result of a single successful military action, their Southern brethren would return to the Union, and the Northern volunteers, their work done, would return home better citizens for their brief experience as soldiers.

While the men of the 23d waited at Camp Diven for their turn to cross the river and join McDowell's growing field army, their biggest worry remained the possibility that they would miss the coming battle that would decide the war. When the false rumor circulated through the camp that the Rebels were seeking an amicable settlement of their differences with the North, Lieutenant Andrews noted that "loud and bitter crys arose against such a course." One enthusiastic Hornellsville soldier thought "it would do us good to see a battle"; he boasted, "When we get at them you will hear of some tall fighting, for we are just the boys that can clean their flues for them."[20]

On July 16, 1861, McDowell's 35,000-man army left Washington by three main routes followed by a number of civilians in carriages and on horseback hoping to witness the grand spectacle of war. The Southern Tier Regiment, however, had to remain behind. On the day that McDowell's advance began, Colonel Hoffman reported to his superiors that his regiment, 780 strong, was in no condition to take the field. Its weapons, he wrote, were "mostly worthless," and he had only ten thousand ball cartridges. He assessed that his men had only a fair proficiency in battalion drill, little or no skill in skirmish or bayonet drill, and only limited experience with the use of firearms, gained mostly from civilian life. In addition, he had no wagons for the transportation of supplies. Apparently only Surgeon Churchill's medical department was ready for active service.[21]

At Manassas Junction McDowell would face about equal numbers of Confederates under the overall command of Brig. Gen. Joseph E. Johnston, whose troops were drawn up behind a stream called Bull Run. The initial clash of the armies occurred at Blackburn's Ford on July 18. In this brief fight Pvt. John W. Walter, from Preble, of the Homer company (D), 12th New York Infantry, became the first battle death from Cortland

County. For the next two days the opposing forces maneuvered for position along the stream before engaging in the climactic battle on Sunday, July 21.

The Southern Tier men on Meridian Hill waited anxiously throughout the morning of the 21st for any news of the battle. Beginning around nine in the morning they could hear the rumble of distant cannon fire. At six, after evening dress parade, Colonel Hoffman formed his men into a hollow square to announce early word of a glorious Union victory. Although Hoffman warned them against a premature celebration, when Major Gregg called for three cheers, "Cheer upon cheer went up," along with hats and anything else the men could get their hands on and toss aloft.[22]

A few hours later messengers arrived from the battlefield with the grim truth of McDowell's terrible defeat. Sgt. Maj. Archibald DeVoe called all of the captains of the 23d together in the colonel's tent to receive new orders for the command to start for the front at four o'clock the next morning with two days' cooked rations. The captains immediately dispatched their orderlies into the company streets to rouse the men from their tents and start the company cooks preparing rations. "During the whole night, the camp was in an uproar," recalled a Company G man, "cooking, packing and preparing," and, added Seymour Dexter, generally "hallooing around." Then they waited and waited, without receiving the order to march. During the gloomy, rainy day that followed the day of battle, the men remained in camp, their emotions having swung "from exultation to despondency."[23]

On the 22d day of July the poet Walt Whitman stood on the rain-soaked streets of Washington to observe the sad return of the "baffled, humiliated, panic-struck" Army of Northeastern Virginia. The dirty, often unarmed soldiers arrived back in the city shamefaced, with no flags flying and no bands playing, to drop down in merciful sleep on doorsteps and in alleyways.[24] The news of the disaster spread rapidly, sending shock waves rippling throughout the North. But rather than plunging the nation into despair and collapse, the defeat only galvanized Northerners to greater effort. The day after the battle Lincoln called for an additional 500,000 volunteers for three years of military service.

The results of the First Battle of Bull Run (Manassas) support the contention of historian Bruce Catton and others that the Civil War ushered in the era of modern warfare. Gone were the days of limited warfare, decisive single battles, and the ritualized "honors of war" for the vanquished.

When the anticipated and longed-for early settlement of the conflict by a single campaign did not materialize, Northerners hunkered down to escalate the conflict, upping the ante in men and resources or whatever else necessary to achieve final victory on the battlefield. As Catton points out, however, one consequence of this "modern" approach to war was that men would no longer control war, it would control them.[25] Modern warfare quickly takes on a logic and momentum of its own that often leads the participants down paths they did not at the outset intend to travel.

After a sleepless night at the White House, President Lincoln on July 22 set to work to reform the broken regiments returning from the battlefield into an effective counterforce to deter a possible Confederate advance against Washington. That same day he sent for Maj. Gen. George B. McClellan to come east from service in western Virginia; he gave McClellan full authority to bring order out of the chaos resulting from McDowell's defeat and to direct the effort to rebuild the nation's military forces.[26]

McClellan appeared to be the perfect choice for the job. Just thirty-four years old, he had graduated second in his class at West Point and received two brevet promotions for superior service in the Mexican War; later he had had a successful career as a civilian engineer and railroad president. He was young, handsome, energetic, bright, and well grounded in the technical and organizational skills essential for the hard work ahead of turning the rag-tag units that fought at Bull Run into a trained and disciplined army.

When McClellan arrived in Washington on July 26 he discovered "no army to command, a mere collection of regiments cowering on the banks of the Potomac, some perfectly raw, others dispirited by their recent defeat." Confronting this deplorable situation with an air of confidence and ability, he immediately became the hero of the hour. The national leadership in Washington deferred to him in all military matters. "All tell me that I am held responsible for the fate of the Nation," he wrote his wife, "and that all its resources shall be placed at my disposal." McClellan's future seemed bright indeed.[27]

Strengthening the defenses on the Virginia approaches to Washington became McClellan's first order of business. On July 23 the Southern Tiers, and with at least four other regiments, crossed the Potomac to assist in securing the Virginia shore. By this time the 23d had received its supply wagons and had replaced its old muskets with 1853-pattern British Enfield "Rifle-muskets."[28] They departed Camp Diven at two in the afternoon and marched into the city "with music playing and colors flying, amidst the shouts of the multitude that lined either side of the route." The martial spirit in Washington must have revived somewhat from the day before, for officers had to instruct their companies not to stop or acknowledge the "endless demonstrations of approval" by civilian spectators. The Cortland Volunteers became the exception when, marching behind the regimental color guard, Captain Clark authorized his men to return the salute of a "beautiful young lady [who] tantalizingly waved the Stars and Stripes from a second story window."[29]

The column passed the base of the unfinished Washington Monument, then proceeded down Fourteenth Street to Long Bridge over the Potomac. The mile-long wooden bridge, described by Lieutenant Andrews as a "crazy old affair," had two draws for the passage of ships and ended on the Virginia shore at a small fortification called Fort Jackson. While crossing they passed ambulances still carrying wounded men from the battlefield to the Washington hospitals. Once on the Virginia shore the 23d marched past an old racetrack to a campsite on the right of the large (twelve-acre) Fort Runyon. The new campsite occupied a flat sandy area about fifty feet above and one-third of a mile back from the river. The Alexandria branch of the Chesapeake and Ohio Canal ran along the back of the camp, and about a mile beyond on a bluff overlooking the city the men could see the massive front pillars of the Robert E. Lee family mansion, "Arlington."[30]

During their brief two-week stay near Fort Runyon, the Southern Tier men tried to make their hot, treeless, mosquito-infested campground more livable. Following the common practice of "hawk striking," they raided a former camp of the New Jersey Regiment, where they found usable cooking utensils, table furniture, sugar, and other cast-off articles, including a bottle of Worcestershire sauce. From a local brickyard they took enough bricks for each company kitchen to form a fireplace using two rows of bricks a foot apart. For shade they cut down the slender red cedar trees lining the banks of the canal and stood them up between the tents and in ten-foot circles around the kitchens. The men of the company messes supplemented their rations with fresh perch and sunfish caught in the Potomac or with items purchased from local "high-priced hucksters" who sold bread for five cents a loaf, butter for thirty cents a pound, and milk for ten cents a quart.[31]

The soldiers' efforts at comfort notwithstanding, the camp of the 23d had little to recommend it. The swampy area, called by the medical personnel of the regiment a "miasmatic district," added a number of cases of treatable malarial fevers to the regiment's sick list.[32] As compensation, the site offered a magnificent view of the nation's capital across the river. Sandstone and marble buildings and structures reflected amber in the soft evening sunlight, and the long view down the sparkling Potomac served up an array of interesting sights. Seymour Dexter spoke of observing on the river the "trailing smoke of the steam tug or the sails of the schooner and now and then the more majestic form of a man-of-war, from whose sides salutes from thundering cannon pealed forth upon their arrival or departure."[33]

On July 24 and 25 the men had a chance to test out their new Enfields at the firing range. The highly regarded British Enfields, issued to fifty-seven out of 136 New York regiments formed in the first two years of the war, measured seventy-three inches in length with bayonet attached and weighed 9.2 pounds. Their barrels were "rifled," their interiors cut with lands, or spiral grooves, to spin the bullet when fired, thus giving the weapon greater range and accuracy than the older smoothbores that were in use throughout the war. One exceptional shot from Company K bragged, "I struck a target eight inches wide, three times out of six, at a distance of 150 yds, and upon increasing the distance to 200 found that the balls were more sure to strike the mark."[34]

The "ball" mentioned above was actually an elongated lead bullet of .577 caliber with a hollow base plugged by a wood insert. When fired, the base would expand, causing the soft lead to "bite" the rifling, which gave the ball a spin as it left the muzzle. The Hardee light infantry training manual (published in 1855 by William J. Hardee, now a Confederate brigadier general) in use by Colonel Hoffman and his officers called for a loading and firing procedure of nine steps. The soldier first placed the butt of his Enfield on the ground. He then reached into his cartridge box, which held up to forty rounds, to retrieve a paper cartridge consisting of a lead bullet combined with a premeasured amount of black powder in a greased-paper cylinder. The soldier opened the cartridge by tearing off the powder end with his teeth. He then poured the powder down the barrel, followed by the ball and paper. He disengaged the ramrod from its runner below the barrel and used it to ram down the bullet and seat it over the powder. After returning the ramrod, he lifted the weapon to open the nipple pathway to the powder by pulling back the hammer to half-cock. Reaching then into his cap box, located on his belt, he took a copper firing cap and placed it over the nipple. Pulling back the hammer to full cock, he was ready to fire. With training, a good soldier could get off three shots a minute.

On August 4 McClellan proceeded to organize his available infantry regiments into twelve brigades. The 23d, along with the 25th, 35th, and 37th New York regiments, formed a brigade under Brig. Gen. David Hunter, a veteran of the Battle of Bull Run. The next day, after burning all of their cut cedar trees in giant bonfires, the 23d marched up from the "mosquito coast" inland to a new camp less than half a mile beyond Arlington House. On first sight, however, the new ground seemed no more hospitable than the previous camp, being located beside a farmer's field "in a dense grove of white oak, peopled with flying squirrels, lizards, black snakes, and all manner of buzzing things."[35]

Hunter's brigade was positioned to support the construction of a chain of forts in Virginia running from Chain Bridge on the Potomac above Washington to near Alexandria below. The camp of the 23d sat between and a little back from two forts being built by the army engineers with soldier labor: Fort Jefferson on the left front (later named Fort Tillinghast) and Fort Ramsay on the right (later Fort Cass). A farm road led from near their camp out beyond the forts about three miles to Ball's Cross Roads, where the Union picket line was established. The 23d camped between the 35th New York on the left and the 2d Wisconsin of Brig. Gen. William T. Sherman's brigade on the right. General McDowell, in overall command on the Virginia front, occupied the Arlington house and grounds as his headquarters.[36]

Despite the "momentary thrill" of several alarms, the uneventful passage of days after the Bull Run defeat dissipated fears of a rapid Rebel advance against the capital. Instead of advancing, Johnston had his Confederate forces dig in on the heights near Centreville, Virginia, about twenty miles west of Washington. By going over to the defensive at this time, Johnston lost the best chance the South would have to bring the North to its knees, at a point when it was militarily and psychologically most vulnerable.

As the Union defensive works took shape, Northern troops gradually regained their confidence. Seymour Dexter, although admitting that the future looked "covered over with dark clouds," found new determination to remain in service for as long as it took "until the disgrace which our arms have suffered has been wiped away." Frederick Burritt of Company H assured his readers in the *Elmira Advertiser* that the soldiers were of "the right material" to get the job done and awaited only "Generals of skill and military education" to provide the needed training.[37]

Once settled into their Arlington camp, the Southern Tier Regiment went to work. Lieutenant Andrews wrote on August 29 that "the spirit of idleness that had so long hung over us, has flown, and now we are doing duty enough to please the most industrious. Hardly a day but every man of our company is drawn for duty of some kind,—either picket, guard, police, clearing land, building roads, at work on forts, or hewing out stockades." When a man did not draw any duty, according to Burritt, "his leisure [was] occupied with gun cleaning, bringing water, cooking, drying his clothes or some other pastime equally profitable."[38]

At the end of each workday, when the regiment assembled on the parade ground for dress parade, Adjutant William W. Hayt stepped out in front of the men to announce, "Attention to orders!" He then proceeded to read out the duty assignments for the next day. The duty day began at sunup, when Pvt. George Edgcomb and his fellow fifers and drummers sounded reveille, at which the men fell out on their company streets. After roll call by the first sergeants, sick call, and breakfast, the work details were formed. Typically seventy men of the regiment reported to the engineers building forts, 150 drew axes for felling trees, thirty reported for picket duty, and others were assigned to various camp duties. Occasionally one or more companies went out toward Ball's Cross Roads on reconnaissance to probe the enemy picket lines.[39]

Of the many possible duties that could be assigned them, the Southern Tier men liked chopping wood the least. Daily, fifteen to twenty-five men from each company under two captains and two or three lieutenants would cut trees in front of the camp to create obstructions against the enemy, clear ground for forts, or build roads. By August 24 a soldier in Company D estimated that hundreds of acres of local forest had been leveled by Yankee axes. The "havoc and waste" to the landscape continued apace into the summer. On September 15 one man speculated that General Lee would not have recognized his Arlington property had he returned.[40]

With so many young men entering the woods wielding axes, it is not surprising that the regiment experienced a number of accidents. On August 16 James Pease of Company C became the first member of the regiment to die, after receiving a blow to the head from a falling tree while on a chopping detail near Fort Jefferson. The company buried Pease in the Military Asylum (Soldier's Home) Cemetery in Washington, D.C.[41]

In contrast to chopping wood, duty on the picket line was, according to Pvt. William P. Maxson, "the pride and delight of the regiment. There was excitement in it, but not unattended with danger." On August 7 the 23d assumed responsibility for the sector of the picket line extending from near Ball's Cross Roads across two miles to Hunter's Chapel on the Columbia Turnpike (modern Route 244). The line consisted of a chain of three-man stationary posts, about a hundred yards apart, protected in front by a 220-yard belt of cut trees and bushes. A mobile cavalry picket guarded the no-man's-land between the Union pickets and General Johnston's picket line beyond the Alexandria, Loudoun, and Hampshire Railroad. The picket line acted as an early-warning system to detect any Confederate movement. Professor Thaddeus S. C. Lowe supplemented the picket screen with observations from the basket of his balloon, *Union,* hovering high over Fort Corcoran near Aqueduct Bridge over the Potomac.[42]

Although the Union pickets were instructed not to fire their weapons unless fired upon and not to leave their posts under any circumstances, Burritt confessed, "the disposition to reconnoitre pervades us, and is almost irresistible." The pickets would wander off between the lines to gather peaches and corn and "have some 'fun' with the rebels" by provoking their fire and then searching for the spent projectiles to bring back to camp as souvenirs.[43] Burritt wrote that Union pickets became "quite reckless in their sports and freaks when on duty." An opposing picket in this sector of the line one day observed a Yankee climb upon a fence and, while in full view of the Confederates, start "cutting up, going through such antics as twirling his fingers on his nose, shaking his fists, and dancing." Even Union officers joined in the picket "sports." Lieutenant Andrews and Sgt. Alvin F. Bailey went out one day to "reconnoitre" and received for their effort a bullet hole in Andrew's coat; the tassel of Bailey's Zouave-style cap was shot away. Another group of ten men out for some peaches came under fire from concealed Confederates. The Yankees quickly "put for the road," looking back to find only a black man visible. "Let. [Sgt. Lester D. Hawley, Co. G] was bound to shoot the nigger, but we thought he had better not, and so we started for the camp."[44]

At times, although strictly against orders, the opposing pickets would greet each other and even meet on neutral ground where, in the words of Colonel Hoffman, they "blackguarded together freely." One well-publicized meeting involving an officer of the 23d took place along the Alexandria, Loudoun, and Hampshire Railroad on the morning of September 2. A Confederate captain named Saunders approached the railroad waving his hand and asking for a parley with a Yankee of equal rank. Capt. Marshall M. Loydon of Company B, 23d, advanced and saluted, and the two men shook hands. The officers then sat down on the railroad embankment for a friendly chat. They agreed, among other things, that the "inhuman and barbarous" practice of shooting pickets was contrary to the rules of civilized warfare and not sanctioned by either side. The two officers parted amicably, Loydon giving Saunders a gift of cigars to share with his fellow officers.[45]

Life on the picket line turned more serious when, on August 25, Brig. Gen. James Longstreet advanced his troops to Upton's and Munson's hills, close to the railroad and only about three miles from Ball's Cross Roads. Soon U.S. congressmen on Capitol Hill could see a large Rebel flag flying over fortifications on Munson's Hill only about eight miles distant. In response to Longstreet's initial forward movement, on August 27 Colonel Hoffman sent out his right-wing companies, D, F, and A—jokingly referred to as the "Dutch Wing" of the regiment—to beef up his picket force at Ball's Cross Roads. Three companies of the 14th New York State Militia (84th New York Volunteers) went along, all under the command of Lieutenant Colonel Crane from the 23d.[46]

Leaving a reserve at the crossroads, Crane advanced the three companies of the 23d to occupy the brow of a hill overlooking the railroad, which in this area ran through a ravine. Crane sent Company A less than a mile to the north to a cornfield on Hall's Hill, where they served as a flank guard. He placed Company F in line of battle facing south behind a ditch bordering the main road. Company D joined the right of Company F, forming an angle along a crossroad, facing southwest. Soon after getting his men into position, Crane sent scouts under Lt. Newton T. Colby (Co. D) out beyond the railroad to locate the enemy.[47]

Sometime between two and four o'clock in the afternoon Crane heard skirmish fire erupt in his front. Then Colby's men came running back with the enemy in close pursuit, the Rebels "howling like maniacs" and yelling, "Shoot the sons of bitches!" Cpl. Thomas Carroll of Elmira and about five others were caught out in the open attempting to return and came under Rebel fire. Carroll fell dead with a ball through his heart, and two others received wounds. Crane had his troops in the road fall flat as the first Confederate musket balls flew whizzing over their heads. They then returned fire for a short time before Crane, whose orders had directed him not to bring on a general engagement, pulled his companies back to his reserves stationed at Ball's Cross Roads. Longstreet's troops pursued a short distance, but they did not push their attack.[48]

Although hardly living up to the name "Battle of Cow's Run," the skirmish of August 27 exposed a portion of the regiment to the trials of the battlefield and provided the men their first opportunity to test their fears in the face of Rebel fire. At an 1885 regimental reunion, Lieutenant Colonel Crane would candidly tell a group of 23d veterans that before the first fight "my greatest anxiety was for myself, whether I would have the nerve to face the chances of battle without showing the fear that was within me." He must have breathed a sigh of relief when one of his men wrote in his hometown paper of seeing Crane mounted on his black mare directing the fight with "perfect composure" as the "bullets fell like hail around him. . . . The boys who were with him say that they are willing to follow him into any battle. They have implicit confidence in his bravery." Other men contemplating their first battle during this period suggested similarly that their relationship with comrades provided a primary motivation for them to stand fire. An officer in the 35th New York admitted in the pages of a Corning newspaper: "As for myself, I believe I am too big a coward to run. For a choice I would prefer to meet balls of the rebels than the scoffs of my friends; that is the way I feel about it." Hosea H. Rockwell of the 23d in 1885 marveled in his speech to veterans at the power of the common trials and dangers of war to "knit men's hearts together" and give them courage.[49]

The Cow's Run skirmish provided the regiment with its first heroes and its first martyr. On August 29 many from the regiment attended Carroll's Catholic funeral. The Hornellsville paper wrote the epitaph: "He fell like a warrior, facing the foe." Sergeant Bailey in the Cortland paper declared, "Thus the first blood of our regiment has been shed in the cause of our country, and we live to avenge it."[50]

Blood was also spilled that August by the Cortland Volunteers in actions of a less ennobling kind. Horseplay between two men on the picket line resulted in the accidental shooting of one of them, Palmer Olmstead. During the same period the accidental discharge of a weapon wounded bystander Edgar Lincoln. The day after Edgar was shot, the body of a corporal in the 25th New York was brought in to camp; he had been shot mistakenly by one of his own sentries. Lieutenant Andrews recognized the victim as the man "who swallowed swords and ate pebbles for the amusement of the crowd at the last Cortland Co. Fair." No one, of course, found these tragic accidents amusing. Corporal Burritt wrote: "I trust that after the accidents and mishaps . . . there will be less boys play with loaded guns."[51]

Sickness also added to the losses in the regiment. The medical officers diagnosed fifteen cases of typhoid fever in the Arlington camp, of which two died. Even more prevalent were the "remittent" and "intermittent" malarial-type fevers, commonly called "Virginia fever." Lieutenant Andrews described the symptoms: "Imagine yourself lying some hot afternoon in your tent. . . . All at once you became aware of the attempts of a swarm of bees to congregate in your head." As you try to rise, "trees, tents, barns and fields are rolling around in terrific confusion," and you must sit. All the while your breakfast takes a notion to "secede." The doctor arrives to check your pulse and tongue. His treatment consists of a dose of about thirty grains of quinine, which sends you "franticly grasping for a canteen [to] inundate your internal economy as a counter irritant."[52] "Intermittent fever" struck down Lt. Alvah Waters the first week of September, requiring him to leave camp in an ambulance for treatment in Washington. He soon resigned his commission for health reasons. That resulted in Benjamin Andrews's becoming first lieutenant of Company H, with Sgt. Leonard F. Hathaway, a twenty-two-year-old farmer from Cuyler, Cortland County, replacing Andrews as second lieutenant.[53]

Despite the hard work and reduced ranks of the regiment, the extraordinary number of extant photographs of the 23d in camp at Fort Runyon and at Arlington Heights seem to confirm, outwardly, at least, the description of the regiment by one of its members as "the gay, jovial and jocose 23rd!!"[54] One Sunday Lieutenant Andrews looked out from his tent to describe an appealing scene for his newspaper readers. He noted that from one tent came voices singing "How Sweet This Sight unto the Lord." At the same time a black man passed by singing "Away Down South in Dixie," and down the way a violinist in Company K played "Roy's Wife." Nearby, "a talented swearer vociferates that he will 'go two better.'" All the while Samuel Palmer could be heard "blowing furiously upon a fife," producing a "very large noise." Palmer and drummer Edgcomb, along with their counterparts in other companies, provided much of the ubiquitous camp music that set the rhythm of the soldiers' day, from reveille at sunup to the tune "The Girl I Left behind Me" at tattoo.[55]

Inwardly, however, the men felt the strain of their long absence from home. Private Edgcomb wrote to his family on August 7 that the night before he and tent mate Sam Palmer had lain awake far into the night listening to the tree toads and talking over "old Cortland times." Captain Clark confessed to a friend that at times he "wished myself back in my cozy little room at the Cortland House [Hotel] reclining in an easy chair . . . with a good 'Havana' in my mouth." He went on to reminisce about "those more happy days. I knew no care—managed to pay my board—lived independent—was a lord of creation." The familiar sounds of a train whistle and the ringing church bells in Washington set Lieutenant Andrews to pondering "how it came about that I, or the great world around me had changed so, since those don't-care-a-fig days."[56]

Underlying many of the soldiers' nostalgic thoughts of home was an unsettling feeling that in their extended absence old friends and loved ones would forget them, that the towns where they had grown up would prosper just fine without them. A Solon man after two months' service wrote home in a humorous vein, "I presume the girls will all be married off before I get home and I shall have to live an old Bach all the days of my life. Now would not that be a pitty." Drummer Edgcomb on September 5 commented on the upcoming changeover to gas streetlights in Cortland and predicted, "By the time I get back you will probably have street cars running your streets and omnibuses and carts so thick that you can not cross from one walk to another."[57]

Long thinking of home could result in severe homesickness, or "disease of the heart," as Andrews termed it, which could be as debilitating to a regiment as Virginia fever. Pvt. Joseph Peek of the Cortland Volunteers, an illiterate twenty-three-year-old farm laborer from Homer, provides a case in point. Captain Clark noted that Peek always seemed "unwell" when any alarm sounded, and he at times became "so affected as to cry." On September 20 Peek took a pistol and a pail down to the spring at the foot of the hill for water. A shot rang out, and soon Peek returned with his right thumb hanging from his hand by a piece of skin. Pulling the thumb free, Peek claimed his wounding was accidental. Clark thought he had shot himself on purpose, knowing that, now unable to cock his Enfield, he would be sent home. Clark gladly signed Peek's discharge paper, noting on the form, "He has been happier since [the "accident"] then before."[58]

As their time in service lengthened, the soldiers increasingly worried about the deleterious effect that military life might have on their personal lives. Before the Civil War Americans had not held the professional soldier in high regard. If considered part of society at all, the soldier was thought of as a misfit, appropriately exiled to the wilds of the frontier, which better suited his indolent nature.[59] Certainly the vast majority of Civil War volunteers had no interest in following the profession of arms. They worried as much as their civilian leaders about the corrupting and degrading influences of soldier life, and they took to heart Congressman Diven's warning to be on their guard against the temptations that they would face while in uniform. They understood the paradox of the citizen-soldiers returning home corrupted from the war, unworthy as citizens and thus unable to realize the benefits and virtues of democratic society that they had left home to preserve.

By the fall of 1861 many Southern Tier men were writing of the harmful temptations and spiritual dangers they encountered in camp. Captain Clark confirmed: "This is really the most detestable kind of a life to lead. . . . We see no society, have no inducements to grow better, but every inducement to degenerate. . . . [We are] thrown among men whose whole caste is vulgarity and sensuality. Let any man follow it for life and he becomes a barbarian." Seymour Dexter concluded, "No pure mind can *like* to be a soldier"; he lamented, "Oh, I would like to spend one Sunday in civilized life." Lieutenant Andrews provided his Cortland newspaper readers a chilling scenario of the poisonous effects that military life might have on their sons, husbands, and fathers if left unchecked. He invited them to imagine the "turning loose upon the order loving North, 400,000 men, grown lawless and reckless, two years behind the age, in mental, moral, and social improvement, a home life grown distasteful to them and with a penchant for a wild roving order of things."[60]

Members of the 23d reported on the "works of the Devil" they struggled with in camp. Ami W. Osgood (Co. G) thought that a man must possess "extraordinary strength of character to withstand the temptations, for he is surrounded by every kind of bad influence. . . . Men who came in good faith to fight the battles of their country, who would have scorned the utterance of an oath, will now swear and bluster with the most vile, and play cards without hesitation." Seymour Dexter claimed, "There is but one officer in our whole regiment besides our chaplain but what uses profane language." Corporal Burritt sadly commented on fellow soldiers stealing, or "hawk striking," private possessions within the company. His description of one young Cortland Volunteer printed in a newspaper article must have caused many a Cortland mother to blanch: "We have a belligerent member of Co. H, aged 15 years and 18 days—a precocious warrior . . . , who can keep his arms in order, endure fatigue, illustrate the theory of self denial, use expletives, adjectives and interjections in conversation, and chew tobacco as well as 'any other man.'"[61]

The antidote to this condition, it was generally understood, was for the soldiers to cleave to the values, institutions, and familiar social bonds of home. Lieutenant Andrews praised the imprint of Cortland on their lives, which, he said, has "gone before us like a pillar of fire, and I hope we may never be so far removed, as to be entirely begone its cheering influence."[62]

The primary link with home remained the personal letters written and received by the soldiers. Andrews lectured the Cortland community on the importance of their letters to his men. "If you have a friend in our company, write to him long and often. Let all write. I think of no more holy influence brought to bear upon our boys than that emanating from home-born letters. Write about everything that will remind the boys of home, if it is nothing more than how the peas grow in the back garden. Send them a clover leaf, a flower, and the fragile tribute will form a link in the chain that shall bind them in all their ramblings to the 'Old Hearth Stone.'" Private Dexter described his letter writing as an intimate experience. He told his sweetheart that he liked to take his writing materials into the woods "beyond the turmoil of the camp, to have a cozy talk with you." All encouragement was given to soldiers to write home. Congressman Rodolpus H. Duell (R) offered to extend his congressional franking privileges to Cortland men of the Southern Tier Regiment if needed. By October 1861 an average of a bushel of letters a day left the Southern Tier camp for posting in Washington.[63]

Newspapers also kept the soldiers abreast of hometown news and the course of national events. Captain Clark begged the home folks to "send us some of your papers; you can't imagine how we would prize them." In addition, the soldiers could purchase copies of the New York, Philadelphia, and Washington papers. Lieutenant Andrews claimed that the men of the 23d received or purchased about five hundred papers per day.[64]

To a considerable extent, the regiment functioned as the soldiers' extended family, with its own structure of authority and strict code of ethics. Colonel Hoffman represented the primary authority figure in the lives of his men. Like a stern father, he attempted to sublimate their youthful impulses in daily hard work and focused effort. He limited the number of passes issued to the men to visit Washington and established a corporal of the guard to patrol the camp, arrest all men found gambling or firing their weapons within the lines, and "preserve order generally." As a result a soldier could report in the *Corning Journal* that "the regiment is very orderly—no drunkenness—no quarreling, and good attention to duties gives promise that it will reflect honor upon the counties from which it has been gathered." Burritt contrasted the camp of the 23d with that of the 35th nearby, where he saw "every seated group absorbed in the game of 'Bluff' [poker]; the hard earnings of a soldier scattered and staked in profusion—a pastime not tolerated here." Lieutenant Waters proudly reported that the men of the Cortland Company were determined "to preserve untarnished their morals," pledging, among other things, "to drink no intoxicating drinks during the term of enlistment."[65]

In the closed male society of the military camp, Hoffman encouraged the civilizing and refining presence of women. Women visitors from home were a frequent sight around camp. Two women, as mentioned previously, stayed in camp with their husbands. On August 14 the wives and family members of the field officers arrived and took up residence in a large tent specially fitted out into seven apartments. Mrs. Sarah Morse appeared on the official roster of the regiment from June 30, 1861, to October 1861, under appointment as a hospital nurse.[66]

Other civilians working as officers' servants or employees of the regimental sutler maintained a hometown presence in camp. Captain Clark, for example, hired Peter Jackson, a black hostler from the Cortland House Hotel, where Clark had had a room before enlistment, to act as his camp servant. Consistent with state law, Hoffman authorized a civilian to act as the regimental sutler, providing to the soldiers (often at exorbitant prices) familiar small luxuries not available from the army quartermaster. Sutlers, referred to as a "necessary evil" by the Paymaster General of the Army, traveled with the regiment and came under the authority of the colonel. In the fall of 1861 "Blossom and Jillson" are mentioned as sutlers for the 23d (the former presumably Enos Blossom, a past proprietor of the Brainard House Hotel in Elmira). Later O. G. Judd became the sutler for the regiment, at the head of an organization that Judd described as including three assistants, two black employees, two wagons, and six horses.[67]

The chaplain of the regiment represented the religious values and moral standards of the soldiers' home communities. Chaplain Ezra F. Crane, a respected Baptist minister from Elmira referred to by the men as a "kind father," also served the regiment as postmaster and occasionally brought the sick into his tent for special care. General McClellan underscored the importance of religious instruction for his troops in General Orders No. 7 (September 6, 1861), in which he set aside Sundays after inspection for rest and divine services. McClellan claimed it a "sacred duty" for the men to observe Sundays as a holy day in order to "deserve the benign favor of the Creator" in achieving the objectives of their "holy cause."[68]

Chaplain Crane assumed a major role in the day-to-day life of the men. In addition to conducting Sunday service, he held evening prayer meetings and organized a Bible class, which was regularly attended by sixty members of the regiment. Private Edgcomb thought in many ways the pious atmosphere of the Arlington camp reminded him of the Methodist camp meetings of his youth, except that "there are not quite so many of the fair sex to be seen or not so many wagons around." In September Crane assured the Chemung River Baptist Association that the "Spirit of the Lord" was "effectually at work" among the 23d. Private Dexter agreed, describing an appealing scene of soldiers each evening sitting on the ground in front of the chaplain's tent, the oak leaf canopy above them for a church and the silver moon for light. "It would be so romantic," he concluded, "were there not so much wickedness around."[69]

The obverse of holding Cortland up as a "Pillar of Fire" was that the soldiers would not tolerate in the home front any signs of weakness or lack of determination in supporting them. In one letter Edgcomb apologized to his family for "scolding" them about not writing more. Lt. Hugh J. Baldwin (Co. E) criticized his sister, "I think you and Ma show yourselves very childish in borrowing so much trouble about 'my coming home.'" He expected them to show "at *least* courage enough" to support him in fulfilling his military obligation. Chauncey Judd, an eighteen-year-old farm laborer from Cortlandville, bluntly told his dependent mother that "their mabe such a thing that I shall get shot but never mind. That I could not come home now if I had a chance for my country needs me and I went in and I shall stay till I get my discharge. Keep good courage and I shall be back before long."[70]

Although separated from Cortland in distance, the three line officers of Company H continued to exert a powerful influence over their home communities through their letters and statements printed in the local newspapers. The three men had been relatively unknown lawyers before the war but quickly gained prominence and respect in the county once they became leaders of Cortland's young soldiers serving at the front. Their youth, vigor, and positions of leadership contrasted favorably in the eyes of the citizens with the stodgy town elders like Henry Stephens, who, to some degree, faded from public attention into their conservative law offices on Main Street.

When the directors of the Cortland Volunteer Fund failed to pay promptly the expenses of Clark's company before their departure, Lieutenant Waters chided them in the paper: "Gentlemen, you should have paid those bills." When Sgt. Alvin Bailey returned to Cortland in September to recruit for the company, he complained about what he perceived to be a different level of patriotism in the county from five months before. He found himself in competition with recruiters from the 10th New York Cavalry Regiment and a new three-year Cortland County regiment (76th New York) forming at Camp Campbell on the county fairgrounds near Cortland Village. Nelson W. Green, a former cadet at West Point, had been given authority by the governor to raise the regiment from Cortland County and the surrounding area. Only about forty county boys initially joined the 10th (mostly in Companies A and C), and only about three hundred from the county went with the "Cortland County Regiment" (mostly in Companies A, B, D, F, and G). Bailey complained to Clark that after September he could find no one in Cortland to enlist in the 23d, that the other recruiters had torn down his handbills and pressured prospects not to talk with him. Green attributed his recruiting difficulties around Cortland at this time to what he perceived to be a "decided disloyal sentiment" existing in the local counties. Clark called the treatment of Bailey by the local authorities "dammed mean" and thought that if he had been Bailey he would not have tolerated it. "Damned pretty patriotism," he concluded, "but they will repent it."[71]

When Lieutenant Andrews learned of a so-called "peace meeting" to be held by the more conservative Democrats in Cortland, he took up his pen to lambaste the community in the *Republican Banner*. If the town supported such treason, Andrews fumed, "then do I renounce all allegiance, all loyalty, all respect and regard for the town we had loved." Speaking for the company, he offered to give back to the county the flag that *they* had "sullied and dishonored," so that they might, in turn, give it to the Confederate president, Jeff Davis. He complained that the Cortland Volunteers had always anticipated the time when they would meet the Rebels on the battlefield, "but it never entered our hearts to guard the home side of ourselves."[72]

In fact, forty county Democrats did meet at the Eagle Tavern on September 3, producing a resolution calling for a more conciliatory national policy toward the South with the immediate objective of restoring the shattered Union through an armistice and compromise. Since this thinking was not inconsistent with the thinking of many Northerners at this stage in the war, the paper seemed hardly justified in proclaiming the attendees "Breckinridge Conspirators in Conclave," giving "Aid and Comfort to Armed Traitors!" The paper went on to identify the other sympathizers, so-called Peace Democrats, in the county; they, it suggested, should be shunned by the community and "avoided as we would avoid the pestilence." The paper warned these men to watch what they did and said, and provided a cautionary tale concerning Noyes Palmerter, who lived in Scott. An outspoken opponent of the war, Palmerter had one evening found his house surrounded by thirty or forty angry neighbors and a martial band playing patriotic airs. Only after a boarding party laid a ladder against his house did Palmerter emerge to "renounce his secession principles." Once satisfied, the mob left Palmerter in peace. Lieutenant Andrews, who had helped stir community emotions with his fiery printed statements, tried to calm things down by writing on September 17, "So long as the bone and sinew of the old County is all right we don't trouble our heads about the excrescences."[73]

In truth, during this stressful period Cortland remained a "Pillar of Fire" in support for her soldiers. Many Northern communities had difficulty raising troops in the fall of 1861 after the initial rush to arms. Cortland recruiters had to reach deeper into the pool of available men, as evidenced by the profile of the four hundred county enlistees in the 10th New York Cavalry and the 76th New York. The average age of recruits had risen from twenty-two in the spring of 1861 to twenty-four, and almost 25 percent of the men in the new regiments were married.

Cortland also continued to support President Lincoln and the Republican politics of war. Charles A. Kohler and the "Peace party" of former Breckinridge Democrats represented only a small minority of Cortland residents. The leading Democrats, Horatio Ballard and Hiram Crandall, readily lent their support to the new nonpartisan Union party, made up of like-minded Democrats and Republicans who backed administration policies to prosecute the war to the fullest. Henry S. Randall, who before the war had led, with Kohler, the Breckinridge faction in the county, subordinated his politics to support various soldier relief efforts.[74]

From the very start of the war Cortland women pitched in to do their part. Henry Randall's wife, Jane Rebecca (Polhemus), volunteered to serve as county agent for the New York Women's Central Association of Relief (WCAR), and later, in early 1863, she accepted an appointment as associate manager of the Sanitary Commission for Cortland County. When the WCAR first put out a call for needed hospital stores after the Battle of Bull Run, Cortland women, despite the demands of the harvest and haying season, plunged into the work. They formed sewing circles in their homes and went house to house to gather cloth to take to the courthouse for separation and shipment. One "spirited" lady from McGrawville, the local paper reported, made some thirty shirts. "Other ladies' sewing machines, too, hummed day and night, for the three or four days during which the good work was in progress." Randall collected the packages of goods in her house and then sent them on to WCAR offices in New York City, often at her own expense. She could do no less, she explained, having been moved so by the number of local women who arrived at her doorstep with their precious packages. "I almost weep," she wrote, "when these plain rural people come to send their simple offerings to absent sons and brothers, fighting and dying under the banner of the Republic."[75]

Although Randall promised to not "let the fire flag" in Cortland, she faced many obstacles to her work. "This is a charming rural region," she explained to WCAR authorities, but it contained only small lots of poor soil, suitable for the most part only for grazing. The people were frugal and included no "thieves or beggars," but, she offered, "there are not a dozen opulent individuals in the county! Nineteen out of every twenty articles I have sent to you have been made by the personal labor of people who employ no servants."[76]

Undaunted, Randall continued the work of the WCAR throughout the war. She repeatedly issued newspaper appeals calling on county women to show as much or more devotion to their cause as the women of the South. "Are we not as affectionate, resolute and as self-sacrificing as they?" one article challenged. In addition, she organized lectures to raise operating funds and published lists of items sent from particular communities "as a strong reminder to the backward regions to do their duty!" By war's end she had accomplished the enviable record of forwarding 189 packages of goods and supplies from the Cortland area.[77]

Many Cortland women also sent boxes of supplies directly to their soldiers in the field. Favorite items included dried beef, cheese, butter, cake, canned fruit, bread, current wines, socks, shirts, "housewives" (small kits of pins, sewing thread, and needles), bouquets of dried flowers, and "havelocks" (linen military cap covers that draped over the back of the neck to keep off the sun). Lieutenant Andrews responded in the local paper to the receipt of one such shipment with the words, "Gentle females, you are kind, and good, and nice, and we are thankful, and grateful." Burritt at one point had to call tactfully upon the ladies to stop making the useless havelocks, which only served to keep any breath of cooling air from parched necks.[78]

By the fall of 1861 both Cortland soldiers and civilians had emerged from the Bull Run defeat with a greater understanding of the seriousness of their undertaking and an acceptance of the need for greater sacrifice and personal commitment in the cause of Union. A young girl from Solon wrote her soldier friend that "it is right that you should go, I suppose, but it seems hard to have our friend[s] leave us and especially when they are in so much dainger. . . . But oh, I cannot think that all of our friends are going never to return. We must not think so, we must look at the bright side and do all of the good we can. . . . The boys that leave their pleasant home and friends, to free their and our country can never be forgotten, no never. If the Cortland boys are sick we will come and take care of them if we are needed." A Virgil mother wrote to her soldier boy, "Forgive me for every unkind word I have ever spoken to you. I often regret that I have not made things more pleasant for you . . . than I have, now that you have it so hard." When Sergeant Bailey recruited two of four brothers in October 1861 for the 23d New York, he met their parents, "who with tears in their eyes, and with hearts full of devotion to their country, cheerfully offered them all. Said the old gentlemen to me, 'I wish that I could go with them, sir, but I am too old, but I willingly give them up; they will never run.'"[79]

The soldiers likewise thought deeply on their service to their country and how they must now endure even greater hardships if they were to see the crisis through. Captain Clark wrote to a friend in early July, "I find that great responsibility makes me serious and I am having a load to carry now. I am living fast—that is seeing a great deal of the world in a short time. Around as far as eye can see lies tented fields and it means something. If one stops to think, he can not really be light hearted or reckless." A young Solon recruit spoke for most of his comrades when he wrote, "This war must be put down and I am one among the many who have left their homes for a while to fight for our country's freedom, not as our fore Fathers fought to gain it, but to retain it. And when that is accomplished I am comming [sic] home." Seymour Dexter struck a common theme of both civilians and soldiers after Bull Run with his words, "It is not now time for affection to rule the heart, stern duty points the way."[80]

CHAPTER 3

A Hundred
Circling Camps

O nce settled into a permanent camp, the Southern Tier men turned
their attention to the "stern duty" of becoming soldiers. They understood what was expected of them. "Each must sacrifice his indi-
viduality, personal comfort and private plans," wrote Fred Burritt,
"and become a mere automatic item in the machinery of a great offensive
and defensive weapon of the Nation."[1] Their transformation from civilians to soldiers had begun when they first donned the common uniform
of blue and joined the "family" of their company to live under its rigid
structure of military rules and regulations.

Training began with the "School of the Soldier." Instructors taught
the men coordinated marching, facing and wheeling movements at different rates of speed, the manual of arms, and the loading and firing of
their Enfields in the prescribed nine steps. Advancing to the "School of the
Company," the men learned their position in the basic two-rank "battle
line," upon which most of the tactical battlefield movements of Civil War
armies depended. Once deployed, a company battle line moved in a solid
bricklike formation with the two long closed ranks, or lines, of men touching elbows, the ranks separated by only thirteen inches of space. The fixed
positions of line officers and noncommissioned officers formed the matrix
or outline of the battle line according to rank (the captain, for example,
took his post on the far right of the front line), with the troops filling
the long spaces between. Given the inevitable losses of men during an

active campaign, the battle lines could be maintained and adjusted at any time by having the men form into line, tallest men on the right, and then count off from the right in each rank by two. The men thus established a four-man grouping (an odd and even file) called "Comrades in Battle," in which they would subsequently locate and with which they would identify themselves. Through repetitive drill and practice it was intended that the movements of the men into and out of line and column would become automatic, without the need for individual thought or decision.

Further integration into the "machinery" of the army proceeded with instruction in the "School of the Battalion" or regiment. Here the company practiced with the nine other companies of the regiment to form an extended battle line segmented by companies, and forming essentially the long base of a flat triangle. The solid base served as a firing platform from which sprouted, from both ranks, five hundred leveled rifle-muskets. Behind the firing line layers of staff and field officers took specific positions of control, with the entire formation thus narrowing back to the point of the triangle, where sat the colonel, mounted on horseback, overlooking and directing all.

The complicated training manuals used by Civil War officers were designed to instruct commanders in the two essential tasks thought necessary for the successful operation of the army. First, they must move troops and their supply wagons in long columns across great distances under often adverse conditions of weather and terrain to arrive on the battlefield with the units intact and ready to fight. Second, once on the field of battle, officers must quickly form battle lines and advance them like rigid plow blades, within larger brigade or division formations, at times in headlong frontal assaults across open ground against prepared enemy positions. Once coming face to face with the enemy, just within effective enemy musket range, the men would, in theory, halt, level their weapons, and deliver a devastating, concentrated volley of fire intended to derange and soften their opponent's battle formations. A decisive battle, so the thinking went, would then culminate with the fixing of bayonets, a soul-stirring cheer, and a charge over the remaining distance under fire to close with and overwhelm the weakened opponent in close combat. The inevitable and anticipated shock of battle in hand-to-hand fighting favored the better trained and disciplined force, which, by its ability to maneuver and deliver volley fire under great emotional and physical stress, gained the critical momentum and psychological advantage of the contest.

Actually, however, there was great disparity between the theory and actual practice on the battlefield. Few commanders could maintain their regimental alignments for long after the start of an attack, particularly over broken ground or under enemy fire. When going up against a prepared and fortified defensive line, the task proved almost impossible. One man in the 9th New York at the Battle of Antietam found it "astonishing how soon, and by what slight causes, regularity of formation and movement are lost in actual battle. Disintegration begins with the first shot. To the book-soldier all order seems destroyed, months of drill apparently going for nothing in a few minutes."[2]

A number of factors explain why the Northern volunteer did not, for the most part, live up to the strict standards of battle tactics detailed with such precision in contemporary training manuals. First and foremost, the Northern volunteer considered himself a citizen-soldier accepting military service on his own terms, under a temporary agreement with Uncle Sam to serve with the limited goal of defeating Rebel armies on the battlefield and restoring the Union. In general, he did not fight with a passion for conquest or personal gain or with a deep-seated hatred toward his enemy. He saw himself less as a warrior than as a carpenter, using the tools of war to repair the crumbling political house of the nation.

Poor leadership also reduced the effectiveness of the Northern volunteer, especially during the first two years of the war. Observers of New York troops attributed the problem to the pernicious state practice of having members of regiments elect their commissioned and noncommissioned officers. The skills that got officers elected, the critics pointed out, were "generally incompatible with the power to enforce subordination and discipline."[3]

The Union defeat at Bull Run (Manassas) provides many examples of the effects of poor leadership in battle. The story of the Homer Company (D), 12th New York, is illustrative. Capt. George Stone, a popular twenty-one-year-old former student, resigned before the battle, accepting a paymaster position in the navy as, presumably, more suited to his talents. During the fight at Blackburn's Ford on July 18, 1861, two companies of the 12th broke and ran when they first came under enemy fire, precipitating the unauthorized retreat of the regiment and threatening the outcome of the battle. The remaining original commissioned line officers in the Homer company (Lucius Storrs and George Snyder) resigned on October 23, 1861, citing their own incompetence as officers. Indeed, of

Washington, D.C., late summer of 1861. Note the unfinished Washington Monument and dome of the Capitol. The camp of the 23d New York is indicated by the red cedar trees cut from the banks of the canal (light-colored strip of earth running across photo from buildings on left) and placed among the tents. The Long Bridge is visible at upper right. *(Boston Athenaeum. See also OR Atlas, plate 6, no. 1)*

the commissioned officers in the thirty-eight two-year state infantry regiments, two-thirds never completed their term of service, resigning or being discharged, and at least one-third resigned within the first six months after enlistment. Subsequent to the Battle of Bull Run, both state and Federal authorities attempted to remedy the situation by authorizing military boards to examine and rule upon the qualifications of volunteer officers. New York State General Order 78 (July 30) stated that henceforth the governor, as commander in chief of the state's forces, would appoint all

field officers. Candidates would have to pass an examination for fitness before receiving their commissions.[4]

The improved weaponry of the period also restricted the ability of Civil War soldiers to employ linear tactics on the battlefield effectively. Long-range artillery and rifled shoulder arms inflicted casualties among an attacking force often as soon as it deployed for an assault, creating a littered landscape of cast-off equipment, dead and wounded men, and horses. Men advancing in lines over such ground would naturally break ranks to clear obstacles, avoid trampling the dead, or stop and assist the wounded. Once they broke elbow-to-elbow contact, the entire line trembled on the edge of dissolution and collapse. "Men fight in masses," explained one soldier of the 79th New York.

To be brave they must be inspired by the feeling of fellowship. Shoulder must touch shoulder. As gaps are opened the men close together, and remain formidable. But when the ranks are torn by artillery, the cohesion begins to fail. Then expose the men for several hundred yards to a murderous fire of musketry, and front rank man is gone, rear rank man is gone, comrades in battle are gone too. A few men struggle along together, but the whole mass has become diluent [diluted]. Little streams of men pour in various directions. They no longer are amenable to command. The colors must be drawn to a place of safety, and in time the men will gather around it again.[5]

Thus, when measured against the severe standards of professional European armies, the Northern volunteer did not seem to make a very good soldier. He lacked the iron discipline and blind obedience to the impersonal rules of early nineteenth-century warfare that foreign observers thought so essential to victory on the battlefield. In general, he griped constantly, malingered when convenient, straggled during long marches, and occasionally, just occasionally, ran from the terrors of battle.[6] Yet despite whatever shortcomings he might have had as a soldier, he and his comrades would endure four long years of trial and suffering, and eventually achieve all of the goals for which they had gone to war—and much more.

In the summer of 1861 no one understood the importance of military organization and training for the new volunteers better than General Mc-Clellan. On August 4 he formed his troops into twelve brigades, ten of the twelve brigade commanders being graduates of West Point. McClellan directed his generals to "at once establish schools of instruction" for the training of field officers and as many subordinate officers as possible.[7]

Further army organization continued throughout the summer. For a short time after Gen. David Hunter became ill, his brigade, which included the 23d, came under the command of Col. John Sedgwick as the Ninth "Reserve Brigade," to be stationed on Arlington Heights.[8] The men had little time to complain about this "reserve" status before they again became a field brigade under the command of the fifty-three-year-old Brig. Gen. James S. Wadsworth.

The brigade quickly came to love General Wadsworth. One of his men fondly described him as having "a form erect, a keen, piercing eye, hair frosted over . . . , with a Roman nose, and a step elastic as a boy." Unlike most of the other brigade-command appointees, Wadsworth could

The "Cedar Tree" camp of the 23d New York outside of Washington, summer 1861. Officers of the Cortland Volunteers (Company H): from left, Lt. Alvah Waters, Capt. Martin C. Clark, and 2d Lieutenant B. B. Andrews. Note the flag, which had been presented to the company at Cortland. *(Author's collection)*

claim no previous military experience beyond a stint as a volunteer aide to Gen. Irvin McDowell during the Bull Run campaign. His was a political appointment, he being the scion of a prominent upstate New York landholding family and an influential leader in the state Republican party. Despite his lack of military credentials, however, Southern Tier men took to him right away in response to his many kindnesses toward them and his paternal concern for their welfare.[9]

On August 24 General Wadsworth's brigade joined Brig. Gen. Erasmus D. Keyes's New York brigade to form a division under General McDowell in McClellan's newly named Army of the Potomac. Two days later the men got a good look at both McClellan and McDowell when the division paraded before them on an old race course near Fort Runyon. McDowell had just gotten his eight New York regiments formed across the broad meadow when a cloud of dust on the road announced the

"Cedar Tree" camp, summer 1861. Company street of the Cortland Volunteers. *(National Archives)*

arrival of President Lincoln and Secretary of State Seward in an open carriage accompanied on horseback by McClellan and his staff. The troops dressed their ranks and presented arms as a military band struck up the "Star Spangled Banner." The subsequent review by the dignitaries came off without a hitch, much to the satisfaction and delight of the troops. Lieutenant Andrews called it a "splendid spectacle," during which observers could see the "measured tread and meaning glitter of the bayonets of over 6,000 soldiers."[10]

It can be said of both Generals McClellan and McDowell that few other Northern generals began the war with more desirable credentials, more self-confidence in their ability to organize and lead victorious armies, or more opportunity to see their ambitions realized. Both failed, conspired against by circumstances and dragged down by the frailties and limitations of their own personalities. Both would emerge from the war as tragic figures—in the case of McDowell, almost comical.

As for McClellan, from the time he first took command in Washington he seemed to personify the thoughts and aspirations of his men. They could identify with his youthful spirit, self-confidence, earnestness of

Another view of the Washington camp, summer 1861. Pvt. George Edgcomb is thought to be in this group. On August 7, 1861, he wrote that he and his tent mates had their photograph taken "sitting in front" of their tent. *(Katcher Collection, USAMHI)*

purpose, and apparent unconcern for the trappings of rank. Lieutenant Andrews seeing McClellan for the first time gushed, "Imagine a school boy of about twenty [he was actually thirty-four], light, waving hair, an open, frank, and yet strongly expressioned eye, a slight, muscular form, and a perfectly careless and unassuming manner."[11] His handsome appearance and physical vigor became the stuff of lore (a reporter passed on the story that McClellan "has been known to take a two shilling piece between his thumb and forefinger and bend it double").[12] A fellow officer tried to give some idea of McClellan's appeal by relating his typical reaction when receiving the cheers of his troops. He "gave his cap a little twirl, which with bow and smile seemed to carry a little of personal good fellowship even to the humblest private soldier."[13] When the men responded to his gesture with delight, McClellan beamed back, looking "as pleased as a child with its toy."[14] One man effused, "All are in love with our young General, and ready to follow him." Another added, "We believe in his star."[15]

Another view of the summer 1861 camp. Group includes Cpl. Daniel O. Clough. *(Author's collection)*

The forty-two-year-old General McDowell, on the other hand, took a little more getting used to. Seymour Dexter described him as five feet, nine or ten inches tall (most other sources say he was about six feet tall), "very broad through the chest, and quite fleshy, of a sandy complexion with a very round face and with a short chubby nose." On the surface he seemed to possess all the qualifications of a successful commander. He was knowledgeable and well versed in his chosen profession, having studied military science in France and at West Point, where he later taught tactics. He valued loyalty to superiors and approached his assigned tasks with a determined energy based not on politics, in which he had little interest, or self-promotion, but a deeply felt patriotism and sense of duty.[16]

At the same time, however, McDowell came across to his fellow officers as a cold fish—aloof, arrogant, excitable, and fault finding. He often barked orders in a rough, irritatingly metallic voice. He nodded off to sleep easily when fatigued, often at the most inopportune moments (even standing up), and he habitually forgot names and faces. In appearance he tried to project the image of an important, historic figure, strutting about the grounds of Arlington in his uniform and a white helmet topped by a glistening metal spike that complemented a persona of a "marshal of the First Empire."[17]

During his Civil War service McDowell remained a man of odd contrasts. He swore off all stimulants, including tobacco, tea, and coffee, but he made up for it by becoming a "Gargantuan feeder" at the table. During one meal at his Arlington headquarters an officer watched in awe as McDowell became "so absorbed in the dishes before him that he had but little time for conversation." After gobbling his way through a number of offerings, he consumed an entire watermelon, enthusiastically pronouncing it "monstrous fine!"[18]

He was not prepossessing in appearance. He had an oddly formed body, short legs supporting a large frame, with "broad rolling hips that worked up and down when he walked." His misproportioned shape rendered him an uninspiring horseman who frequently tumbled from the saddle. Awkwardness on foot and horseback, however, apparently proved no hindrance to a passion for the waltz or to an ability to twirl his large "beefy" frame across the dance floor with "sylph-like grace."[19]

By mid-September 1861 it had become apparent to all observers that McClellan had worked miracles, doubling the protective forces near Washington to 85,000 men and infusing a new confident spirit in the army. In a short time he had transformed the landscape surrounding Washington into a vast fortified camp. Sentries now walked the eight-to-ten-foot earthen walls of forts near Arlington. Each fort mounted powerful cannon and boasted a hundred-foot flagpole defiantly waving the Stars and Stripes in the face of the Confederate "Stars and Bars" that flew not four air miles away on Munson's Hill.[20]

Statements from members of the Southern Tier Regiment during this period reflect the heightened morale in the Army of the Potomac. Pvt. H. H. Rockwell of Company K wrote, "I have never been in better health than at present, nor enjoyed myself better since we entered the service, and I think this is the case with most of the boys." He added that in his successful transition from a civilian to the fighting trim of a soldier he had dispensed with half of the possessions that he had initially thought essential to carry into service. Pvt. George F. Dudley of Company K wrote on September 15, "We are all ready and anxious to try the mettle of the enemy, as we are tired of this inactivity, and are anxious to know how the 23rd, as a Regiment, will stand fire." "In short," echoed Burritt on September 12, "[the] men generally demand a fight and are impatient to fight, and would rather fight then drill." "We have had theory long enough," Burritt added, "now let us apply it."[21]

McClellan found an opportunity to test the condition of his army on September 28, when Gen. Joseph E. Johnston gave up any pretense of attacking Washington and drew back his forces from Munson's and Upton's hills to the fortified heights near Centreville. McClellan responded by ordering McDowell to advance his troops quickly from Arlington Heights to strike Johnston's rear guard. Wadsworth's brigade would lead the infantry.

Near five o'clock on the 28th, many of Wadsworth's men were either on dress parade or preparing their evening meal when mounted orderlies galloped into the camps and reined up before the quarters of the colonels. Soon George Edgcomb and his fellow drummers were sounding the loud repetitive rattle of the "long roll" over a dozen miles, first from near Fort Cass in the camp of the 21st, then picked up by the 23d and 25th, and echoed down to the left by the 35th. The peaceful camp scene immediately became transformed into one of mass confusion, "the officers running hither and thither" and the men racing to find their place in company ranks. Some rose from their sickbeds or obtained releases from the guardhouse in order to participate in the pending action.[22]

Colonel Hoffman directed his men to gather up their weapons, forty rounds of ammunition, two days' rations, and full canteens, and to report to the regimental color line in "light marching order"—that is, without knapsacks or tents. A short time later he formed the men into column, closed them up, and addressed them on the importance of obeying orders and keeping cool in the face of danger. At his command, the drum corps struck up a beat, the flags lifted to the breeze, and, according to Seymour Dexter, "all in the gayest spirits away we started for the enemy."[23]

The 23d joined the brigade on the familiar road to Ball's Cross Roads. Col. William Rogers of the 21st, the ranking colonel in the brigade, took the lead. Once clear of the woods the column broke into a double-quick step, or "smart trot," as one soldier called it, which soon fatigued the men. After passing Ball's Cross Roads and the Alexandria, Loudoun, and Hampshire Railroad, the men struggled to load their weapons as they began to climb Upton's Hill. When the 21st reached the crest it found the Rebels gone and only "humbug fortifications" in evidence, including an old stovepipe mounted on wheels to give the appearance of a cannon.[24]

When the 23d started up the hill behind the 21st, it met McClellan and his staff coming down. As the general rode past them he shouted to the perspiring column, "Take it easy, my lads," indicating that the crisis had passsed. That night the 23d bivouacked on the eastern slope of the hill, with General Keyes's brigade camped below them near the railroad. Without tents or blankets the men had to make do by building shelters of cedar boughs or cornstalks. Keyes's troops kept the evening chill off by building large bonfires. One man from the 30th New York later remembered the striking scene of General McDowell draped in his military cloak standing on the bank of the road silhouetted by the tall flames of a fire behind him. His pose reminded the soldier of one of Napoleon's field marshals.[25]

That night the men got little sleep. At one in the morning the camps were alarmed by the sound of musket volleys to the northwest near Falls Church. The men later learned that the firing had come from troops of Brig. Gen. William F. "Baldy" Smith's command shooting at each other as they stumbled about in the dark, resulting in the death of seventeen men and the wounding of thirty.[26]

The next day, after thirty or forty wagon loads of the Southern Tier equipment and baggage arrived from the old camps near Arlington, things began to return to normal. Soon supply trains regularly ran between Arlington and Falls Church, and military engineers completed a telegraph line between Arlington and Wadsworth's headquarters at the home of Charles H. Upton. Professor T. S. Lowe commenced five-to-six-hundred-foot balloon ascensions from near the Upton house, sometimes with McDowell on board, to peer through his telescope at the peaceful Confederate camps fifteen miles distant, near Centreville. Work also began on Fort Upton (later Fort Ramsay) on Upton's Hill; Fort Buffalo, built by the 21st New York; Fort Taylor, named after a nearby tavern owned by William H. Taylor; and Fort Munson on the hill named for its owner, Daniel O. Munson.[27]

Not long after Wadsworth's brigade occupied Upton's Hill, McClellan had seven Union army divisions at his disposal in Virginia. McDowell's division was increased on October 15 to three brigades: Keyes's First Brigade (14th New York State Militia [NYSM], 22d, 24th, and 30th New York), Wadsworth's Second Brigade, and Brig. Gen. Rufus King's Third Brigade of western troops (2d, 6th, and 7th Wisconsin, and 19th Indiana). The division, which had an effective force of about ten thousand men, also included the 2d New York Cavalry and two batteries of regular (U.S.) artillery.[28]

In early November Wadsworth's brigade completed its final reorganization with the addition of the 20th New York State Militia (also designated 80th New York Volunteers), under the command of Lt. Col. Theodore B. Gates. The brigade, in order of the seniority of regimental commanders, then consisted of the 21st, 23d, 35th, and the 20th NYSM, representing the primarily rural New York counties of Allegheny, Chemung, Columbia, Cortland, Dutchess, Erie, Greene, Jefferson, Lewis, Madison, Schuyler, Steuben, Tioga, and Ulster. The night that the 20th NYSM regiment arrived in camp, Wadsworth and his staff personally greeted Gates's men and, by the light of lanterns they carried, helped settle them into their campsite near Fort Upton. The general also provided stacks of firewood and hot coffee for their comfort as a gesture of welcome.[29]

Wadsworth's brigade assumed responsibility for about three miles of the Union picket line in front of Falls Church facing west toward Fairfax Court House. The regiments took turns for duty on the picket line in forty-eight-hour reliefs. For the most part during the following autumn months this duty remained uneventful. On November 8, however, two Southern Tier pickets of Company I were surprised at their post by a company of the 1st Virginia Cavalry and were captured. McDowell thought the incident demonstrated a laxness in the guards, whom he claimed had been sitting around eating dinner when taken and not on the watch.[30]

As winter approached McClellan broke the monotony of camp life by staging a number of military reviews. These military spectacles impressed all who witnessed them, including the Boston writer and poet Julia Ward Howe, who returned to Washington on November 18 after attending a review of McDowell's division near Bailey's Cross Roads to write the words for the "Battle Hymn of the Republic."[31] McClellan always claimed that he held these military reviews not for public show but as training exercises to "accustom the regiments to move together and see each other, to give the troops an idea of their own strength, [and] to infuse [in them] *esprit de corps* and mutual emulation." The culminating Grand Review held on Tuesday, November 20, not only caught the attention of the nation but left McClellan confirmed in his purpose, "completely satisfied and delighted."[32]

The Grand Review took place on a mile-square open plain between Munson's Hill and Bailey's Cross Roads about eight miles from Washington, where the Columbia Turnpike (modern Route 244) crossed the Leesburg and Alexandria Turnpike (modern Route 7). McDowell, whom

McClellan placed in overall charge of the event, ordered Keyes's and Wadsworth's troops of his division to begin preparing the ground a week before by clearing brush, filling in ditches, and taking down fences.[33]

The morning of November 20 dawned raw and chilly. The sky remained "leaden" throughout the day, but occasionally the sun broke through to light up the review field "as if by magic."[34] The first troops began arriving about nine in the morning. Wadsworth's brigade entered the field to the tune of "Dixie," played by the Union Cornet Band. The band had joined the 21st New York from Buffalo, New York, on September 27 and had quickly become the joy and pride of the brigade. Behind the 21st marched the 23d, sporting new trousers it had been issued the night before.[35]

For the next three hours troops poured onto the field at Bailey's from all directions, outfitted in sky-blue overcoats and black knapsacks, bayonets fixed and flashing, and banners flying. Altogether there were seven divisions gathered, comprising seventy-six infantry regiments (sixty thousand men), seven cavalry regiments (eight thousand), seventeen batteries of artillery with caissons and limbers, the division ambulances, and at least fifty military brass bands. In addition, McClellan allowed Washingtonians to attend as spectators, easing for that day restrictions on travel into Virginia. Consequently twenty or thirty thousand government clerks, businessmen, families, peddlers, and many others poured out from Washington and the surrounding area in carriages, on horseback, or on foot. They clogged all the roads and caused long delays over Long Bridge and on the Columbia Pike. A number of vehicles broke down en route, and there were a few serious injuries from accidents. The early arrivals, in a holiday mood, swarmed over Munson's Hill for the best view of the field. Young boys eagerly climbed into the tall trees nearby. Cavalry guards stationed along the converging roads kept the civilians back from the parade ground.[36]

The great masses of troops slowly found their assigned positions, forming a vast semicircular arrangement of stacked divisions facing a reviewing stand located on a slight elevation near the Lewis Bailey house.[37] McDowell's division occupied the left of the formation behind the divisions of William B. Franklin and Fitz John Porter, about three-quarters of a mile from the knoll. The artillery massed on the left of the infantry near the foot of Munson's Hill. Each division formed generally with its brigades side by side, in line and in proper order, with the regiments in the brigade

71

each showing a two-company front of fifty to seventy men. The other eight companies of the regiments aligned behind the first two in pairs closed up to the front. Thus each of the seven divisions present on the rolling field formed a solid blue rectangle of troops with a frontage of perhaps six hundred men. Above the troops could be seen the sheen of steel bayonets and the colorful regimental flags unfurled. A reporter noted that when occasionally the sun broke through the gray clouds, "the hills are covered with a robe of golden sunshine, and the bayonets dance and gleam in its flitting rays, and the scarlet facings [lining of uniform jackets] of the cannoniers are all aglow with its warmth."[38]

The effect of the massed troops was stunning. Never before had so many soldiers been gathered at one location on the continent, and certainly no American officer had ever commanded such an immense army. "It was a sight that only comes once in a man's life time," wrote a soldier in the 21st New York, "and any man who was in this vicinity and did not see it will have it to regret for the remainder of his days."[39]

McClellan with his staff and escort of 1,800 cavalrymen got caught up in the traffic jam coming out of Washington and did not reach Bailey's until after midday. The president and Mrs. Lincoln, who had arrived earlier in an open carriage, rode down from Munson's Hill to meet the general near the reviewing stand. A host of dignitaries were also on hand for the event, including cabinet secretaries, political leaders, and foreign ministers. When McClellan galloped onto the field, four artillery batteries thundered forth a prearranged salute, and a tremendous cheer burst from the plain, making the ground tremble and stirring the emotions of all present.[40]

McClellan and Lincoln mounted horses, and, followed by a great cavalcade of generals and their staffs, trotted out to inspect the troops. As they approached each division the regiments lowered their banners and their bands played "Hail to the Chief." Some regiments silently and appropriately raised their weapons to "present arms"; others gave way to wild cheering, the waving of hats, and shouts of "Uncle Abe" and "Little Mac." The massed cavalry in its turn sliced the air with polished sabers. One soldier noticed the contrast between McClellan, a graceful horseman, lifting his hat with a flourish to accept the tribute of his soldiers, and the awkward Mr. Lincoln, who struggled to keep his tall silk hat in place as he bobbed up and down in his saddle. It took the cavalcade an hour to circle the troops and return to the reviewing stand.[41]

Next the divisions formed to pass in review up a hundred-yard corridor between McClellan's group and a large crowd of civilians opposite.[42] McDowell and his staff took the post of honor at the head of the
long column of regiments, each arranged in a column of two companies
abreast for infantry and a single column of companies for cavalry. From
the perspective of a reporter viewing the movement from Munson's Hill,
"the distant strains of the regimental bands arose and fell on the still air,
long rows of flashing steel came gleaming on, and when at one time the
sun burst through a cloud, the whole field seemed to wave to and fro in
the light." It took at least four hours for all of the troops to quick-time
past the reviewing stand and exit the field to return to their camps.[43]

McDowell's division brought up the rear of the column. Despite the
lateness of the hour, the crowd remained enthusiastic, clapping and waving handkerchiefs at the sight of a particularly well disciplined or impressive unit. The pompous drum major of a regiment in King's brigade
caused quite a sensation as he strutted by, whirling his baton as he "snuffs
the air and spurns the ground like a war horse." McClellan acknowledged him while he was "in a top loftical gyration of his baton," causing
the man such consternation that he dropped it; consequently, "from the
topmost height of glory he was plunged into the deepest gulf of despair."
McDowell suffered a similar embarrassment that day when his horse became entangled in a wire fence and he tumbled to the ground.[44]

The next day the national press showered praise on McClellan for the
demonstration of national strength and pride that they had witnessed at
Bailey's. One reporter wrote that McClellan "wears a look of confidence
to-day that was not there before, and to-day the men seemed animated
with an unwonted enthusiasm." The final realization of more than forty
miles of garrisoned forts circling Washington and an army of over a hundred thousand well-equipped, trained soldiers blotted out the humiliation
of the North's recent defeat and added new laurels to the man they began
calling the "Young Napoleon." One officer said of the Grand Review, "in
the realization of all observers, . . . the army was born that day."[45]

The debut of the Army of the Potomac at Bailey's Cross Roads represents an important benchmark in the course of the Civil War. One Union
officer wrote that the experience that day forged a special pride and bond
among the troops, a spirit "which afterwards so thoroughly pervaded that
army, and made it one of the best in the world."[46] Indeed, it was an army
that was to withstand the rejection of its creator and the Union disasters

of Second Bull Run and Fredericksburg to emerge in the spring of 1864 as a battle-hardened instrument of war ready for use by its new general in chief, U. S. Grant, in achieving final Union victory.

Private Dexter of the 23d described the Grand Review as "one of the most magnificent sights I ever beheld." Despite the fact that his heavy knapsack "began to take some of the poetry off before night," he found in the scene, a "grandeur that makes one feel inspired." A *New York Times* reporter spoke the obvious when he identified the gathered army as symbolically representing the nation: "From Maine to Iowa, there is not one county of the North, or the East, or the West, that has not its representatives in these columns." Indistinguishable in their nation's uniform marched farmers' sons away from their villages for the first time, alongside adventurers who had traveled overland across the continent to California or furled the sails of America's ships in exotic tropical ports halfway around the world. Within their serried ranks stood the poor from the docks and dirty alleyways of the large coastal cities beside the sons of the richest and most prominent families of America. Beneath the one flag on this field was added the strength and vitality of new immigrants, among them thousands of Irish and German. If this army was not fully representative of America's promise for all its people (blacks, rejected by the states as volunteers, stood on the sidelines), it was nonetheless a profoundly symbolic moment, as Dexter eloquently reflected in his journal. "The idea that they were citizens who had voluntarily left their happy homes and family [to] meet the temptations, the disease and dangers of the camp and field to maintain their country's honor," he wrote, "magnifies and elevates that grandeur to an almost unboundless limit."[47]

From its introduction at Bailey's the Army of the Potomac carried with it the hopes and fears of the nation. Although the western armies arguably were to have better leaders and would be fully equal in fighting abilities, the North always looked to the Army of the Potomac as a measure of the war's progress. Like the statue of Freedom with shield and sheathed sword that would soon grace the top of the new capitol dome in Washington, the Army of the Potomac protected the nation's symbolic center and stood guard over its democratic institutions. The army represented both a shield, to protect Washington, and a sword, unsheathed and thrust forward toward Richmond. Come whatever the future brought, this army was destined either to strike the deathblow of the rebellion at

Richmond or defend the last bastion of the dying republic on the banks of the Potomac.

But as the political leaders of the North patted McClellan on the back for his great achievement, they asked the question, what now? Since his troops had marched to Bailey's with full canteens, haversacks, and cartridge boxes, many soldiers anticipated that the army would advance directly from the parade ground to another confrontation with General Johnston at Manassas.

McClellan, however, did not intend to launch his magnificent army precipitately on a wanton and destructive campaign of conquest against the South, an option that in his mind would simply "waste life in useless battles" and demoralize his troops. Rather, when ready, he would advance in overwhelming numbers, as an expeditionary force, to "strike at the heart" of the rebellion decisively, at Richmond. He believed that only by "thoroughly defeating" Richmond's defenders and capturing the Confederate capital, while at the same time adhering to a "rigidly protective policy as to private property and unarmed persons, and a lenient course as to common soldiers," might the country soon "hope for the permanent restoration of peaceful Union."[48]

McClellan's strategy reflected the thinking of many if not most Northern leaders in 1861. Even after the Battle of Bull Run, there remained a general revulsion at the very notion that civil strife could consume this great experiment of a nation that had been founded on such noble principles and ideals, so hard won in the war of independence. McClellan always maintained the hope that by demonstrating its superior military resources and capabilities the North's "misguided and erring brethren" in the South would see the futility of their cause, come to their senses, and voluntarily return to the Union. That could only be accomplished, thought McClellan, by conducting the war to the extent possible from a high moral plane, with the professional skill of a surgeon using a scalpel to remove an operable cancer. He rejected the abolitionist cause as an unwelcome distraction from his primary goal of reuniting the nation; he asked his influential friends to help him avoid the volatile slave issue—or, as he put it, "dodge the nigger." The worst fear at the time, expressed by President Lincoln in December 1861, was that the conflict could intensify and "degenerate into a violent and remorseless revolutionary struggle," resulting only in endless bitterness and sectional hostility.[49]

After the Grand Review, much to the regret of his soldiers, McClellan sent the army not into battle but into winter quarters. During a string of unusually warm days in early December, quartermaster Myron H. Mandeville laid out a new site for the winter encampment of the Southern Tiers. He chose a sheltered area three-fourths of a mile southeast of their old position, at the back of Munson's Hill and on the south side of a ridge thickly covered with small pine trees. Groups of three or four men then set to work building about two hundred pine, cedar, or chestnut log cabins typically eight feet square and five feet high. They chinked the logs with mud mixed with pine needles and made the roof by fastening or nailing tent sheets to the top log. Each cabin's occupants, or "shanty mates," often purchased a small sheet-iron camp stove for three to five dollars to use for heat or cooking. Others built fireplaces using two old barrels for a chimney. The area quickly took on the appearance of a small village, with graded company streets decorated with evergreens. The members of Company K built over the entrance to their area an elaborate evergreen archway from which hung a large shield and eagle.[50]

Mandeville also managed during the winter to bring order and regularity to the distribution of rations within the regiment. Pvt. Ira Carpenter, a designated cook for the Cortland Volunteers, wrote home on November 19 that the eighty-seven men of the company who drew rations received two full meals a day and were "all good hearty eaters." He said the company received a hundred pounds of fresh beef twice a week and a barrel of pork every two days. They boiled the beef in three large kettles of water to make up a single meal. They fried the pork, saving the grease to make soup or to sell to civilian peddlers.[51]

The army supplemented the supply needs of the troops by numerous authorized foraging expeditions into the Virginia countryside. On December 27, for example, troops from Wadsworth's brigade escorted a train of 120 wagons on a nine-mile trip toward Fairfax Court House. When the column came to a farm site, the lead wagon with a guard would pull off to load up the farmer's stored corn, hay, potatoes, or whatever else they found by way of provisions. The wagon then returned to camp while the remaining wagons in the column continued down the road to the next farm. The procedure worked so efficiently that Captain Clark could state with some truth a week and a half later, "There is not a bushel of corn between here and Fairfax." Some of the Cortland men expressed regret at having to take a fellow farmer's livelihood; Private Edgcomb admitted that he could "hardly help feeling sorry for the families as they would beg so. But that was of no avail." The farmers could request a receipt for property taken for later reimbursement by the Federal government on demonstration of loyalty to the Union.[52]

At the same time that Mandeville established "Camp McDowell" near Munson's, Surgeon Seymour Churchill scouted up the road in Falls Church for a suitable place to relocate the regimental hospital. Falls Church, located along the Alexandria, Loudoun, and Hampshire Railroad, consisted of a tavern, blacksmith shop, three churches, and about twenty houses. Churchill decided to occupy two large, well-ventilated rooms in the Columbia Baptist Church to shelter many of the sixty patients under his care. Most of them suffered from typhus and typhoid fevers, which had first appeared at Arlington and then swept through the camps at Upton's, causing the deaths of at least ten men in the 23d. Hamilton Squires was the first of the Cortland Volunteers to die of "camp fever," on December 4, followed by three others before the end of the month. Captain Clark had the sad duty of writing condolence letters to the next of kin.[53]

Hamilton Squires and his brother Lucien were two of the four men recruited in Onondaga County by Sergeant Bailey the previous October. Soon after arriving in camp, Hamilton came down with dysentery. Lucien cared for his brother as best he could, even trying a home remedy of white oak bark that Hamilton refused to eat, as Lucien reported home, "because it did not taste good." Dysentery led to typhoid and Hamilton's death on December 4. Captain Clark raised seventy dollars from the members of the company to send the bodies of Hamilton and Henry Cooper home, accompanied by Lucien. Many of the companies did this early in the war, although the practice quickly disappeared due to the high costs involved and the increasing number of deaths.[54]

On December 9 civilian W. J. Gilbert visited Churchill's Falls Church hospital and reported critical observations in an article for the *Corning Journal*. Adjutant W. W. Hayt defended Churchill in another article by saying that the hospital had just begun operations at the time of Gilbert's visit. Still, in the 23d, the number of deaths (sixteen by December 18), sick in hospital (forty-five on December 18), and disability discharges (seven in the Cortland Volunteers alone in September and October) gave concern to the Southern Tier home communities. In a letter to his brother, drummer Edgcomb added his criticisms of conditions in the regimental hospitals, saying that he hoped he would "never be obliged to enter one a sick man." (According to his Civil War service and pension records in the National Archives, he never did.)[55]

Daily drill continued into the fall and winter, enlivened occasionally by mock battles "with all the noise of musketry, artillery, and a grand charge of cavalry." Since a large portion of the regiment was often unavailable for one reason or another, Colonel Hoffman resorted to "pole" or "skeleton" drills to train his officers in the science of battle-line movements and facings. The front rank of each company battle line was represented on the drill field by four corporals carrying the ends of two fifteen-foot poles. A private without arms stood behind each corporal to indicate the second rank. The sergeants and commissioned officers occupied the positions they would have, had the company been present and at full strength.[56]

In late winter Hoffman concentrated his efforts on drilling his regiment in the manner of light infantry. The "Light Infantry" and "Riflemen" designations applied to the 23d at this time indicated a specially trained unit, swift-moving and capable of independent action and initiative. Light infantry specialized in skirmishing, sharpshooting, and scouting; guarding and protecting the army's front, flank, and rear; and "developing" enemy positions (that is, establishing their size and location by making contact) on the battlefield. Training emphasized target shooting at distances of two hundred, 350, and five hundred yards; bayonet and skirmish drill under the direction of bugle calls; and physical conditioning to include boxing with gloves, "turning over a pole," and the unexplained "riding a wooden circus." Despite its light-infantry identification, however, the 23d's operations in subsequent campaigns were for the most part no different from those of any other regiment in the division.[57]

Although by late February 1862 Hoffman had noted good progress in drill and discipline, the regiment's sharpshooting skills left much to be desired. For example, out of 180 shots that his men fired at two hundred yards, only thirty-two hit the target. Lieutenant Andrews's offer of one dollar to anyone in the Cortland Volunteers who could hit the five-hundred-yard target went unclaimed.[58]

Winter days of rain and snow (the first snow fell January 3) kept the soldiers close to camp. The officers busied themselves serving on various military boards and courts or poring over their military manuals under threat of having to demonstrate their professional competence before a review board. Sergeant Bailey of the Cortland Volunteers formed the company noncommissioned officers into a society that held nightly meetings to discuss the martial, moral, and social betterment of their charges.[59]

The primary concern of the officers that winter settled upon the increase of drunkenness they observed in the regiment, particularly after the men received two months' back pay in January. Seymour Dexter decried the presence of liquor in camp, which he called a "foul fiend" and "serpentine charmer" that revealed itself "in the bloated faces, in the blood shot eyes and unnatural stare, in the foolish demeanor and brutish degradation" of those that partook of it. Chaplain Ezra F. Crane took the bull by the horns and organized a division of the Order of the Sons of Temperance within the regiment, at once signing up about forty members.[60]

The men passed the dreary winter days by writing letters or reading newspapers. Seymour Dexter, a former Alfred College student, boasted that his cabin library included such titles as Charles Dickens's *Great Expectations* and Sir Walter Scott's *Ivanhoe*. On Sundays many of the men attended church services at Falls Church or in their own log church, erected in February 1862. Other pastimes mentioned in soldier letters of the period included visiting friends, collecting photographs of generals, trading gold pens, playing chess, and battling a general infestation of lice.[61]

The holidays provided a welcome break in the monotony of camp life. The men spent Christmas together in song and laughter, enjoying boxes of fruit and cookies sent from home, or mince pies and other holiday treats purchased from the sutler or camp peddlers. They welcomed the New Year with the unauthorized firing of their weapons (unintentionally alarming the people of Washington). On Washington's Birthday in February, artillery salutes and illuminations accompanied the readings of General Washington's farewell address to his troops.[62]

The holidays also brought with them the inevitable melancholy thoughts of home. Seymour Dexter wrote on Christmas Day, "We are all letting our minds wander over the past and contemplating on the future." Edgcomb reminisced in a letter to his sister-in-law about the pleasures of Christmases past, with brightly decorated trees and stockings hung before Christmas morning. In one letter he noted his old friends at home getting married and the passing Cortland scenes. "Is Alice as pretty as ever?" he asked, and he added, "give my best respects and love too to Louise Hunter. I tell you anything from home looks good."[63]

During the winter of 1861–62 Uncle Sam offered the men of the 23d two opportunities to transfer honorably out of the regiment. In November 1861 Capt. John Gibbon of McDowell's command received authorization to bring his regular battery (B, 4th U.S. Artillery) up to strength from the ranks of volunteer infantry regiments of McDowell's division. From November 20 until June 8, 1862, twenty-eight members of the 23d from Companies B, D, F, and G transferred to Gibbon's battery to serve out their enlistments. Enough men joined Gibbon that he permanently assigned one gun to those transferring from the 23d and allowed them to fly a silk pennant with their volunteer number and state in gold letters.[64]

A second opportunity to leave the regiment came on February 15, 1862, when Hoffman formed the regiment on the parade ground to read aloud a call for volunteers to man the Union gunboats operating on the western rivers. The authorities accepted only five men from the 23d from dozens of applicants. Fergus Moore (a sailor before enlisting in the company in Elmira) went from the Cortland Volunteers. Burritt, for one, regretted seeing him go, stating in his newspaper column, "We have lost our wit, wag and clown." Apparently, however, Moore was of a class of malcontents that the officers of the regiment were happy to get rid of. Moore never reported to gunboat service and was listed as a deserter from the 23d. He subsequently enlisted in the 193d New York in March 1865, only to desert that regiment six months later.[65]

In the spring of 1862 the Southern Tier Regiment emerged from the winter and nine months' training, its men confident in their ability as soldiers and eager to meet the foe. Burritt bragged in February, "When next McDowell undertakes a journey southward it will be in command of soldiers, and not with such a disgraceful rabble as were the pest of good citizens at the Elmira Rendezvous last Spring, and a grease spot on our country's fame at Bull Run." The men felt that they had successfully passed through their initiation as soldiers, and they looked back almost with nostalgia on the experience. They fondly remembered "the sword presentations and speeches, the flags intrusted to our keeping, the round of gayety, the hearts lost and won, the joy and sadness of those days of preparation." They now wanted no more to read of the great battles in the West while they remained inactive in Virginia or played at mock battles that accomplished little more than "the vexing of about 9,000 men with late suppers and very dirty guns." It was time they made their own history. They felt ready to fight and were confident in the outcome of the coming contest. Lt. Newton Colby (Co. D) wrote home on September 11 to assure his friends, "We do not fear anything the Rebels can do—for we are ready for them."[66]

CHAPTER 4

McClellan
Makes His Move

D espite the persistent "On to Richmond" calls from the Northern press, McClellan spent the winter months slowly developing plans for a spring offensive. Early on he rejected another advance directly on Manassas Junction, as well as a tedious hundred-mile overland campaign stepping down the rungs of numerous and easily defended river barriers to reach Richmond. He decided instead to transport his army by water down the Chesapeake Bay to land near the mouth of the Rappahannock River at Urbanna, just fifty miles from Richmond. He expected that once Confederate commander Joseph E. Johnston found McClellan's troops on his right flank near Urbanna, the Confederates would abandon Manassas Junction and march to the defense of their capital. McClellan then anticipated engaging Johnston with the advantages of initiative, time, and favorable terrain.

McClellan had to rethink his plans when Johnston in early March suddenly withdrew from Manassas Junction along the Orange and Alexandria Railroad to a less exposed position south of the Rappahannock River. McClellan then had to adjust his primary landing point farther south to the Union-held tip of the Virginia Peninsula between the York and James Rivers at Fort Monroe, about seventy miles southeast from Richmond.

Once McClellan confirmed Johnston's withdrawal on Sunday, March 9, he ordered his army to move in pursuit. He intended to strike Johnston's retreating rear guard or at least disrupt his opponent's plans while he continued the work of assembling the fleet of vessels at Alexandria, Virginia, on the Potomac, needed to carry his army south. He also thought that a strenuous march would serve to test the machinery of his new army and shake off the lethargy of his troops after dull months spent in winter quarters.[1]

Brig. Gen. William B. Franklin's division led McDowell's command in the advance to Manassas. Sunday evening's tattoo had long passed when Adjutant W. W. Hayt of the 23d alerted the Southern Tier captains to prepare for a rapid march beginning the next morning at five o'clock. There followed a sleepless night of "hurry and bustle" for the officers who had to see to the many details of preparation. Among other things they had to recall the men on special details and the guards, roust the cooks from their sleep to prepare three days' cooked rations for the men, and identify sick and half-duty men unable to make the trek.[2] Some managed to scribble out final letters home. Maj. William Gregg wrote a friend that night to assure him of their coming victory—the Army of the Potomac, he said, "cannot be conquered." He also confided that the prospect of battle was not so "frightful" to him as it had once been, although he realized that many would soon die. He asked his friend to be a "father and friend" to his young daughter, if he happened to be among the slain.[3]

At three in the morning the call "General" sounded to the familiar tune of "Yankee Doodle," alerting the men to break camp. Bonfires along the company streets rose up in the darkness fed by the cast-off straw from soldiers' beds, unused firewood, and any other combustibles considered excess baggage for the movement. By the fires' glow, officers and men rushed about filling canteens, packing knapsacks, drawing ammunition and rations, and storing away medical and commissary stores, animal forage, officers baggage, and camp equipment in the four four-horse wagons allowed to each regiment. To lighten the load McDowell specified that officers were allowed transportation for only one carpetbag or valise each. Their troops had to carry all of their baggage with them. For an infantryman this amounted to forty or fifty pounds of equipment, including rifle-musket, bayonet, full cartridge and cap boxes, knapsack, blanket, change of clothes, overcoat, haversack with rations, tin canteen and cup, tent fly and poles, and personal items. The week before the regiment had had to give up its comfortable "A" tents and received instead one square piece of cotton cloth per man, approximately five feet by five; these, when buttoned together with two similar cloths and held up by poles, formed smaller three-man tents. Although the new tents at least kept off the rain, the men derisively called them "dog tents," from the need to crawl into them on all fours.[4]

At half past four in the morning the bugles sounded "Assembly," calling the troops into their company streets with all of their equipment for inspection and roll call. One half-hour later the call "To the Color" directed the companies to fall in on the camp color line. Without ceremony, Colonel Hoffman then formed them into column, four abreast, and ordered "Forward, march!" As the sun rose in the east, the men happily turned away from their log city. At Fort Buffalo, the 23d took its proper place within the brigade and division. When the long column reached Annandale, Virginia, the division artillery fell in behind, and the entire column turned onto the Little River Turnpike heading toward Fairfax Court House.[5]

Moving an army in columns across great stretches of countryside proved one of the most difficult challenges that Civil War commanders faced. Excessive straggling or march fatigue could severely compromise the effectiveness of an army before the first shot of battle was fired. On the march the columns normally ranged over the landscape, following every possible avenue of advance like lava flowing down a mountainside. Union commanders operating in Virginia had a particularly hard time of it; unlike their opponents, who most likely had local boys within their ranks who knew every road and farm path, Union officers had few road maps or guides to assist them. In Virginia, troops typically had to travel over a confusing maze of crisscrossing, unmarked roads of fine claylike soil that on hot sunny days rose up as irritating dust at any disturbance and in a rainstorm quickly turned to a sucking quagmire. The column would inevitably accordion out on long stretches and bunch up when attempting to negotiate the numerous crossroads, obstructions, or bridgeless streams. Under ideal conditions—meaning dry, hard-surface roads such as the Little River Turnpike—a column of well-conditioned soldiers could average two and a half miles per hour for an eight-hour marching day.

To maintain the strength of their commands by minimizing straggling, commanders relied upon discipline, training, and strict adherence to the rules of the march set down in the training manuals or issued in special orders. An advance began with the men in formal close-order formation (a column of men marching four abreast, closed up to the front), the drum corps beating cadence, and the men's weapons carried at "right shoulder shift" or slung over their shoulder by the sling. The mounted field officers with their staffs and orderlies rode in front of the column, followed by the "field music" (the musicians), the ten companies in order, each led by its captain on foot, and in the rear the servants, ambulances, and wagons.

Once a column got under way the colonel passed back the voice command "route step" to the captains, resulting in a general flurry of activity all along the line of march. The music stopped, and the men fell into a walk, carrying their rifle-muskets in whatever manner they found most comfortable. Normally the regiment's second in command and the surgeon rode back along the column to take up a position behind their troops. At the same time, the ten company captains dropped to the rear of their respective commands. Henceforth, if a soldier needed to drop out of the column for any reason, such as to adjust his equipment or respond to a call of nature, he first had to get his captain's permission. He then left his weapon and knapsack to be carried by one of his comrades, thus ensuring the anger of his friends if he did not return promptly. If sick, the soldier had to get a written pass from the captain allowing him to drop out of the column with his equipment and report to the surgeon. The medical officer would then either send the soldier running back to his company or allow him to ride in a wagon or ambulance. Stragglers found without a pass by the division provost guard were subject to arrest and punishment. To keep track of his men while on the march the captain had the roll called at least five times a day.[6]

The march continued in this irregular fashion, with the rifle-muskets and two standards with cased colors projecting above the long blue columns like pins stuck in a pincushion. The column at times would make its own way according to circumstances, straightening out curves in the road, bypassing obstructions by cutting across fields, or flattening fences to walk on more solid ground beside the road. All the while the marchers had to compete for space in the roadway with stragglers from the forward units, broken-down vehicles, and the eager young aides and orderlies of the commanders, who often rode up and down beside the column carrying messages or orders.

No matter how fatiguing or wearisome the march, however, and whether under a pouring rain or broiling hot sun, the youthful spirit of the men seemed always to prevail. One Union soldier described a typical march: "Sometimes, for hours, only the steady tramp of feet is heard.

. . . Then something sets all their lips awag, and the woods and fields echo with their shouts and laughter. They comment on everything—on the houses, the fields, the trees, the road; they jibe at and joke with one an-other;. . . and their laughter is as care-free and contagious as that of happy children."[7] At other times, "an occasional silence would be broken by the starting of a familiar song, and very soon the whole regiment would join in the singing. Sometimes it would be a whistling chorus, when all would be whistling." When the men spied a pretty girl along the route someone might acknowledge her with an obvious cough or sound, or shout out "Guide right!" or "Guide left!" depending on which side of the road she had appeared.[8]

At regular intervals of about an hour or more the bugle announced a ten-minute break. The column then closed up, and the men fell out to the side of the road: "In an instant, almost, the men assume all varieties of postures—some sitting, some lying down. . . . The stragglers come up, one by one, and drop in with their commands. Then the bugle sounds again, and all start to their feet. . . . in a few moments, [they] fall into their old, irregular, go-as-you-please step and route."[9]

Midday the soldiers greeted the dinner call with an enthusiastic shout, for it meant a longer rest, hot coffee, and a lighter haversack thereafter. The men stacked arms (producing pyramids of four or five rifle-muskets resting on their butts and hooked at the fixed bayonets) and dispersed to prepare a quick meal. "A few moments later, little volumes of smoke— hundreds and thousands of them, as far as the eye can reach along the road—roll up, and the atmosphere is filled with the perfume of burning pine, the aroma of coffee, and perhap[s] the savory smell of bacon."[10]

Around noon on March 10, Wadsworth's brigade entered the town of Fairfax Court House displaying its colors "for the gratification of the few forlorn inhabitants." Then it turned down the Warrenton Turnpike (modern Route 29) near Jermantown (Germantown), where Wadsworth learned that Johnston had escaped to the west beyond his grasp. Wads-worth's brigade went into bivouac within three miles of Centreville, with the 23d stacking arms in a pinewood near the graves of fifteen Rebel sol-diers who had died of camp measles the previous October.[11]

When going into bivouac for the night the columns dissolved into three-man squads. "One of the men would get wood and water, another would pitch the tent and the third would attend to the cooking." One by one the cooking fires sprang to life amid "the murmur of a thousand voices mingling with the ring and jingle of arms, the crack of brushwood, and the short, sharp echo of the axes." Once finished with their camp duties and their "meager menu" for a meal, most of the men wearily crawled into their "little apology" for tents and fell into a heavy sleep until reveille. Others, whatever the weather, would relish the opportunity to sit around blazing campfires wrapped in their overcoats or oilcloths smoking, drinking coffee, and swapping stories with comrades. A wag might spin some yarn about "how widow somebody's big black ram butted Deacon somebody else over a four rail fence then jumped over and butted him back through it." Finally tattoo sounded, the last of the men retired, the fires slowly died away, and the bivouac fell silent except for the tramp of the guards.[12]

Wadsworth's brigade occupied this bivouac site for five days. On the 12th it marched to Centreville to participate in a mock attack against the empty Rebel works. The Centreville area at the time presented a scene of ruin and desolation, resulting from months of military occupation and the rapid Confederate withdrawal. The Yankees found only a decaying, empty landscape of tree stumps, rutted impassible roads, lines of abandoned earthworks, and the rotting carcasses of an estimated 1,500 horses. The men took much interest in the famous "Quaker guns" (logs painted black to look like cannon) that the national press found so amusing, much to the chagrin of Union leaders.[13] The soldiers also took advantage of every opportunity to visit the nearby sites of the Battle of Bull Run as tourists.[14]

While camped near Centreville, General Wadsworth received an appointment as military governor of the District of Columbia in command of the defenses of Washington. His troops were crestfallen at the thought of his leaving. They remembered the warm woolen gloves that he had bought for them at his own expense the previous winter, and the particularly stormy night when he had taken sympathy on a sentry guarding his headquarters and sent him back to his dry quarters. When he and his staff departed on March 13, his troops crowded both sides of the road to say good-bye. With tears running down his cheeks Wadsworth told them, "God bless you boys. I do not want to leave you, I desire to go with you on the *field* but I am *ordered* off. Never leave your colors, boys." After raising his cap in salute to the colors of the 23d, he disappeared down the road, repeating with a husky voice, "God bless you all!" as the Union

Cornet Band played "Auld Lang Syne." The senior colonel, William Rogers of the 21st, took temporary command of the brigade.[15]

On March 15, McDowell's troops broke camp and marched back on the Little River Turnpike toward the river port of Alexandria, where McClellan planned for them to embark as the vanguard of his waterborne expedition against Richmond. McDowell, meanwhile, remained in Washington completing the organization of his newly formed army corps, to be designated the First Corps of the Army of the Potomac. The quiet and unassuming forty-eight-year-old Brig. Gen. Rufus King, formerly in charge of the brigade of western troops, took command of McDowell's old division. King, a member of a prominent New York family, was a West Point graduate who had become an educator and newspaper editor in Milwaukee, Wisconsin. Major Generals William B. Franklin and George A. McCall commanded McDowell's two other divisions.[16]

King drove his division east on the pike toward Alexandria through a heavy rainstorm. One of the Southern Tier men remembered the general misery of that particular march, with the rain "beating in our faces" and soaking their cloths and blankets. King allowed them few rest breaks. The men could only curse when they passed the men of another regiment warming themselves around an abandoned building that they had set on fire. Despite the efforts of the men to lift their spirits by singing hymns and popular songs, many in the regiment broke down and fell out of the column as stragglers. Lieutenant Colonel Crane and Major Gregg of the 23d rode along the line shouting encouragement to the sufferers and offering to carry the traps of the weakest men so that they could keep up. The column finally came to a halt before a washed-out bridge over a swollen stream three miles west of Alexandria. Burritt commented on the woebegone appearance of the men as they stood in a downpour: "Teeth chattered, human frames shivered as with ague and trembled like ashen leaves, muscles were becoming rigid, joints inflexible and mouths almost speechless." Most of the division bivouacked that night beside the road.[17]

The following day, because of delays, bad weather, and the lack of transports at Alexandria to carry McDowell's corps, King ordered his men to return to their snug cabins at Upton's. Two days later, on March 18, the division set out again for Alexandria, reaching a point two miles below Bailey's Cross Roads on the Leesburg Pike (modern Route 7) before going into camp. Here they remained under new orders placing them not in the vanguard of McClellan's movement to the Peninsula but bringing up the rear.[18]

Brig. Gen. Charles S. Hamilton's division of Samuel P. Heintzelman's Third Corps was the first to begin embarkation at Alexandria, on March 17, utilizing about thirty craft of all description. In the weeks that followed, McClellan's troops would stream into Alexandria, filling the deserted streets and massing before the long wooden wharves that jutted out into the Potomac. At times more than a hundred ships and boats would crowd the broad river, their forest of masts flying gaily colored flags and banners. Small tugs churned the water between them, nudging the large steamships into the slips to commence loading their cargoes of men, animals, and war material, before drawing out to anchor in midstream. At the same time, other oceangoing craft took on men and supplies upriver at Georgetown or alongside Washington's Sixth Street Wharf; these vessels then moved down to Alexandria, where they joined the great fleets of vessels assembling for the two-hundred-mile trip south.[19]

In the evening the work of embarkation continued by the light of bonfires set along the wharves. Soldiers confined to the ships at anchor remained on deck to enjoy the lively and animated scene. Across the extent of the busy harbor rose a steady murmur of activity that occasionally erupted in bursts of laughter and cheering, the shouting of commands, and the neighing of the horses being penned up in barges or lifted in slings up over and into the holds of the larger ships. At dark, fingers of light skimmed across the water from the shore fires, while colored signal lanterns blinked between the vessels. In their cramped quarters, men's tempers flared, especially when fueled by whiskey. On one ship the soldiers somehow managed to smuggle a barrel of contraband whiskey on board; "All got very drunk and noisy and were fighting all night." A colonel finally ended the bacchanal "by knocking three of them down the hatchway and kicking two others after them."[20]

At daylight the harbor heaved with movement as the larger ships raised anchor and maneuvered into formation behind the flagship carrying the division commander. All watched and cheered as the fleet got under way. The soldiers remained crowded on the decks to celebrate their departure and view the passing historic sites as they sailed down the Potomac. "Like schoolboys out for a holiday, [they] cheered and sang and laughed." The bands played "Red, White and Blue" and "Hail Columbia"; when passing George Washington's home, Mount Vernon, they reverently struck up

Gen. Marsena R. Patrick. *(Courtesy of the Civil War and Underground Railroad Museum of Philadelphia)*

"Washington's March" and other appropriate tributes. "Such enthusiasm I never dreamed of," wrote one officer, "excepting in reading the history of 'The Crusades.'"[21]

Watching them go with a knowing smile was Clio, the muse of history. Over a hundred years before, in the spring of 1755, she had watched the troops of Maj. Gen. Edward Braddock march out of Alexandria to fight the French on the Monongahela, aroused by the same self-confidence, the same impulsive, indomitable spirit of youth.

Meanwhile, the 23d New York languished back at "Camp Nowhere." Captain Clark sourly expressed on March 29 his disappointment over what he considered a depressing turn of events. He blamed McClellan for their difficulties, now calling him an "imbecile and entirely unfit for the command of such an army." Drummer Edgcomb, although he agreed that "it does seem as if there was some mismanagement somewhere," was willing to give McClellan the benefit of the doubt. "It is a different thing," he challenged the growing number of McClellan's stay-at-home critics, "to live in a place of quiet and peace and *talk;* than to be *on the field* and experience what we do." For himself, Edgcomb appreciated the opportunity McClellan had given him to test himself against adversity.

Although still sore from his recent marches, he proudly stated, "I did not know I could stand so much. I am now ready for another tramp."[22]

On March 25, Brig. Gen. Marsena Rudolph Patrick took charge of Wadsworth's old brigade. Although both brigade commanders were in their early fifties and had come from rural upstate New York backgrounds, the two men could not have been more dissimilar in their politics, outlooks on life, and approaches to command. Wadsworth's rank sprang from his wealth, political influence, and schooling at Harvard. Patrick, the youngest of ten children, had run away from home at an early age to try his hand at various jobs, including those of a driver on the Erie Canal and a schoolteacher. He later struggled through his studies at West Point, to graduate in 1835 toward the bottom of his class. While Wadsworth could claim little military experience, Patrick had served in both the Mexican and Seminole wars. In his politics Wadsworth remained a Republican. Patrick, along with McClellan, Colonel Hoffman, and many of their fellow officers, supported the more conservative policies of the War Democrats.[23]

At the outbreak of the war Patrick, having resigned his commission in 1850, was pursuing an interest in scientific farming at Ovid, in Seneca County, New York, as president of the New York State Agricultural College (a forerunner of Cornell University in nearby Ithaca). New York Republican governor Edwin D. Morgan appointed him inspector general of New York State forces organizing at the various state depots—a position later expanded to include inspector of New York troops "in the field" as aide and advisor to McClellan. He was appointed a brigadier general in volunteer service on March 17, 1862, and got his first official look at his new brigade at inspection on the 25th. That same day he led the brigade at a review of McDowell's corps held at Fort Ward outside Alexandria.[24]

After all of their heartfelt tears shed over General Wadsworth's departure, the men shuddered at the thought of their future with General Patrick. His reputation as a prickly personality and severe martinet had preceded him. One of his former associates in the governor's office in Albany spoke of Patrick's "irascibility" and admitted that even Morgan was "anxious to get rid of him."[25] Before taking over the brigade Patrick was seen snooping around the camps, his uniform concealed by "a Mexican blanket hanging over his shoulders and enveloping his form— his head passing through a hole in the centre of this odd garment." In his talk to associates he made no bones about the fact that he thought

Wadsworth had spoiled the brigade and spoke of how he planned to correct the situation.[26]

To observers, Patrick presented a "somewhat fierce appearance and manner." He was quick of temper and "savage when provoked." He had cold eyes, a thunderous voice, "heavy and powerful," and an expressionless mouth concealed by a thick "patriartical" beard. An acquaintance described him as "a self-disciplined Presbyterian fearing God only, he had the air of an Old Testament prophet with a dash of the Pharisee." One soldier put it more succinctly: "He looks as though he could bite the head off a tenpenny nail, and would like to do it." From the very start of his association with the brigade, as one man told his father, Patrick was "both feared and hated." Nevertheless, for better or worse, Patrick would direct the fortunes of the 23d for much of its remaining service and imprint his strong personality on the character and development of the brigade.[27]

The saga of King's wandering division took yet another turn in early April as a result of a dispute between the president and General McClellan concerning the number of troops needed for the protection of the capital. Lincoln finally decided to detach McDowell's corps from McClellan's army and retain it as a defensive covering force in front of Washington. On April 4 two military departments were created: the Department of the Shenandoah under Maj. Gen. Nathaniel P. Banks west of the Blue Ridge Mountains in the Shenandoah Valley, and the new Department of the Rappahannock under General McDowell. McDowell had authority over the territory east of the mountains, to include the District of Columbia.[28]

While McClellan fumed from the Peninsula over the loss of McDowell's corps to what he considered a Washington cabal working against his success, McDowell's troops prepared for yet another march. This time their destination was not Alexandria but rather Manassas Junction once again, where the corps would take up a defensive line along the Orange and Alexandria Railroad between Manassas Junction and Warrenton Junction. King's division had orders to occupy Bristoe Station.[29]

On April 4 the division left Bailey's Cross Roads in heavy marching order with three days' rations and a herd of beef cattle. It traveled along familiar roads through Annandale, Fairfax Court House, and Centreville. Crossing Bull Run over a temporary bridge half a mile below Blackburn's Ford, it entered Manassas Junction about noon on the 6th. A boy, hawking Washington newspapers for ten cents each, met the men as they entered the "village" of Manassas Junction, consisting of only a few buildings in broken-down condition. Patrick thought Manassas "one of the most miserable places I ever saw." Another observer added, "A foul smell of charred animal matter hung about the place, and flights of crows were feeding upon the garbage strewn on every side."[30]

King quickly departed Manassas along the route of the Orange and Alexandria Railroad, passing through Milford before coming to Broad Run. As the men halted before the stream, "shoes and socks were slung over the shoulder, pants elevated, and with laughs, jests, songs and shouts, we splashed across." After taking the time to divert some water playfully through two abandoned mills to get the big water wheels turning, the Cortland Volunteers moved with the brigade to bivouac in some woods near the Warrenton road about a mile or so southwest of Bristoe Station. Close by they discovered a Rebel cemetery holding about seventy marked graves of soldiers from the 10th Alabama who had died of disease. General King took up his headquarters in a white frame building facing the tracks near the station.[31]

The day after their arrival at Bristoe a late-season snowstorm announced three days of cold and wet weather. Their shelter tents proved "little better then sieves," letting in water from above while additional water seemed to bubble up from the soggy ground below. The men tried to keep warm by building huge fires before their tents, resulting in a constant cloud of smoke hanging over the camp. To add to their discomfort, promised rations from Alexandria did not arrive on schedule, due to apparent mismanagement of the railroad.[32]

The men sought to supplement their meager rations by foraging in the neighborhood. They felt perfectly justified in doing so, since they were in enemy country and suffering from a lack of supplies. Also, foraging provided a source of adventure. On April 7, Lt. Hugh Baldwin of Company E, 23d, admitted in a letter, "While I write the boys are out shooting sheep 'on the sly' as it is contrary to the *Genl's orders*. . . . Soldiers will *take* things: There is no use talking, they of course belonged to Rebs."[33]

McDowell's generals, however, took a decidedly different view of the practice of foraging. They felt it undermined Northern efforts to restore Southern loyalties to the Union and destroyed the discipline of their troops. The same day Baldwin wrote his letter, General King issued General Orders No. 36 calling the activity of foraging nothing more than criminal thievery, perpetrated most often against "peaceable and unoffending citizens." The order stated, "The soldiers of the Republic are here to enforce, not violate, the laws, and to give protection to persons and property. If it be disgraceful in a citizen to steal, it is doubly so in the soldier, for he wears a badge of authority, and the public look up to him for protection, not indignity and insult." King threatened that anyone caught stealing from local farms would be sent to Alexandria and jailed to await trial in civil courts.[34]

The issue of foraging came to a head on April 12, when Pvt. Joseph UpdeGraff of Company K, 23d, tried to slip through the guard to go on a hunt with a comrade. Caught by the sergeant of the guard, David L. Hamer of the 24th New York, UpdeGraff apparently resisted arrest. The confrontation resulted in Hamer shooting UpdeGraff dead with his comrade's weapon. Updegraff's many friends in the regiment thought the incident amounted to murder. General Patrick ruled Hamer's action "fully justified" and considered the death a good lesson for the rest of his command. Burritt commented on the event: "May God hasten the time when we shall commence the destruction of the common enemy and cease killing each other."[35]

Patrick refused, however, to let the UpdeGraff matter drop. The next day, Sunday, April 13, was set aside by the secretary of war to give thanks for recent Union victories in the West at Shiloh and Island Number 10 on the Mississippi. After morning inspection, the regiments of the brigade assembled on their respective parade grounds for prayer and the reading of the secretary's proclamation. Patrick used the occasion to lecture his men on their recent behavior. He visited each regiment and said a few words "according to circumstances." His themes included the bad habits of some who stole and used "obscene and profane language." He lectured the 23d on the importance of obeying orders and related the shooting of UpdeGraff as a cautionary tale.[36]

Before the men of the 21st New York, Patrick leveled a broadside on a theme that he would return to again and again in the coming year:

Be men. Learn to respect yourselves, and others will respect you. A good soldier ought to be a good moral man—and a bad man is not likely to make a good soldier. Rise above temptation to do wrong. Suffer yourselves to contact no habits while here which you will be ashamed to carry home with you, or which will make the virtuous and good shun you, or be afraid of you, or despise you. I am an old soldier, and have been in the Mexican war. And among the western regiments that shared in that war were many who, while there, became so demoralized, that on their return home, whole communities where they dwelt became deteriorated for years and years, through their defiling contact. Let us hope better things of you, so that when this war is over, and you go back to your friends, who will rejoice over your return and your honorable exploits, they will not have occasion to blush for your vices, and perhaps wish, in bitterness, that you had rather died than be morally blighted by ever entering on so ruinous a service.

Patrick's gloomy speech on this intended day of celebration did not advance him in the estimation of his men. One reported that the sermon "fell upon heedless ears."[37]

On April 9 McDowell broke up his headquarters at the Episcopal Seminary and High School near Alexandria and set out to join his troops along the Orange and Alexandria Railroad. He traveled in style, riding in a new carriage pulled by a team of four dappled gray horses. He was accompanied by his escort, the 1st Pennsylvania Cavalry under Col. George Bayard, and a large entourage, including two French cooks and John La Mountain, transporting his observation balloon *Atlantic*. Arriving at Catlett's Station between Bristoe and Warrenton Junction on the 12th, he established department headquarters at the Nimrod Mark property. From Catlett's McDowell could control the roads to the Rappahannock—especially the road to Falmouth and Fredericksburg via Weaversville, Bristersburg, Spotted Tavern, and Hartwood Church. Here he could also maintain communications with Banks's Department in the Shenandoah Valley via Chester, Manassas, and Ashby's gaps in the Blue Ridge Mountains.[38]

When McDowell took up his headquarters at Catlett's, his corps had been reduced to about twenty thousand effectives formed into two infantry divisions of three brigades each, under the command of George McCall and Rufus King. In addition, two cavalry regiments were attached to the corps, the 2d New York and the 1st Pennsylvania, joined soon by a third, the 1st New Jersey. King's division consisted of Brig. Gen. Christopher C. Augur's First Brigade, Patrick's Second Brigade, and Col. Lysander Cutler's Third Brigade, formerly commanded by King. King's division had four artillery batteries attached: Capt. J. Albert Monroe's Battery D, 1st Rhode Island Artillery; Capt. George A. Gerrish's, Battery A, 1st New Hampshire; Capt. George Durell's Independent Pennsylvania Battery D; and Capt. John Gibbon's Battery B, 4th U.S. All of King's infantry regiments carried rifles, and his twenty-four cannon were divided evenly between bronze smoothbores and ten-pounder rifled Parrotts.[39]

Although McDowell understood that the posture of his command was to be defensive in nature, as a covering force protecting the nation's capital, in mid-April he received verbal authorization from Secretary of War Edwin Stanton to advance his corps from Catlett's to Falmouth on the Rappahannock. If feasible he could cross the river and occupy Fredericksburg. McDowell had previously argued for the move, saying that he could just as easily defend Washington from the Rappahannock, while at the same time he could better check the activities of Brig. Gen. Charles W. Field's Rebel brigade operating, with about 2,200 men, near Fredericksburg.[40] Once on the Rappahannock he could also smooth out his communication and supply line to Washington by opening the Union railroad and supply base at Aquia Landing on the Potomac about ten miles from Falmouth. Chafing over his imposed exile from the fighting forces on the Peninsula, McDowell also sought by aggressive action to remain a player in McClellan's grand campaign against Richmond. He sent McClellan a verbal message to the effect that his advance to Fredericksburg, just fifty miles from Richmond, was also intended as a demonstration in McClellan's favor.[41]

The twenty-seven-mile march from Catlett's to Falmouth began at sunrise on April 17. General Augur's First Brigade led the division, joined by men of the 1st Pennsylvania and the 2d New York cavalry regiments and eight guns from Gibbon's and Gerrish's batteries. McDowell directed Augur to move quickly, drive in any Confederate outposts north of the Rappahannock, and save one or more of the three wooden river bridges from destruction by Field's Confederates. He also warned Augur to prevent straggling or marauding by enforcing "the most rigid and inflexible discipline . . . not hesitating to shoot on the spot any one whom you may find firing houses, committing violence on women, or other crimes."[42]

Some seventeen miles out from Catlett's beyond Spotted Tavern, Lt. Col. Judson Kilpatrick's 2d New York Cavalry drove in Field's advanced pickets. Learning from a local black resident that a Rebel camp lay a few miles down the road, Kilpatrick formed a swift-moving column of cavalry and infantry from the 14th NYSM regiment and put his force in motion. The infantrymen, dead tired after hours of marching in the hot sun, could keep up only by handing up their rifles to the horse soldiers and holding on to their saddle stirrups. Kilpatrick later reported that he struck the

Rebel camp "with a shout and a blow," scattering the enemy and losing only one man shot dead. Augur's command came up and bivouacked in the abandoned Rebel camp near Berea Baptist Church, grateful for the rations that Field's men had left behind in their precipitous retreat.[43]

Despite Augur's extraordinary efforts that day, darkness found him miles from his objective with Field's troops still blocking his path. Late that night a local civilian professing loyalty to the Union appeared in Augur's camp claiming that Field intended to make a stand before Falmouth and had prepared the Falmouth bridge for destruction. Bayard quickly organized a striking force of about seven hundred horsemen. At two o'clock they set out in the moonlight down a side road by which they hoped to reenter the main road below the enemy and capture the bridge. Being unfamiliar with local roads, however, the men returned to the main road prematurely and were soon brought up short by the sound of musket fire ahead. The cavalrymen drew their sabers and charged up an incline in the road near the home of Miss Lucy Ann Payne, where the Rebels had thrown up a barricade of rails and posted infantry with a flank force of cavalry. Two Union cavalry charges broke before the concentrated Confederate musket fire, the second charge thrusting the cavalrymen to within twenty-five yards of the rails. Bayard fell back to await reinforcements, leaving five of his dead and sixteen wounded on the battlefield.[44]

By six in the morning on the 18th, Field had decided to abandon his positions north of the river. Crossing his force into Fredericksburg, he set fire to the three Rappahannock bridges, two steamers in the river, twenty schooners at the Fredericksburg wharf loaded with grain, and fifteen to twenty thousand dollars' worth of cotton stored in warehouses. The smoke from the fires rising above Fredericksburg spurred Augur's troops on to greater effort. At daylight the lead elements of his force pushed on toward Falmouth past the scene of the skirmish that had occurred the night before. The soldiers discovered one wounded man still on his hands and knees, his intestines protruding from a gaping saber wound in his side. Another man's face was partially shot away and swollen beyond recognition. Men were detailed to care for the wounded, while others from the passing column thought to cover the faces of the dead with their caps.[45]

A spirited dash by Union cavalry to the river managed to save only about one-third of the Falmouth bridge before the rest of the structure was consumed by fire. Gibbon's guns unlimbered on a high hill overlooking the town but managed only to fire a few rounds at the tail end of Field's infantry column seen disappearing over Marye's Heights behind Fredericksburg. Not long after, Augur's men entered Falmouth with their music playing and flags flying. "The Nigers were all a'grinning," one soldier from the 24th New York Infantry said of their reception, "but the white folks looked rather sober."[46]

Patrick's Second Brigade followed Augur's on April 18. Two days before they had marched over from Bristoe to Catlett's in high spirits, encouraged by the popular songs played along the way by the Union Cornet Band. At Catlett's, Patrick found department headquarters in a festive mood, with "whiskey and water still flowing freely."[47] Patrick's men marched past the station, described as a shed and a station house in "mournful dilapidation," to a pleasant bivouac site on the William Quisenberry plantation, "Airly," with a picturesque view of the Blue Ridge. King made his headquarters at the main house, while Patrick established his brigade headquarters near the overseer's cottage.[48]

On the 18th, after a night of singing and music at King's headquarters, reveille sounded for the brigade at four o'clock. Because of the large amount of accumulated baggage to be loaded in the wagons, the march did not begin until seven. To lighten their marching loads many men threw away all nonessentials—described by one soldier as including "books, brush brooms, checker-boards, surplus shirts and drawers, and 'Yankee notions' of all descriptions."[49]

The march from Catlett's began well enough. After a brief halt at Elk Run to build a bridge for the wagons, the infantry continued down the main road; Patrick took a number of slower wagons and two artillery batteries down a parallel route. The men marched under a brilliant blue sky past peach and cherry orchards in full spring bloom, bright green hundred-acre fields of four-inch-high wheat, and meadows of blue violets and fragrant wildflowers. Every half-mile or more they passed well-tended homesteads with the houses set back from the road in groves of shade trees. In contrast to the fearful white landowners, who stayed back out of sight, the slaves swarmed to the roadside to witness the "splendid pageant" with emotions ranging from childlike curiosity and caution to "extravagant manifestations of joy." One self-appointed black spokesman rode up to the passing column driving a two-wheel wagon pulled by a donkey and announced, "We's mighty glad to see you gentleman; been specting you long time; the more of you we sees, the gladder we is." The soldiers and slaves began a lively banter, with many of the slaves walking through the fields along the road to keep up with the moving column.[50]

The first encounter between Patrick's New Yorkers and the numerous plantation slaves reveals their very different perceptions of one another. Blacks saw the Union army as the authority willing and able to deliver them from slavery. Dexter wrote on April 22, "I have not yet heard one express his opinion but what he wished to be free." Another Southern Tier man reported that "they seemed anxious for freedom, but did not seem to understand how to obtain it." Nor, apparently, did they understand what freedom meant in terms of their daily welfare or the welfare of their families. Despite the obvious dangers in trying to escape their masters, many on the spur of the moment fled the plantations to join the rear of Patrick's column, often with literally nothing more than the clothes on their backs.[51]

Many soldiers viewed the slaves they encountered simply as humorous objects of curiosity. Colonel Hoffman in a letter of April 22 to his brother reflected on the large number of slaves he had seen, referring to the area through which they passed as "a kind of niggar breeding district," producing "odd looking objects of all shapes, sizes and colours. . . . It was very amusing to me," he continued, "to catch short conversations with them and hear them talk and see them act." Sergeant Crandall of Company D interpreted their general enthusiasm to mean that they were content with their lot. Many other soldiers had great fun encouraging them in their ignorance. "Do what you like, and go where you please," one soldier flippantly told one man, "you don't belong to Massa ___ anymore than Massa ___ belongs to you." Colonel Hoffman wrote that Major Gregg remained in the rear of the 23d giving "good advice" to the escaping slaves about keeping "their eye on the North Star, etc."[52]

Soon after Patrick's men had begun their march to Falmouth, things started to go wrong. The wagon train became hopelessly lost trying to travel over unmapped and unfamiliar roads. Also, the day turned out to be one of the warmest in the season. Blisters rose on the men's feet, sweat streaked down their dust-covered faces, and the straps of their heavy knapsacks cut into their shoulders and compressed their chests. Their thirst became unbearable. Knots of soldiers loaded down with their comrades' empty canteens eddied from the column to crowd around scarce wells and jostle with each other for the precious water. Some of the more desperate men simply drank yellow water from roadside ditches. Toward afternoon their march route became littered with cast-off blankets, overcoats, and even knapsacks. Eager local blacks contested for the spoils "like a swarm of hungry flies," and "many a hearty laugh was caused by the strife between them." Other blacks "followed in our wake on horseback and with light wagons picking up booty."[53]

Despite numerous halts for rest, the men began to straggle. Adjutant Hayt spent much of his time "riding hither and yon, doing my best to encourage the poor fellows who were constantly leaving the ranks." Hoffman finally issued passes for a number of men to fall out and follow in the rear of the column as best they could. Patrick, in contrast, showed little sympathy for the plight of his men. He kept the brigade marching long after sunset under a severe thunderstorm that brought high winds, vivid flashes of lightning, and a downpour of rain. Finally, around eight at night, after covering a total of twenty miles in thirteen hours, the brigade bivouacked with the baggage train near Spotted Tavern. After roll call the men scattered to gather firewood for boiling coffee and drying out clothes. Others sought whatever available shelter they could find to keep off the rain. Stragglers continued to stumble into camp throughout the night, listening for their company letters frequently shouted out in the dark to identify bivouac sites.[54]

Patrick complained that his men that night "burned fences and ran riot" and were "perfectly unmanageable." He formed special police patrols to keep them under control. One squad of the 23d that had broken into a cooper's shop was just getting comfortable before a warming fire when some of Patrick's security men drove them back out into the rain. One of the victims wrote, "That night alone is sufficient to make a lifelong impression of him [Patrick] in our memory."[55] Some of the officers of the Cortland Volunteers found shelter in a house owned by an old couple "as ignorant as poor." Patrick himself "took possession" with his staff of the James Briggs home, "Stony Hill."[56]

The next day, the 19th, the rain gave way to a clear but chilly morning. Because of reports of Rebel cavalry operating in the area and the confused march of the day before, Patrick became more cautious in his advance. He directed Durell's and Monroe's artillery to take the lead, followed by the infantry, the wagons, and finally the 23d acting as rear guard. As the march began, the warm morning sun raised steam from the men's damp uniforms. Much refreshed from the trials of the day before, the men sang "Dixie" and other airs as they marched past many appreciative local blacks, who continued to hail them with "broad smiles and comical remarks and gestures."[57]

When a woman confronted Patrick to complain that one of his soldiers had stolen her horse, the general organized a force of "reliable" men to march at the head of each regiment. When the lead regiment came to a roadside residence, one of these men would drop out to guard it until replaced by a man from the next regiment coming up. The guards had authority to "shoot down" any officer or soldier who attempted to enter a house uninvited or gain access to private property except for wells or springs. From Patrick's perspective, these actions had "an excellent effect upon the Troops."[58]

By midafternoon Patrick's brigade had marched past Augur's headquarters and entered Falmouth. One soldier described the town as having "a church, a factory, a mill, and several stores, and about eighty dilapidated frame houses." As they passed through the village they amused themselves by shouting "rude greetings" to some "slatternly women [who] thrust their heads through broken windows," while at the same time speaking "blunt expressions of admiration" to the few embarrassed pretty young girls among them. Climbing the steep hill out of Falmouth they passed the brick Union Church and hospital, near where a burial party was at work interring the Union dead from the skirmish on the morning of the 18th. They continued on downriver for about a mile to a site opposite Fredericksburg, where they laid out a camp on a broad plain near the tracks of the Richmond, Fredericksburg, and Potomac Railroad. The camp sat about a mile back from the river near an imposing Gothic Revival–style brick home owned by the wealthy Alexander Keene Phillips. The two batteries with Patrick unlimbered on high ground near the Phillips house and pointed their guns over the infantry toward the spires of Fredericksburg visible across the river.[59]

Toward evening the Union Cornet Band advanced down to the riverbank to stand in the front yard of the J. Horace Lacy house, "Chatham." Below them, across the river, the city of Fredericksburg appeared "like a place of the dead" with no human movement visible and the buildings appearing gray and cold in the evening shadows. After unfurling a large national flag on a pole stuck in the ground, the band began playing the "Star Spangled Banner." The music drifted out over the river in the still night air and settled onto the town. When finished, the bandsmen waited in silence, hearing only what they took to be a distant mocking laugh. Then two figures emerged from the shadows on the Fredericksburg shore. It was a woman, holding the hand of a child. "Her arm was raised toward us, and something white fluttered in the night wind above her head."[60]

CHAPTER 5

Fredericksburg

T he town of Fredericksburg boasts a rich history dating back to the 1720s, when it was first established at the fall line, the head of navigation, of the Rappahannock River. At the time of the Civil War the river here spanned four hundred feet; the main channel could reach twelve feet at tide and accommodate vessels of up to 140 tons.[1] From the founding of the town, the Rappahannock had given Fredericksburg an outward-looking perspective based upon commerce and water-powered industry.

The sister communities of Falmouth and Fredericksburg grew up on opposite sides of the river less than a mile and a half apart below uneven fifty- to hundred-foot heights that here turn and direct the river on its remaining 125-mile course to the Chesapeake Bay. Stafford Heights on the northern, or left, bank held Falmouth close to the river, while Spotsylvania Heights climbed more gradually away behind the town of Fredericksburg (see map p. 233).

Leaving Falmouth the river abruptly turns south a short distance, fronting Fredericksburg before resuming a southeastward course. Fredericksburg grew within this elbow of the river, expanding from the shoreline over parallel ridgelines formed by a previous course that the river had abandoned long ago in geologic time. Enterprising local entrepreneurs before the Civil War diverted water from the river above Falmouth down the old river channel to turn the great waterwheels of local mills. A supportive transportation network—the north-south Telegraph Road; the Richmond, Fredericksburg, and Potomac Railroad; the westward Orange Plank Road to Orange and the road to Culpeper Court House; and the forty-five-mile Rappahannock canal system above the river's fall line—seemed to assure Fredericksburg a prosperous future.

In 1860 Fredericksburg had a population of about five thousand inhabitants (including 1,291 slaves and 422 free blacks).[2] Despite its growth, however, Fredericksburg retained the features of a quaint colonial town, with many historic buildings and solid historical pretensions based upon famous early residents, including James Monroe and Brig. Gen. Hugh Mercer. George Washington walked the streets as a boy, growing up on the "Ferry Farm" in Stafford County opposite the Fredericksburg town wharves and steamboat landing. George's mother, Mary Ball Washington, lived and died in a frame house on Charles Street in Fredericksburg and was buried near a prominent, grass-covered rock outcropping at the edge of town.

Ironically, when war came, Fredericksburg's many geographic advantages proved its undoing. Jefferson Davis once remarked that Fredericksburg stood "right in the wrong place."[3] Located astride the Telegraph Road about equidistant between the two opposing capitals[4] and controlling the primary crossing point of the Rappahannock River barrier, Fredericksburg was destined to play a critical role in the coming military campaigns in the East. As indicated earlier, it was the strategic location of Fredericksburg that drew McDowell's army to the banks of the Rappahannock in the spring of 1862.

On April 18, after Gen. Charles Field's Brigade set fire to the bridges and military stores in Fredericksburg and fled south, the townspeople felt abandoned and at the mercy of the enemy. They gathered anxiously along the burning waterfront to watch the Stafford shore, where they expected the Yankee host to appear at any moment. Out from the pall of smoke that blanketed the river came makeshift civilian rafts being poled toward the Fredericksburg shore past the still-burning ships and clear of the flaming bridge timbers that occasionally fell hissing into the water. Some of the rafts carried entire families, with their slaves and horses.[5]

A black waiter at the Shakespeare House hotel later described the "wild confusion" of the hotel diners when excited Rebel cavalrymen first announced the arrival of Yankees in Falmouth. "Every where was hurried words and hasty foot steps," he remembered. Outside on the street,

Wartime Fredericksburg, Virginia. *(National Archives)*

wagons and carriages piled high with personal items struggled for space in the column of vehicles trying to escape in the wake of departing Confederate troops. Stores and businesses closed, and those residents remaining in town sought refuge behind locked doors. Soon the streets were deserted except for groups of curious blacks that gathered on street corners or on rooftops to gaze toward Falmouth with feelings of "new born hopes."[6]

Fredericksburg's mayor, Montgomery Slaughter, reacted to the crisis by calling an emergency session of the governing council. Recognizing the proximity of the first anniversary date of Virginia's vote in convention to adopt an ordinance of secession (April 17), the council boldly asserted Fredericksburg's undying devotion to the Confederate cause. The mayor then formed a committee to meet with the invaders—first with Union officers on the 18th near the Chatham Bridge site,[7] and the next day with General Augur at his Falmouth headquarters in order to surrender the town.[8] When a committee member, Commonwealth's Attorney Thomas B. Barton, reported on the surrender proceedings to General Field, he acknowledged Fredericksburg's helpless situation: "We are in the hands of the Philistines."[9]

McDowell moved quickly to secure his hold on the northern bank of the river. General King arrived in Falmouth with his remaining infantry and artillery on April 23. King ordered Augur to deploy his men along the riverbank above the J. Horace Lacy house, "Chatham," with Patrick's troops similarly placed below the house, under instructions to prevent any unauthorized river crossings of goods or persons. "In a very rude manner," according to Patrick, King's staff took charge of the Alexander K. Phillips house and grounds for division headquarters. Patrick consequently moved his headquarters from the Phillips property farther out the Belle Plain Road[10] to the Gustavus B. Wallace house, "Little Whim," where he established his brigade camp on April 28–29. Before the end of the month, McCall's division arrived at Falmouth, giving McDowell a total of twenty thousand available troops. In addition, on May 1, after the repulse of Stonewall Jackson's troops by General Banks at the Battle of Kernstown in the Shenandoah Valley (March 23), Lincoln ordered Brig. Gen. James Shields's eleven-thousand-man division of Banks's command transferred to McDowell's department. McDowell directed Shields to join his main force by marching to Catlett's Station on the Orange and Alexandria Railroad, where he would be in a position to guard McDowell's right flank and rear.[11]

McDowell established his headquarters at the Peter Hedgeman house, about two and a half miles from Aquia Creek along the sixteen-mile stretch of the Richmond, Fredericksburg, and Potomac Railroad, which ran between Fredericksburg and its terminus at Aquia Landing. At Hedgeman's he could personally oversee the critical work of securing his supply and communication line between Falmouth and Washington from bases on the two estuaries of the Potomac—Aquia and Potomac creeks. The needed work included restoring the telegraph line; repairing damage to three miles of railroad track, three railroad bridges, and the wharf at Aquia Landing; and maintaining the twelve miles of the Belle Plain Road from the Rappahannock to the old stage landing at Potomac Creek. The engineer Herman Haupt, an aide to McDowell in charge of the railroad repair, later wrote that McDowell visited his work sites almost daily "to watch the progress and encourage the men by his presence. He said he had never heard sweeter music than the click of the hammers when we were working all night near his Headquarters, spiking rails by the aid of lanterns, the men soaked with rain and the ties laid in mud." On April 27 McDowell reported with pride that two locomotives had been landed and mounted on the tracks at Aquia Landing. By May 3 he felt that the work had progressed far enough that he could officially move his headquarters from Hedgeman's to "Chatham."[12]

Meanwhile, Patrick struggled to instill greater discipline in his troops by establishing a rigorous schedule of drill and guard duty. He thought the task an uphill battle. He considered his officers "a set of drones, generally, and [who] do not care a fig for discipline or duty." The troops, he wrote, behaved badly, "like a pack of Demons," with some of them "plundering houses, insulting women and committing depredation for miles around." He admitted, "I am almost discouraged in my efforts to get thieves, skulks and political scribblers to become soldiers."[13]

On April 27 Patrick stood bareheaded before the brigade gathered for Sunday service. With "gleaming eye, burning with fervor," and in a slow, deep voice, "raised in exhortation," he firmly stated the superior claims of morality and religion on the lives of his soldiers. Although his words "hushed and awed" all who heard them, in effect they only encouraged the growing number of his critics in the ranks who thought him too strict and overbearing with the men and at the same time too soft in his dealings with Southern civilians.[14] Burritt, who probably qualified in Patrick's book as a "political scribbler," stated the case against Patrick's policies in a letter published in the *Elmira Advertiser* of April 29. He complained about their "protecting the property of known enemies of the government, which we represent, and whose laws, in the absence of civil officers we propose to enforce."

The unscheduled appearance of Gen. James Wadsworth in camp the day of Patrick's sermon nicely contrasted the attitude of the men toward their two brigade commanders. When Wadsworth came down the road near camp with his son and staff, the sudden call "Old Waddy's coming!" brought nearly two thousand men from his old brigade running in various states of dress to surround and touch their beloved former leader. The Union Cornet Band struck up "Hail to the Chief." Wadsworth, his hat off, "leaned from his horse, shaking the hands of his boys, the tears streaming down his furrowed cheeks, and unable to speak an audible word." When he turned to leave, pushing his horse through the crowd to reach the road, the band played "The Days of Auld Lang Syne." Mc-Dowell happened by soon after, and the men, still excited and primed to cheer, let out a fusillade of hurrahs that startled the general's horse. After an awkward moment as he struggled with the reins to control his mount, McDowell touched his cap in recognition and rode on.[15]

Despite the trials of army life and the "cold looks and scowls" coming from the local white inhabitants, King's men found their days at Falmouth not altogether unpleasant. Tent cities sprang up along Stafford Heights, and a division bakery began turning out 2,160 loaves of soft bread a day. "Soon the town was filled with our sutlers, store-keepers and photographers, who gave new life to it."[16] A variety of vendors began selling everything from canned fruit and ready-made clothing to books. With such a large audience of Americans with money in their pockets came the "inevitable showman." One entrepreneur draped an immense canvas sheet down the outside of a deserted shanty on which was an image of the "largest snake in the world." For a fee the soldiers could eat peanuts and gingerbread, drink lemonade, and inside the building see the amazing "*Duck Man,* born without arms!"[17]

In contrast to the scowls of the white population, the soldiers received unwavering support from local blacks, who welcomed the Yankees as their liberators. On April 27 Burritt reported that a "stampede" of joyful escaped slaves passed through the Union camps, including twenty young men who had fled from a single plantation.[18]

The Southern Tier men looked upon the local black population with mixed emotions. In their writings they disparagingly referred to them as "niggers," "coloreds," "darkies," "shades," and "contrabands." They sympathized with their plight as slaves but did not consider blacks in any way their equals in life, and they expressed resentment toward the blacks as a cause of the war. Drummer Edgcomb, while casually watching a group of black women carrying baskets of manure on their heads to a local pumpkin field, mused, "What a trouble this afflicted race has been to us as a nation and what will be the end?" Capt. Luzerne Todd (Co. D) of the 23d questioned the ability of former slaves to live as freemen. "I would like to see them free," he explained, "yet I believe that those I have seen are better off here than they would be to go North." A thoughtful Cortland County officer serving in Virginia in June 1861 argued against the immediate freeing of the slaves. He reasoned that the "immediate physical comfort of the slave, on the whole, would not be promoted by emancipation, and his intellectual and moral condition could hardly stand the test of so sudden and great a change." Sgt. Albert Crandall of the 23d took the extreme view that given what he had seen thus far in Virginia, "slavery, in itself, is right, and when well regulated proper too." Crandall considered the vexing problem of what to do with the many former slaves he saw, "every one of which, I wish would shoulder an Irishman and leave the Continent."[19]

Although most of Patrick's men hated the institution of slavery, few would claim that the abolition of slavery and the freeing of the slave were the reasons for their service or the banners under which they fought. Surgeon Seymour Churchill chided the abolitionists in a letter to the Owego, New York, newspaper: "This is not a war for the sole purpose of exterminating slavery, but for a higher and more noble purpose, that of upholding our once free and happy country, and the sustaining of her laws." He supported the emancipation of the slaves in the occupied South but only as a war measure to deny the Confederacy the labor and wealth by which to pursue the war. If slavery was abolished as a consequence of these policies, Churchill reasoned, all the better, but he insisted that abolition remain "the *means* and not the *end* of our mission." Lieutenant Andrews succinctly summed up the soldiers' thinking: "I am an abolitionist . . . not because I love an African. I am one because I think it the most takable point in which to touch them. A joint is loose in their armor there."[20]

Captain Todd recognized the obvious disparity between Northern soldiers' attitudes toward slavery and the perspective of the runaway slaves, who had staked everything on freedom and "look[ed] upon the Union army as the men that are here for that purpose instead of being here as we are to put down the rebellion."[21] The freedmen soon found themselves straddling a fence between two worlds, without a foothold in either.

From the time of their first arrival at Falmouth, Union troops did everything they could to separate the slaves from their masters. They termed the slaves "contraband" property, subject to seizure by Union authorities without compensation to owners. They encouraged local slaves to desert their masters and held out the offer of support and protection for those arriving within Union lines. A member of General Augur's staff employed a local black to scour the countryside encouraging other slaves to escape. Major Gregg delighted in the success of these efforts as evidenced by the increasing numbers of runaways seen about the Union camps. "It does me a great deal of good," he wrote, "to see eight to fifteen hundred dollars' worth of property walking away from our enemies."[22]

Once the former slaves arrived within Union lines, the soldiers rebuffed all efforts of their former owners to reclaim their property. In one publicized incident a group of Union officers rescued a young black girl being beaten by her master on the street. Local citizen Betty Herndon Maury commented that by mid-May whenever any "little difficulties" and conflicts sprung up between local whites and blacks, "in every case the soldiers have interfered in favour of the negroes."[23]

After the former slaves arrived in Falmouth, many of the able-bodied males remained in town seeking work while the aged men, women, and children continued north to Washington. The military hired many of the men as guides, laborers, informers, cooks, or servants. McDowell's engineers employed a number of them as laborers on the railroad. They were formed into work gangs, issued distinctive badges, and set to work repairing track for fifty cents a day, one ration per day, and five cents an hour for extra work. Many other blacks found work as camp servants. "Each officer has one," one soldier claimed, "and many of the privates have them to black their boots or clean their brass." A man of the 23d added on May 2, "At first they asked large prices for their labor, but now we can hire a pretty good waiter for four dollars a month."[24]

The men enjoyed and benefited greatly from their association with the local black population. Each morning blacks would arrive in camp balancing upon their heads baskets containing hoecakes, eggs, and tobacco to sell or trade for coffee. In the evening they danced in the company streets for sutler's exchange tickets to the accompaniment of hand "pats" from two or three of their fellows. On April 22 a more formal dance was got up on the parade ground of the 21st New York for a number of "good looking, gaily dressed, young ladies of pure and unmixed African blood." The regiment's brass band played "as a substitute for the banjo." The men delighted in these amusements, especially finding the "wild, fervid religious dances, with their accompanying chants . . . the most wierdly [sic] exciting, yet ludicrous performances imaginable."[25]

For former slaves traveling on to Washington by foot or train, the Northern capital proved far from the Promised Land of freedom. On May 13 a soldier in the 26th New York met a group of blacks returning disappointed to Falmouth. The trip north had been full of dangers. The railroads would not carry them beyond Washington without a bond, and there was always the fear, particularly for those entering Maryland, of being arrested as fugitives and sold back into slavery. Also, they had met hostility from the black residents of Washington, who complained that the new arrivals ("country darkies") were generally driving down wages.[26]

For blacks stranded in Falmouth there remained few options. A *New York Herald* reporter on May 8 wrote that some chose to return to slavery, "declaring the road to freedom not so smooth as they anticipated" and lacking "the care of those to whom they have been wont to look for assistance." Others took advantage of the opportunity to emigrate to Haiti. On July 11, 1862, a bark outfitted by James Redpath, general agent of the Haitian Bureau of Emigration, anchored off the wharf at Aquia Landing, and within ten days the ship set sail with 450 new black colonists.[27]

Despite the hardships and danger of escaping slavery, the presence of a rapidly growing fugitive black population in Falmouth, supported and encouraged by Federal authorities, emboldened other slaves south of the river to flee plantations deep in Spotsylvania County. Many remained in Fredericksburg, beyond the control of the weakened civil authorities and under the protection of Union guns on Stafford Heights. The new arrivals wandered the streets reveling in their newfound freedom and demanding wages for their labor. Fredericksburg whites refused to hire them, citing applicable state laws against it, as well as a higher claim, expressed by resident Jane Beale, that the black race was "ordained of high Heaven to serve the white man and it is only in that capacity they can be happy, useful and respected." The Yankees would soon find out, she warned, that freeing the slaves would result in "the great evil of a useless, expensive and degraded population among them." Betty Herndon Maury expressed similar concerns as she warily watched the growing number of "very independent and impertinent" blacks who wandered idly about the town. "I am afraid of the lawless Yankee soldiers," she wrote, "but that is nothing to my fear of the negroes if they should rise against us."[28]

On April 25 General King demonstrated to the Southerners Fredericksburg's vulnerability by launching a bold predawn cavalry raid against one of General Field's picket posts south of Fredericksburg. Eighteen horsemen of the 1st New Jersey Cavalry, guided by two former slaves, slipped across the river by small boat and rode out to capture five enemy soldiers, returning with them without loss. That same afternoon a convoy of ships down from Alexandria arrived at Fredericksburg, including a shallow-draft steam ferryboat, two gunboats, and two steamships towing twenty canal boats intended for use in bridging the river. The fleet floated at anchor just below the ruins of the railroad bridge.[29]

Because of high water from recent rains, work on the canal-boat bridge did not begin until April 28. A captain directed the work crews, which included a thirty-man detail from the Southern Tier regiment under Sgt. Daniel O. Clough of Company H. The men began the bridge from a point opposite the Fredericksburg town wharves under the protective guns of Gerrish's New Hampshire battery positioned on a grassy elevation nearby. Spanning the four-hundred-foot river would require seventeen or eighteen boats anchored side by side twelve to fifteen feet apart, and connected by stringers supporting a smooth plank surface that would be laid on. On the 29th a pontoon train lumbered past Patrick's camp down the Belle Plain Road, each wagon pulled by a ten-mule team. The train carried the India-rubber pontoon boats that would provide McDowell a second bridge if needed.[30]

From the time his troops first arrived at Falmouth, McDowell chafed at his purely defensive role protecting Washington while McClellan battled Gen. Joseph Johnston before Richmond and Maj. Gen. Nathaniel Banks chased Stonewall Jackson up the Shenandoah Valley. As early as April 26 McDowell sought permission from Washington to send a force across the river to occupy Fredericksburg. He argued that by crossing the river he could gain greater control over the river traffic and more effectively check a growing Confederate counterforce located about twelve miles south of Fredericksburg (Brig. Gen. Joseph R. Anderson's Army of the Rappahannock, about ten thousand men). He also wanted to seize Confederate stores and supplies remaining in Fredericksburg and provide the protection requested by a number of pro-Union citizens being harassed by Confederate authorities. Five or six Union men of Fredericksburg had reportedly been arrested and carried south for incarceration in Richmond. Also, although he did not state it in writing, McDowell anticipated using Fredericksburg as a springboard for an overland campaign against Richmond in support of McClellan. Finally, on April 30, Secretary of War Edwin Stanton gave McDowell approval for the occupation of Fredericksburg, but only "with such force as in your judgment may be necessary to hold it for defensive purposes, but not with a view to make a forward movement."[31]

Meanwhile, work continued on the canal-boat bridge before the gaze of curious and chatty civilian onlookers drawn to the riverbank by all the activity. Completed before five in the evening on May 2, the bridge particularly impressed Jane Beale, who thought it had the "appearance of strength and perfect adaptation to its purpose."[32]

When King and his staff rode up to inspect the finished bridge, the general directed Sergeant Clough to deliver some papers to Mayor Slaughter. When King asked him if he had a white handkerchief to use as a flag of truce, he replied, "No sir, I have not seen one in six months." King gave him one and Clough set out on his mission. King and General Patrick, along with their staffs and a squad of cavalry, followed Clough into the city to meet briefly with the mayor and then ride down Caroline and Princess Anne Streets to locate posts for pickets and to identify property needing special protection.[33]

When Patrick first rode through Fredericksburg, he took note of the "indignant" reaction of the whites he encountered: "It was amusing to see the manner in which the Secesh women showed us their Backs. They were all looking until about the time the Cavalcade would get opposite their doors then, with a grand air they would throw back their Crinoline, as Stage Ladies do." The one bright spot for Patrick came from the "refreshing" smiles from the attractive daughters of Union man Peleg Clarke Jr., who waved their white handkerchiefs in welcome. Major Gregg of the 23d added that the black population, in contrast to most whites, offered them joyous greetings with such comments to the soldiers as "God bless you massa, we is so glad you have come."[34]

On the evening of May 2 Captain Todd, leading Company D, crossed over the bridge and pushed through a crowd of anxious citizens asking in loud voices "why we were here, and why we did not stay at home and let them alone?" He immediately established a cordon of soldiers around the bridgehead and assumed the position of provost marshal, with headquarters at the Alexander Keene Phillips brick warehouse, located on the riverbank near the bridge landing. The next day he organized patrols of the town to keep order and search for military stores and weapons. During the following week Todd reported seizing 25,000 bushels of corn and about a thousand barrels of flour. On May 5 several of Todd's men knocked on Betty Herndon Maury's door to investigate a tip that she was hiding weapons. Five old swords were all that she could produce; she attributed the "humiliating" experience to the vengeful talk of her bitter and increasingly "insolent and unbearable" black servants.[35]

McDowell worked quickly to consolidate his hold on Fredericksburg and secure his supply bases. He established telegraph communication with Washington by the first week of May. On Sunday, May 4, he rode on the first locomotive from Aquia Landing over the 150-foot long Accakeek Bridge near Brooke Station, which his engineer-genius Herman Haupt had built in fifteen hours. Earlier that same morning, as the church bells rang out in the river valley to call the Fredericksburg faithful to worship, work started on a pontoon bridge from the mouth of a ravine near Chatham about a mile above the canal-boat bridge. Late in the day the sound of cheering rose from the valley on the news that Yorktown had fallen to

McClellan's forces. At sunset McDowell topped off the rewarding day by relaxing with guests at Chatham, to music provided by a military band.[36]

Early on May 5 the engineers completed the pontoon bridge, protected by six Parrott rifled guns of Durell's Pennsylvania battery positioned on a bluff near Chatham and by Company C of the 35th New York, which had crossed over the night before to secure the landing site.[37] In the afternoon Generals McDowell, King, and Patrick, along with the 2d New York Cavalry, crossed over the bridge to visit Fredericksburg. Captain Clark of the Cortland Volunteers accompanied McDowell's party and later related a humorous incident. Passing a number of ladies standing on a porch, McDowell "gallantly" raised his cap in greeting. "The ladies put on as contemptuous an expression as they could, accompanying it by turning their backs to the General, much to the amusement of the escort, and even to the General, who spoiled the joke by laughing as heartily as any as soon as they arrived in camp."[38]

At first Patrick hesitated to send an organized independent force over to occupy Fredericksburg. He did not think his regimental commanders were up to the task, preferring to employ individual companies so he could "control them myself." By five in the evening of May 5, Patrick had sent to the south bank Companies D and A of the 23d, three companies of the 20th NYSM, and one of the 35th. He placed Col. Theodore B. Gates of the 20th in overall command in Fredericksburg as provost marshal, with headquarters first at the corner of Pitt and Princess Anne streets and later, on May 6, at the stone warehouse near the ruins of the old Chatham bridge. Capt. Theodore Schlick of Company A took up his headquarters in a gas-lit room at the train depot.[39]

On the 6th, however, Patrick, "troubled" by the increasingly tense situation developing in Fredericksburg, decided to replace the Fredericksburg troops with a full regiment, giving the honor to Colonel Hoffman and the 23d. Hoffman, however, did not have Patrick's full confidence. In a journal entry Patrick worried, "I do not know how he will keep his men." (The next day, after Hoffman had occupied Fredericksburg, McDowell was to step in to order Patrick across the river with his entire brigade and assume himself the position of military governor.)[40]

By eight o'clock in the morning on May 7 Colonel Hoffman had his men all packed and ready to march. They stood on their parade ground "with clothes brushed, shoes blacked and brass polished." Hoffman led them silently and without fanfare or music down the Belle Plain Road and over the canal-boat bridge to their new headquarters at the three-story, brick, tobacco-factory building at the corner of Prussia and Princess Anne. Taking possession of the building, Hoffman ordered Sgt. Maj. Archibald M. DeVoe and Color Cpl. Ebin E. Crocker (Co. D) to unfurl the regimental Stars and Stripes from the rooftop for all of Fredericksburg to see.[41]

In the days to follow, Hoffman established a protective eight-mile cordon of pickets enclosing the bend of the river that cradled Fredericksburg. Pickets took up a line from a point on the river above Fredericksburg near the home of John Stansbury, "Snowden," across to a point below the town near the mouth of Deep Run. At about the center rear of the picket line Hoffman placed the camps of Companies H and C. The camps stood about half a mile apart on a narrow, uneven ridgeline, forty to fifty feet high and nine hundred feet long, known as Marye's Heights (pronounced "Marie"). The heights ran parallel to and about a mile back from the Fredericksburg shoreline and beyond the outskirts of the town. From the town Marye's Heights appears as a high salient or balcony of land projecting forward from the higher Spotsylvania Heights and separated from them by a ravine and the stream Hazel Run.

Marye's Heights gave Hoffman command of the major roads entering the town from Richmond, Orange, and Culpeper. The camp of Company C controlled the Orange Plank Road; its pickets extended to Alum Springs.[42] Captain Clark with the Cortland Volunteers occupied the southern extension of Marye's Heights on Willis Hill. From this position Clark could command the important Telegraph Road running between Washington and Richmond. Emerging from town the road crossed a six-hundred-yard open plain checkered by fences before reaching Marye's Heights directly below Willis Hill. The road then turned south a short distance along the base of the heights before it swung around the southern end of Willis Hill, crossed Hazel Run at a grist mill and dwelling, and then disappeared up the wooded slope of Spotsylvania Heights. Hoffman's pickets watched the Telegraph Road from Spotsylvania Heights; their line extended across to the Richmond, Fredericksburg, and Potomac tracks at Hazel Run and to the Bowling Green Road (modern Route 2), where it crossed Deep Run.

Companies K, G, and B of the 23d directly supported the two companies on Marye's Heights from camps nearer to town. Company A guarded the railroad depot, I and D the canal-boat bridge, E the line of the railroad through town, and Company F the pontoon bridge. Two companies of the 2d New York Cavalry also joined Patrick in Fredericksburg to extend his reach. One of them, Company L, bivouacked near the Cortland Volunteers below Willis Hill on Hazel Run. On the Stafford side of the river three of the four division batteries protected the bridges: Gerrish at the boat bridge, Durell near Chatham at the pontoon bridge, and, as of May 10, Monroe's Rhode Island battery in position to cover the men at work on the railroad bridge.[43]

General Patrick, although in poor health and obliged to travel in a carriage, established his headquarters in Fredericksburg at the Farmers Bank of Virginia on Princess Anne Street. He quickly found himself "overrun with business," getting little sleep and often bothered by the meddling McDowell, who, Patrick complained, "hangs on terribly." At the same time the situation in Fredericksburg remained tense and perilous. Patrick had fewer than seven hundred men with him, their backs to the river, facing an active and numerically superior enemy force. Numerous picket clashes kept him and his men on edge; stories circulated of atrocities committed by partisans against unwary Union soldiers caught outside of the security of their camps. An article appearing in the *Philadelphia Inquirer* on May 9 reported that two men of the 30th New York who strayed from their regiment had been found dead—one hanging by his heels from a tree and both with their throats cut. Patrick himself kept the pot simmering by not hesitating to exert his authority when he felt the need. On May 9 and 10 he ordered out cavalry patrols beyond Union lines to arrest several citizens and bring them in to Fredericksburg.[44]

On the evening of May 10 Patrick attempted to bring the rest of his brigade across the river, causing as little alarm or disturbance as possible. That night the moon showed through a thick haze. Near eight o'clock a red light signal burned for a minute from the tower of the courthouse in Fredericksburg, to be answered immediately by each of Patrick's three regiments on the Stafford side of the river. Soon the dark column of troops slipped across the canal-boat bridge and marched up through the deserted streets past the railroad depot and out to a bivouac site "snug out of sight" at "Hazel Dell" beside the mill dam on Hazel Run below Willis Hill. The movement, which Patrick thought "beautifully done," resulted in a substantial increase of his available force, to more than 1,500 men.[45]

In direct support of Patrick, General King placed his Third Brigade, under the newly appointed thirty-five-year-old Brig. Gen. John Gibbon, in position near the boat bridge, ready to cross at any time. General

Augur's First Brigade remained at Falmouth, and McCall's division was camped back along Stafford Heights. On May 16 McDowell created an additional ten-thousand-man division within his department, under Maj. Gen. Edward O. C. Ord, to include the brigades of James B. Ricketts and George L. Hartsuff. That same day McDowell reported that he had a total of 30,112 officers and men near Fredericksburg and Falmouth and an additional 1,361 at Aquia Landing and Belle Plain. On May 16 General Shields's division passed through Chester Gap in the Blue Ridge Mountains en route via Warrenton, Virginia, to join McDowell and take up a position at Catlett's Station.[46]

The first significant test of Patrick's Fredericksburg defenses occurred on Sunday, May 11. The eventful day began with a reconnaissance down the Bowling Green Road by a squadron of the 2d New York Cavalry under the flamboyant Maj. Alfred Napoleon Alexander Duffié. About four miles out Duffié surprised and captured one of Gen. J. R. Anderson's picket posts.[47] In late morning, when word of this success arrived back in Fredericksburg, Patrick rode out toward Hazel Dell to meet the returning patrol and question the Rebel prisoners. While Patrick was in conversation with the prisoners, an excited courier reined up to announce that Duffié had stirred up a hornet's nest—a strong Rebel force was rapidly approaching on the Bowling Green Road. Patrick immediately alerted Colonels Hoffman and Rogers to the impending danger.[48]

By midday, the religious services and inspections having ended in Patrick's camps, "the men were enjoying a comfortable afternoon, lying in the shade of the trees, writing letters to friends at home, sleeping, amusing themselves as they would." Suddenly cavalrymen galloped through the camps, firing their guns or otherwise giving the alarm. Drummers stepped forward to sound the "long roll," and soon "men were running at breakneck pace to join their companies, and the officers were clamorously shouting to their men to fall in."[49]

Patrick rode with his aides toward the point of danger, picking up the 35th New York on the way. His regiments advanced from across fields and over fences to converge at a point in support of a thin line of cavalrymen stretched across the Bowling Green Road near Deep Run. When Hoffman arrived he deployed Companies A and K of the 23d as skirmishers, supported soon after by Companies E, B, and G. The 35th formed behind the skirmishers in line of battle, while the 20th NYSM and 21st regiments advanced to the right of the 35th along the railroad. The Rebels quailed before this show of force and retreated after firing only a few shots. One well-aimed bullet sung past the neck of Patrick's horse, just missed the general, and killed an orderly's horse—the only Union casualty in the skirmish. Afterward Hoffman advanced his pickets to the properties of the brothers Alfred and Arthur Bernard near the Rappahannock and returned with the rest of his men to camp.[50]

The excitement of the day continued into the evening with false alarms and the six o'clock arrival of the news that Norfolk had fallen to Union troops and that the Rebels had destroyed their famous ironclad *Virginia* (originally the U.S. steam frigate *Merrimac*). Word of these victories spread rapidly, and soon, according to Patrick, cheers rose up in the darkness from "15 or 20 thousand throats that fairly shook the town." The townspeople listening to the cheering thought it sounded "hideous," for it reminded them of the growing numbers of loved ones and acquaintances wounded and dying on far away battlefields. Betty Maury wrote in her journal that night, "Each cheer strikes to my heart like the knell of some dear one." Similar emotions surfaced earlier that day when residents saw Confederate prisoners being led through the streets under guard on their way to Union headquarters. The local women along the route stopped to silently watch them pass. A few sympathetically motioned to the captives with their handkerchiefs.[51]

When McDowell learned of the ruckus at Deep Run, he instructed General King to impress upon Patrick that "the object of our troops there [Fredericksburg] is not an offensive one. A collision is to be avoided, if possible." For the next two months King would authorize no more dashing cavalry raids. To avoid further clashes, on McDowell's orders, King had Patrick draw in his forces as close as possible to Fredericksburg under the cover of artillery. Officers instructed the pickets not to fire their weapons except to give alarm or to defend themselves if fired upon.[52]

For most of May, except for some isolated arrests of civilians, Fredericksburg remained relatively quiet. On Willis Hill the fifty-one members of the Cortland Volunteers laid out their camp on a luxuriant twenty-three-acre clover pasture along the crest.[53] From this vantage point Clark's men had a magnificent view of Fredericksburg, the Union camps on Stafford Heights, and the valley of the Rappahannock to the southeast. Here the days passed quietly in drill, picket guard, and the cutting of timber on Spotsylvania Heights for the construction of military blockhouses and stockades to protect the railroad and the bridges.[54] Below them near Hazel

Run restive cavalrymen of the 2d New York, with the moratorium on cavalry raids in place, lounged about with little to occupy their time. A visiting newspaper reporter on May 13 described the camp of the 2d as a scene of repose and tranquility: "The once gay and dashing Colonel lay lazily in his tent, permitting a cigar to burn itself slowly away between his lips, . . . while behind his chair stood two contraband attendants with fans."[55]

Although the month of May marked the anniversary of the Cortland Volunteers' first year of service, few among them seemed in a mood to celebrate. On May 4 Ira Carpenter became the fifth man in the company to die from typhoid fever. On the 7th the popular Lt. Benjamin Andrews resigned, citing ill health; thirty-seven others of the company languished in hospitals from Falmouth to Washington. On May 3 Clark reflected on his regiment's losses and its current inactivity, confiding to a friend, "I am not as cheerful as I was one year ago. All the visions of those days have vanished and I fancy the men who stayed at home showed the best sense." Clark himself went on extended leave (May 17–June 28) "to regain my health," under a cloud of suspicion by his men that he was faking sickness to get home. Private Edgcomb asked his family to observe Clark's health closely after he arrived at his mother's home in Groton. When Edgcomb learned to his satisfaction that the suspicions concerning Clark's "illness" were justified, he grumbled, "justice is a pretty scarce article in a military life"; he added fatalistically, "It won't last always."[56]

During this period the town of Fredericksburg also reflected a sullen mood. To one Federal occupier it seemed like "a city of the dead," the only audible sounds the "beat of the guard-house drum, and the interminable howling of the dogs." Across the river on Stafford Heights, in contrast, the hillsides were "alive with men. They look like so many ants running out of their tents. At night the camp fires are beautiful. The hills appear to be covered with balls of fire, ranged in regular order of the company streets. The brigades on the summits of the hills have every appearance of a large city with street lamps all lighted and burning brightly. It is really a very beautiful and grand sight."[57]

Fredericksburg began to stir from its lethargy on May 9, when the pro-Union *Christian Banner* newspaper, shut down at the start of the war, began publishing again under the protective arm of McDowell's forces. The first issues stated the case for the North's conduct of the war based on the so-called conservative principles advocated by many Northern Democrats in Congress and by, arguably, most of the North's military leaders, including Generals McClellan and Patrick. The paper began by telling the citizens that the cause of their current troubles rested squarely with radical Southern hotheads and with "Jeff. Davis and his click" of leaders, whom the *Banner* denounced as "traitors, madmen and fools." The paper editorialized that once such traitors no longer ruled the South, the people had every reason to anticipate an amicable settlement to the conflict and the peaceful restoration of national rule. When peace did come Southerners would once more flourish under the rule of law based upon "the preservation of all personal rights and privileges, the protection of private property, and . . . continuance of the accustomed business pursuits of our citizens." Reconciliation with the North must be the goal, the paper stated, for it "is our *only* hope of any peace or happiness in the future."[58]

Patrick's actions as military governor of Fredericksburg reflected such thinking. A soldier of the 23d wrote that when they first occupied the town, "guards were posted upon the principal corners, and the strictest discipline enforced for the maintenance of order and the protection of the citizens in their legitimate pursuits. The patrol guard arrested all soldiers found in the streets, not upon some authorized business; and no one, private or commissioned, was allowed to enter a house or hold a discussion with any of the inhabitants." Captain Clark explained, "Depredation of all kinds are strictly prohibited, and the citizens treated with respect and dignified courtesy—we wish to show them by our conduct that we are not the ruthless marauders they have been taught by their unprincipled leaders to believe we were."[59]

McDowell also made every effort to treat the local citizens within his department fairly and with respect. On May 7 he issued General Orders No. 8 stating that no supplies of any kind could be taken from citizens without the authorization of division commanders and unless written receipts were given. When McDowell learned that a woman's grave in Falmouth had been vandalized by Union troops, he ordered General Augur to have it repaired. On May 13 King issued a circular apparently designed to spare the local females embarrassment, stating that there "shall be no bathing in the Rapp. River between the hours of 6 o'clock a.m. and 7 o'clock p.m. at any point opposite the town of Fredericksburg."[60]

McDowell expressed outrage when he learned of a rape committed by a Union straggler; the victim had been the daughter of a man living a few miles from the Potomac Creek railroad bridge. If left unpunished, he wrote, the crime would become a stain attached to all "good men of the army, to the service, to the country, to the sisters, daughters, mothers, and wives of all. . . . That we are here with arms in our hands, and that the people have no practical redress from our wrong-doings but heightens our obligation to protect the helpless." On May 16 he issued his draconian General Orders No. 12, which established division-level military commissions to try such cases, with the power to render summary judgments. The order stated, "The punishment for rape will be death; and any violence offered a female, white or colored, with the evident intent or purpose to commit a rape, will be considered as one." Death for those found guilty of rape could be by hanging, "or by shooting if the former should not be convenient."[61]

General Patrick sought to curb the marauding tendencies of both officers and men by keeping them busy and on a short rein. Captain Todd wrote on May 11, "Our new General is a man of discipline, and so long as every officer toes the mark all goes right." "When he gave an order," wrote another man from the ranks, "if it was not obeyed, the punishment was sure, swift, and severe." Punishment for minor offenses took the form of extra duty or various modes of public humiliation. Pvt. Chauncey Judd of the Cortland Volunteers described how when Patrick caught a man sitting on guard duty or not walking his rounds with his weapon at "support arms," he had him arrested, forced to plant a pole in the ground, and then tied to it for twenty-four hours. When Herman Haupt visited Fredericksburg during the Patrick regime he noticed fifteen to twenty soldiers standing along the curbstone "with boards on their backs stating their offenses, such as 'I stole a ham,' 'I broke into a private house,' etc." Other punishments included "bucking and gagging," "making a spread eagle," carrying a knapsack filled with rocks, and wearing a barrel or "wooden overcoat." Patrick's methods, though harsh, seemed to accomplish their intended purpose. The *Christian Banner* of May 27 reported, "General Patrick is certainly a fine disciplinarian, and his men know how to deport themselves."[62]

One of a soldier's most severe punishments was being "drummed out of camp." On May 24, Pvt. George House of the 35th suffered that disgrace after receiving a dishonorable discharge and three months' imprisonment for desertion. At the appointed hour, House was brought from the guardhouse to the parade ground with

coat off, hands tied behind him, a newspaper hat on a yard long running to a point, and surmounted by a goose quill, two boards with large letters, "deserter," painted on them, hanging on his neck, four guards were placed behind him some three feet, standing at charge bayonet, and behind them our martial band, were formed with lips puckered, drums muffled sticks raised, ready to play the "rogues march." The regiment was drawn up in line of battle, without arms. . . . The arrangement perfected, the procession marched down the front of the regiment out of the camp, thence to the depot. The ranks were silent, and many a blush mantled the cheeks of our noble soldiers at witnessing this painful, yet ludicrous scene, and departure of a fellow comrade.[63]

Patrick's troops, unlike many of their officers, despaired of the local Fredericksburg population's ever becoming reconciled with the Federal government, and they deeply resented what they perceived to be Patrick's misplaced deference to the rights and property of the enemy. Captain Clark admitted, "The people are almost universally our enemies. It is folly to attempt to disguise a truth of such importance. There are some Union men here but they are few." When Patrick sent some of the Cortland Volunteers to guard the hams and chickens of the avowed secessionist Alfred Bernard, Sgt. Maj. Fred Burritt once more openly challenged his "conservative" approach, in a letter published in the *Elmira Advertiser.* He protested Union policies that resulted in "much solicitude for the future welfare of menacing, defiant and unscrupulous insurgents who have not yet even pretended to regret the most dire consequences of their criminal acts." How ludicrous the thought that "by the exercise of Christian graces, smiles and courtesies," the "willfully wicked" population of Fredericksburg could resume citizenship under the old flag. "In the name of justice and righteous retribution," he asked his readers, "how much longer will an indignant people tamely submit to the practice of such humiliating 'conservatism'?"[64]

When the soldiers spoke of the willfully wicked population of Fredericksburg, they referred most often to the white females. The white males, mostly old men and boys, said little and walked about the streets with downcast eyes. Burritt attributed their prudence to two instances where soldiers had applied "the potent and opportune administration of heavy sole leather" to their persons. Their total silence also indicated a strong Confederate influence remaining in Fredericksburg, supported by General Field's soldiers lurking just outside the Union picket line. Consequently, as one citizen stated, "A man is a fool who comes out for the Union in Fredericksburg."[65]

As for the local white females, however, almost every soldier writing from Fredericksburg in the summer of 1862 made some reference to the intense hostility they encountered from them. An early indication of things to come occurred when Patrick's men first arrived in Falmouth and noticed a woman on the Fredericksburg shore "tantalizing" them by waving a black flag emblazoned with the skull and crossbones. Once the soldiers occupied Fredericksburg, whenever they approached a woman on the street, "a sweeping aside of skirts, or a detour into the middle of the street, with a flashing of disdainful eyes, was the very least we could expect." Fredericksburg women refused all acknowledgement of the Stars and Stripes, which must have presented them quite a problem, for by mid-May Union troops had hung Old Glory everywhere—over stores, public buildings, and bridges, and from lines stretched across the major streets. The women defiantly wore secession badges and threw tracts and sermons on the rebellion upon the sidewalk for the edification of the misguided Yankees. One woman acknowledged that she approached the Southern cause as a religion, telling a Union soldier that "she considered it a religious duty to hate the Yankees." "Ah!" sighed the teenaged firebrand Lizzie Alsop, "they [Northerners] little know the hatred in our hearts towards them."[66]

Burritt wrote that when the men of the 23d began their duties in Fredericksburg, the women would "hourly tantalize officers and soldiers of the guard . . . by the most insulting, odious, aggravating, indecent and unladylike language and deportment." Chauncey Judd wrote, "[They] call us Dam Yankee Sons of Biches and every thing they have a mind to." They spat on the soldiers from windows, hissed at them on the street, and, wrote Pvt. C. C. Hanks of the 20th NYSM to his mother, "[gave] a fellow invitations to kiss them in locations that I never thought of applying that token of affection." Mothers encouraged their children to confront the Yankees freely on the street with shouts of "hurra for Jeff. Davis and the Southern Confederacy." One officer reported stones thrown at him by a gang of impudent young boys. Burritt concluded that the women of Fredericksburg "hardly deserve the protection universally accorded to their sex, and are little more to be respected than she wolves, or rattlesnakes."[67]

There is little doubt, however, that Patrick's benign rule in Fredericksburg and his tight control over his troops had the beneficial effect of reducing the tensions generated by the Union occupation. Betty Maury had to admit on May 13, "I am much struck with the superior discipline of these Yankee soldiers over ours. I have not seen a drunken man since they have been here." On May 25 a correspondent for the *New York Tribune* reported, "in consequence of the energetic yet judicious administration of Gen. Patrick, a marked change has taken place in the sentiment and conduct of the entire community of Fredericksburg. Our soldiers now are not insulted as they pass through the streets."[68]

Once the Union occupation became a fact of life, the town began to emerge from its torpor. On May 24 one soldier reflected that "Fredericksburg is beginning to look more lively. Mr. Hunt of New York, alias Farini, the tight-rope walker, has opened the Shakspeare [*sic*] House [hotel]. . . . Some fine stores are opened, and the necessaries of life, beef, beer, billiards, etc. are available." The Planters Hotel on William Street reopened, providing lodging for ten dollars a week and a "dinner" of bacon, bread and butter, and tea for fifty cents. O. G. Judd, the sutler of the 23d New York, leased a store in Fredericksburg and offered the general public such luxuries as shoes, salt, and coffee, not previously available locally because of the Union occupation and the tightening Federal blockade of Southern ports. Burritt noted with some satisfaction that many of the local "she wolves" managed to "overcome their aversion to the Yankee as to buy his goods with avidity at four times the prices they could have been obtained for a year ago." Jane Beale explained this phenomenon: "I do not admire *naked martyrdom,* so we abuse the Yankees to our heart's content, but buy their goods still."[69]

On Sunday, May 18, the local preachers open the doors of their churches to Union soldiers and toned down their sermons. The day turned out beautiful, warm and sunny. After services the soldiers strolled through the town, occasionally stopping on the sidewalk to listen to the sweet music of a piano and the pleasing sounds of female voices that drifted out of parlor windows, reminding them of their Northern homes. In the afternoon many soldiers crowded around the "gay looking" young Captain Worthington of General Anderson's staff, who had come into town under a flag of truce with a message for McDowell. The captain rode a black stallion and wore a "splendid gray uniform" trimmed with gold. As he was being led through the streets under guard, hundreds of Union soldiers stood by to gawk, "delighted to see a live rebel."[70]

Meanwhile, on May 17, with the military situation quiet in the Valley, McDowell received the long-awaited authorization from Lincoln to begin his advance overland to join McClellan before Richmond. McDowell anticipated first engaging and defeating General Anderson's troops six to eight miles out along the line of the Richmond, Fredericksburg, and Potomac Railroad. He then expected to join McClellan's right flank near the Pamunkey River about fifteen miles north of Richmond. After Shields's division arrived at Catlett's on May 19, McDowell would have forty thousand men, a hundred pieces of artillery, and eleven thousand animals available for the campaign. If all went well, the jaws of McDowell's and McClellan's armies would slowly close on Richmond, sealing the fate of the Confederacy.[71]

In the final days before the start of the campaign, McDowell pushed the work to complete the infrastructure of bridges, railroad track, and roads needed to support his army as it moved south. The town rang with the sound of hammers as men repaired the track near the depot and erected the trestlework to complete the Chatham and railroad bridges. Yankee mechanics occupied and put back in operation the extensive Hope foundry operation on Princess Anne and Charlotte streets. A large locomotive under repair sat incongruously in front of the building on a specially built rail line that by late May ran down Princess Anne Street to a warehouse near the railroad depot. The industry that McDowell's troops displayed in their many engineering projects brought grudging admiration from the local citizens. Jane Beale acknowledged, "This is a wonderful people with whom we have to contend, their resources appear unlimited [and] their energy inexhaustible."[72]

McDowell's crowning achievement came late on May 19 with the completion of the rebuilt railroad bridge over the Rappahannock, establishing a rail connection between his supply base at Aquia Landing and Fredericksburg. Constructed by about three hundred soldiers in fewer than fifteen days, the span, six hundred feet long and sixteen feet wide, rose on trestlework forty-three feet above the water. Planking allowed the passage of wagons, artillery, and troops. The first locomotive to attempt a crossing pushed before it a car full of scrap iron; it would trigger any explosive device attached to the tracks by a saboteur. Finding the tracks safe and sturdy, soldiers illuminated the bridge, and the first train arrived in Fredericksburg amid much celebration, to the music of a military band on board. Workmen completed the Chatham trestle bridge three days later to be used as a wagon bridge connecting William Street with the Belle Plain Road, which led to the old steamboat landing on Potomac Creek. Once the workmen completed the Chatham Bridge, the engineers moved the pontoon bridge upriver to Falmouth. McDowell now had four Rappahannock bridges to use for his campaign against Richmond.[73]

Bridge security became one of McDowell's major concerns. After an unidentified man attempted to derail a train near the depot and flee into a crowd of civilians, McDowell warned Mayor Slaughter not to allow any large gathering of people along the tracks. "If another attempt of the kind is made," he threatened, "an indiscriminate fire will be directed against the source whence the attempt comes." Blockhouses and stockades guarded the southern approaches to the bridgeheads and the railroad crossing at Hazel Run, and by May 24 a gunboat had taken station on the river near the railroad bridge.[74]

The added flurry of activity from headquarters in late May alerted Union troops to the start of the long-anticipated movement. An ammunition supply train arrived on May 21 from Aquia Landing, and a specially outfitted train of nine hospital cars made the return trip carrying away the sick and disabled from two of McDowell's divisions. The civilian aeronaut John La Mountain appeared at Falmouth from Catlett's and prepared his observation balloon for an ascent in order to scan the routes south for enemy activity. Meanwhile, McDowell's redoubtable engineer Herman Haupt busied himself in the construction of a prefabricated bridge frame ready to replace a bridge the Rebels were expected to destroy in their retreat. At the railroad depot huge coils of telegraph wire and an eleven-car supply train with the locomotive in the rear sat ready to follow and support the advance. At the same time, Patrick ordered his brigade officers to press forward their pickets, load the regimental wagons with five days' rations of hard tack, coffee, sugar, and salt, and have the men draw two days' rations for their haversacks and two pairs each of shoes and gaiters.[75]

On the night of May 20 McDowell found time to relax with friends and staff members at his Chatham headquarters. In the preceding month he had accomplished much. He had occupied Fredericksburg and tied down Anderson's force that General Johnston sorely needed on the Peninsula; now he stood poised to open a second front against Richmond in support of McClellan. Despite the dark and rainy night, McDowell and friends sat on Chatham's porch overlooking terraced grounds that sloped down toward the river opposite Fredericksburg. The silhouettes of the sentries moved slowly along the dark garden walkways between the sweet smelling shrubs and rose bushes, while before the porch four military bands played alternately under the tall shade trees; the flickering candles that illuminated their sheet music added a magical effect. Perhaps for the first time since his humiliating defeat at Bull Run almost a year before, McDowell could find new confidence in the thought of fresh victories to come.[76]

On Friday, May 23, President Lincoln, several members of his cabinet, and guests, including the French minister, traveled to Falmouth to confer with McDowell and give the troops a formal send-off. Early that morning Lincoln disembarked from the *Martha Washington* at the Aquia wharf amid a host of craft that crowded the harbor flying colorful flags and banners for the festive occasion. He then continued his journey by train, stopping briefly at the Potomac Creek bridge to marvel at Haupt's handiwork. McDowell claimed proudly that the trestle bridge, built by soldiers from May 6 to 13 with logs cut from neighboring forests, ignored "all the rules and precedents of military science as laid down in books." Lincoln later bragged, "That man Haupt has built a bridge . . . about 400 feet long and nearly 100 feet high, over which loaded trains are running every hour, and, upon my word, . . . there is nothing in it but beanpoles and cornstalks."[77]

Lincoln arrived at Falmouth about nine in the morning. He spent some time talking and joking with McDowell's generals in the entrance hall of Chatham. Despite the wilting ninety-degree temperature, Lincoln mounted a spirited black horse to visit the various Union encampments on Stafford Heights. When Lincoln reviewed McCall's division, "the troops presented arms, the colors drooped, officers saluted, drums beat, trumpets sounded, and a salute of twenty-one guns [was] fired." Whenever the soldiers caught sight of the president they spontaneously cheered. One rather unimpressed observer, however, thought Lincoln "a queer figure on horseback, his long legs reaching well toward the ground." At one point Lincoln walked his horse along the line of a brigade, asking the name of each regiment and "talking with the boys as though they were old friends."[78]

In the afternoon Lincoln and Secretary of War Stanton paid a relatively low-key visit to Fredericksburg. Patrick escorted Lincoln's carriage, pulled by four iron-gray horses, from the canal-boat bridge up Princess Anne Street through the town. Apparently no contact occurred between Lincoln and local officials, and, as one observer noted, "there were no

demonstrations of joy" from the local residents. Lincoln visited and reviewed Patrick's troops near Hazel Dell and stopped for a brief meeting
at his headquarters in the Farmer's Bank. Patrick then "said adieu" to his
honored guests as they disappeared over the new bridge near Chatham.
After an evening meal in the crowded dining room of Chatham and a final review at dusk of Shield's division on the open plain in the rear of the
house, Lincoln and his entourage returned to Washington. While at Chatham the president agreed with McDowell that since Shields's division
had arrived at Falmouth the day before deficient in supplies and equipment, McDowell would, in Lincoln's words, "take a *good ready*" and not
begin the campaign until Monday morning, May 26.[79]

CHAPTER 6

The Summer
of Forlorn Hopes

W hile President Lincoln conferred with General McDowell at Chatham on May 23, events in the Shenandoah Valley combined to unravel McDowell's well-laid plans. When General Shields left the valley on May 16 to join McDowell, Gen. Nathaniel Banks remained behind with seven thousand men at Strasburg astride the hard-surface Valley Turnpike (modern Route 11) near where the Manassas Gap Railroad enters the lower valley through Manassas Gap in the Blue Ridge Mountains. From Strasburg, Banks could protect the lower valley and the three important gaps in the Blue Ridge (Ashby's, Manassas, and Chester) that gave the most direct access to Washington, as well as to the right flank and rear of McDowell's forces at Falmouth. Banks placed a thousand of his men between Manassas Gap and Strasburg at Front Royal. Brig. Gen. John W. Geary's 1,800-man force occupied Rectortown, on the Manassas Gap Railroad between the Blue Ridge and Manassas Junction.[1]

Early on the afternoon of the 23d Stonewall Jackson led seventeen thousand of his men north down the valley to strike Banks's outpost at Front Royal, twelve miles east of his isolated main force at Strasburg. Banks's force retreated to Winchester and eventually across the Potomac out of the valley on May 26. Geary's panic-stricken troops burned government stores near Gainesville on the Manassas Gap Railroad and fled back toward Manassas Junction spreading wild rumors of having been forced back by Jackson's advancing troops. Thus in one swift stroke Jackson successfully emptied the lower valley of Union troops, cleared the mountain passes, and threw the Lincoln administration into the crisis of an impending Confederate strike against Manassas Junction and possibly Washington.

In the days that followed, President Lincoln stepped in as commander in chief to orchestrate the Union response. At five o'clock in the evening on May 24 he ordered McDowell to lay aside, "for the present," his advance toward Richmond and send twenty thousand men, or about half of his force, to the Shenandoah Valley. He intended that McDowell plug the gaps in the Blue Ridge and act in concert with other Union forces being sent to cut off Jackson's anticipated retreat south along the Valley Pike from Winchester. "Everything now depends upon the celerity and vigor of your movement," Lincoln wrote McDowell, adding that he expected the first of McDowell's forces to reach Front Royal by noon on May 30.[2]

Although McDowell immediately instructed Shields to return to the valley, he conveyed to his superiors that he had "a heavy heart in the matter." He pointed out to the president that given the distances and obstacles facing the proposed march, success was doubtful and not worth the paralyzing effect it would have on the strategically more important objective of supporting McClellan before Richmond. "I shall gain nothing for you there [the valley]," he explained, "and shall lose much for you here." By ignoring McDowell's sound analysis of the situation, Lincoln inadvertently played into the Confederate strategy of neutralizing McDowell's threatening force at Fredericksburg.[3]

By the afternoon of May 25 McDowell had set his army in motion moving in different directions. Shields began his march of almost a hundred miles back to the valley via Catlett's, Manassas Junction, and then along the line of the Manassas Gap Railroad to Front Royal. In addition, McDowell directed Ord's division to Aquia Creek for transfer by boat to Alexandria. From Alexandria Ord's troops would travel by rail to Manassas Junction and then march to Front Royal behind Shields. At the same time, refusing to abandon totally the benefits of the movement toward Richmond, McDowell ordered King's division to begin a reconnaissance in force south from Fredericksburg to probe Rebel positions and investigate reported indications of Confederate general J. R. Anderson's withdrawal from his front. McCall's division remained at Falmouth to maintain McDowell's foothold on the Rappahannock. Late on the afternoon of the 25th, Augur's and Gibbon's brigades crossed over the river into Fredericksburg and marched out on the Richmond Telegraph and

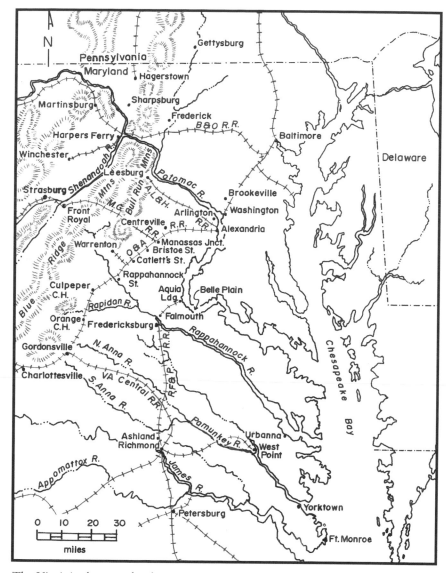

The Virginia theater of military operations. *(John Heiser)*

Bowling Green roads, respectively. A specially formed "Flying Brigade" of troops made up of cavalry, infantry, and artillery under the cavalry chief, Brig. Gen. George D. Bayard, supported the movement.[4]

Patrick had orders to advance his brigade out the Orange Plank Road once he had provided for the orderly transfer of provost duties in Fredericksburg to his successor. In preparation, Patrick moved his headquarters to the William Y. Downman house, "Idlewild," on the Plank Road and advanced three of his regiments to near Salem Church. Half of the 23d remained temporarily in town. The rest of the regiment under Colonel Hoffman (Companies C, E, G, H, and K) moved over to protect the far right flank of the division two miles from Fredericksburg on the river road. Meanwhile, McCall took up King's old headquarters at the Phillips house, and King moved over to an office in the Farmer's Bank in Fredericksburg. On May 28 McDowell established his headquarters at the William J. Weir house, "Liberia," at Manassas Junction, from where he could personally expedite the movement of his troops to the valley.[5]

With all the commotion caused by troops marching back and forth through Fredericksburg and by Union sutlers and civilians fleeing for the bridges with all the possessions they could carry, wild rumors of pending military action freely circulated through the community. Several frightened women came to their doors to ask passing Union staff officers if the Yankees intended to shell the town. Their fears increased when a tremendous explosion rocked the depot area about midmorning on the 25th. An accidental spark had ignited a munitions magazine in a detached brick building about 150 yards from the train station. The blast destroyed the structure and shattered the glass in the adjacent buildings. The sentry on duty, Southern Tier Pvt. William March of Company A, had both legs torn from his body in the explosion, which killed him instantly.[6]

Townspeople also became concerned over Patrick's designated replacement as military governor, Brig. Gen. Abner Doubleday. Doubleday had arrived at Falmouth on May 23 in command of an independent demibrigade consisting of the 76th and 102d New York regiments. The 76th, or "Cortland," Regiment had been organized in September 1861 at Camp Campbell, near Cortland Village on the county fairgrounds. The regiment listed on its rolls many friends and relatives of men in Company H of the 23d, including George Edgcomb's brother, Sgt. Martin Edgcomb.

By the 23d word had reached Patrick of how disappointed the Fredericksburg population was over the appointment of Doubleday. Leading citizens signed a letter to McDowell asking to have Patrick remain as military governor. "I feel sad myself," Patrick wrote, "at the thought that these helpless families are to be left to the tender mercies of an Abolitionist."[7] Indeed, Doubleday began his duties expressing his opposition to Patrick's previous kid-glove policy for dealing with secessionist Fredericksburg. "I found it quite impossible," he wrote, "to carry out a policy, the effect of which was simply to discourage the Union men in every possible way and favor the rebels." He criticized Patrick for not having done more to protect Union men, who were still being carried off with their hands tied behind their backs for alleged violations of city ordinances and other offenses. He also refused calls to restrict the increasing flow of fugitive slaves across the river to freedom. After only two days on the job, McDowell replaced Doubleday with the more agreeable Brig. Gen. John Fulton Reynolds, who commanded a brigade of Pennsylvania troops in McCall's division.[8]

On May 26 General Reynolds led his brigade across the new Chatham trestle bridge and, with unfurled flags and martial music playing, marched "merrily" up William Street.[9] Patrick then moved most of his troops over to the Telegraph Road to join Augur's brigade, bivouacked six miles out at Massaponax Creek. The Southern Tier Regiment, thus relieved from guard duties, reunited at Salem Church before joining the brigade the next day on the banks of the Massaponax.[10] Confederate troops had previously occupied the new bivouac site, leaving behind still-smoldering campfires and other evidence of a hasty retreat. Signs nailed to the trees expressed Rebel contempt for the "damned Yanks" and promised an early return. One sign pointing south had the words written in charcoal, "30 Miles To Richmond! Come And See Us!"[11]

Actually, Anderson had been withdrawn from McDowell's front on May 24 under orders to support Brig. Gen. Lawrence O'Bryan Branch's Brigade, near the Pamunkey River at Ashland. By occupying the strategically important Ashland–Hanover Court House area, Gen. Joseph Johnston could block any attempt to combine McDowell's and McClellan's forces northeast of Richmond. On May 27 Branch tangled with the advance division of Brig. Gen. Fitz John Porter's Fifth Corps reaching out from McClellan's right flank in an attempt to clear the obstruction of Branch's forces and keep the way open to receive reinforcements from Fredericksburg. On the same day, Bayard's Flying Brigade made a reconnaissance down the Telegraph Road from Massaponax Church to within earshot of Porter's guns.[12] Porter managed to push aside Branch and capture Ashland, but left hanging by the failure of McDowell's forces to join him, he could do little beyond the important work of destroying bridges and cutting the rail lines before having to withdraw. On the 31st Johnston then checked any further Union activity near Ashland by engaging McClellan east of Richmond in the Battle of Fair Oaks, or Seven Pines.

During this hectic and confusing period, Lincoln and Secretary of War Edwin Stanton, admitted novices in their roles as military commanders, continued to struggle with the details of the rapidly changing military situation in Virginia. On May 26 Lincoln suggested to McDowell that he send most of his remaining troops at Fredericksburg to Manassas Junction or Alexandria. Two days later, after reports indicated that Jackson did not threaten Manassas Junction as the excited Geary had indicated, Lincoln changed his mind and authorized McDowell to continue King's advance to join Porter near Hanover Court House. McDowell finally ended all discussion late on May 28, when, after receiving a bogus report that Anderson's troops had marched to join Jackson in the valley, he ordered King's division to join the movement of his two other divisions to Front Royal. He knew that King could not arrive in time to be a factor in Jackson's capture, but as he explained, "I think it better to concentrate than to divide the force now in the field."[13]

Late on the night of May 28 McDowell reported to Lincoln from the Weir house at Manassas Junction, "I beg to assure you that I am doing everything which legs and steam are capable of to hurry forward matters in this quarter." On the 28th Shields's leading brigade reached Rectortown, about thirty railroad miles from Manassas Junction and within a two-day march of Front Royal. With his troops closing in for the kill, McDowell confidently sent Geary's brigade to Ashby's Gap to discourage a surprise early visit by Stonewall Jackson east of the Blue Ridge. That same day Bayard's Flying Brigade left Fredericksburg, crossed the pontoon bridge into Falmouth, and headed for Catlett's. McDowell's deficiency in cavalry meant that he needed Bayard to spearhead both King's and Shields's efforts. In other words, Bayard had to leapfrog from King's advanced position south of Fredericksburg back in the opposite direction to the full length of his marching columns to reach the head of Shields's troops approaching Front Royal. King's division followed Bayard the next day, dragging along a large supply train and three hundred beef cattle. Col. Herman Haupt, McDowell's newly appointed chief of railroad construction and transportation, took charge of the railroads and available rolling stock to push forward supplies. On the morning of the 29th McDowell could note that the telegraph and the Manassas Gap Railroad were operational as far as Rectortown. McCall's division and Doubleday's brigade stayed behind at Falmouth to secure Fredericksburg.[14]

Early the same morning Augur's brigade led King's division out of

Fredericksburg down Princess Anne Street toward the Falmouth pontoon bridge. As Patrick's brigade waited for Augur's troops to clear the bridge, many Fredericksburg citizens, including the mayor, arrived to see Patrick off and wish him well. As Patrick rested on the steps of the Douglas Gordon house on a high bank overlooking his troops standing in the road, servants emerged from the Gordon house and a neighbor's to offer him pie and a cool drink of milk. Patrick quoted them as saying that their mistresses had sent the refreshments in gratitude for his kindness toward them and for "the protection he has given us and the perfect quietness and order he has preserved in the Town." Patrick's men, as usual, viewed the events of the day quite differently. One man of the 23d remembered only dusty streets crowded with citizens "rejoicing over our disaster in Bank's [sic] department, and bidding us a taunting 'Good bye.'"[15]

On Friday, May 30, 1862, the head of Shields's division reached Front Royal at half past eleven in the morning—on schedule. Shields's small cavalry force quickly captured the town and secured the Shenandoah River bridges. Ahead lay a twelve-mile march to Strasburg and the Valley Turnpike, where he expected to block Jackson's retreat in cooperation with Maj. Gen. John C. Frémont's force (seventeen thousand approaching from the west).[16] At the same time, Jackson's force (twelve thousand)[17] continued to march rapidly back up the valley along the pike and had reached a point twenty miles north of Strasburg. Sensing that the denouement of this exciting drama was at hand, McDowell boarded a train at Manassas Junction for Front Royal.

When his train arrived at Rectortown, McDowell found that the head of Ord's division had only reached Piedmont Station (Delaplane), with the tail of the column stretching back along the tracks. His wrath fell on the distressed General Ord, who, claiming illness, turned his division over to Gen. James B. Ricketts. Meanwhile, back at Catlett's, Bayard's Flying Brigade arrived and separated. The cavalry trotted up the road toward Thoroughfare Gap in the Bull Run Mountains. The infantry boarded railroad cars for a roundabout trip, first east on the Orange and Alexandria Railroad to Manassas Junction, then back west on the Manassas Gap Railroad toward Front Royal.[18]

McDowell, now caught up in the chase, encouraged his commanders to greater effort with the call that "the whole country is looking with anxiety and hope."[19] King, bringing up the rear of the column, managed a twenty-mile march on the 30th from his bivouac near the William Irvine place "Hartwood" to Elk Run, about four miles short of Catlett's. Before departing that morning Patrick had to shoo away some of the 23d men from their "lady friends" at the Irvine house and settle up with the family by issuing government vouchers for damage done to their property by Union troops. For the rest of the day the men of the 23d trudged along, some of them carrying their heavy knapsacks hung from their rifle-muskets. A number of local inhabitants tried to deny them precious water by throwing their well buckets and windlasses down the shafts. In the afternoon it started to rain.[20]

The drenching rain of the next day (May 31) did not dampen the spirits of McDowell's troops as they closed in on their quarry. McDowell arrived at Front Royal in a flurry of activity focused on bringing up Ricketts and Bayard and getting the railroad fully operational. Ricketts's troops marched through a pouring rain to reach Manassas Gap that night, stopping briefly as some of the men took boyish delight in pushing some wrecked railroad cars crashing eighty to a hundred feet down an embankment. McDowell later reported to Washington that Ricketts's troops had reached Front Royal "considerably aroused by the excitement of an approaching battle."[21]

Meanwhile, King continued to cool his heels at Catlett's waiting for nine promised trains that would carry his troops toward the valley via Manassas Junction. Patrick used the time to slaughter cattle and distribute rations and mail. Augur managed to send off his troops by train the afternoon of May 31, followed about dark by the 21st and 35th regiments of Patrick's brigade. For lack of train transport, the rest of the division had to remain at Catlett's, now thoroughly despoiled after countless occupations by Union troops. Patrick described Catlett's as "that vilest of vile places." The 23d bivouacked along the railroad tracks "amid filth of every description, stench intolerable, bugs, worms, gnats, flies, lice, lizards and wood ticks in profusion and variety."[22]

King's men riding on the trains that night fared much worse. Since each company generally had to crowd into a single boxcar, many soldiers opted to ride between the cars or on top, wrapped in their rubber ponchos to keep off the rain and clinging to the brakeman's foot plank, which ran down the center of the cars. The trains plowed on slowly through the dark, rainy night, traveling on average ten miles per hour, until a tragic accident put a halt to the movement. The lead train, carrying the 2d U.S. Sharpshooters of Augur's command, having passed through Thoroughfare Gap in the Bull Run Mountains, was trying to climb a difficult grade when its engine gave out, bringing the overloaded train to a stop. The safety lantern on the rear car had gone out, causing the second train to crash into it. The force of the impact lifted two flatcars carrying the Sharpshooters and sent them crashing into the forward boxcars, full of sleeping or resting troops. Miraculously, the accident resulted in only one man killed and forty-three injured.[23]

At half past eight on the morning of June 1, King dispatched his supply train up the road from Catlett's following Bayard's route to Thoroughfare Gap via Greenwich and Haymarket. Cavalrymen from the 2d New York led the column, followed by about two hundred wagons, regimental ambulances (five per regiment), three artillery batteries, and a guard of one infantry company from the 20th NYSM. By evening the three-mile column had reached Haymarket, described by one soldier as "a small village of half a dozen houses and huts, and a large brick church." Augur's brigade that day reached Front Royal, along with the 21st New York of Patrick's brigade. The 35th got as far as Piedmont Station. King remained at the Quisenberry house near Catlett's impatiently waiting with Generals Patrick and Gibbon for more train cars to carry their troops forward.[24]

Lincoln's campaign came to an abrupt halt on the afternoon of June 1, when McDowell's troops, led by a cavalry squadron from Bayard's Flying Brigade, finally crossed the north fork of the Shenandoah River from Front Royal and advanced on Strasburg. They reached the crest of a low hill overlooking the pike just in time to see the tail end of Jackson's eleven-mile column (including 2,300 Union prisoners) safely passing south through Strasburg. The Union movement that Lincoln had counted on to destroy Stonewall Jackson's force had failed. A dejected McDowell sent King a terse note: "The enemy has flown[;] . . . halt your division wherever it may be on receipt of this message."[25]

Due, however, to a temporary break in the telegraph line between Front Royal and Manassas Junction, King did not receive McDowell's directive. Not having heard from McDowell, the anxious King met with his subordinates on June 2 and decided to march with the rest of his command behind the wagon train to Haymarket. Around noon Gibbon's brigade took the lead, followed by Patrick's remaining regiments (23d and 20th NYSM) and the herd of cattle. Once under way, Patrick and his aides rode ahead to catch up with the head of the column near the Charles Green house, "The Lawn," in Greenwich. Patrick stopped at the house to watch the column pass along the road and take tea with the owner. The column bivouacked at Broad Run about two miles short of Haymarket.[26]

During the afternoon of June 2 McDowell rode through the continuing rain into Strasburg to try to salvage the rapidly deteriorating situation. He decided to send Bayard and Shields with Frémont's force farther into the valley after Jackson. He ordered Ricketts to remain for the time being at Front Royal, while King was to collect his division near Haymarket. Stonewall Jackson would later turn to fight McDowell's advance in the battles of Cross Keys and Port Republic before joining forces with the Confederate divisions near Richmond to form the Army of Northern Virginia under Gen. Robert E. Lee.

In the final analysis, McDowell's hard marches and extraordinary efforts of late May did little but scatter his forces and break down about four thousand of his men. The 23d ended the campaign "vexed and jaded," occupying a wet and soggy camp along Little Bull Run above Haymarket—altogether "a sorry sight, gloomy beyond description."[27] At the end of May, the 23d mustered only 587 men present (down from 629 in April); only forty-four men were reporting present for duty in the Cortland Volunteers.[28]

Herman Haupt summed up the campaign best: "The move had been a horrible one; rain, mud and no shelter, army demoralized, the public clamorous, critics numerous, the President discouraged, a victim demanded." McDowell, whose reputation had never fully recovered after his Bull Run defeat, provided an easy scapegoat. General Patrick wrote on June 4 that "McDowell has lost the confidence of his men, entirely—They speak very strongly against him." Patrick's criticism extended to General King, who, he stated, "amounts to nothing and his staff are worthless."[29]

The dramatic conclusion to Lincoln's ill-conceived expedition to Front Royal came on June 4, when the rain-swollen rivers and streams swept away the Shenandoah River bridges and the important railroad bridge over Bull Run near Manassas Junction. In addition, the new Chatham trestle bridge over the Rappahannock at Fredericksburg collapsed in the flood; the floating debris carried away the railroad and canal-boat bridges. The gunboats in the river managed to get out of the way in time, and luckily the pontoon bridge had been taken up the day before by Union troops as a precautionary measure. At the first alarm, Fredericksburg citizens gathered along the riverbank and "as each structure gave way they demonstrated their joy by loud cheers and the waving of handkerchiefs."[30]

McDowell arrived back in Washington on June 6 to meet with Secretary Stanton and receive welcome orders to secure Washington with his forces, hold Fredericksburg, and proceed, "as speedily as possible in the direction of Richmond, to co-operate with Major General McClellan." McDowell wrote McClellan on June 8, "For the third time I am ordered to join you, and this time I hope to get through." He planned to reach McClellan with his forces within ten days.[31]

On June 5, before King returned to Fredericksburg from Haymarket, he received orders to march his division on a twelve-mile side trip into Fauquier County to counter a Rebel cavalry force of 1,500 men reportedly occupying the town of Warrenton. Gibbon's brigade led the march on June 6, turning down the Warrenton Turnpike (modern Route 29), followed by Augur's brigade, and finally by Patrick's men, who guarded the division wagon train from the rear of the column. The 21st remained behind to guard a supply depot established at Gainesville on the Manassas Gap Railroad. Gibbon reached Warrenton that same evening to find the place empty of Rebel cavalry and the area quiet except for "small parties of mounted men hunting up and carrying off negroes South."[32] Patrick's brigade bivouacked about one mile before the town.

The town of Warrenton impressed Patrick and his men. The white population seemed to Patrick not so "full of spite as those of Fredsburg [sic]," and their dwellings, as one of his men recorded, "for beauty and costlieness, [to] excel anything we have seen this side of the Potomac." On June 8 the division started back toward Fredericksburg, marching out of town with flags unfurled "to the gaze of gaping, but unappreciative groups of spectators, old men, cripples, women and children." With many escaping blacks in tow, the column headed down the branch line of the Orange and Alexandria Railroad to where it met the main line at Warrenton Junction (Calverton). That night Patrick took quarters at the abandoned Randolph plantation home, "Eastern View," where many prominent Virginians, including Robert E. Lee, had received their early educations.[33]

On June 9 King's division returned to Catlett's Station (the 21st joined on June 11) and settled in for an extended stay in the area between Cedar Run and Elk Run. During this period Patrick complained that as a result of the recent campaign his men had become "indifferent and feel that they are acting without an object, or a purpose; consequently they behave badly, strolling over the country, stealing, destroying fruit trees loaded with partially ripened fruit, etc. etc." On the 9th Patrick arrested twenty-one men for "sheepstealing and hog killing." Subsequently he let all but four of the sheep stealers go after the rest agreed to pay five dollars each in recompense. Patrick dismissed another man hauled before him for stripping milk from a cow directly into his mouth with the exclamation, "You great calf! Go to your regiment!" In truth, the men did feel a good deal of frustration over the recent turn of events and cheated in their desire to come to grips with the enemy. They rebelled against the waste of their time marching in circles or standing sentry over Southern property. Burritt reported in the *Elmira Daily Advertiser* that "the brightest hope of the present hour among this community is that our skeleton battalions may soon join the *working party* [italics mine] now before Richmond."[34]

Patrick moved his brigade on June 13 to a more healthy camping ground a few miles down the road at Tullis Mills on Town Run. Here it remained with Monroe's and Durrell's batteries while the rest of the division returned to Falmouth. The Tullis site consisted of an "old decayed, worm-eaten tenement, on a small brook, erected at an early day for a flouring establishment." For eight relatively happy days the men killed time eating ripe red and black cherries, "fishing, frog catching, snake killing," and by taking many delightful "cool refreshing baths in the mill-pond and under the water-wheel of the old mill." Major Gregg tried to satisfy the men's hunger for reading material by riding ten miles to obtain copies of four Washington papers, which he gave out from his tent as "mental rations."[35]

On the afternoon of June 14 a number of wagons under cavalry escort arrived in camp from Falmouth carrying about twenty-five bushels of mail representing a two-week brigade accumulation. William P. Maxson thought of mail from home as "almost as valuable as rations" and remembered that particular event as one of the happiest moments in the history of the regiment. As the call of "Mail!" spread quickly through the camps, the men crowded into their company streets. One soldier spoke of the common intense feelings of either "real pleasure" or "bitter disappointment" that accompanied the appearance of the orderly sergeant with his heavy bundles of letters and newspapers.

Pleasure, when friends at home have remembered us; harrowing disappointment, either when the mail fails to bring the letters written, or friends fail to write the letters expected. . . . All were eager and cheerful [with expectation], and as letter after letter was counted off, a stream of jokes followed the happy recipients to their tents. The seals were hastily broken, and an observer could plainly guess the various contents of the missives by watching the changing expression on the countenance of the soldier.[36]

While Patrick remained near Catlett's, McDowell, on June 11, reestablished his headquarters at the William Weir house near Manassas Junction and initiated plans to redirect his troops from the valley toward Richmond. On June 18 he suffered a serious accident when his horse Ohio reared up and fell over backward onto the general, rendering him temporarily unconscious. The next day, convalescing at his headquarters, he assured President Lincoln, who had come down from Washington to express his concern for his ailing commander, that he was well and eager to continue the work of his department. Many of his soldiers upon hearing the news of the accident wished the worst for their unpopular leader. One man wrote, "It is a pitty he did not breake his neck or some thing worse."[37]

The first element of McDowell's command to depart, McCall's division, left for the Virginia Peninsula by ship on June 9 from hastily built wharves at Gray's Landing on the Rappahannock seven miles below Fredericksburg. Shields's division reached Bristoe Station on June 23 and six days later boarded steamboats at Alexandria to follow McCall. McDowell held back King's and Ricketts's divisions, along with Bayard's Flying Brigade, to protect Washington and to attempt once more to advance overland to Richmond (this time via Bowling Green, Virginia). Banks's command, with Geary's brigade attached, resumed responsibility for protecting the lower Shenandoah Valley.[38]

With McCall's departure, General Doubleday assumed temporary command at Falmouth. On June 10 Doubleday sent the 76th New York over the river to occupy Fredericksburg, with Maj. Charles E. Livingston acting as military governor and Capt. John E. Cook as provost marshal. Livingston caused quite a sensation in the local community on his first day in office when his cavalry picket rode fifteen miles south to a point near the railroad to arrest the prominent J. Horace Lacy, owner of Chatham, who was serving at the time with the Confederate army. By June 15 word had reached Patrick from Fredericksburg that because of Livingston's activities, "the people are very hostile and their demonstrations very disagreeable." When General King arrived back at Falmouth on June 15 he relieved Livingston of his duties in Fredericksburg and replaced the 76th with two companies, commanded by Capt. John Mansfield, of the 2d Wisconsin Infantry. On June 17 King wrote to headquarters that he was anxious to have Patrick's brigade join him at Falmouth: "The Fredericksburg ladies all want to see Father Patrick."[39]

Patrick's troops returned to Falmouth on June 24 to take up their old campsite between the Wallace house, "Little Whim," and a nearby mill dam. The night before Patrick's arrival the rain-swollen Rappahannock River for the second time swept away the river bridges, leaving only the ferry to carry troops across to Fredericksburg. Thus, as Patrick's men marched out of Falmouth, by all appearances very little had changed since they had first marched through town nearly two months before.

On June 26 President Lincoln continued to dabble in military affairs by organizing the independent Union forces operating in northern Virginia into a single army. By executive order he created the Army of Virginia, to consist of Frémont's First Corps, Banks's Second Corps, and McDowell's Third Corps (Ricketts's and King's divisions and Doubleday's brigade). To command this new army Lincoln chose the son of a prominent Illinois judge and family acquaintance, Maj. Gen. John Pope, who at the time was serving in the western theater. He instructed Pope to secure Washington, clear the lower Shenandoah Valley of enemy forces, and threaten the Confederate supply and communication lines in the direction of Charlottesville. Apparently he envisioned McClellan kicking in the front door of Richmond as Pope came around the back.[40] Although the plan had the potential of breathing new life into McClellan's stalled Peninsula campaign, the Union command never got the chance to implement it. On the very day that Lincoln created the Army of Virginia, General Lee launched a series of hammer blows known as the Seven Days Battles that sent McClellan backpedaling down the Virginia Peninsula.

For the rest of June and most of July, while Lincoln held Pope in Washington to serve as his military advisor, King's First Division of McDowell's Third Corps, Army of Virginia, remained at Fredericksburg to secure Pope's hold on the Rappahannock. King had with him about twelve thousand men, including three infantry brigades, General Doubleday's unattached brigade, four artillery batteries, the 2d New York Cavalry, and the battery of mountain howitzers at Manassas Junction attached to General Bayard's Flying Brigade. From his Chatham headquarters King directed the restoration of the river bridges, the occupation of Fredericksburg, and the patrolling of roads toward Richmond to watch for any renewal of Confederate activity from that direction. Gunboats from the Potomac Flotilla frequently visited Fredericksburg, looking ominously like crocodiles floating near the railroad bridge.[41]

On June 27 Patrick moved his brigade across the stream near his "Little Whim" headquarters a short distance out the Belle Plain Road to a new camp in a meadow on the Peter King farm. Patrick named the camp "Rufus King," in honor of the division commander. He positioned the regimental camps side by side in brigade formation across a gentle slope. Nearby in a luxuriant pine grove Patrick's men erected seats and a pulpit for church services. The men made their new camp as comfortable as possible, securing their tents to raised platforms made from tree branches and covered by pine boughs.[42]

Almost immediately, much to Patrick's displeasure, the new camp swarmed with "all sorts of Peddlers, Dealers and Ambrotype men." A man of the 35th said that after sending a portion of their most recent pay home, many spent the rest "purchasing watches and jewelry . . . [or] paying it out liberally for a little very poor whiskey." Private Edgcomb wrote home on June 29, "Peddlers are seen in every direction with crowds around them. Paying 21 [cents] for a pie. 5 to 10 cents for lemons and oranges. 30 cents for eggs. Cucumber pickles 3 cents each." Patrick moved to immediately "arrest some and break up others."[43]

Maxson of the 23d remembered that "the severest drill and the hottest days of summer were the main features of this camp." The typical workday for the soldiers in late June began at five in the morning with reveille and roll call; at half past five, breakfast; from six to eight, police the camp putting rubbish in a pile; at eight, guard mount; from eight to half past nine, company drill; at noon, dinner call and roll call; battery or brigade drill beginning at half past two; at half past five, dress parade in full service uniform; at sundown, retreat and roll call; at nine, tattoo and roll call; and at half past nine, lights out. On especially hot days Patrick ordered a reduced schedule of brigade drills at seven in the morning and battalion drills at six in the evening. Only Sunday inspection and religious services, mail calls, and the rare payday broke this boring routine. With warm weather, swimming in the river near the pontoon bridge and herring fishing with seines became popular sports, despite three deaths by drowning.[44]

While at Camp Rufus King, many from the 23d returned to the ranks from the valley march or from sick leave, including Colonel Hoffman and Captain Clark. Still, the total number of troops "present" in the 23d continued to decline—from 629 in April to 587 in May. On June 25 the 23d had only 506 present of a paper strength of 768 men and officers. Sgt. Maj. Burritt reported absentees to include two prisoners of war; seven "by authority"; five absent without leave; fifty-two on detached duty, mostly with the artillery; and 128 sick in hospital. Before returning to his company from sick leave, Captain Clark had visited about twenty of his men in hospitals in and around Washington. He found them all better than expected but "a little inclined to profanity at McDowell for the long march they had taken and nothing effected." [45]

On July 4, 1862, Federal authorities at Fredericksburg suspended all camp duties in order to celebrate Independence Day. At sunrise, Patrick's men erected an evergreen-canopied speaker's platform on the brigade drill field and decorated it with their brigade flags. At ten o'clock the troops marched to the site without weapons, except sidearms for the officers, and formed into a hollow square, each of the four regiments facing one side of the platform. At the command "Rest," the men made themselves comfortable on the grass. They were joined by the bands of the 21st and 25th New York regiments and two howitzers from Gerrish's New Hampshire battery. [46]

The sun rose bright in a clear sky. The band of the 25th played "Hail Columbia" to open the festivities and the chaplain of the 20th NYSM read a prayer, followed by the band of the 21st playing "The Star Spangled Banner" and the hymn "God Save Our Native Land." The chaplain of the 21st read the Declaration of Independence, and the howitzers fired a thirty-four-round salute to the states. Patrick, although quite ill, alighted from the seat of a wagon to mount the speaker's stand and give a few "pertinent" remarks. He spoke of the great numbers of men killed in the recent battles near Richmond and provided the sobering statistic that the number of dead was twice the number of men in their whole division. He told them that he expected momentarily to hear confirmation of the "floating rumor" that Richmond had fallen, and he urged all present to "hope and pray from now till night" that the "God of Battles, of Jacob and Joshua, might be with McClellan and his command." At the mention of McClellan's name the men impulsively jumped to their feet, waved their caps, and cheered. Patrick called for three more cheers for McClellan, which were enthusiastically given. Other short speeches followed, including a humorous anecdote contributed by Colonel Hoffman. The ceremonies ended before noon with "a prayer by the chaplain of the 23rd [James DeBois], the benediction and Yankee Doodle."[47]

Patrick's men had the rest of the day to themselves until evening dress parade. Many walked down to the open plain between Chatham and the Phillips house to watch other commands conduct horse races and an unusual mule race. Twenty or so mule riders whipped and encouraged the mules of competitors around a circular track while trying to hold back their own in order to come in last and so win the "race" for a purse of ten dollars. Back at Camp Rufus King, the 20th NYSM staged sack, hurdle, and foot (one man per company) races. They also erected a debarked and greased pine pole with ten dollars strapped to the top for anyone bold and daring enough to claim. Perhaps the most ludicrous scene of the day occurred when hundreds of Patrick's men chased about the field trying to grab the tail of a hundred-pound shaved and greased pig.[48]

At evening dress parade, roles were reversed in some of the regiments, with the privates giving the orders, "with a mock gravity," to the officers. In the camp of the 23d, Adjutant William Hayt called the regiment to early dress parade so that the noncommissioned officers could surprise Colonel Hoffman with the gift of an eighty-five-dollar sword. The privates had similarly contributed for a sword presented at the same time to Lieutenant Colonel Crane. Hoffman accepted his sword in a moving speech. Soon, he told them, they would all be tested in battle. "When that time comes," he said, "as come it must, I pray that Heaven will so nerve my heart and strengthen the arm which you have intrusted to wield this beautiful weapon, that I may meet the shock in such a manner that you may not be ashamed of the gift."[49]

That night "hilarity reigned" in the camps of King's division. The gunboats in the river were illuminated, and celebratory bonfires dotted the hillsides. Over the broad fields behind Chatham "the heavens were ablaze with rockets throughout the whole evening, their magnificence being embellished with the fiery balls of Roman candles, fire wheels, colored lights, etc." Private Dexter described the nine o'clock scene at Patrick's camp: "Everybody is jubilant, sky rockets are mounting with their streams of brilliant fire. Fire crackers are crackling in all directions, while now and then are explosions from heavy guns. The drums and bugles are now playing tattoo." Patrick watched the evening fireworks from Chatham with General King and others. Afterwards the eager spectators called the generals out onto one of the porches for speeches. Patrick finally returned late that evening to his Wallace house headquarters, where, after "taking my little toddy like an old toper," he climbed into bed at ten.[50]

The remaining dog days of that particularly hot Fredericksburg summer passed uneventfully. Without an immediate Confederate threat, Union authorities relaxed their grip on the area. As a result, the thin line of pickets girding Fredericksburg proved quite porous to authorized and unauthorized traffic alike. Newspapers and private correspondence arrived on a regular basis from both Washington and Richmond, and Fredericksburg civilians could, to some degree, come and go at will. On July 3 Federal authorities allowed a number of civilian carriages to travel south on a humanitarian mission to aid the mounting number of Southern casualties resulting from the battles on the Peninsula.[51]

King also loosened the restrictive policies in regard to the flood of fugitive slaves seeking passes to cross the river from Fredericksburg and travel north. The *Christian Banner* of July 2, 1862, acknowledged that by midsummer Fredericksburg had become the gateway to freedom for slaves fleeing from all points in Spotsylvania County and from other Virginia counties as well—Hanover, Louisa, Caroline, Orange, and Albemarle. They arrived daily in groups of ten and twenty at a time, "with their packs on their backs and handkerchiefs tied over their heads—men, women, little children, and babies." One woman came with five small children, the youngest four weeks old, having walked twenty-five miles all night and morning. That same day thirty-three came in with "two yokes of oxen and two carts, and one splendid horse, all of which, was the property of their masters." The "stampede" of blacks reaching Fredericksburg numbered, according to an estimate in the *Banner* of June 18, on average two hundred a day. The paper painted a pathetic picture of the growing number of black men, women, and children "strolling through the town and country unprotected, uncared for, homeless, penniless, and friendless, not knowing where to go, what to do, nor what's to be-come of them." Another reporter found the extent of their blind faith in the prospects of freedom extraordinary. Despite their condition, they wandered about "looking on the wonders of creation, careless and indifferent as to the future, and seem to be perfectly happy."[52]

The great number of blacks remaining in the area seeking work, travel passes, or transportation north soon became a nuisance for the Federal authorities. Many of them settled in migrant camps, where they scavenged for subsistence from the military camps. On July 22 Patrick "attended" to about thirty-five or forty contrabands who lived near the outskirts of his brigade camp "by stealing and plundering." He "captured" some of them and sent them on to Washington.[53]

By late July 1862, the Federal occupation of Fredericksburg had imprinted a decidedly Yankee cast upon the town. Betty Maury sadly observed in late June that "the town is intensely Yankee, and looks as though it never had been anything else. Yankee ice carts go about selling Yankee ice. Yankee news boys cry Yankee papers along the streets. Yankee citizens and Yankee Dutchmen have opened all the stores on Main Street. Some of them have brought their families and look as if they had been born and bred here, and intended to stay here until they died. One man has built him a house!" Burritt in July confirmed that a great number of "transient northern traders, Sutlers and Jews . . . have moved in to make their fortunes." The Yankees came to dominate all aspects of the economic, political, and social life of the town. When a dramatic company arrived in late June and opened the Fredericksburg Theater, soldier-actors assisted the troupe in presenting a number of productions, including the popular summer comedy, *The Mischievous Negro*. A Union cavalryman on July 24 described Fredericksburg as a "horrible place" of a mongrel character. He observed the "principal features" of the town as being "the soldier—firm, unyielding, and knowing his power—the excited, anxious citizen, resigned old ladies in mourning—girls bitter and defiant, camp followers, lewd women, and the eager contraband, wild for freedom of which he has no correct knowledge."[54]

Every day five men from each company of the 23d received passes to visit Fredericksburg, where they might see the sights, attend church services, purchase small luxuries, or simply stroll the streets eyeing the many pretty young girls. From the time of the soldiers' first contact with the local females their approaches to them ranged from sheepish side glances to "unsuppressed and blunt expressions of admiration." Pvt. Chauncey Judd of the Cortland Volunteers admitted that despite the hostile, anti-Yankee sentiment exhibited by the women and the strict Federal nonfraternization policy in effect, the men still attempted to meet them and "have a talk with them once in a while on the sly." Most of the soldiers, away from home for more than a year, looked upon the haughty Fredericksburg women with feelings not of reciprocal anger and contempt but of longing and desire. The ache of their desire led some to visit the growing number of prostitutes plying their trade in Fredericksburg. Thomas

Dodd of the Cortland Volunteers admitted that "a number of the boys" sought the sexual services of "nigger wenches," particularly one "old black Ann," resulting in cases of venereal disease reported in the company. Most of the men, however, responding to the powerful ties of family and home and to the "Pillar of Fire" that Cortland represented in their lives, remained content with and grateful for opportunities simply to gaze upon the wondrous beauty of the female face and form. One soldier reasoned, "It was more agreeable to see even the back of a woman's bonnet than no woman at all."[55]

General Patrick, of course, was never one to settle back and enjoy a peaceful summer's day. He continued to rail against the undisciplined nature of his soldiers and their deficiencies in "general conduct and bearing toward . . . superiors." On Sunday, July 6, clean shaven except for his moustache, Patrick assembled his men for readings from his favorite two books—the Bible and army regulations. On July 10 he had his headquarters moved from "Little Whim" to a campsite in a prominent position at the center of Camp Rufus King, from where he could keep an eagle eye on his entire command. On July 15 he dressed down a thirty-five-year-old captain in the 23d for intemperance, causing him to weep, "like a child"; on July 20 he lectured a surgeon from the 35th New York for "intemperate language about Rebels and Rebeldom." He also described with obvious relish a confrontation he had with an abusive teamster: "I jumped down upon him, took him by the throat and gave him a sharp cut or two with my riding stick, which shut him up." He declared war on all liquor sellers hanging around camp and in late July, consistent with orders from army headquarters, stopped all passes into Fredericksburg for soldiers except when on official business. Patrick even lectured himself. After once consuming "blackberries, and some cake, and some cucumbers and ...a cup of chocolate over all," he commented in his journal, "if I am not sick it will not be my fault."[56]

Part of Patrick's distress during this period stemmed from the apparent ascendancy in power and influence of the Radical Republicans in Congress and their allies within the army who sought the expansion of the war aims to include punishment of all Southerners for the actions of their leaders. Lincoln's July 17 signature on the harsh Second Confiscation Act sent an unmistakable warning of things to come. His appointment of John Pope also signaled an intended shift in the conduct of the war. Although Pope as a military commander could claim some military successes in the western theater, more important to the administration were his political credentials as an outspoken antislavery and anti-McClellan Republican.[57] With the sympathetic Pope standing by his side as an emblem of the new order, Lincoln in mid-July pursued discussions concerning his controversial proposal to emancipate the slaves within those states still in rebellion.

From the time he first arrived on the scene in Washington, Pope set out to contrast himself with McClellan. He thrilled his supporters with bellicose statements of his intent to carry out an aggressive war against Southern forces. "I mean to attack them at all times that I can get the opportunity," he told the Committee on the Conduct of the War—"day and night" if necessary "until his forces are destroyed, or mine." On July 14 he chided his troops to abandon McClellan's influences. "I have come to you from the West," he proclaimed, "where we have always seen the backs of our enemies." He told them to discard their concerns for "lines of retreat" and "bases of supplies, . . . which I am sorry to find so much in vogue amongst you." He prodded them, "Let us look before us, and not behind. Success and glory are in the advance, disaster and shame lurk in the rear." He scoffed at McClellan's kid-glove approach to the war: "War means desolation and death," he said bluntly, "and it is neither humanity nor wisdom to carry it out upon any other theory. The more bitter it is made for the delinquents, the sooner it will end."[58]

During the last two weeks of July Pope backed up such words with the controversial General Orders No. 5, 6, 7, 11, and 13, to his Army of Virginia. These directives confronted directly McClellan's and the Democrats' more conciliatory approach to Southern noncombatants and gave teeth to the Second Confiscation Act. Pope directed his army to live off the land when possible, providing vouchers to owners for property taken. Southerners could later receive compensation, but only upon proof of loyalty to the United States. Adult male citizens living within Union lines had to sign an oath of allegiance to the United States or be sent south. Any attack against Union soldiers or U.S. property by civilians would bring immediate and harsh retaliation. Those caught in partisan acts of destruction could be summarily shot; all residents within five miles of an incident could be fined or forced to repair the damage, or both. No unofficial communications between the lines would thenceforth be allowed, and no guards could be placed over private houses or property. Soldiers had come south to fight, Pope explained in General Orders No. 13, not to be "wasted in protecting private property of those most hostile to the Government."[59]

In general, the North embraced the tone, if not all of the particulars, of Pope's directives. The *New York Times* commented in the July 27 issue, "It seems now as though . . . [we are] to wage war in downright, deathly earnest. The recent orders of Gen. Pope are the key-note of this new policy." Pope's soldiers responded with mixed feelings. On the one hand they resented the readiness of this pompous general of what they considered unproven ability to make bombastic speeches critical of their fighting abilities. For example, they referred to his July 14 proclamation as "Pope's Bull" and thought the tone of it, in Patrick's words, "very windy and somewhat insolent." On the other hand they saw in Pope someone who was willing and apparently able to engage the nation's resources fully in order to bring the conflict to a speedy and successful conclusion. Seymour Dexter wrote, "His orders have sounded like war and has [*sic*] made his entire command feel that they are not sacrificing their lives in 'playing' with the enemy." "*Now,* all men feel encouraged and satisfied," Burritt added, "that their united power will be wielded to a righteous purpose, and end in the enforcement of laws and the punishment of guilt." Major Gregg rejoiced at Pope's appointment, declaring, "I thank God that the sweet sounding term conservative has lost its charm; that it is played out and will delude the people no more."[60]

Predictably, Generals McClellan and Patrick and the more conservative Democrats were appalled by Pope's actions. Patrick thought Pope's directives "the Orders of a Demagogue!" As a result of them, he wrote, his troops "believe they have a perfect right to rob, tyrannize, threaten and maltreat any one they please, under the Orders of Gen. Pope." McClellan reacted with similar outrage. On August 9 he issued General Orders No. 154 to his Army of the Potomac by which, he told his wife, he would "strike square in the teeth of all his [Pope's] infamous orders and give directly the reverse instructions to my army—forbid all pillaging and stealing and take the highest Christian ground for the conduct of the war—let the Govt. gainsay it if they dare." He vowed, "I will not permit this army to degenerate into a mob of thieves, nor will I return these men of mine to their families as a set of wicked and demoralized robbers—I will not have that sin on my conscience."[61]

The citizens of Fredericksburg and Falmouth soon felt the sting of Pope's heavy-handed policies. On July 21 King ordered Patrick to remove all Union sentries guarding Rebel houses and property. One of King's men happily noted on July 24, after observing ten empty wagons leave camp to obtain potatoes and other produce from local farmers, that "the foraging business is being gone into now with full vim, under General Pope's orders." The *Christian Banner* on July 30 reported that the order directing Southerners to take an oath of loyalty to the Union "has fallen like a thunderbolt from a clear sky on the citizens of this community." A *New York Tribune* reporter noted on July 27 that at least thirty of the town's leading Rebels had led their families to Richmond rather than take oath. The situation in Fredericksburg became increasingly tense as a result of Pope's orders; Patrick soon came to believe that it was spinning rapidly out of control. He criticized King's apparent inaction, attributing it to his being "frightened" of pro-Pope newspaper reporters.[62]

Pope's hard-line policies in dealing with Fredericksburg civilians, however, gave voice and influence to the small and long-suffering pro-Union segment of the community. This group succeeded on July 25 in having Provost Marshal John Mansfield of the 2d Wisconsin Infantry removed from his position by accusing him of disloyalty, for his alleged pro-Southern sympathies. At the instigation of General Doubleday, a committee of loyal citizens met with Pope to complain about the ongoing arrest and harassment of area Union men by Confederate authorities. Pope ordered that hostages be taken from the community for the safe return of those Union men previously arrested. General Patrick had the difficult task of choosing four prominent Fredericksburg men for arrest from a list of eight candidates. Patrick's soldiers took the men "from their beds" during the night of July 22 and then the next morning sent them by train to Washington for incarceration in Old Capitol Prison. During the next three weeks, fifteen additional Fredericksburg men joined them, including Mayor Montgomery Slaughter; a total of seven Union men had been taken and sent south.[63]

Pope, at Lincoln's request, remained in Washington during this period while his forces awaited the consequences of McClellan's reverses on the Peninsula. Franz Sigel's First Corps camped near Sperryville, just east of the Blue Ridge. Banks's Second Corps moved to a position between First Corps and Ricketts's division of McDowell's Third Corps, near Warrenton. Then, in mid-July, Pope directed Banks's cavalry to occupy Culpeper, thirty-five miles northeast of an important railroad junction at Gordonsville and about thirty-five miles northwest of King's division of McDowell's corps at Fredericksburg. On July 17, with the wheels of a new campaign slowly starting to turn, McDowell shifted his headquarters from the Weir house at Manassas Junction to the Rice W. H. Payne home, "Mecca," in Warrenton.[64]

The Union occupation of Culpeper provoked General Lee to action. With McClellan's army for the moment quiet, on July 13 Lee took the gamble of splitting his army and sending two divisions under Stonewall Jackson by train from Richmond on the Virginia Central Railroad across General King's front to Louisa Court House and Gordonsville.[65] As early as July 3 McDowell had warned King of just this possibility and directed him to watch for activity along the line of the Virginia Central between Hanover Junction and Gordonsville. King on July 4 began sending out paid spies and cavalry patrols to gather information. Under Pope's orders, in late July King sent two cavalry raids of about three hundred men each down the Telegraph Road to strike the railroad and disrupt traffic. The first raid (July 19–20), by the 2d New York, reached Beaver Dam Station. The second (July 22–23), made up of equal numbers from the 2d New York and the 3d Indiana cavalry regiments, advanced as far as Anderson's Turnout, ten miles below Beaver Dam Station and less than thirty railroad miles from Richmond. Despite Northern claims to the contrary, however, neither cavalry raid significantly interfered with the transfer of Lee's troops and supplies from Richmond along the line of the Virginia Central.[66]

On July 24 King issued orders for General Gibbon to form a "light column" of troops to move rapidly out the Orange Plank Road on a reconnaissance in force to determine the extent of the Confederate presence in the area of Orange Court House and Gordonsville. Gibbon's force consisted of the 23d and 30th New York regiments, the 2d Wisconsin, companies C and D of the 3d Indiana Cavalry, Companies A and C of the 2d U.S. Sharpshooters, and the six twelve-pounder Napoleon guns of Gibbon's former Battery B, 4th U.S. Artillery. The 1,500-man column left Fredericksburg at three in the afternoon in light marching order—that is, without a burdensome supply train and leaving behind all nonessential personnel, including the regimental musicians. The infantrymen carried only weapons, bayonets, fifty rounds of ammunition, and two days' rations of salt pork, hard tack, and coffee. After covering thirteen miles in seven hours under a hot sun, they spent the first night lying out in the rain without tents. Thirty-three men from the 23d gave out on the first day and had to be sent back to Fredericksburg.[67]

The advance continued early on July 25 under strict provisions for security. Gibbon forced all adult male civilians encountered along the route to join the column as prisoners, to prevent them from alerting the enemy of their approach. The sweep netted quite a crowd, including two mail carriers coming up from Richmond. At road intersections pioneers felled trees to block crossroads so as to deter surprise attacks on the column's flanks and rear. Gibbon halted for the night about four miles short of Orange after a march of twenty-five miles.[68]

Gibbon expected to compensate for a deficiency in supplies by having his men live off the land, in conformance to Pope's General Orders No. 5. As the column went into bivouac Colonel Hoffman dispatched two men from each company to forage the countryside looking for fresh meat. On the second night out the foragers "discovered and surrounded" a flock of sheep and "forty fine fat muttons were soon stretched upon the grass." One Southern Tier man admitted that "some of the boys like to put their own construction on said order, which they think gives them the privilege of going into any house on the road, [and] taking anything to eat that they can find." The men took whatever they could consume or carry and showed little sympathy for their victims. Major Gregg did relent once, finding and returning a stolen horse to a widow after he had witnessed her "wonderful demonstration of grief and indignation." It can also be recorded that members of the 23d paid at least one farmer for his chickens—in counterfeit Confederate five-dollar notes. The local outrage over these Union practices knew no bounds. One furious woman charged that the Yankees had stolen her missing child. Another woman appeared at her doorway shaking her fist at the passing troops and yelling, "I hope you *all* will get killed, every one of you. . . . I hope you will all get your throats cut."[69]

On the 26th Gibbon formed a small striking force to pierce the Rebel picket screen before Orange. He advanced the 2d Wisconsin, his cavalry, sharpshooters, and two artillery pieces. Gibbon's remaining units formed a line of battle across the road in a wood, the 23d and 30th in line with the four artillery pieces positioned in the road. Colonel Hoffman gave the command "In place rest" to his troops, allowing the men to sit in small groups between lines of loaded, stacked arms. As the minutes passed, Hoffman walked down the line of troops quietly talking to the captains and giving them instructions. He ordered the small number of black camp servants that had joined the expedition to the rear under the command of Captain Clark's servant, "who was created their Lord

Lieutenant for the occasion." Clark hung his old flannel blouse on an oak twig and sat on the ground to wait.[70]

Gibbon's vanguard drove forward to within one and a half miles of Orange, where Gibbon witnessed Rebel infantry swarming from the town to meet him. Having satisfied his orders by identifying a sizable Rebel presence near Orange, and not wanting to bring on a general engagement, Gibbon beat a hasty retreat. By ten in the morning the column was in motion, retracing its route back to Fredericksburg. It continued through a heavy rainstorm while maintaining a strong rearguard to fend off any Rebel harassers and also to drive forward any Union stragglers. A few of the mounted field officers of the 23d strove to keep the weary men moving by "continually aiding these men by cheering words, carrying their guns, and even dismounting, compelling the weary fellows to ride." After bivouacking near Chancellorsville, the column arrived in Fredericksburg around two on the afternoon of the 27th, having marched almost eighty miles in three days with not one man killed or wounded. The 23d did not get back to Camp Rufus King until four, appearing, according to one observer in the 35th, "as tired and dusty looking set of men as I ever saw." Many had worn out at least one pair of shoes, for which Uncle Sam would charge them $1.95 from their annual forty-two-dollar clothing allowance.[71]

The men of the 23d returned to Falmouth to find that General Patrick had once again taken up duties in Fredericksburg as military governor. On July 25, King, having been criticized by Pope for his management of affairs in Fredericksburg, called upon Patrick to help calm tensions and restore order. Patrick agreed to resume his duties as military governor in Fredericksburg only after King granted him full powers to act. By July 28 Patrick was back in his old office in the Farmer's Bank. The 21st and 20th NYSM regiments crossed the river with him to guard the town and enforce martial law; the 21st camped along the Plank Road near Poplar Springs, and the 20th NYSM was split between the John L. Stansbury's "Snowden" (four companies) and John Ferneyhough's "Sligo" properties (six companies). On July 31, six companies of the 3d Indiana Cavalry arrived and camped along Hazel Run, augmenting Patrick's Fredericksburg force.[72]

The 35th New York, joined early on July 29 by the 23d, bivouacked together under Colonel Hoffman at "Camp Washington" on the former George Washington family property on the Stafford side of the river opposite the Fredericksburg wharves and close to the canal-boat bridge. The 23d camped about 150 feet from the water, where lay at anchor the wooden gunboat *Anacostia*, nicknamed "The Gray Mare" by Hoffman's men.[73] From Camp Washington the two regiments guarded the river bridges, including the new wire suspension bridge near Chatham. Hoffman sent Company K of the 23d across the river into Fredericksburg to assist in guarding government stores and property.[74]

When Patrick took charge of Fredericksburg, he found the town "full of Brothels and Prostitutes and drinking saloons and all sorts of vile institutions." He established beyond the town a picket line that he described as "so very close that nobody can get in or out." He instituted a system of passes for those wishing to cross the river, requiring even officers to get written authorization from their brigade and division commanders. He also placed severe restrictions on sutlers and broke up "all grog shops and dens of debauchery" whenever his guards discovered them. On August 4 he gathered together "quite a number" of arrested prostitutes and sent them north on the eleven o'clock train. To handle the "hegira of Negroes," as Patrick termed it, heading north, he designated quarters to be used as a holding area where they could remain for up to a day while being processed. Patrick set aside one or two train cars for blacks on the daily run to Aquia Landing.[75]

Patrick also clamped a strict nine o'clock curfew on the town. Each night the drum corps from either the 35th or 23d regiments marched up through the town beating the tattoo and filling the air with the tunes "Yankee Doodle" and the "Star Spangled Banner." A company of soldiers followed, breaking into squads to scour the byways and ensure that doors were closed, all lights extinguished in public buildings, the streets clear, and all military personnel safely back at their camps. Second Lt. John Prentiss of Company G of the 23d reported on July 30, "We have got the citizens tight. They can't get out of town, all that refuse to take the oath, are drove out of town." Patrick also acted swiftly to stamp out any pro-Confederate activity within the reach of his authority. On August 8 he sent six companies of the 23d (A, B, C, D, E, and G) and a portion of the 20th NYSM with a squad of cavalry and two artillery pieces down the Bowling Green Road to capture and bring in William Taylor and William Dickinson and their farm animals.[76]

Patrick's actions and manner during this period won him few friends in Fredericksburg and lost many supporters of his earlier administration. A visitor to Patrick's headquarters found his demeanor "*all military,* pious,

rigid, if not severe." As Patrick bore down on the community and the summer temperatures soared some days to over a hundred degrees, tempers
flared. On August 5 Patrick admitted, "My reputation in Fredericsburg
[sic] is lost, completely, I expect, as I have caused a number of persons to
be searched, and it has raised a great row—well! It was necessary." When
challenged by a citizen to explain the contrast between his present actions
and his more lenient policies of the past spring, he explained, "*Then* I
was doing according to the *Gospel, now* I am doing business *according
to law*."[77]

By the end of July Pope harbored little doubt that Stonewall Jackson
had occupied the Orange-Gordonsville area with a large force of at least
thirty thousand men. On July 29 he finally managed to leave Washington,
on a special train "handsomely decorated with flags," Maj. Gen. Henry
W. Halleck having assumed the function of general in chief of the Union
armies.[78] When Pope arrived in Warrenton he met with McDowell, his
acting, unofficial second in command, and the two set to work preparing
the Army of Virginia for battle. On August 3, Lincoln, through General
Halleck, added greatly to Pope's responsibilities by directing the sluggish
McClellan to quit the Peninsula and send his troops by ship back to the
Potomac to be combined with Pope's army under Pope's command.[79]

At Pope's heralded arrival in Warrenton, the general appeared to one
officer a troubled man, "jaded and irascible." He had but a short time to
organize the pieces of an army that were handed to him, meet and take
the measure of his commanders and troops, and gain some understanding
of the terrain over which he would soon have to fight. His three fractious
corps commanders had no inclination to work or function together, much
less serve under the upstart Pope, whom they outranked (Frémont refused
outright to subordinate himself to Pope and was replaced as commander
of the First Corps by Sigel). Pope then faced the even more difficult task
of integrating troops loyal to his archrival McClellan into his Army of
Virginia while in the course of an active campaign. Pope later stated in
his memoirs that he approached the campaign with trepidation, believing
that he was being "offered the command of a forlorn hope under the most
unfavorable conditions possible for success."[80]

Pope also later claimed that his command problems stemmed in large
part from the sinkhole of Washington politics, which, he said, permeated
the air with the "moral odor of sewer gas." He chose to ignore in such

assessments the negative impact of his own caustic and arrogant personality and his eagerness to play the role of lightning rod for the Radical Republicans in Congress. In the heat of battle, his aggressive and confident persona was to melt away to reveal his true insecurities and incompetence as an army commander. So complete would be Pope's defeat and humiliation that one must question Lincoln's initial judgment in staking so much on a commander of such limited experience and ability.[81]

In early August, however, McDowell prepared for the new campaign by ordering his two divisions to unite at Culpeper. Pope agreed to this action, but only after the twelve thousand men of Maj. Gen. Ambrose Burnside's Ninth Corps first replaced King's troops at Fredericksburg. Burnside's force arrived by ship at Aquia Landing from Fort Monroe on August 4, but King could not begin his march until his troops completed another raid toward Hanover Junction in a further attempt to break Lee's Virginia Central lifeline. On August 5 General Gibbon led two columns made up of troops from his own brigade, two cavalry regiments, and two batteries of artillery over the canal-boat bridge into Fredericksburg. One column struck at Fredericks Hall Station and caused considerable damage to the track and railroad facilities. All of Gibbon's troops returned on August 8.[82]

While King remained at Fredericksburg, his division underwent further reorganization. General Augur's old brigade was given to Brig. Gen. John P. Hatch, General Banks's former cavalry chief, who was in disfavor with Pope for his apparent lack of aggressiveness while serving in that capacity. General Doubleday's three regiments became the Second Brigade. In accordance with the seniority of the brigade commanders, Patrick's four regiments became the Third Brigade, and Gibbon's westerners became the Fourth Brigade. Four batteries were assigned to the division: Company B, 4th U.S. Artillery (Capt. Joseph Campbell); Company D, 1st Rhode Island Artillery (Capt. J. Albert Monroe); Battery A, 1st New Hampshire (Capt. George A. Gerrish); and Company L, 1st New York Artillery (Capt. John A. Reynolds).

Patrick spent the first week of August tying up loose ends in preparation for the march to Culpeper. On August 7 he brought the 23d across the river to join the rest of the brigade and placed the Southern Tier men in bivouac on familiar ground near Hazel Run. The next day, when Maj. Gen. Isaac Stevens of General Burnside's command replaced Patrick as military governor of Fredericksburg, Patrick moved his headquarters once again to the Downman house, "Idlewild," west of town on the Plank Road. Colonel Hoffman, suffering from jaundice, left for Washington on the 9th, turning over his command to Lt. Col. Nirom M. Crane.[83]

In late July Patrick met with his officers to prepare them for their coming trial on the battlefield and to explain what he expected of them. He told them basically, "I don't want to make regulars of you, you are a different class of men, but I do want you to do your duty."[84]

On Sunday, July 27, Patrick called his brigade together to talk to the men as a group, perhaps for the last time for many of them. He assembled his three regiments (he excused the 23d, just back from its tiring march to Orange) around an old oak tree at Camp Rufus King. In the still of twilight with the sun just setting above the trees, a gentle breeze fluttered the leaves of the chaplain's prayer book as he read passages of hope and salvation. The general then rose and in a voice "husky with emotion" spoke of the need for spiritual preparation for the work ahead and how noble was the sacrifice of the soldier who died on the battlefield for the good of mankind and in a just cause. The men listened "with hushed breath" as Patrick finished. An aide then rose to read a hymn, but he became overcome by emotion, and his voice faltered.

"'Give me the book,' said Patrick, and with his deep tones full of the believer's fervor, he read the hymn beginning,

> Rock of ages, cleft for me,
> Let me hide myself in thee.

And a thousand voices rising on the evening air, told the woods and hills how Christian soldiers prepared for the day of battle."[85]

CHAPTER 7

Pinched Bellies and a
Hell of a Fight

The morning of August 9, 1862, dawned with the promise of another sultry day. Late in the afternoon the first of Gen. Rufus King's two columns departed Fredericksburg on the Plank Road for the thirty-five-mile march to Culpeper. Although a distant rumbling in the direction of Culpeper indicated that a battle was in progress, the column, consisting of Patrick's and Doubleday's brigades and Gerrish's New Hampshire battery, advanced only nine miles before bivouacking near Chancellorsville. The next morning it continued on to a crossing of the Rapidan River at Ely's Ford. As Patrick's men splashed across the stream, King led a second column of Gibbon's and Hatch's brigades, Campbell's U.S. (regular) battery, and the 2d New York Cavalry northwest from Falmouth to cross the Rappahannock River at Richards' Ford. Early on the 11th the two columns converged in the narrow neck of land between the rivers at Richards' Cross Roads (Richardsville), whereupon they hurried forward under General Pope's urgent orders. General Burnside's two divisions remained near Fredericksburg to guard the nearby Rappahannock River crossings and maintain the vital link between Pope's left flank near Culpeper and his forward bases at Falmouth and Aquia Landing.

The fourteen miles from Richards' Cross Roads to near Culpeper severely tested King's men. The road was "ankle deep in dust, which continually rose in choking clouds, filling ears, eyes and mouth."[1] King had to order a halt at Stevensburg for his many stragglers to catch up, and consequently it was well after dark before King's command bivouacked along the road south of Culpeper. The men fell into a sound sleep, undisturbed by the steady commotion of passing ambulances carrying wounded soldiers to Culpeper from the Battle of Cedar Mountain, fought two days before.

Although Patrick arrived too late to participate in the fighting at Cedar Mountain, he continued his personal struggle against what he considered the corrupting influence of Pope's now infamous orders on his men. The march began, according to one man from the 23d, with the "general" execution of Pope's General Orders No. 5. Adjutant Hayt complained that all along the route the men chased after hogs, cattle, sheep, poultry, and "all else eatible wherever they find it." Even Lieutenant Colonel Crane joined in the general pillage of the countryside, ordering a soldier to kill a farmer's hog in order to feed his hungry men.[2] Consequently, Patrick charged, his brigade arrived at Culpeper "completely demoralized." On August 14 he wrote in his journal that he needed to provide transport for a family to Culpeper "to save the daughters from violation by our soldiers." The previous day he wrote "I am so utterly disgusted that I feel like resigning and letting the whole thing go—I am afraid of God's Justice, for our Rulers and Commanders deserve his wrath and curse."[3]

While his army rested near Culpeper, Pope took the time to inspect the troops of King's division. At midmorning on the 14th, King's four brigades, two batteries, and the 2d New York Cavalry formed in two lines on a small field near their campground. Although only two of King's sixteen infantry regiments had yet seen any significant fighting, months of active campaigning and the fatiguing march from Fredericksburg had reduced the division to fewer than nine thousand men present. The 23d counted about five hundred ready for battle.[4] Consequently, when the bewhiskered and portly figure of General Pope arrived on the field in a flourish of military music, the men did not respond with much enthusiasm. A year of fruitless campaigning without the promised victory had made them skeptical of their leaders. As one soldier wrote, "Few were inclined to take him on trust."[5]

Patrick took the opportunity when meeting Pope to detail abuses against civilians engendered by his controversial general orders. Pope assured Patrick that his intentions in issuing the orders had been misunderstood; he showed Patrick an as-yet-unissued new directive by which he expected to set the record straight. The order stated unequivocally that wanton acts of pillage and outrage "are disgraceful to the army, and have neither been contemplated nor authorized by any orders whatsoever; the perpetrators of them, whether officers or soldiers, will be visited with a punishment which they will have reason to remember." Patrick welcomed Pope's correction: "With this in my hand I can fight anything." On the morning of August 16 he read aloud Pope's new General Orders No. 19 to the troops of his brigade and added to it his own sweeping instructions—which, he confided in his journal, "I mean to have . . . obeyed." "And we all knew him too well," admitted one listener, "to doubt the consequence of disobedience."[6]

After the Battle of Cedar Mountain Stonewall Jackson withdrew his men to the south bank of the Rapidan River where Gen. Robert E. Lee joined him with the other wing of the Army of Northern Virginia, under Maj. Gen. James Longstreet. Lee intended to concentrate his army of about 55,000 men on the Rapidan and strike at Pope across the river before McClellan's troops could arrive from Aquia Landing and Alexandria to form an immense army of more than a hundred thousand men. After his severe losses on the Virginia Peninsula fighting McClellan, Lee did not look for a major and costly confrontation with Pope. Instead, he planned to seize the initiative and then, by a strategy of maneuver, fighting only when necessary or advantageous, to break the tightening grip of Union armies in Virginia, clear the central part of the state before the fall harvest, and force Northern commanders into a static defensive strategy to protect their capital.

Pope concentrated his army of 52,000[7] men south of Culpeper near Cedar Mountain in a position to protect his supply line along the Orange and Alexandria Railroad and confront Lee from the north bank of the Rapidan. On August 18 he learned from captured documents that Lee intended to strike a blow against his left flank by crossing troops over the Somerville and Raccoon Fords of the Rapidan. If successful, Lee would sever Pope's connection to Fredericksburg and be in a position to cut off his retreat routes across the Rappahannock. Despite Pope's previous promises of a new aggressive spirit in all of his military actions, he ordered his army to retreat to a stronger, more defensible line behind the Rappahannock where he might feel secure and await reinforcements from the Army of the Potomac. Pope ordered three columns of retreat, each proceeded by a wagon train and followed by a covering brigade of cavalry. Banks's Second Corps and McDowell's Third Corps, followed by

Gen. George D. Bayard's cavalry brigade, would make up the center column, following the line of the Orange and Alexandria Railroad to its river crossing at Rappahannock Station (near modern Remington).[8]

Pope ordered the retreat to begin late on the 18th. On that day King's division occupied a most unpleasant camping ground on the Cedar Mountain battlefield eight miles south of Culpeper. Although more than a week had passed since the fighting ended, buzzards still circled overhead, and the cloying smell of death floated in the air. The men thus felt relief when orders finally arrived to break camp, draw three days' rations and extra ammunition, and send all the wagons back toward Culpeper. Their initial excitement over the prospects for battle, however, soon turned to disappointment when they realized that the great cloud of dust rising to the north indicated not an advance but a retreat.

Once the withdrawal began, the streets of Culpeper became a bottleneck for the passage of supply wagons. An average division, such as King's, might have forty ammunition and fifty forage and subsistence wagons, twenty or thirty ambulances, and sixty regimental and headquarters wagons. A typical supply wagon drawn by four or six horses or mules required about a hundred feet of road. Consequently division train occupied over three miles of roadway. The backup of wagons trying to get through Culpeper extended more than ten miles.[9]

At dark, King's division still had not budged. Campfires twinkled across the vast plain below Cedar Mountain as the men stacked their arms and lay down in their formations to rest and wait. Soon a light rain began to fall to add to their discomfort. Daylight found them wrapped in their rubber blankets, "cold, cross and hungry."[10]

Throughout the night the clogged streets of Culpeper heard the constant creaking of wagons, the crack of whips, and the clamorous swearing of teamsters and shouts of "Yea Mule." Pope rode among the mass of vehicles driving on the teamsters with "salutations of profanity" in the manner of a "Mississippi stevedore."[11] McDowell was spotted sitting on his horse in the middle of a small creek just east of Culpeper snapping a large "black snake" whip over the heads of dilatory teams and at times their recalcitrant drivers.[12]

Soon after midnight King received the order to march. His soldiers piled fence rails on their campfires to deceive the enemy as the shadowy columns of troops passed out between them into the dark night. King's division, being at the tail end of McDowell's column, did not get off until after daylight. Before departing, his men destroyed everything that they could not carry.[13]

"And Such a March!" wrote Patrick, "Halting and moving—moving and halting, without system." The route became marked by a great number of smoldering, broken-down wagons shoved to the side of the road and set ablaze. Entering Culpeper, a soldier of Ricketts's command encountered townswomen who "insulted us in every way they could. Standing upon the sidewalks and in doorways they made grimaces as we marched by, and quoted from Pope's grandiloquent orders." The Union retreat was further hampered by the stream of escaping slaves that followed the army "on foot, on horse or mule, in old broken-down vehicles tied with straps and strings, in all manner of costumes grave and gay." Near midnight, King's men turned off the road into a wood less than three miles from the railroad bridge spanning the Rappahannock.[14]

Before crossing the river early on August 20, the dust-caked men of the 23d bringing up the rear of the infantry column stripped naked and plunged into the river and a nearby millpond to wash. Their revelry was cut short, however, when storm clouds of dust raised by enemy troops appeared above the trees behind them. Hurrying to the north bank the men looked back and, joined by Generals Pope and McDowell, watched as the last Union stragglers darted across the bridge or plunged into the sixty-foot-wide river to swim across to safety. Pope ordered General Ricketts to keep a small force of artillery and infantry on the south bank of the river to maintain a fortified bridgehead.[15]

Pope settled into an excellent defensive position along approximately ten miles of Rappahannock riverbank extending from below Sulphur Springs downriver to Kelly's Ford. He could take additional comfort in the knowledge that the first division of McClellan's troops, under Brig. Gen. John F. Reynolds, would soon join him from Falmouth. Lee, however, could not allow Pope time to fortify his position and calmly collect his reinforcements. Early on the 21st, elements of Jackson's wing sidled upriver to probe for weak points along Pope's right flank. At Beverly Ford the 5th Virginia Cavalry with two cannon splashed across the river and drove in the panicked Union pickets. McDowell, conspicuous that day in a large, white civilian hat, happened to be nearby. He called upon Patrick, whose troops were stationed in the area, to lead his brigade and Reynolds's Battery L, 1st New York, forward to defend the ford.[16]

Patrick positioned the artillery behind the crest of a small ridge over-looking the ford. He deployed the 21st New York as skirmishers and had the rest of the brigade lie down en masse behind the guns. When he saw the Rebels withdraw back across the river before his show of force, he ordered the infantry to follow them down to the riverbank. Here they remained until Patrick saw a battery on the south bank moving into posi-tion to deliver enfilading fire down the ravine where his men had taken shelter. About dark the New Yorkers beat a hasty retreat up the bank under fire, suffering the loss of one man almost cut in two by solid shot. The 23d arrived back behind Reynolds's guns practically unscathed from their baptism of fire as a regiment. Crane expressed pride in the soldierly bearing of his Southern Tier men, boasting in his after-action report that "not a man flinched from his duty."[17]

On August 22 each side tested the defenses of the other with artillery duels and forays of troops across the river. One "action" occurred around noon when a herd of Rebel cattle made a slow advance on the Union posi-tion at Rappahannock Station and were "captured" by Ricketts's men.[18] In a more determined effort, Confederate cavalry chief J. E. B. Stuart launched a dramatic twenty-five-mile raid with 1,500 troopers and two cannon, crossing over Waterloo Bridge and an adjacent ford about four miles upriver from Sulphur Springs. Stuart passed through Warrenton around and behind the right flank of the Union army to strike Pope's Orange and Alexandria Railroad supply line at Catlett's Station. At the same time Jackson ordered a strong force of infantry to cross the river near Sulphur Springs. Both efforts came to naught, however, when a sud-den and heavy rainstorm swelled the river a number of feet above normal. The rain prevented Stuart from burning or destroying a wooden railroad bridge near Catlett's and forced him to hurry back across the river the next day. Jackson's infantry was not so lucky; the rising water stranded Brig. Gen. Jubal Early's Brigade plus the 13th Georgia and two artillery batteries on the north bank. Pope, seeking to take advantage of Early's predicament, ordered Franz Sigel's troops of the First Corps to strike him by marching upon the springs. He also ordered McDowell to support Si-gel by pulling his troops back from the river to Warrenton.[19]

Early the next morning, August 23, McDowell's troops destroyed the railroad bridge at Rappahannock Station, burned the depot, and set out on the road to Warrenton. Brig. Gen. John Hatch temporarily took command of King's division after a debilitating epileptic seizure forced King to travel in an ambulance.[20] At Warrenton, General Reynolds's command of 4,700 men arrived from Falmouth and reported for duty with McDowell's Third Corps. McDowell now had three divisions, totaling approximately 23,000 men. The corps bivouacked that night in and around Warrenton with the expectation of a fight the next morning.

Morning light revealed that General Early had escaped back across the river. For many in the Union ranks this represented the final indignity, resulting from what appeared to be Pope's senseless cat-and-mouse game with Lee. The tedious marches, short bivouacs, and insufficient rations only added to their frustration. Two new army directives had the effect of spreading additional gloom through the Union camps. One restricted all correspondence by soldiers from leaving the army, for reasons of security. The other order discharged the popular regimental bands as unneeded in the field. The historian-soldier of the 21st commented that when the Union Cornet Band marched away toward home on August 16, "with them departed half the remaining romance of our lives."[21]

General Patrick joined the chorus of complainers. Suffering from various health problems and a "violent pain in my bowels" that he treated with "a great deal of opium," he took out his hostility on Pope and McDowell. He wrote on the 24th that Pope "seems to be universally detested by the Citizens[,] and our Troops are loud in their expressions of disgust." Turning on McDowell, to whom in other writings Patrick derogatorily referred as "his Magnificence," Patrick stated, "I am so thoroughly disgusted with the management of *this* [McDowell's] Corps, that I am anxious to leave it. I feel that disgrace *here* is inevitable. . . . All is confusion."[22]

Capitalizing on Pope's confusion as to Confederate movements, Lee seized the initiative to pursue his strategy of maneuver. On August 24 Lee met with his commanders in a field near the small community of Jeffersonton; there they outlined on the ground an audacious plan of action.[23] Jackson would take his army wing of about 24,000 men and his artillery and march in a wide arc around Pope's right flank through Thoroughfare Gap in the Bull Run Mountains to strike the Orange and Alexandria Railroad in Pope's rear. Longstreet would remain behind with 28,000 men to keep Pope occupied at the Rappahannock. Pope, the thinking went, must then abandon his strong position and attempt to restore his supply line along the railroad. With Pope in the open and off balance, Lee's two wings could reunite and deliver a destructive if not decisive blow. Great risk went with a divided army separated by a strong and aggressive foe, but Lee was willing to take the risk for the advantages that might be gained. Jackson's men departed their bivouacs at dawn on August 25 — to where, they did not know.

As soon as Pope received indications of Jackson's move north, possibly into the Shenandoah Valley, he ordered McDowell to push a strong force from Warrenton across the river at Sulphur Springs and Waterloo Bridge to investigate. Patrick's brigade with the New Hampshire battery led the seven-mile march from near Warrenton to the Springs under the mistaken belief that Ricketts's division had preceded them and that the passage of the river would be undisputed. At half past nine on the morning of the 26th the brigade arrived at the still-smoldering ruins of the famed Sulphur Springs Hotel; there the men rested while Patrick and his staff rode forward four hundred yards to the riverbank in search of a suitable crossing.

Before the war, Fauquier White Sulphur Springs had gained a reputation as an elegant summer resort serving fashionable members of Virginia society who sought the local foul-smelling sulphur waters for their supposed medicinal powers. Six hundred guests could comfortably lodge in a complex of whitewashed brick buildings clustered near the 188-foot-long, four-story main hotel building known as "the Pavilion." A semicircular row of smaller detached cottages flanked the main building, eight to a side. Lead pipes carried the heated mineral waters to a bath house containing twenty tubs. Nearby, an octagonal spring house, or "temple," covered a bubbling fountain of drinking water watched over by a life-sized statue of Hygiea, the Greek goddess of health. During the summer season the spacious green lawns hemmed by beautiful flower gardens rang with the sounds of "bowls and quoits," and hunting horns bleated above the yelping of hounds. No summer at the Springs was complete without the tournament of knights. Dashing young horsemen donned silks of bright colors to compete with lances against a target for the honor of choosing the "Queens of Love and Beauty" to reign over the evening's fancy-dress ball. On cool summer evenings couples walked among the swaying willow trees along the riverbank or down shaded pathways through stands of exotic trees that harbored deer and enclosures for monkeys and strange, beautiful birds.[24]

For Patrick's men standing in the Warrenton Road, this elegance was no more. The resort had become transformed by war into a scene of "riddled and broken brick work, scattered furniture, partly in fragments, open doors and windows revealing naught but bare and defaced walls, charred and withered trees, smoke, ashes and desolation." The Springs had begun a sharp decline at the start of the war; the final blow had occurred the day before Patrick's arrival, when the 9th New York Cavalry rode down from Waterloo Bridge with four cannon to clash with Confederate forces occupying the resort. During the artillery duel that ensued, shells struck the Pavilion and another building, setting them on fire, and resulting in the final destruction of the complex.[25]

Meanwhile, down along the stream, a disappointed Patrick looked out from beneath a broad-brimmed gray felt hat to find that nothing remained but the pilings of the bridge the Federals had previously constructed. When he turned to some men nearby to inquire about a suitable ford, one of his staff, recognizing the individuals as Confederate soldiers, yelled "Gray Coats!" Patrick instinctively drew his sword and waved it menacingly over his head. The Rebel Muskets flamed, sending the first group of Union officers galloping back to the infantry column near the hotel. Patrick followed, acting as if nothing terribly unusual had happened. In a normal voice he turned to Colonel Rogers of the 21st and said, "You may deploy two companies, one on each side of the road and advance to the river."[26] As the companies formed and started forward, Longstreet's artillery opened from the opposite bank, picking up the tempo of the fight and prompting Patrick to deploy the rest of his brigade. The 21st and 35th regiments advanced along the road, while the 23d and the 20th NYSM moved off to guard the left flank. The 23d had to double-quick across an open field under intense artillery fire for a quarter of a mile to reach a position in the corner of a wood. Companies G and K of the 23d went forward to clear the riverbank of Rebels and act as skirmishers. For the remainder of the day the artillery dueled across the river while the infantry hugged the ground for cover. The 23d reported no casualties.[27]

Toward evening the firing slackened as a lone Rebel horseman appeared on the opposite heights carrying a flag of truce. Thousands of soldiers watched as the man rode slowly down to the crossing leading a group of infantry who guarded a woman prisoner dressed as a Union soldier. Suspecting that the requested parley for the woman's release was being staged as a ruse to allow the Rebels to withdraw some of their troops to safety, Patrick abruptly ended all contact with the enemy and sent his men back within their own lines.[28]

At the same time the woman in blue interrupted the fight at the Springs, far to the rear of Patrick's brigade the leading cavalry regiment of Jackson's 24,000-man column was pounding down the road from Gainesville to Bristoe Station on the Orange and Alexandria Railroad. Jackson's men had traveled fifty-five miles in two days under a hot August sun to arrive squarely athwart Pope's communication and supply lifeline back to Alexandria and Washington. Brushing aside slight Union resistance, Jackson's men entered Bristoe, wrecked two trains, and cut the telegraph line. Early the next morning Jackson's main force pushed east three and a half miles along the tracks to Manassas Junction, where Pope had stockpiled supplies for his army. For much of August 27, Jackson's hungry troops at the Junction broke open Yankee boxcars and storehouses to feast on everything from common soldier fare to such delicacies as canned lobster that had been ordered up for Union officers' mess tables. The total success of the operation must have surprised even Jackson.

Pope did not panic. Although he now had to abandon his strong Rappahannock line, he saw an opportunity to defeat Jackson's isolated wing before Longstreet could come to Jackson's rescue. Moreover, he now had with him the additional strength of Maj. Gen. Samuel P. Heintzelman's Third Corps and Maj. Gen. Fitz John Porter's Fifth Corps from the Army of the Potomac. Before dawn on the 27th, Pope directed his army, now totaling about 75,000 men, to turn east and converge on Jackson's force of 24,000.[29] McDowell fell back with his own and Sigel's corps through Warrenton and onto the turnpike toward Gainesville. Maj. Gen. Jesse L. Reno's Ninth Corps and part of Heintzelman's corps took a parallel course through the village of Greenwich. Gen. Joseph Hooker's division of Heintzelman's corps led Porter's corps along the railroad to Bristoe Station. Banks's Second Corps, owing to the losses it had suffered at Cedar Mountain, remained in the rear as a reserve. In the critical hours that followed, Pope repeatedly pleaded with his commanders to push forward their attack. If they moved quickly, he promised, "We shall bag the whole crowd."[30]

King's division, with King now back in active command, left Sulphur Springs about noon on August 27. McDowell rode along the moving encouraging and threatening—"savage as a meat axe," one aide remembered, in verbally punishing any man he perceived to be a shirker or straggler. In return, one soldier noted, "many a deep and bitter curse with threats to shoot McD[owell] when occasion offered were uttered by the men."[31] When Patrick asked McDowell at Warrenton to let his command halt and receive rations, the commander responded that they would "have pinched bellies and a Hell of a fight before we could eat or rest." The march continued into a rainy night so dark that Patrick's staff occasionally had to dismount and literally feel the ground for the road. Arriving at their bivouac site between New Baltimore and Buckland, a line of men took position across the road to snag stragglers before they unwittingly stumbled past in the dark.[32]

At nine o'clock on August 27, Pope issued new orders for the next day's march, by which he intended to "bag" Jackson at Manassas Junction. Sigel's corps would lead the advance from Gainesville along the Warrenton Turnpike. Once he crossed the Manassas Gap Railroad Sigel would pivot to the southeast, keeping his right flank on the railroad as a guide to the junction. McDowell would follow Sigel on the turnpike connecting with and extending Sigel's left flank toward the Manassas-Sudley Road (modern Route 234). The resulting immense arc of advancing Union troops, stretching from Bristoe Station to near the Manassas-Sudley Road, would fix Jackson at the junction and block his escape routes north for a possible reunion with Longstreet.[33]

Had Pope concentrated his forces at Gainesville, he would have remained between the two wings of Lee's army. But unbeknownst to Pope, Jackson, about the same time Pope issued his nine o'clock order, dispatched his lead division from Manassas Junction to the north up the Manassas-Sudley Road. Jackson intended, once all of his troops had been gathered in the area of Sudley Church, north of the Warrenton Turnpike and about five miles from Gainesville, to lie low, rest his command, await Longstreet (approaching on the route of Thoroughfare Gap, Haymarket, and Gainesville), and look for new opportunities to fight. Thus, McDowell, in conformance to Pope's orders directing him to Manassas Junction, would in effect pass Jackson moving in the opposite direction; as a result, Pope lost his best chance to snare his wily opponent.

On the morning of August 28, McDowell's command advanced on the turnpike in the order of Sigel's corps, Reynolds's division, and then King's division. McDowell sent Ricketts's division to Haymarket to watch for Longstreet's expected arrival at Thoroughfare Gap. Sigel, instead of aligning on the Manassas Gap Railroad as ordered, turned down the Manassas-Gainesville Road (modern Wellington Road) as a better and more convenient route to the junction.[34] Reynolds and King continued to march along the turnpike toward the crossroad community of Groveton, ready to find and align on Sigel's left flank.

Jackson, meanwhile, continued to harass and baffle Pope and Mc-Dowell from his position near Sudley Church. He advanced Col. Bradley T. Johnson's infantry brigade to occupy the high ground near the John C. Brawner farm, just west of Groveton along the turnpike. From there Johnson could block the turnpike from Gainesville to Centreville and thus stand across the path of Reynolds and King. When the head of Reynolds's column neared the crossroad of Pageland Lane, Johnson's artillery fired a few rounds at them, causing some casualties in the 8th Pennsylvania Reserves. McDowell and staff, riding at the head of the column, seemed to draw Johnson's fire. ("They must have recognized McDowell's Japanese washbowl," one aide joked in reference to the general's white hat.) Coming under fire, Reynolds's column halted while McDowell dismounted to sit under an apple tree near a small stream and study his maps.[35]

Around midday Reynolds deployed his troops and pushed forward to skirmish briefly with Johnson's troops. McDowell watched the action from high ground south of the pike known locally as Monroe Hill. At one point McDowell noticed a distant cloud of dust above the trees to the north and east, indicating a moving wagon train, and concluded that the enemy troops Reynolds faced consisted of only a plucky wagon-train guard. McDowell directed Reynolds to leave the turnpike and cautiously sweep south cross-country toward Manassas Junction, in cooperation with Sigel on his right.[36]

Like a fly hitting a spider web, Reynolds's action drew out more of Jackson's men from Sudley Church along Stony Ridge, within striking distance of the Warrenton Turnpike. Jackson's movement, for its part, had the effect of stretching out his line westward toward Longstreet's troops, who were at the time approaching Thoroughfare Gap.

The day was waning when King's division, marching behind Reynolds, took center stage along the turnpike. A little more than a mile before reaching Groveton, the head of King's column turned down Pageland Lane to fill the developing gap between Sigel and Reynolds. They had advanced but one mile, three of King's four brigades having made the turn, when the arrival of orders from Pope's headquarters to McDowell brought the column to a halt. Union troops had entered Manassas Junction to find only smoking ruins. Additional reports indicated that a strong Confederate force had passed through Centreville (actually one of Jackson's divisions under Gen. A. P. Hill joined him at Sudley Church over a roundabout route from Manassas Junction through Centreville). As Pope struggled to understand the confusing rush of conflicting events, King's division received a most welcome rest.[37]

Patrick's brigade that afternoon served as the division wagon-train guard, marching behind the wagons at the rear of King's column. When the order to rest came down the column, the men fell out to lie down in the shade of roadside trees or to attempt to satisfy their hunger by foraging the countryside for apples or corn. Some men of the 21st New York must have rubbed their eyes in delighted disbelief when a heavily laden sutler's wagon suddenly appeared, seemingly out of nowhere, like a plump deer walking out of the forest. The men were hot, tired and famished, and not about to pay the exorbitant prices of a "rascally sutler." "Clean him out!" someone from the 21st yelled. "There was a momentary swarming of blue jackets and caps, and then cheeses, loaves, jars, chains of sausages, and black bottles flew in every direction, so that all might share, and in less time than you have been reading it, all was over; the wagon stood empty and forlorn, and the crowd had dispersed."[38]

Late in the afternoon McDowell received an order from Pope to move King's division from Pageland Lane back to the turnpike and march it directly east to Centreville. Hatch's brigade took the lead, followed by Gibbon, Doubleday, the wagon train, then Patrick. The division artillery batteries spread out along the column.[39]

As the men groaned to their feet and formed a column of march, Mc-Dowell anxiously scanned the eastern horizon toward Centreville through his field glasses. His three divisions had become separated across eleven miles of countryside and were moving in different directions. Ricketts was marching west toward Thoroughfare Gap to counter Longstreet, King was traveling east on the turnpike toward Groveton through the area where Reynolds had previously skirmished with Jackson, and Reynolds had disappeared toward the southeast en route to Manassas Junction. Focusing his attention on the Groveton area, McDowell could see no evidence of Rebels in King's path. Just to be sure, he dispatched two cannon three hundred yards north of the pike to unlimber near the Brawner farm and fire exploratory rounds to the northeast toward Stony Ridge.[40] No response! Satisfied that King faced no immediate danger, McDowell rode off to catch up with Reynolds and meet with Pope somewhere near Manassas Junction.

With his division in motion, General King accepted an invitation from one of his battery commanders to take a meal "picnic fashion" at a shady spot beside a pond east of Pageland Lane and just south of the pike. As King sat and chatted with his staff, his troops passed slowly on the pike nearby. Across the road in the distance the bright red pants of Hatch's skirmishers [Zouaves] shone bright in the soft evening sunlight. The men seemed to glide up the grassy slope toward the Brawner farm and disappear into the woods to the east. One weary 6th Wisconsin soldier, not looking forward to yet another tiresome march, spoke for many when he turned to a comrade to say, "I tell you, this d—n war will be over and we will never get into a battle!" Up ahead Hatch's leading cavalry escort reached Groveton without incident. Apparently no one in the column advancing "quietly and serenely" along the pike realized that not three-quarters of a mile to their north more than twenty thousand Confederates were astir in the last fevered preparations for battle.[41]

Stonewall Jackson had earlier ridden out from Stony Ridge to a vantage point near the Brawner farm, where he could look down upon the slow-moving blue line of troops. Pondering the situation for a moment he realized that although Longstreet had yet to clear the mountain gap visible eight miles to the west, he could not simply watch King's troops pass his front to join with McClellan's reinforcements on the fortified heights of Centreville. At the same time, Jackson knew that if he revealed his position, Pope would surely turn all his forces against him. Jackson chose to give battle, first by sending his artillery out near the Brawner house to shell King's mile-long column of troops.

The first explosive "crack" from Jackson's guns jerked the tired eyes of King's men open and turned them toward the puffs of smoke visible along the far ridgeline. More rounds fired in quick secession left them in no doubt as to their peril. King and his officers immediately jumped up from their meals and scrambled for their horses. One man leaping into the saddle looked back astonished to see the general prostrate on the ground in the throes of another epileptic seizure.[42] King's division was thus plunged into the fight with Jackson near the Brawner farm without an overall commander. Each brigade was left to fight on its own.

The first of Jackson's artillery rounds struck the head of Hatch's column, sending his troops diving for cover. Most, later admitted one soldier, immediately dropped down flat and "lay so close to the ground that we must have left our impressions in the soil!"[43] A shell tore one man's head nearly from his body; around them fence rails exploded in a shower of splinters, and a round struck a nearby artillery caisson full of ammunition, which went up with a roar and sent great plumes of smoke skyward.[44]

Cannon fire quickly swept down the column to reach Gibbon's and Doubleday's troops. A small square of woods between the road and the Brawner farm screened Gibbon's westerners, but Doubleday's brigade found itself caught out in the open. Captain Noyes of Doubleday's staff later remembered, "For a single instant the ranks paused, as if uncertain what to do." About a half-dozen men were seen leaping the fence south of the road and running off. Others hugged the ground or furtively looked for cover from the exploding shells. Col. William Wainwright of the 76th New York ("Cortland Regiment") attempted to calm his men by riding out between the column and the source of danger and speaking to them. Significantly, he did not issue threats or demand from them the discipline of trained professional soldiers, which he knew to be impossible; nor did he appeal to their patriotism or the cause for which they fought. No, in a tone more pleading than angry he called out to his volunteers, "Oh, my boys, don't run, don't run. Think a moment how it would sound to say, 'the Seventy-sixth ran!'" His words had a "magic effect" and brought nearly every man back to his place.[45] They responded from a strong sense of duty and a fear that their actions would bring shame upon themselves, their regiment, and their families back home. Once Doubleday had steadied his brigade he moved it up behind Gibbon under the cover of the woods.

The men of Patrick's brigade, just west of Pageland Lane, watched the Rebel shells "piling the men of Gibbons' [sic] and Doubleday's brigades right and left upon the road." Then they came under fire themselves. The explosions stampeded the division trains and threw everything, according to Patrick, "into the greatest confusion and smash up." It was almost dark before Patrick managed to get his men and wagons into the woods south of the road and move them up along the road shoulder to within supporting distance of Gibbon and Doubleday. Patrick had only three of his regiments in hand; the 20th NYSM, wrote Patrick, "*had fled* and I could not get their whereabouts for more than two hours." The 23d took position on the left of the division near Pageland Lane, with Companies G and K advanced north of the pike as skirmishers.[46]

Gibbon, meanwhile, decided to send his battle-hardened 2d Wisconsin up through the woods to root out the irritating Rebel artillery. Emerging into a field they encountered not just artillery but also Brig. Gen. William B. Taliaferro's Division of infantry from Jackson's wing moving down on them from Stony Ridge in long battle lines. Gibbon rushed up the rest of his brigade in support, along with the 76th New York and the 56th Pennsylvania from General Doubleday's command. Patrick, however, refused to enter the fight on orders of the most junior brigade officer without direct instructions from his division commander, prompting Gibbon's bitter comment in his after-action report of the fighting: "Patrick's brigade remained immovable and did not fire a shot." Fighting practically alone, Gibbon felt; "I was permitted to be sacrificed."[47]

For the remainder of the battle Patrick's men stood inactive south of the road as the bright streaks of musket flame near the Brawner farm pierced the night like lighting. Technically, Patrick was right, since King had not officially relinquished command.[48] But given King's obvious poor physical condition and the opportunity to affect the battle, Patrick's inaction, in hindsight, seems inexcusable.

Around ten o'clock the battle lines disengaged, and Gibbon ordered his battered command back down to the turnpike. Patrick sent the 23d and 21st up to the battlefield to secure the area and assist in bringing back the wounded to torch-lit aid stations established near the pike.[49] During the night Jackson's troops settled back into a strong defensive position along the cuts and fills of an unfinished railroad bed two and a half miles long between Sudley Church and the Brawner farm (the grade had been prepared, but the ties and rails had not been laid).

Toward the end of the battle King recovered sufficiently to reemerge and meet with his brigade commanders. In the glow of a campfire at a fence corner along the pike they discussed what to do next. Initially, King proposed to have his troops remain in the area and await reinforcements. Hatch and Gibbon argued that the division was isolated and would be at a disadvantage if it stayed; Confederate prisoners had erroneously reported that King faced between sixty and seventy thousand of Jackson's men. Doubleday apparently spoke most strongly for staying and fighting it out. Years later Patrick implied in a letter to King's son that he did not attend the fateful meeting and thus had only a minor role in King's ultimate decision to fall back during the night seven miles to Manassas Junction.[50]

General Pope bristled with anger when he learned of King's decision to withdraw. Pope knew that both Sigel's and Reynolds's commands were working their way back toward the battlefield along the Manassas-Sudley Road (under his earlier Centreville orders) and would be in a position to support King at Groveton by daylight. Also, Ricketts, after battling Longstreet at Thoroughfare Gap, had fallen back to Gainesville, only two miles down the road from King. Had King massed this artillery and infantry on the dominating high ground from Monroe's Hill to Groveton, Longstreet could not have hinged upon Jackson's line the next morning south of the turnpike, and the battle would have progressed quite differently.

Patrick did not learn of King's intended movement to the junction until early morning. About three o'clock his men hurriedly gathered up what wounded they could carry and followed the rest of the division down a narrow farm lane south of the turnpike to the Manassas-Gainesville Road. Their stomachs ached from lack of food, and their senses were numbed from having had almost no sleep since six the previous morning. At sunrise they arrived in sight of the blackened ruins of Manassas Junction, and, after Patrick scavenged some hardtack and coffee for them, they lay down along the railroad tracks and fell into a sound sleep.[51]

Dawn of August 29 revealed Pope's grand strategy in disarray. King's retreat had opened the way for the two wings of Lee's army to combine near Groveton in a favorable position to give battle. McDowell could not be found, having the night before become lost attempting to ride from Manassas Junction back toward the sounds of battle. King appeared at Union headquarters at the William Weir home, "Liberia," declaring that for health reasons he could not exercise command of his division. After saying good-bye to Patrick, King departed for Washington, leaving Hatch to take temporary command of the division.[52]

Discouragement and failure seemed to dog Pope's every effort. Still, he did not waver from his single-minded obsession to "bag" Jackson. He convinced himself that the night before King had stumbled onto Jackson while the Confederates were trying to retreat toward the Shenandoah Valley. On the morning of the 29th Pope directed Sigel to attack Jackson at first light and bring him to bay as the rest of his army closed in on Groveton. He ordered Gen. Fitz John Porter at the head of the Fifth Corps from the Army of the Potomac to pick up King's wandering division at the junction and lead it back up the Manassas-Gainesville Road toward Jackson's right flank, thought to be somewhere near the Brawner farm.

After but a few hours of sleep, Patrick's men awakened on the 29th to the sound of cheering. Porter's corps, including two brigades of regulars, was passing out on the road to Gainesville. Patrick's voice bellowed above the noise calling upon his men to prepare to march: "Rapidly my men! Rapidly!" he shouted. Before departing, Patrick addressed the brigade, "My men! We *return* to the battle ground of last night. You fight in good company. You follow the regulars." Lest this statement of admiration for the reputed discipline and soldierly qualities of the regulars be misunderstood, Patrick added: "*You fight well.* I've no fault to find. Keep well closed up, and be prompt to obey orders. Colonel Rogers, lead off by the right flank." The New Yorkers swung in behind Porter's troops, and Patrick rode forward to join Porter at the head of the column as a guide.[53]

Patrick's troops had marched to a half-mile beyond Bethlehem Church when McDowell arrived, wearing a long duster coat and his "Chinese summer hat," to reclaim his division. McDowell ordered Patrick to cut across to the Manassas-Sudley Road and follow the rest of the Third Corps troops to the battlefield.[54] In late afternoon Patrick's brigade arrived on ground fought over thirteen months before during the First Battle of Bull Run (Manassas). His regiments took position in reserve on the Benjamin Chinn farm west of the Manassas-Sudley Road. Fighting could be heard north of the turnpike, and the acrid smoke of battle hung in the warm, still air.

From dawn to dusk on August 29 Pope ineffectually hurled at least four separate and uncoordinated attacks against Jackson's strong defensive line along the unfinished railroad. Around eleven o'clock that morning Lee arrived with Longstreet's troops from Thoroughfare Gap. Lee placed Longstreet's men on Jackson's right flank to extend the Confederate line south of the Brawner farm and turnpike to a point beyond the Gainesville Road, thereby effectively blocking Porter's path. By evening, Lee had secured his position. His two wings formed powerful jaws ready to close on and crush any Union advance westward along the turnpike.

Pope, however, continued to labor under the illusion that Jackson still sought an opportunity to escape. At dusk on the 29th he seized upon sightings of Rebel wagons moving west on the pike as a further indication of Jackson's intent and ordered that the "pursuit" be pushed. McDowell responded by ordering Hatch to double-quick his troops out the pike and disrupt Jackson's plans. In the twilight Hatch led Doubleday's brigade and his own (under Col. Timothy Sullivan) north on the Manassas-Sudley Road to its intersection with the Warrenton Turnpike in a bowl of low ground formed by Young's Branch. As he approached the intersection he noticed McDowell and his staff in the yard of the prominent red sand-stone house and drovers' tavern owned by Henry Matthews. McDowell called out to him, "The enemy is in full retreat." Pointing out the pike to the west, he shouted, "Pursue him rapidly!" The eager, cheering, column briskly turned onto the pike and disappeared beyond a rise of ground into a brilliant golden sunset.[55]

About dark Patrick's brigade followed Hatch from its position near the Chinn house. A short distance out the pike it turned off the road on the right to support a line of Union cannons on a high ridge near the house of John Dogan, "Rosefield." About one mile ahead, in the gathering dark-ness, Hatch's men were engaged with troops of Longstreet on the heights near Groveton. Strangely, the men back near Dogan's could see but not hear the fighting. Lt. Col. David Hunter Strother, serving on Pope's staff, watched fascinated in the stillness as "the sparkling lines of musketry shone in the darkness like fire-flies in a meadow, while the more brilliant flashes of artillery might have been mistaken for swamp meteors."[56]

Patrick had not been long at Dogan's when Colonel Sullivan galloped up to say that his command had been cut to pieces and to ask him for assistance. Despite the darkness, Patrick pushed his brigade forward to occupy the crest of the intervening ridge between the Dogan house and Groveton. His regiments formed battle lines to the right of the road with the 35th and 21st directly in front of the 23d and 20th NYSM. When skir-mishers from the 21st tried to advance a short distance into a cornfield they made contact with the enemy. Patrick had his men lie down on the back slope of the ridge and wait for the enemy to appear above them on the slight rise of ground, where they would be silhouetted against the night sky.[57]

Slowly the remnants of Doubleday's and Sullivan's brigades fell back, uncovering Patrick's front. At one point a squadron of the 2d New York Cavalry under Lt. Col. Judson Kilpatrick came thundering along the turn-pike past the Southern Tier men in a wild charge designed to check Long-street's advance and capture a Rebel battery. The Confederates allowed the riders through an opening in their ranks and then turned to shat-ter their formations with converging point-blank musket volleys. Only a small number of horsemen returned out of the blackness to find safety behind Patrick's isolated strongpoint.[58]

A lull in the fighting occurred as Longstreet reformed his lines for a re-newal of his attack. Soon Patrick's pickets ran in to alert the prone soldiers that the Rebels were coming. The New Yorkers nervously checked their rifles for the last time and scanned the forward crest for any discernable movement. The minutes passed slowly, then:

> We hear them; first a subdued murmur, then the clanking of arms, and the "scuffing" tread of feet in the dry grass, and then the words of command and exhortation . . . and then we clearly hear the "halt" and "close up," echoed along their line, and the subdued voices of angry officers urge up the laggards and the grumblers. Every word is now distinctly audible, but nothing can we see; their line is evidently halted to restore order, and in a moment they will advance again. Suddenly—"*crash!*" and a stream of flame bursts from our left and dashes in repetition along the line.[59]

The Rebel volley flew over the heads of the 35th lying next to the road. The men instinctively jumped to their feet to return fire, presenting their animated forms to the frightened men of the 23d behind, who fired into them by mistake. Caught between the two fires, the commander of the 35th yelled out to his men, "Cease firing, fix bayonets, forward, double-quick, charge!" Their bold attack checked the enemy advance momentarily until a Confederate flanking movement on Patrick's right forced his entire command to fall back behind the Union guns near the Dogan house.[60]

Riding back with his staff toward the Dogan house, Patrick had reached a dry ditch when he received a challenge from an unknown column of troops in the road. When Patrick identified his brigade, the reply shot back, "Surrender or we fire." Patrick's group bolted for safety up the rise toward the house. A sharp volley followed, wounding two of Patrick's staff—one being Lt. John V. Bouvier, great grandfather to First Lady Jacqueline Bouvier Kennedy. After putting his men into bivouac for the night along the ridge behind the guns and in the pike just west of the Stone house intersection, Patrick took up his headquarters in the Dogan house. Many of the wounded from the fight took refuge in Matthews's Stone house, and throughout the night they filled the air with their cries.[61]

On the night of the 29th, General Lee could look with satisfaction on the events of the day. Since Pope seemed willing to squander his army's strength and blood against Jackson's strong defensive position, Lee concluded to let Pope continue his costly attacks on the 30th. If, on the other

hand, Pope refused battle, Lee planned to pursue his campaign of maneuver by sending Jackson to turn Pope's right flank via the Little River Turnpike (modern Route 50) to Jermantown (Germantown), thereby placing
his troops between Pope and Washington.[62]

Pope spent a difficult night at his headquarters on a high knoll behind
the Stone house known as Buck Hill. A bright sunrise on the 30th did
little to help clear up his muddled thinking about the battlefield situation. Strother observed him nervously smoking and pacing the ground
by himself "evidently solving some problem of contradictory evidence in
his mind." Pope knew by this time that Longstreet had joined Jackson on
the battlefield, but he persisted in believing that Longstreet had kept his
troops north of the pike behind Jackson to facilitate a general Confederate withdrawal. In a state of mental paralysis, Pope refused to consider all
evidence to the contrary. Twice General Patrick rode to Buck Hill to warn
Pope and McDowell of a strong and aggressive enemy force remaining
in their front blocking the turnpike. "You are mistaken," they told him
on one occasion, suggesting that if he "get off and get some coffee" he
would "feel better natured." "Pursue them with your whole command,"
they chided him, "for we can't afford to let them escape." At one point
McDowell repeated Pope's chant, "We have got to bag them." Frustrated,
Patrick left Buck Hill wondering out loud to McDowell on which side of
the "bag" they would soon find themselves. Strother later remembered
the two commanders spending the morning together under a tree, "waiting for the enemy to retreat."[63]

A lull in the fighting allowed for the shifting of troops to new positions. Porter's Fifth Corps arrived from the far Union left to relieve Patrick's brigade near the Dogan house. Patrick then marched his brigade up
the Manassas-Sudley Road to support the Union right flank near Sudley
Church. Time passed slowly until around noon, when Pope finally shook
himself from his torpor and issued orders for his troops to renew the
"pursuit" of Lee.[64]

Porter would command the advance, made up of his own corps and
King's division under Hatch. Patrick's brigade then rejoined the division
by marching back down the Manassas-Sudley Road through the great blue
drifts of soldiers, from Pope's army, that covered the adjacent hillsides.
Many of Pope's soldiers readily accepted the notion that the Rebels were
retreating and jeered at Patrick's troops marching by with their stretcher
bearers prominently placed in the column. Reaching the turnpike, the New

Yorkers halted to rest and kindle fires with dry cornstalks for a comforting cup of coffee.[65]

While they waited, George Edgcomb took the opportunity to visit the Stone house near the road intersection. He entered the hallway and continued up the stairs to the second floor, where he found a wounded Union soldier whose leg had been amputated above the knee. Edgcomb gave the man water from his canteen but could do no more, as the call came for the 23d to advance.[66]

Plans called for Porter first to break the crust of Jackson's rear guard along the unfinished railroad and then sweep to their left front and overwhelm Lee's vulnerable army in retreat along the pike. Porter had available two of his own divisions, amounting to eight thousand men and at least five thousand men under Hatch. Hatch's troops followed Porter's out the pike and then to the right, across fields fought over the day before and still littered with the blackening corpses of both blue and gray. They formed for the attack on Porter's right in a thick strip of oak and chestnut on the east side of the Groveton-Sudley Road facing and within striking distance of Jackson's line along the unfinished railroad. Confederate artillerymen noticed the Union troops getting into position and opened a harassing fire. Hatch's men paid little heed to the danger and even found amusement in the antics of a large Newfoundland dog that leaped about the fields chasing spent and ricocheting cannon balls.[67]

Porter's attack would cover about a half-mile of front and have a quarter-mile of depth. Hatch, holding the right of the line, ensured that his force had the punch needed to breach Jackson's line by stacking his brigades into seven lines of battle. Sullivan's brigade would spearhead Hatch's advance, the 30th and 24th New York regiments in front of the 22d and 14th NYSM. Next came Patrick's brigade, the 35th and 21st in front of the 23d and the 20th NYSM. Farther back formed the battle-weary and depleted brigades of Gibbon and Doubleday. Since the railroad grade gradually closed with and crossed the Groveton-Sudley Road to the right of Hatch, his troops had less distance to travel than Porter's men did before crossing bayonets with the enemy.[68]

The regiments of Porter's Fifth Corps on Hatch's left had the difficult task of charging across about five hundred yards of open pastureland. The final hundred yards rose up a steep slope to the railroad grade in an area known as "Deep Cut," named for its nearly vertical man-made excavation, ten to fifteen feet deep. As soon as his troops emerged from the woods, they would be subject to the fire of Col. Stephen D. Lee's eighteen-gun artillery battalion, aligned forward of and perpendicular to the railroad bed on high ground near the Brawner farm, about three-quarters of a mile off Porter's left flank.

Porter's commanders knew that the prospects for the attack did not look good. Few in the Union ranks had any doubt that Jackson's men still occupied a strong defensive position in force. Before the assault General Hatch was heard to order his artillery placed where it could cover an anticipated retreat.[69]

The attack got under way about half past two in the afternoon. First a thin line of green-clad skirmishers from the U.S. Sharpshooters emerged from the tree line to clear the pasture of Confederates preparatory to the main assault. Three cheers then rose from the woods followed by the slow advance of the Union battle lines. Each regiment formed in the standard two ranks, the men standing shoulder to shoulder, with a thin third line of file closers made up of lieutenants and noncommissioned officers intent on keeping the forward ranks aligned properly during the advance and filling in any gaps caused by Rebel fire.

The lines flowed out from the trees and across the road, collapsing the rail fence as they entered the pasture. "The advance began in magnificent style" one Confederate officer looking down from the railroad cut would remember, with "lines as straight as an arrow, all fringed with glittering bayonets and fluttering with flags." But soon little puffs of smoke appeared above the ranks where S. D. Lee's artillery rounds exploded, and below each puff "lay a pile of bodies, and half a dozen or more staggering figures . . . leaning on their muskets and then slowly limping back to the rear."[70]

The 30th and 24th New York regiments of Hatch's command could advance only a short distance before the dark lines of the enemy rose above the railroad embankment to fire a devastating musket volley that felled a third of the 24th and staggered both regiments. The officers immediately stepped forward to try and re-form the dazed and disoriented survivors. File closers shouted their threats and entreaties above the din of battle for the men to close up, keep steady, and do their duty. Officers raised their swords ready to strike with the flat the back of any man who showed the first sign of fear that might infect comrades and compromise the integrity of the moving line. The file closers of the 24th had instructions to shoot any man who attempted to run.[71]

The New Yorkers managed to close ranks to the center as the colors were advanced. Again they pushed forward elbow to elbow into the smoke that now obscured the field. With nerves raw and frayed, they flinched at each shell that exploded overhead and shrank from the thudding sound of comrades being hit. Pressing on, they tried to avoid stepping on the dead or the living wounded, who pleaded with upraised arms for assistance. As they crossed a meandering trace of a wet-weather stream midpoint in the field, another fusillade of enemy bullets threw them back, "literally spending their force in the bellies of the victims." The lines disintegrated and melted away. Only by the greatest exertions of the officers did a number of men brave the deadly storm of projectiles to reach the railroad embankment. Too few to continue, one man recalled, they "lay as flat to the slope as we could, crawling occasionally to the top, and discharging our muskets, held horizontally over our heads, in the direction which seemed to afford a chance of hitting somebody on the other side of the grade."[72]

Sullivan's second line, having witnessed the destruction of the forward regiments, hesitated to move forward from the cover of the woods and roadbed. At the same time, Patrick's brigade struggled forward through the dense woods, which had filled with the shirkers from other commands and wounded men who were trying to make their way to the rear. When the 35th and 21st regiments neared the road, Patrick had them lie down and await further orders.

The attack had stalled near the streambed when General Hatch emerged through the smoke yelling orders for Patrick's men at the road to move forward in support of the hard-pressed troops fighting at the embankment. The 35th tried to advance but soon became pinned down by S. D. Lee's artillery on the left front and could do little. Colonel Rogers on the right shouted to his men, "Rise up Twenty-first! Fix bayonets! Forward! Double-quick! March!" Bayonets clattered onto rifles, and the line dressed as if on parade. Giving out a cheer, the men entered the road, now filled with the dead and wounded. After they had climbed what remained of the roadside fence and reached the open field, the officers dressed ranks and swung the left of the line forward to align on the embankment. Though hit by searing "hell-blast sweeps" of rifle and artillery fire, the 21st managed to stumble forward through the smoke. "Screams of agony and hoarse commands mingle," one 21st man recalled the experience, "and all around men are lying down to die." Survivors pushed in toward the streambed, where they found scant cover from which to add their meager contribution of lead against the strongly posted Confederates. No other regiment from Patrick's brigade ventured out into the storm-swept field except the 20th NYSM, from the brigade's second line, which bravely advanced through woods close to the embankment to protect the right of Hatch's attack. Late in the fight the 23d moved up to the road but went no farther.[73]

As additional troops piled up behind the streambed, the slaughter intensified. Battle lines dissolved as quickly as officers could form them; the fight degenerated into a confused free-for-all, with individuals displaying the broad range of human emotion from cowardice to extreme bravery. All the while the "pounding breath" of S. D. Lee's guns continued to scythe with solid shot and exploded shell fragments the crawling, seething, mass of humanity that desperately clung to the shallow ditch in the center of the open field. When one stunned and severely wounded man of the 21st arrived at the dry ditch he discovered that it had become wet with blood. In shock from his wound, he could comprehend little of what transpired around him. "Like a dream in which minutes are ages, . . . I dimly see the shifting changes of the fight. The ditch is deep with the wounded and the dead. . . . All around [men] are dropping, quietly, or crawling to the ditch or toward the rear; the thick smoke envelopes all, the ceaseless roar of batteries and musketry . . . the shriek and crash of shell and shrapnel, the yells of excited officers and blood maddened men, mingle wierdly [sic] in my befogged brain, as I lie here between the dying and the dead."[74]

Not half an hour after the fight had begun, General Hatch, despite a painful head wound, sought out Porter to protest against any further slaughter of their troops. With only about three of his available brigades fully engaged, Porter concluded that the attack had been a failure, and he ordered everyone back to the road.[75]

Many of the men hugging the embankment were hesitant to cross back over the killing ground near the ditch to reach the safety of the woods beyond the road. One soldier looking back on the torrent of artillery rounds striking the ground and throwing up dirt was reminded of a millpond in a shower. Some simply surrendered rather than face what appeared to be certain death in retreat. Others made it back as best they could, every man for himself. General Porter tried to halt them at the road calling, "Form here, men." Too shaken and demoralized to listen, many continued to the

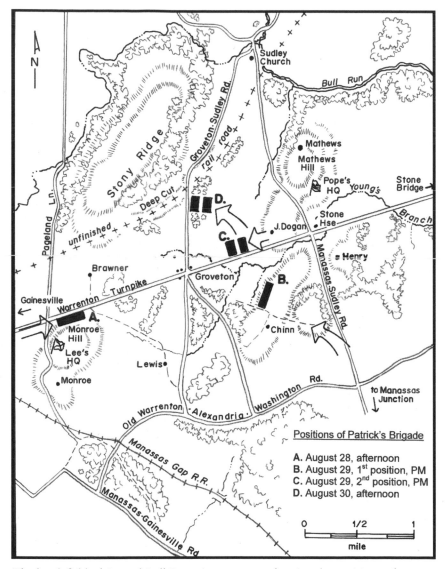

The battlefield of Second Bull Run, August 1862, showing the positions of Patrick's brigade. *(John Heiser)*

rear, where Porter had established a cavalry screen to halt the fugitives and prevent a general panic.[76]

The rapid Union retreat left the 23d practically alone at the edge of the woods. Soon Jackson's victorious soldiers appeared on the heels of the retreating Yankees, while Union artillery fire ranged dangerously close. Fearing that the Rebels might sweep across the road and pocket his command, Lieutenant Colonel Crane ordered the 23d back to the rear by right of companies. In perfect order, color bearer Lorenzo Sykes from Company H led the 23d through the woods and into a field under the gaze of General Patrick. When some of Jackson's men threatened to cut off the escape route of the 23d and 35th regiments, Patrick ordered the 35th to furl its colors to conceal its identity. Patrick managed to lead his men out of danger to a point behind about thirty Union cannon massed on the ridge near the Dogan house.[77]

Now Lee's fighting blood was up. Sensing this as one of those supreme moments on which battles turn, Lee ordered a general Confederate counterattack, which got under way about four o'clock. Longstreet's 28,000 fresh troops stormed east from the area of Monroe's Hill south of the turnpike to rout two isolated New York regiments and drive on toward Pope's left and rear.

Pope and McDowell frantically tried to rush troops south of the turnpike to Chinn Ridge, the Manassas-Sudley Road, and Henry Hill—sites all too familiar to Union veterans of the First Battle of Bull Run. If Longstreet's troops could capture the Stone house intersection or the stone bridge over Bull Run, they would block Pope's retreat route on the turnpike, and Pope's army would face annihilation. The blue lines held, however, not through any leadership by Generals Pope or McDowell but because of the tenacity and courage of the veteran regiments. As these men fought a heroic rear-guard action, thousands of their comrades funneled into the turnpike and headed out the road toward Centreville. McDowell, "looking nearly exhausted with fatigue and excitement," took position near the Stone house harassing the troops with verbal bursts of "Quick! quick! They're driving us!" Eventually he too joined the river of dispirited soldiers heading east toward Washington; he was last seen riding out the turnpike amid a flock of aides shouting, "Make room for the general!"[78]

Before departing the battlefield, drummer Edgcomb returned to the Stone house to discover the wounded soldier he had encountered earlier still present and eager to escape with the army. Edgcomb and a comrade placed him on a stretcher and started down the crowded road toward Centreville. Having to stop occasionally to catch their breath, the stretcher bearers finally gave out and had to abandon the man at the roadside near the bridge. For the rest of his life Edgcomb would wonder about the soldier's fate.[79]

The night of August 30 was dark, with a quarter-moon. Units became so mixed up on the roads that many soldiers spent the night wandering about Centreville searching for the guideboards that identified corps, divisions, and brigades. Pope arrived to find nineteen thousand fresh troops from McClellan's army under Major Generals Edwin V. Sumner and William B. Franklin waiting for him at or near Centreville, but little fight remained in either the defeated Pope or the wreck of his army. Lieutenant Colonel Crane spoke for most of Pope's soldiers at that moment when he later wrote, "No recollections of my short life could bring up an hour of such utter dejection and despondency. I felt as though all was lost."[80]

Early on the 31st Patrick detached the 21st and 23d regiments to guard a wagon train on an eight-mile march to Fairfax Court House. On September 1, the 35th and 20th NYSM joined them just outside Fairfax, and the reunited brigade started back toward Centreville. About halfway in their journey, General Joseph Hooker ordered them to march rapidly to Jermantown on the Little River Turnpike to protect the right of Pope's army against another turning movement by Stonewall Jackson. Hoffman's Southern Tiers spent a rainy afternoon occupying abandoned Confederate rifle pits and listening to the sounds of battle three miles up the road near Ox Hill. The Battle of Chantilly, or Ox Hill, resulted in heavy losses on both sides, including the deaths of Union generals Philip Kearny and Isaac I. Stevens, but it checked Jackson's advance.[81]

Pope's army fell back to Fairfax Court House and eventually to a safe haven within the outer defenses of the capital. As a result of his precipitous retreat, Pope had to abandon his supply bases at Bristoe Station and Falmouth. At Bristoe eleven locomotives and 141 freight cars filled with hundreds of thousands of rations, along with quartermaster, hospital, and ordnance stores, went up in smoke to prevent their falling into the hands of the enemy.[82] At Fredericksburg Union surgeon Daniel Holmes began evacuating 250 of his patients from the Woolen Mill hospital to Falmouth as early as August 28.[83] The next day rumors of a Rebel advance on the city initiated a mass exodus of more than a thousand blacks, who crowded into the train depot and filled the Chatham Wire Bridge on the road to Aquia Landing.[84] Early on the 31st General Burnside ordered the Union evacuation of Fredericksburg and the destruction of all government property that could not be transported.[85] His soldiers spread tar and wood chips over the three wooden river bridges that McDowell's troops had worked so hard to build and maintain throughout the previous summer.

By evening they had set fire to the machine shop and foundry, the three river bridges, the depot and all government stores and facilities; as one cavalryman of the rear guard recorded, "by their light we followed the retreating column toward Aquia." The man also noted, "There was great rejoicing in the city all day, and in the evening grew boisterous."[86]

Pope's army had suffered terrible losses during the campaign: 1,747 killed, 8,452 wounded, and 4,263 missing. Patrick's brigade had 56 killed, 334 wounded, and 178 missing. The Cortland Volunteers had but three wounded. Lieutenant Colonel Crane concluded from the low number of casualties in the 23d (one killed, seventeen wounded, twenty-six missing) that "Providence has thus far seemed to favor us."[87]

Pope and McDowell joined the head of Hatch's column as it marched in retreat along the Little River Turnpike back toward Washington. At Annandale it turned north on a by-road toward Patrick's old camping ground at Upton's Hill. There Pope and McDowell met General McClellan, who had ridden out from Washington on orders to take charge of Pope's defeated army as it arrived within the outlying Washington defenses. McClellan sat stiffly on his horse in full uniform as Hatch's weary, dust-covered column approached. Pope apparently was so absorbed in his thoughts that he rode past the waiting general and had to turn back to meet him. After a short conversation concerning the military situation, the generals bowed to each other in parting, thus ending the Second Battle of Bull Run.[88] Pope then rode off in disgrace to fight Indians in Minnesota, McDowell to languish in western posts until his retirement in 1882.

General Hatch, having previously suffered Pope's wrath while serving as his cavalry chief early in the campaign, could not let the moment pass without adding to Pope's humiliation. Turning his head to face his waiting troops, Hatch shouted, "Boys, McClellan is in command again; three cheers!" The men responded joyously, their cheers reverberating up and down the column.[89]

CHAPTER 8

Battle Autumn

On September 5 and 6, 1862, the weary, ill-equipped columns of Lee's army of nearly fifty thousand men[1] splashed across White's Ford on the Potomac River near Leesburg, Virginia, and headed north into Maryland. Lee intended by this bold stroke to carry the war's burdens from Virginia to the relatively unspoiled Northern soil, to rekindle Southern loyalties of long-suffering Marylanders held forcibly in the Union, and to sustain the momentum of Southern victory begun on the Virginia Peninsula. A successful campaign north of the Potomac would also discourage the Northern war effort and encourage wavering foreign interests to support the Southern cause.

McClellan responded by ordering his field army of about 85,000 men[2] back across the Potomac at Washington, D.C. Patrick's brigade left Upton's Hill about one on the morning of September 7 to join the long columns of men filling the moonlit web of roads leading to the Potomac bridges. After hours of frustrating starts and stops, at daybreak King's division crossed Aqueduct Bridge, marched through slumbering Georgetown, past the White House on Pennsylvania Avenue, and then out Seventh Street northward. Once in Maryland, McClellan's army advanced on a broad arc, intending to maintain contact with Lee's forces advancing north and east of the mountains and at the same time to protect and screen the cities of Washington and Baltimore. King's division marched as part of Maj. Gen. Joseph Hooker's First Corps, which, along with the

Ninth Corps, constituted Maj. Gen. Ambrose Burnside's right wing of the Army of the Potomac.

Late on the afternoon of September 7 McClellan and twenty or thirty of his staff and escort departed Washington to join the advancing army. Riding out Pennsylvania Avenue near H Street, he happened to pass the Secretary of the Navy Gideon Welles, out for an evening stroll with his son. McClellan stopped to say good-bye. Welles, one of McClellan's few remaining political allies, had come to share the growing concern in Washington that the commander lacked the vigor necessary to prosecute the war effectively. Lee's apparent invasion of the North demonstrated that the war was expanding and moving down new paths that McClellan did not seem to understand or appreciate. An air of caution and indecision about him did not bode well for the coming campaign. Still, when McClellan spoke of his intent to launch a bold forward movement, it gave Welles hope. "Success to you, then," he called up to the general, and added, "with all my heart."[3] McClellan turned to rejoin the cavalcade of officers that rode clattering off into the evening shadows toward a dark future.

The lively strains of "Maryland, My Maryland," sung by Southern soldiers as they marched from the Potomac to Frederick, were tempered by the cold reception they received from many western Marylanders. The bonds to the Union remained stronger in this part of the state than many Southern leaders had anticipated. Disappointed but undeterred in his immediate objective of drawing McClellan farther from Washington, Lee turned west from Frederick up through the passes of the parallel Catoctin and South mountain ranges, directing his troops toward a concentration at Hagerstown, Maryland.

Before proceeding to Hagerstown and conceivably into the broad Cumberland Valley of Pennsylvania, Lee halted his army to clear a passage for his troops and supplies through the Shenandoah Valley. Of primary concern to Lee were the Potomac River crossings and especially the Union garrisons at Martinsburg and at Harpers Ferry, where the Potomac slices through the mountains. Lee could not afford to leave these troops poised within easy striking distance of his Valley lifeline. Consequently, on September 10, Lee dispatched Stonewall Jackson with more than half of the Southern army to slip back, and, using the mountains as a screen, surround and capture Harpers Ferry. Lee would remain with the rest of the army, under Maj. Gen. James Longstreet, on the road to Hagerstown while keeping a careful watch on the mountain gaps from Frederick. The Confederate advance would resume when Jackson returned. Thus Lee once again accepted the inherent danger in separating his army in the face of the enemy, believing that the cautious nature of his opponent would provide Jackson time to accomplish his task.[4]

McClellan concentrated his army near Frederick on September 12 and 13. General King's division under General Hatch arrived late on the 13th after a leisurely series of short marches from Washington, covering about forty-five miles in six days. Patrick's men bivouacked that night east of the Monocacy River along the turnpike, overlooking a rich-hued late-summer landscape dotted by thousands of small white tents. The evening was warm and pleasant. After supper the men sat under the stars listening to military music floating up from the camps below.[5]

General Patrick spent the night of the 13th fussing and fuming at his headquarters in a private home beside the road. His corps was in disarray. The hapless McDowell had departed in a huff, dogged by absurd rumors of traitorous and cowardly behavior on the battlefield. McClellan spoke of the corps as being "in bad condition as to discipline and everything else." He had picked "Fighting Joe" Hooker as McDowell's replacement, thinking Hooker could "make them fight if anyone can." Patrick complained about his own division, expressing no confidence in its commander. He criticized Doubleday for his politics, was "disgusted" by Hatch, and called Gibbon, his severest critic since the Brawner farm fight on August 28, a "despicable toady" for his friendship and influence with McClellan. For Patrick the simmering kettle boiled over on the 13th, when he shot an angry note to the wing commander, General Burnside. As Patrick recorded in his journal, "I have said that neither patriotism nor self respect will permit me to serve many days longer in the position that I now hold." Patrick requested a transfer.[6]

McClellan, however, would forever mark September 13 as one of the happier days in his military career. The day began with his triumphal entry into Frederick. A staff member riding with McClellan recalled the streets crowded with cheering citizens and Union flags: "Old men rushed out and barred the passage of our cavalcade to grasp the hand of McClellen. Ladies brought out bouquets and flags to decorate his horse. Fathers held up their children for a kiss and a recognition."[7]

Meanwhile, not far from this joyous scene, the actions of two soldiers from the 27th Indiana would dramatically shift the fortunes of the campaign in McClellan's favor. After a wearisome march in the hot sun, the regiment stacked arms in a meadow west of the Monocacy and sank to the ground to rest. As a sergeant and a private lay chatting, one of them noticed a long envelope propped up by tall grass. Inside the soldiers found fresh cigars and a piece of writing paper. The cigars took precedence until a casual glance at the paper brought stares of amazement. The men held what appeared to be an official Confederate dispatch detailing the movements and destination of all major components of the Rebel army! The paper, marked "Special Order 191," quickly passed from hand to hand up to McClellan's headquarters. Once it was authenticated by his staff, McClellan crowed at his good luck. He now realized that beyond the mountains Lee's army was divided, its elements moving in different directions. A quick thrust through the mountain gaps against the weak Confederate center could save Harpers Ferry and at the same time split Lee's army into two easily digestible portions. Waving Special Order 191 before General Gibbon he exclaimed, "Here is a paper with which if I cannot whip 'Bobbie Lee,' I will be willing to go home."[8]

McClellan directed Jesse Reno's Ninth Corps, followed by Hooker's First Corps of about seventeen thousand men,[9] to advance the next morning out the turnpike along Turner's Gap through South Mountain. At the same time he ordered Gen. William B. Franklin's Sixth Corps to cross the mountain at Crampton's Gap, six miles below Turner's, and drive on to the south about seven miles to rescue the over eleven thousand Union soldiers holed up at Harpers Ferry. Although the plan seemed adequate, it reflected little of the dash or spirit necessary to turn McClellan's incredible good fortune into a decisive victory.

On Sunday, September 14, 1862, Patrick's men, numbering less than a thousand, awoke to the sound of reveille echoing down the valley of the Monocacy. Thousands of campfires sparked to flame, and quickly the smell of coffee drifted in the air. Above the hum and bustle of camp activity came shouted roll calls and orders to march. With battle imminent, General Patrick and Colonel Hoffman, although both quite ill, mounted their horses to take positions at the heads of their respective commands. Captain Clark and Lt. Leonard Hathaway of the Cortland Volunteers had been absent sick since the first week of September, leaving 2d Lt. Archibald D. DeVoe in charge of the company. On command, the column snaked down the hillside and across the stone bridge over the river to take its proper position behind Brig. Gen. George G. Meade's leading division of Hooker's corps. Ricketts's division brought up the rear.[10]

The morning was bright and warm. The spires of Frederick glistened in the sunlight, and church bells rang out their call to worship. An officer in King's division who entered Frederick later remembered the experience as "one continuous waving of flags, fluttering of handkerchiefs, tossing of bouquets, and cheering by our men, who grew fairly hoarse before they had passed through its main street."[11] How different the scene from that cold reception Patrick's men had experienced in Fredericksburg just four months before.

Leaving Frederick, the men grew silent as the sound of the church bells dimmed, replaced by the distant muttering of cannon fire. Wagons, cavalry, and artillery rumbled along the road, while the infantry took the sides, knocking down or clearing any impediments as they went. Gibbon, in the rear of Hatch's column, kept a line of troops spread out across the road to snag stragglers from forward units and send them back to the ranks to the sound of hoots, jeers, and a drum corps playing "The Rogue's March."[12] Cresting Catoctin Mountain, Hooker's troops had a magnificent view of Reno's men advancing across Middletown Valley. The crackling sound of musket fire and the white wreaths of smoke rolling up over the spine of South Mountain eight miles ahead indicated that the fight for the mountain passes had begun.

General Reno had made first contact at nine o'clock, striking the Confederate rear guard at Fox's Gap, just south of Turner's Gap. While Lee turned back additional troops from Longstreet's command to hold the passes, Hooker's corps rested in the noonday sun along Catoctin Creek, approximately four miles from the fighting. Here it remained until midafternoon, the men drinking coffee, listening to the sounds of battle, and possibly speculating on their future with their new division commander, Hatch, who officially took command at this time from the ailing Rufus King. Finally, orders arrived for elements of Hooker's corps to make a diversionary attack against the left of Longstreet's position at Turner's Gap.[13]

Meade's leading division marched out the Baltimore-National Pike toward Turner's Gap accompanied by a crowd of curious local citizens. Before entering the gap, Meade turned right onto the narrow wagon path of the old Hagerstown Road, which skirted the base of the mountain. Passing

Mount Tabor Church, which sat on a knoll to the right of the road, Meade deployed his troops for battle. Patrick's brigade, leading Hatch's four-brigade division, halted near the stone church. General Burnside ordered Gibbon's westerners detached from the division to attack up the pike directly into Turner's Gap.

Hooker and his staff surveyed the battlefield from the yard of the church. Beyond the road and a small stream the ground rose sharply to form a shieldlike hill about a thousand feet high and half a mile across below Turner's Gap. The pike disappeared on the left of the hill as it ascended through the gap. On the right side of the hill a ravine carried the old Hagerstown Road up near the crest, where it followed a narrow plateau before entering the pike at the gap just below the Mountain House Tavern. The hill had a generally open face, with an occasional cornfield, and a crown of hardwoods. As Hooker deployed his troops he could see no enemy activity. However, he did not know what the distant dark woods might conceal.

About four in the afternoon, with only a few hours of daylight left, Meade's Pennsylvanians began their ascent. At the first explosion of a Confederate shell nearby, the civilians tagging along with Meade's troops lost interest in the fight: "The effect upon the sightseers was magical, they breaking through our lines with wild screams, and knocking the boys around like toys. The men, with a bound, cleared the fences, and run like deer, but many of the poor women were left hanging on the posts by their petticoats and hoops, while the terrified children lay upon the ground and shrieked."[14]

In support of Meade's attack, Patrick ordered the 21st New York up the left side of the ravine. Three companies of the 21st deployed as skirmishers, followed by the rest of the regiment in line of battle. Before proceeding far they encountered an old woman who, much excited, warned of Rebels on the top of the hill. "There are hundreds of 'em up there," she exclaimed, waving her arms, "Don't you go. Some of you will get hurt!" The men laughed, breaking the tension for the moment, and the regiment moved on.[15]

Hatch now ordered Patrick to deploy the rest of his brigade and attack directly up the face of the hill. Patrick led the 35th New York forward and deployed the whole of it into an extended skirmish line stretching from near the left of the 21st almost to the pike. While Hoffman waited his turn to form behind the 35th, he tried to steady his 202 officers and men with a

brief speech. "Gentlemen," he shouted, "you all understand your duty as
well as I can tell you. All I ask of you is to do it as well as you know how.
Give strict attention to your business, and obey Orders promptly." The
23d formed their line of battle behind the 35th, and the 20th NYSM took
position similarly behind the 21st. Patrick noted in his journal, "By dint
of hurrying and pressing they got up." Behind Patrick came Hatch's old
brigade, now under Col. Walter Phelps Jr., in column, and behind Phelps,
Doubleday's brigade. Ricketts's division remained at the base of the hill
as a reserve. With the advance under way, the military surgeons scurried
about the stone church in preparation to receive the wounded.[16]

Hooker, staff officers, aides, and observers clustered near the church
to watch the slow blue lines pick their way up the hill unopposed. Their
new corps commander looked confident and showed no hesitance about
the coming fight. "Fighting Joe," six feet tall, clean shaven, and handsome, had commanding blue eyes and an evident restless energy. In battle
he appeared fearless, riding erect in the saddle and personally leading
his men into the thickest of the action. George W. Smalley, a newspaper
correspondent who traveled with Hooker's headquarters during the campaign, thought, "He had to the full that joy of battle which McClellan
never had at all."[17]

Smalley also observed McClellan watching Hooker's advance from a
knoll along the pike. In contrast to Hooker, McClellan "had a singular
air of detachment; almost that of a disinterested spectator: or of a general
watching maneuvers." His wrinkled, ill-fitting uniform, with at least one
button missing, punctuated the impression of casualness toward events.
To Smalley he appeared distracted and deep in thought, as if his mind was
somewhere back at headquarters plotting out grand strategy on a map. In
truth, McClellan had no stomach for the battlefield. Three months earlier
he had admitted to his wife that the field of battle sickened him, "with its
mangled corpses and poor suffering wounded! Victory has no charms for
me when purchased at such cost."[18]

Not far distant from McClellan, Colonel Hoffman halted the 23d
about three-quarters of a mile up the hill along a farm road running parallel with the crest. Here the men left their burdensome knapsacks and after
a brief rest pushed on. Up ahead they could see the skirmishers of the
35th approach the woods. Soon, however, Hoffman reported that he had
lost contact with the rest of the brigade, prompting Patrick to dart back
and forth across the field trying unsuccessfully to restore his lines. At one

point Patrick ventured dangerously close to a concealed enemy skirmish line; a musket volley sent him plunging down the mountainside.[19]

Patrick's and Phelps's brigades eventually engaged Longstreet's skirmishers and drove them back through the woods and into a field beyond a stone wall that bordered the narrow plateau along the crest. In the advance Hatch received a wound while gallantly leading his men, forcing him to turn the command of the division over to General Doubleday. Doubleday ordered his brigade to fix bayonets and join the mass of troops fighting at the stone wall.

The 23d, having lost contact with the troops on their right, veered to the left. It swung around the left side of the hill within three hundred yards of the pike before turning back up toward the crest. The way became rocky, forcing many of the field officers to dismount and walk their horses. By the time they arrived at the left of the mile-long Union line of battle, the evening had become "dark as a pocket." After a fifteen-minute rest to catch their breath, Hoffman directed his men up to the line near the left of the 76th New York of Doubleday's brigade. Due to the darkness, the Cortland Volunteers of the 23d probably never realized that they were fighting alongside Cortland men of the 76th. Hoffman's first volley went ticking through a cornfield identified as concealing the Rebel position. The regiment fired about twelve rounds with little appreciable effect before the order to cease fire arrived from the right of the line.[20]

As the firing sputtered out, the Union lines became broken and entangled. By some mistake the 23d was prematurely ordered off the line, only to be hustled back to meet a new Confederate attack through the cornfield. At the same time fresh troops from Ricketts's reserve division arrived; according to Hoffman, they "came up in the darkness hooting and yelling, running over everybody and throwing everything into even worse confusion than before." In the dark the regiments tended to bunch up instinctively for security, resulting, on one part of the line, in "the men pressing against each other, and firing into the air in a sort of frenzy." This "disgraceful scene," as Patrick described it, threatened to panic the confused mob of soldiers at the wall into shooting each other, as had happened to the 23d at Second Bull Run, or fleeing. It was only with the greatest effort by the officers that the firing was stopped and calm restored. Late that night Hoffman separated out his command from the rest and brought it groping partway down the hill to retrieve knapsacks and bivouac for the night.[21]

In the fight for South Mountain in the area of Turner's Gap the First Corps, originally about ten thousand strong, lost close to a thousand men. The determined attack of Gibbon's men up the pike accounted for one-third of this casualty figure, earning its famous nom de guerre "the Iron Brigade." The 23d emerged from the fighting with but six men slightly wounded, none from Company H.[22] General Lee, feeling hard pressed by Hooker and Reno, decided late on September 14 to abandon his mountain defenses and withdraw northward toward Boonsboro.

The Union soldiers spent the long, chilly night on the mountainside under the stars wrapped in their blankets. In the quiet the soldiers could hear the distant, familiar sounds of a tinkling cowbell and the baying of a farm dog. Looking back up the mountain through the trees they saw flickering lanterns carried by those still searching for the wounded. On a far off ridgeline, a signal torch pierced the darkness as it searched for a response.[23]

Morning emerged slowly through a dense fog. At first light a number of Hooker's men found time to explore the battlefield of the night before, while a few slithered over the wall in the smoky half-light to rob the bodies of the enemy dead. Most, however, happily turned away from the horrors of the battlefield to join the grand concourse of men, wagons, and artillery funneling through Turner's Gap in pursuit of the retreating foe. Nearing the crest, past the Mountain House Tavern, where many Union officers lounged on the porch, the men offered choruses of "Maryland, My Maryland," with words changed to suit the singers.[24]

McClellan spent the morning conferring with subordinates and organizing the pursuit to press his advantage. Although General Franklin had punched through Crampton's Gap as planned, around eight in the morning enemy guns firing on Harpers Ferry fell ominously silent. McClellan was further disheartened by a visit to a temporary field hospital located at a house along the pike. Walking among the wounded in the yard, he shook their hands and thanked them in the name of the country for the victory that they had achieved the day before. After briefly entering the house where the surgeons were at their bloody work, he returned to the road. "Though his face was unmoved," one man recorded, "tears were trickling down his cheeks, and as he came to his horse he dashed them away with his hand, mounted hastily and rode on."[25] About midday a signal station near Turner's Gap alerted McClellan to the fact that Lee's army had turned to bear its bronze cannon across the hills and ridges near

Sharpsburg, Maryland, about eight miles from the gap and two miles short of the Potomac River. With Lee apparently cornered, McClellan turned from the battlefield of South Mountain and rode toward the head of his advancing troops, his spirits restored by cheers that seemed to carry him along the moving columns.

Lee could not continue his march to Hagerstown as long as his army remained divided and McClellan's troops continued to pour over South Mountain. At first Lee thought of ending the campaign, recrossing the Potomac and reuniting his army in Virginia. Then word arrived of Jackson's expected capture of Harpers Ferry. Lee finally decided to remain east of the river near the small German-American farm community of Sharpsburg and accept battle. He placed his ten-thousand-man[26] force in a defensive position across a broad three-mile ridge of land formed by the meandering Antietam Creek in its course toward confluence with the Potomac south of the village. Lee's ragged and hungry soldiers formed a thin line from the Potomac on his left over broken ground east of Sharpsburg, to the Antietam at a point below the Rohrbach stone bridge. The troops did not dig breastworks or in any significant way prepare their position, and Lee did not seem overly concerned that his only available means of escape across the Potomac was narrow Blackford's (or Boteler's) Ford. Despite being drastically outnumbered and with no assurance that reinforcements from Stonewall Jackson's command could arrive in time to help, Lee confidently told his men, "We will make our stand on these Hills."[27]

Why did Lee fight at Sharpsburg? His scarecrow army had reached the limits of its endurance. No victory could be pursued effectively with the forces he had at hand, and defeat in such a vulnerable position invited disaster. Nevertheless, Lee stood to fight. In the waning summer of 1862 the hopes of the new nation rode on the proud shoulders of its victorious armies. Lee had not marched and fought all this way just to end his incredible three-month string of victories by a simple retreat to Virginia. He would fight a battle, not one of grand strategy or for material objectives but soldier against soldier, in a bloody, stand-up act of defiance and commitment to the Southern cause. Lee seemed unperturbed by the overwhelming forces arrayed against him, for he understood the strengths and weaknesses of his opponent, and he had an unshakable faith in the proven fighting qualities of his men.

Predictably, McClellan dallied for two days maneuvering his troops and personally inspecting the Confederate positions in careful preparation for the coming battle. Meanwhile the Harpers Ferry garrison capitulated to Stonewall Jackson early on September 15, allowing the number of Confederate troops with Lee at Sharpsburg to grow to 26,500 by the time McClellan began implementing his battle plan on September 16.[28]

McClellan's orders called for Hooker to land the initial blow against the Confederate left, supported by Joseph K. F. Mansfield's Twelfth Corps and Edwin Vose Sumner's Second Corps. McClellan ordered a supporting attack by troops of Burnside's Ninth Corps against the Confederate right flank at Rohrbach's Bridge—soon to be known as Burnside's Bridge. Pending the success of these attacks, McClellan planned a final devastating blow by Fitz John Porter's Fifth Corps to crush the Confederate center and carry the field. William B. Franklin's remaining Sixth Corps would take position near the Union center to act as a general reserve.

Late on the 16th, Hooker's corps of about nine thousand men left its bivouacs near Keedysville between Boonsboro and Sharpsburg and made the short march to the unguarded upper, or Hitt, bridge over the Antietam.[29] Meade's leading division, followed by Ricketts's, crossed on the stone bridge, while Doubleday's men scampered down the stream bank a short distance below to wade knee deep across a ford. Brushing aside enemy pickets, the three divisions closed to form a flag-studded rectangular phalanx of troops, which continued across the undulating farm fields like a great blue sheet rippling in the breeze.

Hooker's men had to march less than two miles to reach the Hagerstown-Sharpsburg Turnpike, which ran along high ground between the Potomac and the Antietam and led directly south toward Sharpsburg and the Confederate left. Patrick's brigade at one point became separated from the division and for a short distance traveled alone. Cutting across the darkening fields, the New Yorkers knocked down farm fences to clear their path while keeping a soldier's eye out for fruit-laden trees from which to fill their empty haversacks. Confederate artillerymen spotted Hooker's movement and sent shells searching for targets. Patrick's brigade suffered a few casualties from this fire as it took position in a small triangle of woods along the turnpike. Skirmishers from the 23d were sent to the far right near the Potomac; the remaining troops of Hooker's command lay down with their weapons on the damp ground, the air heavy and "perfumed with a mixture of crushed green cornstalks, ragweed, and clover." Many remained awake that evening to watch the occasional arching streamer of light in the night sky burning fuses of fired artillery from the shells. "The fight flashed, and glimmered, and faded, and finally went out in the dark." At nine in the evening, it started to rain.[30]

Hooker established his command post beside a large locust tree on the property of Joseph Poffenberger, whose house and barn overlooked the battlefield from a high knoll and a ridge bordering the turnpike. Hooker clustered his infantry divisions around the base of the hill and placed his supporting artillery in line on the high open ridge near the Poffenberger house. He attended to all of the details of troop placements himself, and in all of his actions he communicated his rising anticipation of battle. He appeared "all alive," one man wrote. "He sits uneasily in his saddle, and his look means mischief."[31]

Although Hooker appeared eager for the coming fight, he had no illusions of an easy victory. Lee obviously knew his every move after crossing the Antietam and no doubt had prepared a stout defense. Whatever doubts Hooker may have felt about the fighting mettle of his men, he sensed that a great moment in the war had arrived. His skirmishers held Lee with his back to the river and vulnerable to the devastating blow he intended to deliver at morning light. Within Hooker's grasp that battle autumn was a harvest of victory after a summer of defeat—a showdown that could destroy Lee's army and break the back of the Confederacy. "We are through for to-night gentlemen," Hooker solemnly told his staff in the evening shadows, "but to-morrow we fight the battle that will decide the fate of the Republic." Hooker took shelter from the rain in the Poffenberger barn, where he spent the night.[32]

Sleep did not come easy for the soldiers that wet and dreary night. Their minds wandered to personal matters and their prospects in the morning's fight. One spoke for many in describing later his feelings as morning approached: "I am not aware that I once wished we should not fight. I know that to stay out or shrink from the battle in any way never entered my head; yet I can venture to say that while we waited in the twilight time flew with slow wings, and the quicker I was in it and through it, alive or dead, the better I thought it would be."[33] All too soon for many, the first light of dawn filtered through a thick fog and framed the distant ridgeline where Lee's men lay waiting. With low voices the officers formed their commands in the gray mist and waited for orders.

Early on September 17, Hooker, in the full uniform of a major general, rode out on a conspicuous white charger to inspect the battleground. The land between the watercourses south of Poffenberger's was rough hewn, marked by numerous hollows, broken ridges, and jagged outcroppings of rock scattered about as if by some ancient horseplay of nature. Most common were square fenced fields of grass and pastureland, often scarred by amber streaks of limestone breaking the surface to vex even the most determined farmer. Pale yellow shocks of corn and grain stood next to an occasional ploughed field, and a few sections of tall corn remained to be harvested. Small separated clusters of hickory, walnut, and oak trees, used by farmers as wood lots, were all that remained of large eighteenth-century forests long since cleared by the hardy, hard-nosed German families who had first settled the region. Their descendents still worked the fields in 1862, and that particular autumn, as for many years past, they looked forward to enjoying the bounty of a productive year of labor. Although hardened to the demands of plow and pulpit, few could have conceived of the horrors about to descend upon their peaceful community.

The morning fog lifted slowly to reveal an overcast sky. From Poffenberger's Hooker looked south down a corridor of farmland four to five hundred yards wide, ending less than a mile away at a cross ridge occupied by the Lee's infantry and artillery. The Hagerstown Turnpike could be seen running near the middle of the corridor until it disappeared over the ridge on its final one-mile descent into Sharpsburg. Conspicuous along the ridge on a wooded knoll near the pike sat the small white-washed brick church of a German Baptist brethren known as Dunkers. The church looked like a schoolhouse, without steeple or adornments, reflecting the pious, humble nature of its members. More important to Hooker, however, the building marked the Rebel left flank and thus provided an objective for his attack.

Hooker directed Doubleday's division to lead his attack along the turnpike, with Ricketts's division on his left and the bulk of Meade's division behind as a reserve. From the very start of the attack Doubleday's right flank would be exposed to raking fire from Maj. John Pelham's Rebel artillery positioned on high ground known as Nicodemus Heights. But rather than driving off Pelham's guns with cavalry or infantry, Hooker planned to neutralize the threat with counterbattery fire from his corps batteries massed near Poffenberger's.

Hooker chose the Iron Brigade to lead his attack. From Poffenberger's, Gibbon's men moved through Meade's Pennsylvanians into a strip

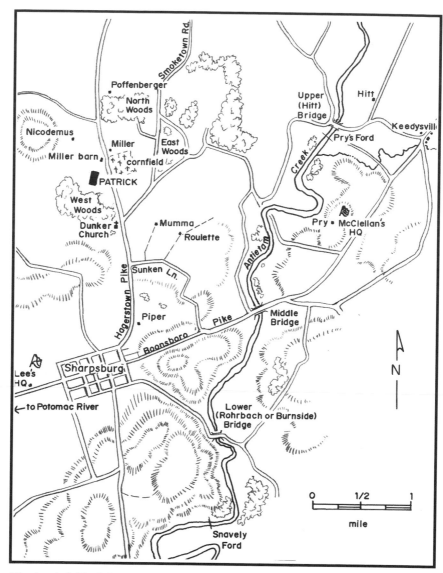

The battlefield of Antietam, September 17, 1862. Patrick's brigade is indicated behind the Rock Ledge, facing the Cornfield. *(John Heiser)*

of open woods that historians call Poffenberger's, or the North Woods. Here they deployed into a battle line amid the thunder of Pelham's cannon and the crash of falling tree limbs from the exploding shells overhead. Beyond the woods the ground rose slightly to an exposed tongue-shaped plateau of ploughed ground about 250 yards in length projecting south from Poffenberger's and running on the left of and parallel to the pike. Generals Hooker, Meade, and Doubleday watched from the edge of the North Woods as Gibbon's skirmishers darted out onto the field swept by artillery fire to drive their Rebel counterparts from the David R. Miller buildings and yard just off the end of the plateau. The Confederate skirmishers fell back past the house and disappeared into a thirty-acre field of tall corn. Gibbon's troops plunged into the corn in pursuit, extending their right across the pike to a clover field in front of the Miller barn. Gibbon's former Battery B, 4th U.S. Artillery, rolled forward to unlimber on the plateau above the Miller house and provide close support for the attacking infantry.

Once Gibbon became engaged, Doubleday sent forward his other brigades to maintain the momentum of the attack. Patrick's small brigade, down to only 824 men[34] present, had been waiting in formation since four in the morning. At about half past five it moved to Poffenberger's and swung in behind Colonel Phelps's brigade. The two brigades then ran the gauntlet of Pelham's artillery fire down the plateau to support Gibbon, who was fighting in what would become famous as "the Cornfield." Phelps halted in the edge of the corn while Patrick's troops hunkered down in the cover of a shallow trough of ground near the Miller house. Doubleday held his former brigade, now under Lt. Col. John William Hofmann, back at Poffenberger's heights to protect Hooker's artillery.

Gibbon's troops struggled to maintain their alignment as they pushed through the thick, head-high forest of broad-leafed corn. Nearing the elevated midpoint of the Cornfield, the musket fire coming from their front right across the road and from the intense musket and artillery fire clipping through the corn in their front forced the westerners to halt and lie down between the corn rows.

Gibbon now focused his attention on the area west of the pike. The ground sloped gently away from the road for about seventy yards until it abruptly fell two or three feet at a natural rock ledge running parallel to the road. Beyond the ledge the ground sank further to a basin of pastureland bordered on the west by woods (the West Woods). The woods continued to the south, eventually closing with the turnpike and almost engulfing Dunker Church. Enemy troops occupied the rock ledge and woods, causing Gibbon much trouble by their enfilade fire. He could not advance farther through the corn and ignore this threat to his right flank.

Gibbon sent the 19th Indiana across the road to clear the rock ledge and enter the West Woods. The 7th Wisconsin soon joined it. At the same time two guns of Battery B arrived at lashing speed along the pike to take a supporting position near some straw stacks just south of the Miller barn. These movements were under way when Patrick's brigade first arrived near the Miller house. Within five minutes after they halted the order rang out, "By the right flank, march!" and they too were off across the road, close on the heels of the 7th Wisconsin.[35]

Passing the Miller barn, Patrick detached his smallest regiment, the 20th NYSM, to protect the guns of Battery B. Shortly thereafter, Patrick sent the 23d on a mission beyond the West Woods to thwart a reported advance of the enemy from that direction. He then directed the 21st and 35th regiments to close up behind Gibbon's two regiments in the woods; Patrick assumed command of all four. When enemy resistance in the woods intensified, Patrick ordered the 21st and 35th to move up on the right of the westerners to form a single battle line parallel to Gibbon's line on their left in the Cornfield and facing toward Dunker Church.[36]

Once Patrick managed to clear the northern edge of the West Woods, Gibbon resumed his advance through the Cornfield. When his troops reached the fence bordering the southern edge of the corn they could see the Dunker Church not eight hundred yards ahead on the opposite side of an open field—open, yes, but for a solid gray barrier of Stonewall Jackson's command, which loosed a shattering musket volley at two hundred yards' distance. The battle now broke out in all its fury. Maj. Rufus Dawes of the 6th Wisconsin would describe how the westerners jumped the fence and struggled forward "loading, firing, and shouting as we advanced." Phelps's brigade merged with the Iron Brigade, and soon "men and officers of New York and Wisconsin are fused into a common mass. . . . Every body tears cartridges, loads, passes guns, or shoots. Men are falling in their places or running back into the corn."[37]

The fight intensified when two fresh Confederate brigades under Brig. Gen. William E. Starke burst from the West Woods to halt at the turnpike fence and fire obliquely into Gibbon's right front. Union commanders effectively shifted their troops to return fire and check this attack. Starke's left brigade of Louisiana troops suffered most, receiving fire from their front, from Battery B spitting shells down the clover corridor between the West Woods and the turnpike, and from Patrick's skirmishers in the northern section of the West Woods. After a thirty-minute fight, Starke fell mortally wounded, and three hundred of his 650 Louisianans lay dead or wounded.[38]

Jackson's lines now started to give way, encouraging Hooker's men to believe that the coveted Dunker ridgeline was within their grasp. In the voice of Major Dawes, "'Forward' is the word.' The men are loading and firing with demoniacal fury and shouting and laughing hysterically, and the whole field before us is covered with rebels fleeing for life, into the woods. Great numbers of them are shot while climbing over the high post and rail fences along the turnpike. We push on over the open fields half way to the little church."[39]

Far above the smoke of battle, General McClellan calmly watched the action from near his headquarters at the Philip Pry house, located on a high ridge east of the Antietam. Whether standing out on the hillside smoking or sitting behind a telescope in quiet conversation with subordinates, the commanding general seemed no more in control of events than the clusters of soldiers and civilians gathered nearby to glean news of the battle.[40] Around seven o'clock, the early enthusiasm at headquarters over Hooker's advance turned somber when a sudden eruption of musketry drew all eyes back toward the billowing clouds of smoke rising above the area of Dunker Church.

Unseen to the spectators at the Pry house, beneath the smoke of battle, two thousand men of Brig. Gen. John B. Hood's Division had swarmed from the West Woods near Dunker Church and deployed for battle in the field between the church and Cornfield. They now drove forward, collapsing Hooker's exhausted forward units and driving the survivors back through the corn. The Texas Brigade advanced close behind Hooker's retreating troops, targeting next the isolated guns of Battery B in the road and Meade's Pennsylvanians trying to form a defensive line in the Miller yard at the northern edge of the Cornfield. The 1st Texas Infantry, followed by Hampton's Legion and the 18th Georgia, used the cover of the corn to approach within easy musket range of the guns.

The Union cannoneers near the Miller barn bravely stood to their guns, repeatedly yanking the firing lanyards, ramming down new charges, and scurrying back to bring up additional ammunition from the limbers and caissons parked nearby. The rest of the battery came galloping out of the smoke to their relief, and soon all six guns formed a curved line blasting fire and iron into the corn and down the road. Many men fell beside their guns from enemy musket fire at point-blank range of seventy-five yards and closing. Volunteers from the supporting infantry ran forward to take the places of the dead and wounded in order to keep the guns firing. General Gibbon rode up at a critical point in the fight to cast his fate with his old battery. Vowing "They shan't have these guns," he took charge of the left piece in the road closest to the corn. Stepping from behind the loaded gun, double-shotted with canister, his face black from powder and streaked with perspiration, he called out, "Give them Hell, boys!" The gun leaped back at discharge and recoiled down the declivity of the road. The shotgunlike blast of cast-iron balls furrowed the dirt in front, while above, through a cloud of dust and smoke, chunks of fence rail, corn stalks, and human flesh were hurled into the air.[41]

The Cornfield became a fiery cauldron of death. General Hooker in his after-action report spoke of the intensity of the fighting there. He remembered "every stalk of corn in the northern and greater part of the field was cut as closely as could have been done with a knife, and the slain lay in rows precisely as they had stood in their ranks a few moments before. It was never my fortune to witness a more bloody, dismal battle-field." When all seemed lost, amid the chaos of booming cannon and ripping sound of musket volleys, Doubleday's servant Temple fell to his knees in the broken corn and prayed heavenward for their deliverance.[42]

The Texans and other Southern units recoiled from the fire of Meade's rallying troops in their front and right, and from the additional threat posed by Patrick's fresh troops appearing on their left. The 1st Texas had to fall back through the corn on their supports after suffering an incredible loss of 182 killed and wounded and four missing out of 211 men engaged.[43]

Patrick had previously made note of Hood's troops passing beyond his left through the Cornfield. In response he ordered the four regiments under his direct control to change front to the left and take position behind the rock ledge between the West Woods and the pike. From the ledge they opened a crossfire that assisted in drawing off the Texans and Georgians in front of Battery B.

The 23d, as noted, had been sent off beyond the West Woods to check a reported enemy advance. A short distance out, Colonel Hoffman discovered that the 10th Pennsylvania Reserve Infantry of Meade's division had preceded him on the same mission. Hoffman's orders were then countermanded, and his men double-quicked back along a farm lane toward the intensifying sounds of battle along the turnpike.[44]

When Hoffman halted his men in the clearing off the northern tip of the West Woods, his limited view to the east offered a confusing picture of the ongoing battle. Beyond the Hagerstown Turnpike drifting clouds of smoke obscured the opposing battle lines. In his immediate front, near the rock ledge, the 7th Wisconsin was engaged with Rebel troops along the road. Hoffman could see the 19th Indiana fighting on the right of the 7th, while the 21st and 35th regiments emerged from the West Woods to deploy their battle lines.

There was no time to lose. While Hoffman surveyed the scene, two of his men from his leading element, Company A, fell wounded. Shouted orders quickly separated the column into companies, which recombined to form a two-rank battle line fifty or sixty yards long. Only eight companies, averaging twenty men each, were present (Company D guarded the division supply wagons, and Company C had not yet rejoined the regiment from picket duty the night before).[45] After Hoffman adjusted the direction of his line by ordering a short wheeling movement, the 23d marched forward into battle, replacing the 7th Wisconsin at the rock ledge.[46]

The ledge provided an ideal defensive position. The three-foot-high limestone outcropping protected the men as they looked across the clover field that sloped gently up to the turnpike in their front. From the ledge the men could see the top rails of the fence along the road sparkling with Rebel musket flashes interspersed with the bright red patches of their battle flags. Officers shouted orders to aim low as the men leveled their rifle-muskets over the ledge to fire their first crackling volley toward the road. The men then began loading and firing at will.[47]

Patrick, wearing a nonmilitary light-colored slouch hat and a plain blue army blouse, fearlessly rode from point to point on the battlefield trying to coordinate the complicated movements of his scattered command. On the left of his line along the rock ledge he squeezed the 35th New York between the 23d and the guns of Battery B. To their right, the 19th Indiana and the 21st New York advanced on their own to the road and beyond into the field. In their impetuous rush to meet the Rebels, a lieutenant in the 21st noticed that their flag bearer stood in the pike jerking the flag aggressively at the enemy. When asked later what he was doing, he said "that he wanted to get a heap of bullet holes in it." They found bullets aplenty, especially when the 19th Indiana collided with Brig. Gen. Roswell S. Ripley's advancing Confederate brigade. When Patrick caught up with his overeager regiments, he ordered everyone back to the road.[48]

The advance of the two Union regiments across the pike forced the 4th Texas in front of the 23d to back away from the fence for fear of being cut off and surrounded. Its retreat drew the 23d and 35th into the vacuum to make their bid for possession of the Cornfield. The men of the 23d leapt up onto the ledge and let forth a burst of hurrahs as they ran in line through the clover field and up to the post and rail fence along the pike. The fence proved too sturdy to knock down, so they climbed over it in order to reach a similar fence on the opposite side of the road. The men knelt down to fire through the rails into the tangled broken mass of cornstalks. By this time most of the enemy had fled except for four or five Rebels huddled by the roadside, who immediately surrendered.[49]

The 23d and the 35th at the fence line fired only a few rounds before a new threat appeared on their right. General Starke's Louisianans, having recovered from their earlier bloody encounter with Gibbon's men and now commanded by Col. Leroy A. Stafford, came barreling up the open corridor between the West Woods and the pike, their lines at right angles to Patrick's, thus crossing the T. Stafford's men concentrated their volley fire on the New Yorkers' vulnerable right-flank companies, which were facing the wrong direction to respond effectively. Patrick's regiments in turn tried unsuccessfully to adjust their lines to the right under fire to meet the new assault. Colonel Rogers of the 21st simply ordered his regiment to "disperse," every man for himself, and then reassemble on the colors back at the West Woods.[50] Most of Patrick's losses in the battle occurred in these brief but bloody encounters. When the 21st fell back it exposed the right companies, A and G, of the 23d to a severe fire, resulting in a number of casualties in the regiment before Hoffman could effect an orderly retreat from the road back to the cover of the rock ledge.[51] The regiments finally rallied to check Stafford's attack and drive the Confederates back into the cover of the West Woods.

A lull now settled over the seesaw battle of the flanks, allowing both sides to back off, rest, and replenish their ammunition. The remnants of Gibbon's brigade, with Battery B and the 20th NYSM, withdrew north on the turnpike and passed out of this phase of the battle. Patrick's remaining three regiments rested in the low pasture near the Miller barn, where after reinforcements arrived they stacked arms, shared their remaining ammunition, and kindled fires for coffee. Although they were still in danger from sporadic enemy artillery fire, this respite after two and a half hours of fighting proved most refreshing. The sun even tried to shine through the clouds.

Hooker wasn't through yet. Now General Mansfield brought up the Twelfth Corps to bolster the flagging First Corps attack and renew the Union drive for Dunker ridge. Col. William B. Goodrich's brigade of the Twelfth Corps reinforced Patrick's sector of the battlefield and took position just inside the West Woods, facing south. Other brigades from the Twelfth Corps entered the Cornfield and battled to reestablish Gibbon's forward position in the field between the Cornfield and Dunker Church. Hooker remained on the battlefield trying to rally his troops and waving off expressed concerns by others for his safety "with an explosion of curses and contempt." About nine o'clock he was riding forward along his lines when one of the many musket balls coming from the West Woods near the church struck him in the foot. Even while being taken to the rear he continued to shout out orders: "Tell them to carry these woods and hold them," he yelled, "and it is our fight!"[52]

General Sumner now led his Second Corps onto the battlefield and took command from Hooker. His nickname "Bull" Sumner at this time might have stood for "bull-headed," for he made little effort to coordinate the attack of his corps with other commands on the field or to attempt to understand enemy positions. Instead, he rode to the front of Brig. Gen. John Sedgwick's division and took it straight across the battlefield, skirting the Cornfield to cross the turnpike and enter the West Woods between Goodrich's brigade and a strong Confederate line advancing on his left from a point southwest of Dunker Church.

At the time of Sumner's attack, Patrick's three regiments had been forced by harassing Confederate artillery fire to lie down under cover of the West Woods behind Goodrich's line. From here they witnessed the grand spectacle of Sedgwick's five thousand men in three battle lines, advancing with dressed ranks and weapons at right shoulder shift, moving deliberately across the pike into the woods. Then came the terrible sound of a Confederate broadside fired into Sedgwick's left flank.

Sensing pending disaster, Patrick directed his men to move once more under the protective cover of the rock ledge. The men waited in tense anticipation, searching the dark shade of the woods for any sign of movement. "Steady, boys—Steady, boys," Hoffman repeated in a low voice. Next they heard a mighty roar like the breaking loose of a great flood of water: "As [the sound] came nearer we could distinguish voices and shouts, the clanking of scabbard, guns and accouterments making an awful din, when suddenly there burst out of the woods close to us a rushing tide of human life, rolling on and on, a disorganized mass of individuals, while riding around in this onrushing tide of men were mounted officers, waving swords which flashed in the sunlight, and calling upon their men to halt."[53]

Sedgwick's panicked troops had tumbled into Goodrich's troops and precipitated a general Union flight to the rear. Colonel Rogers of the 21st New York tried to form a human net across their path, but he found it impossible to stop the stampede. Patrick's troops could not fire upon the pursuing Southerners for fear of hitting Union troops being driven before them. When the Rebels advanced past his position near the West Woods, Hoffman had to fall back. With great composure under trying circumstances, he marched the 23d by the left flank onto the Hagerstown Turnpike. Brig. Gen. Oliver O. Howard of Sedgwick's command noticed their disciplined movement and pointed out the 23d to his own disorganized mob: "Men! that is the way to leave a field. That regiment are acting like soldiers!"[54]

Patrick's brigade was the last of Hooker's corps to leave the battlefield. Marching out the turnpike it filed in behind a fence along the southern edge of the North Woods to watch the enemy, halted in the West Woods. After four exhausting hours of marching and fighting, Patrick's men found themselves no closer to seizing the Dunker ridge position then when they started. Of Hooker's nine thousand troops drawn into the bloody whirlpool of battle in the Cornfield, 2,468 had fallen killed or wounded. Patrick suffered 234 killed, wounded, or missing, out of 824 men present. The 23d had nine dead and mortally wounded, and thirty-two others wounded. Of the Cortland Volunteers, L. Clinton Ball received a wound in the knee, John W. Stebbins one in the ankle, and Edmund O. Campbell was struck in the thigh and left arm. Campbell would later die from the amputation of his arm. The men of the company were thankful for having suffered so few losses. "If you could be placed where we have been," George Edgcomb wrote his family, "you would think it almost a miracle that any could escape."[55]

Before the sun's "Great Red ball of blood" sunk behind the smoky battle haze of September 17, more than twenty-three thousand Americans were to fall at Antietam, to mark it forever as the bloodiest day in

The battlefield at Antietam, September 1862. Dead Confederate soldiers lie along the Hagerstown Pike (road visible between the two fence lines on right). The position of the 23d is visible on top of a rise in the distance along the fence. The dead Confederates could be from William E. Starke's Louisiana brigade. *(Library of Congress)*

American history. Near midday the fighting drifted away from the Cornfield to farmer Mumma's "Sunken Road" and "Burnside's Bridge" over the Antietam. Late in the battle, the attack of General Burnside's Ninth Corps managed to carry the bridge before Stonewall Jackson's last division, under Maj. Gen. Ambrose P. Hill, arrived in time from Harpers Ferry to blunt and drive back Burnside's advance. At day's end the lines stood not far from where they had been at the start of the fighting. On September 18, Lee remained at Sharpsburg, as if defiantly sticking out his chin to challenge a renewal of the fighting, but McClellan had had enough. That night Lee ended his operationally successful, often brilliant, three-month campaign by crossing the Potomac back into Virginia at Boteler's Ford. Although in the days to follow both sides would claim victory in the battle, both actually settled for quite a bit less. In hindsight, in comparison with its costs, Antietam represented a senseless battle, fought with grit, determination, and raw courage but without substantive military objectives or decisive results.

President Lincoln found victory enough at Sharpsburg to issue on September 22, 1862, the Preliminary Emancipation Proclamation, declaring that beginning January 1, 1863, the slaves in the rebellious states were forever free. As an immediate practical matter, it meant little. Slaves in Maryland, for example, would still belong to their masters. But by this stroke of a pen, the Battle of Antietam rose from a tragic orgy of death to a pivotal moment in American history, when the nation veered toward a new destiny. The sectional conflict that had begun as a limited militia war to restore the Union now became a noble revolutionary struggle to resolve the divisive national issue of slavery. No conservative middle ground remained to serve as a basis for sectional reconciliation. For both sides the choices now became victory or destruction, and, after their bloody encounter at Antietam, both sides knew that victory would not come cheap.[56]

Northern soldiers shared Lincoln's evolving vision of the war to the extent that they wished the war prosecuted to the fullest and ended as quickly as possible. They generally supported freeing the slave as a necessary war measure. It did not follow for most Union soldiers, however, that freeing and arming the slaves would place blacks on an equal footing with whites as men or soldiers. A lieutenant of the 23d wrote in a letter published in the Hornellsville paper on August 7, "I am as much opposed to slavery as any of them, but I am not willing to be put on a level with the negro and fight with them. And it is the same with all the soldiers or nearly all." "For every nigger they arm," he mistakenly declared, "they will loose two white soldiers." On October 7 Polly Underwood wrote from Lapeer, Cortland County, to her soldier son Ogden expressing her groundless fears concerning the effect of Lincoln's recent actions on local enlistments. "There will be terrible times," she thought, "for some say they will be shot here at home before they're go and fight for the nasty negroes."[57]

Hooker's corps remained near Sharpsburg for almost a month and a half after the battle. The days immediately after the fighting ended were the most trying. Caring for the wounded became the first concern. Surgeons took over many of the area's public buildings, nearby private farmhouses, and barns and began their grisly work. Surgeon William A. Madill of the 23d occupied the block schoolhouse on the edge of Sharpsburg. For some days after the fighting the cries of the suffering and the sickening smell of death could easily locate these charnel houses. Algar Wheeler, an officer in the 21st New York, took a wounded comrade, Levi Vallier, to a field hospital apparently located along the Hagerstown Pike, later describing what he witnessed:

A great crowd of officers, horses, ambulances, and wounded men were there. The many surgeons were too busy to attend to any but serious wounds—amputations first, if possible. As we passed by one of the windows of the operating rooms, we noticed a pile of legs, arms feet, etc., several feet high and nearly up to the window sill. It made Vallier feel faint. I seated him in a garden on a bee gum, in among a lot of large cabbage plants. While leaning forward with his hand on his wounded head, he nervously moved his sword in its scabbard to and fro, uncovering a freshly amputated human foot under a large cabbage leaf. Some animal must have dragged it there to eat. This gave Levi a second opportunity to faint.[58]

Later that same day, after enduring many similar scenes of carnage, Wheeler happened to see McClellan ride by with a large escort. "We were told he had gained a great victory," Wheeler wrote, but "we wondered where, when, and how." On the night of the 18th General Patrick could not sleep for his anxiety over the possible renewal of the fighting in the morning: "I prayed much of the night—prayed for my country—prayed for my children—prayed for myself—It was a night of wrestling with God—Did he hear?"[59]

The living had the unenviable task of burying the four thousand battlefield dead. An eyewitness wrote, "No sight or stench could be more loathsome than that of those dead, as they were devoured by swarms of insects, with faces black as midnight, heads and necks swollen and hideously disfigured." As late as September 20 Patrick noted, "The stench arising from the decomposition of the dead is almost intolerable." Work details wrapped the corpses in army blankets and placed them in shallow trench graves without markings, save perhaps for a penciled name on an ammunition-box lid. They dragged the dead horses into piles and tried to burn them. For weeks an eerie, empty, atmosphere settled over the blighted, death-shrouded fields. One resident noted that during this period no dogs barked, no birds whistled, and there were no rabbits to run or chickens to crow: "It was a curious silent world."[60]

The spirits of Patrick's men sank further after hearing persistent camp rumors and reports critical of the brigade's actions in recent battles. Patrick fumed at Gibbon's reported grumbling that Patrick's troops had failed to support him in the Brawner farm fight. He wrote in his journal on September 20 that if additional critical remarks attributed to Hooker were true, he was going to ask for an official court of inquiry. Fred Burritt the next day wrote for publication in an Elmira paper: "All the young boys in the ranks feel incensed and outraged at the silly, ridiculous, slanderous, base, defamatory and lying reports of the recent conduct of the 23d, its officers and men in time of battle." When Gibbon and Hooker denied making such comments, Patrick reluctantly let the matter drop. However, at brigade religious services the first Sunday after the battle, Patrick felt the need to note the recent sacrifices of the brigade and assure his men that in his eyes they had never failed to do their duty. After throwing in a lecture on the evils of profanity, the services ended with three choruses of Patrick's favorite hymn, the "Old Hundredth," based on the Hundredth Psalm.[61]

In the first week of October Patrick made the startling announcement that he was leaving his command to join the staff of General McClellan as provost marshal general of the Army of the Potomac. His difficulties with superiors may have contributed to his appointment, and some doubts perhaps lingered over his handling of his troops at Second Bull Run. Still, few could deny that Patrick stood out as the obvious choice for the new position. He had gained a reputation as a strict disciplinarian with his troops, and no doubt McClellan appreciated his evenhanded and humane administration as military governor of Fredericksburg the previous summer.

Patrick's men expressed little emotion over his departure. Burritt simply issued the warning, "Woe to the ruthless pillager who falls into his hands!" The men had grown to respect him as a son would a stern father, but there was never any real affection between them. Some spoke in praise of his personal bravery, his fairness, and how he looked out for their welfare in camp and battle. At the same time, however, they had thought him too demanding and unrealistic in his efforts to minister to both their material and spiritual needs, and they had found it impossible to live up to his high expectations. In his farewell statement to his brigade Patrick asked his men to "touch lightly" on his faults, "in the full conviction that, as their commander, he has endeavored to discharge his duties to them, to his country and his God." The men of the brigade were content to leave it at that and move on.[62]

Along the Antietam, by mid-October autumnal tints had begun to transform the surrounding forests, farmers had returned to repair damaged fences and buildings, and the many stark chains of brown earth mounds scaring the battlefield had started to show healing flecks of green. The brigade occupied pleasant Camp Barnett on high ground about a mile northwest of Sharpsburg near the Potomac. The issuance of new uniforms, the regular arrival of mail and newspapers, and visits by friends, relatives, and sightseers restored a restless routine to army life.[63]

Not long after the battle Captain Clark wrote from his sickbed in Washington to a Cortland friend expressing the general attitude in the army at this juncture in the war. Although he had led the Cortland Volunteers in all the fights in Virginia, "my campaign with Pope played me out, I could not endure any more and it is so with one half of his old Army." Clark noted a general weariness with the war stemming from the horrors of the battlefield, the months of marching seemingly to no effect, the hardships of soldier life, and the failed generals with their catalog of defeats. There remained with him, however, an abiding and sustaining sense of duty and strong identification with the Cortland Volunteers. He had pride in his company. Only one man, he confided, had run in a fight, at Sulphur Springs, but that man had later returned to the ranks and was subsequently wounded in battle. Whatever fate awaited the Cortland Volunteers, Clark planned to share it; he vowed to "be thar" in the next campaign.[64]

President Lincoln arrived at Sharpsburg in early October to review the troops and spur McClellan to follow up his victory aggressively. Not until late October, however, did the army stretch and slowly move south toward the Potomac River crossings. The First Corps marched over South Mountain at Crampton's Gap, halting on the afternoon of October 30 in the streets of Berlin (Brunswick), Maryland, to await its turn to cross the river on a military pontoon bridge. It was a beautiful Indian summer day, "the air soft and balmy, the smoky mist hanging on the mountains." Nearing the crest of the riverbank the men could look down upon the sparkling waters of the Potomac and hear the distant music of military bands along the long visible line of advancing troops. An aide of General Doubleday delighted in the scene: "All our tedious waiting at Antietam was forgotten; only the pleasant reminiscences of our Maryland campaign were left in our memory."[65]

McClellan's army cast its dark shadow down through Loudoun County, Virginia, filling the roads and occasionally igniting the contact points at the mountain passes in the Blue Ridge between the two armies. Marching conditions were excellent. The air was cool and dustless, and the trees along the roadways blazed in their autumn colors like torches heralding the army's passage. Doubleday's First Division spent seven days marching fifty-five miles from the Potomac, through Purcelleville, Snickersville (Bluemont), Bloomfield, Rectortown, and Salem (Marshall), before going into camp southwest of Warrenton, Virginia, on the Sulphur Springs Road. At Warrenton the army could reconnect with its supply line of the Orange and Alexandria Railroad before continuing south. On November 7 a rogue gale swept down from the mountains bringing four inches of snow and cold that froze the water in the soldiers' canteens. The troops took to their tents or huddled before great flaming pyramids of burning rails. The next day the stunning news arrived that McClellan had been relieved from command of the Army of the Potomac.

Lincoln had fired McClellan because he could no longer tolerate the general's sluggish movements in pursuit of Lee. Also, after the midterm fall elections, he could rid the army of McClellan's influence and set a new course without fear of serious political backlash from the Democrats. The year was waning, and little time remained in the campaign season to initiate the aggressive, hard-fighting drive south that Lincoln and the Republicans thought necessary to bring the war to a successful conclusion.

McClellan's soldiers stuck by their commander to the end. His youthful image, his compassion for their suffering, and his ready smile and the twirl of his cap in response to their cheers had won their hearts. He had unconsciously forged an enduring bond of trust and devotion with his troops that had distinguished the Army of the Potomac. But, like so many of the powerful forces of war that he had harnessed to little effect, McClellan never seemed to realize the possibilities that this unique relationship with his soldiers provided him on the battlefield. Even in the final moments of his military career before his cheering men at Warrenton, he was so moved by their emotional outpouring that he tearfully asked a companion, "What do you think of all this?" as if to say, "What does it all mean?"[66]

On November 11, displaying the "appearance of submission and sorrow," McClellan boarded a flag-decorated train at Warrenton for the trip home to Trenton, New Jersey, where he would await new orders that never came. Despite the show of troops along the rail line and the ceremonial firing of cannon, a feeling of melancholy and drift hung over the army at the news of McClellan's departure. The soldiers had believed in McClellan and what he represented: the promise of victory, the power and inevitability of a righteous cause, and the drumbeat, flag-draped pageant of war—all lost now, somewhere back beyond the killing ground of Antietam. At Warrenton Junction some of the soldiers broke ranks to uncouple the general's car in an effort to prevent his leaving. McClellan stood on the car platform and with dignity reminded the men of their duty as soldiers and the loyalty they owed their new commander, Burnside. The men reluctantly reconnected the cars, and the train slowly pulled away from the station. McClellan remained standing out on the car platform, waving his cap, receiving his soldier's last "long and mournful" hurrah and repeating his last "Good-bye lads" as the train receded into the brown Virginia countryside.[67]

CHAPTER 9

White Death
on a Frozen Hillside

The portly and affable Ambrose E. Burnside seemed an odd choice to succeed McClellan at the head of the Army of the Potomac. Burnside neither sought nor welcomed the position. He believed, and he willingly admitted, that the command of more than a hundred thousand men was beyond his capabilities.[1] On November 8, after discovering Burnside "almost crazy" with worry over his appointment, McClellan took up quarters with him at the Warren Green Hotel in Warrenton, where the two men sat up late into the night discussing the military situation. Apparently McClellan could do little to calm Burnside's troubled mind. Early on November 10 a newspaper reporter spotted Burnside pacing the elevated porch of the hotel "in an absorbed, distraught condition, seemingly overwhelmed by the weight of responsibility resting upon him." Brig. Gen. Oliver O. Howard met the new army commander during this time and found him broken in spirit, "sad and weary" from sleepless nights and quick to lament what he considered his terrible predicament.[2]

Early on November 11 Burnside walked with McClellan down to the depot and sat with him awhile in the coach of his waiting train as Union officers filed by to pay their final respects to their former commander. At length, only the two old friends remained. Although their relationship had become strained since the Battle of Antietam, Burnside rose to grasp McClellan's hand warmly in both of his. Placing a hand on Burnsides's shoulder, McClellan spoke parting, and no doubt consoling, words that have been lost to history. A group of spectators on the train platform stood silently with uncovered heads as the train pulled away from the depot, leaving Burnside behind to carry on alone. The depressing scene appeared to one observer more like a "funeral party than anything else."[3]

Vowing, however, to do his best, Burnside sought first to gather the scattered elements of his army and initiate an active campaign before winter's freeze. McClellan had left the army near Warrenton poised to march south along the line of the Orange and Alexandria Railroad as a wedge between Lee in the Shenandoah Valley and Richmond. It was when General Longstreet had slipped east across the Blue Ridge with half of Lee's army to stand in McClellan's path near Culpeper that President Lincoln had sent the "Young Napoleon" packing.

Burnside proposed a shift in strategy. He would abandon the Orange and Alexandria and, after a feint toward Lee's separated army, sidestep east of Longstreet at Culpeper in a thirty-five-mile dash to Fredericksburg. Burnside then planned to reconnect his supply line via the Richmond, Fredericksburg, and Potomac Railroad and gather an immense wagon train carrying subsistence for twelve days before putting his army on the road to Richmond. What Burnside thought Lee would be doing all of this time he did not say. Nevertheless, on November 14 Burnside's proposal to bypass Longstreet and march on Fredericksburg received Lincoln's blessing. "He thinks that it will succeed," reported the general in chief, Henry Halleck, "if you move very rapidly; otherwise not."[4]

Burnside wasted no time in reorganizing his army and setting it in motion. He created three "grand divisions" of two corps each. Edwin V. Sumner's Right Grand Division, made up of the Second and Ninth Corps, led the advance from Warrenton on November 15, covering the distance in two and a half days. It arrived on Stafford Heights overlooking Fredericksburg three days before any sizeable Rebel force could take a position to defend the city.[5]

Burnside ordered his two remaining grand divisions into supporting positions. William B. Franklin's Left Grand Division, including John F. Reynolds's First Corps and William F. Smith's Sixth Corps, followed Sumner on November 17. Abner Doubleday's division of the First Corps (including Patrick's old brigade) marched that day from Fayettesville on the Bealeton-Falmouth Road (modern Route 17) to bivouac that night between Morrisville and Deep Run.[6]

The march to Fredericksburg proved particularly difficult, owing to glutinous mud roads and a lack of animals to haul guns and supplies. A virulent "black tongue and hoof rot" disease had struck that fall, causing thousands of animals to be turned out of camp "limping and famished," so many that the efficiency of the army was threatened. Two cannon of Gerrish's six-gun battery, for example, had to be left behind for lack of horses to pull them. All along the army's route soldiers daily led hundreds of the suffering animals to the side of the road, where they were shot, for fear they might otherwise recover and fall into enemy hands.[7]

The First Corps resumed its march on the 18th in a hard rain. At Hartwood Church it turned up the Stafford Court House Road, crossing the track traveled the past spring by the 23d from Catlett's Station to Fredericksburg. Franklin's Left Grand Division took position near Stafford Court House to protect the reconstruction of a thousand-foot wharf at Aquia Landing and the repair of the single-track railroad from Aquia to near Falmouth. Ironically, Burnside's own troops had caused some of the damage to these structures, on Burnside's orders, during the evacuation of Fredericksburg following the Union defeat at Second Bull Run.

Maj. Gen. Joseph Hooker had recovered sufficiently from his Antietam wound to assume command of the Center Grand Division, made up of the Third and Fifth Corps. On November 19 Hooker halted his troops at Hartwood Church in position to guard the upper crossings of the Rappahannock. The Twelfth Corps at Harpers Ferry and the Eleventh Corps based at Fairfax Court House further protected the outlying approaches to Washington.

Initially exhibiting drive and energy, Burnside won the race to the river opposite Fredericksburg. On the 21st, Gen. Marsena Patrick, now of his staff, appeared at the riverbank waving a white towel to ask for a meeting with Fredericksburg officials. Patrick presented them a written ultimatum signed by Sumner stating that if they did not immediately surrender Fredericksburg, sixteen hours would pass for the removal of women and children before Union artillerymen would "proceed to shell the town."[8]

Burnside, however, was bluffing. The pontoon boats he needed to bridge the river and secure the town were late in arriving; in fact, they would not be available in sufficient numbers for a crossing until November 24. By that time most of Longstreet's forty-thousand-man corps had arrived to block Burnside's advance, and General Lee showed no inclination either to surrender the city or allow Burnside to come across the river without a fight. Thus, for want of small, frail, rectangular pontoon boats, Burnside lost all chances of an early safe passage of his forces to the south bank.

As Burnside studied the growing Confederate force in his front, Patrick's old brigade, now under the command of Brig. Gen. Gabriel R. Paul, settled into an excellent campsite on a wooded hillside overlooking Brooke Station on the Richmond, Fredericksburg, and Potomac Railroad.[9] While here they joined with many of their fellow soldiers to mark a period in the war that might be called the Time of Grumbling in the Union army. Fred Burritt, for example, could be read in the Elmira newspapers complaining of the lice that infested the men's clothes; their want of tobacco, "that indispensable weed, both for chewing and smoking purposes"; reduced rations; lack of communications with the "outer world"; and back pay, about seven months overdue.[10]

The men also grew more vocal in their complaints concerning their officers. They cared little for a general's politics, according to Albert Crandall, but rather judged him on demonstrated "skill, bravery, and his kind considerate treatment of the common soldery [sic]." McDowell and Pope, in particular, had not measured up in their estimation.[11] Army chaplains came in for special abuse. Lt. Hugh Baldwin of Company E called them "emphatically a nuisance." Burritt also attacked chaplains, "who (with a few honorable exceptions) render no service whatever. . . . They often become lazy, fault-finding, selfish and parsimonious, rarely visiting the sick—as distant as possible from death-beds and especially from battle-fields—rarely preaching and more rarely asked to preach— sometimes infidels—they are in very moderate esteem as a class, and they ought to be."[12]

Union officers grumbled over the dismissal of McClellan, which many attributed to cowardly Northern rulers who, for political reasons, "have tampered with this Rebellion till we find a divided North hoping, vainly attempting to reduce a United South." Colonel Hoffman confided to a friend on November 27, "You can't find a man or officer but what has got enough of war the way things are going." He sarcastically offered his own "terms of mediation" for ending the war: "I'd take about 20 abolitionists from the north and the same number of secessionists from the south and all the niggers on the continent and send them in a balloon to some desert island with no harbors that any could land on, and bring off the balloon and let them and all others live in peace." Burritt stated the common refrain of the soldiers during this period: "We are sick of changes."[13]

As the conflict dragged on toward the end of its second year, similar stresses surfaced on the Cortland home front. The winter of 1861–62 had been a period of watchful waiting as McClellan's large and better-trained army took the field with every expectation that it would reverse McDowell's shocking First Bull Run defeat. When McClellan's Grand Army suffered a drubbing before Richmond and General Lee seized the initiative with his drive north, the nation's confidence in its cause and leaders was again shaken. Northerners faced the unsettling prospect of a protracted war, requiring yet greater sacrifices and additional levies of troops.

On July 1, 1862, as McClellan's forces fell back from Richmond, President Lincoln called on Northern states to furnish additional 300,000 volunteers to serve for three years. To meet New York's quota of 59,705 men under this call, Governor Edwin Morgan launched an innovative and creative initiative to raise the needed regiments, mostly infantry. It concentrated authority for organizing the new units in the governor's office while at the same time securing the benefits of a close association between the regiments and their home communities. He directed that each of New York's thirty-two senatorial districts raise at least one regiment. The governor would appoint the regimental commanders; each could then establish a camp of rendezvous and instruction within their district and begin to recruit. The commander would receive his commission from the governor at the time of his regiment's final organization. The other officer commissions would go to individuals authorized by the commander and certified by the governor to recruit for the regiment within the district. Their qualifications for command positions would be subject to testing by state and Federal military review boards.[14]

To maintain local support for the new call, in early July Morgan invested considerable power in local military committees. The committees would be made up of at least twelve influential local leaders appointed by the governor and representing a political cross section within each district. The Cortland group of committee members headed by the conservative Democrat Henry S. Randall included Horatio Ballard, the sitting secretary of state of New York, and Cortland's Republican congressman R. H. Duell. In the following months these men worked selflessly to stoke the flagging patriotic fires in Cortland and lead the county toward meeting most of its manpower obligations.[15]

Cortland County fell within the twenty-third state senatorial district, made up of Cortland, Madison, and Chenango counties and represented in Albany by Republican senator John J. Foote of Hamilton, Madison County. The district would eventually field two infantry regiments: the 114th formed in Norwich, of primarily Chenango County residents; and the 157th in Hamilton, Madison County, made up of Cortland and Madison county men. The governor authorized Madison College professor Philip Perry Brown Jr. to organize the Cortland-Madison regiment. A number of individuals, including B. B. Andrews, formerly of the Cortland Volunteers, received authority to begin recruiting for the regiment in Cortland County.[16]

Recruiting for the district regiments was under way when Lincoln on August 4 issued an additional call for 300,000 men from the state militia organizations for a period of nine months' Federal service. Since the available state militia forces were not sufficient to meet this call, the states faced the prospect of the first compulsory draft of eligible male citizens into state service. Even more onerous to many, the recently revised National Militia Act passed by Congress and signed by Lincoln on July 17, 1862, expanded the powers of the Federal government to step in and administer the state drafts if state procedures failed to raise the required number of troops. The law allowed for provost marshals nominated by the governors and appointed by the War Department to enforce Federal regulations in regard to the implementation of state drafts.[17]

Governor Morgan tried to prepare New Yorkers for a state militia draft by initiating in June a statewide enrollment of all males eighteen to forty-five years of age. Silas Burt of the governor's office acknowledged, however, that with the prospect of compulsory state service imminent after Lincoln's August 4 call great unrest surfaced in the state, and "large numbers attempted to avoid the risk of conscription by fleeing to Europe or Canada." Although no figures can be found of those "fleeing" the state, the general threat of draft evasion prompted draconian measures by the Federal government to prevent it. Lincoln announced through the secretary of war (on August 8, 1862) that all draft evaders were subject to being detained and arrested; in such cases habeas corpus would be suspended. Burt later told the story of one deputy provost marshal going car to car on a train heading west out of Buffalo, New York, questioning all draft-eligible males on their enrollment status. Conservative Democrats and others professing to be the guardians of citizens' rights and liberties under the Constitution were "horrified" by these and other acts of "despotism."[18]

Confusion resulting from the differing terms of the two troop calls created a pressure-cooker atmosphere for Cortland County recruiters. This was relieved somewhat by a determination by Federal authorities that the states could combine their quotas for the two calls and receive credits against this figure for all residents enlisting in any existing active military unit after July 2. Under the two calls Cortland received an initial obligation to furnish 814 men. If the New York counties failed to meet their quota one way or another by August 15 (later extended to November 10), a state draft of the enrolled reserve would commence. Working against this deadline, the Cortland Military Committee plunged into the work of encouraging volunteer enlistments, apportioning the county quotas among the townships, and certifying the list of county residents entering military service since July 2, 1862. Chairman Randall reported in the *Gazette and Banner* of August 28, 1862, that Cortland had four hundred men to go to meet its goal of 814 volunteers.[19]

Although it soon became evident that New York would meet its quotas and would not have to resort to the use of a state draft, the Cortland Military Committee evoked the possibility as a matter of local pride and patriotism in order to encourage enlistments. Randall set the tone by the following appeal published in the local paper:

It is supposed that few counties in the State, or United States, will require to be drafted. Their patriotism will meet the emergency without any compulsion. Shall Cortland County occupy an unenviable position among those counties which must be FORCED to raise troops to save that legacy of our forefathers, the American Union? Every consideration of patriotism, pride and interest respond—NO!

The appeal concluded, "Now let our young men come forward, united, manfully and [following in bold print] Save Our County from this Stigma!" The paper also pointed out that drafted men would not receive any of the available bounties.[20]

While Cortland town fathers encouraged volunteer enlistments, the process of enrollment for the state militia draft continued. The final totals for Cortland County included 4,427 enrolled and 1,742 exempted out of a total county population of about 26,000. Medical disabilities accounted for 654 of the exemptions, for: hernia (eighty-six), lung and throat problems (eighty-one), injury of the joints (seventy-six), heart disease (forty-five), and asthma (forty-four). Other types of exemptions from state service allowable under state or Federal guidelines included: all clergymen; judges; justices and officers of the courts; firemen; current members of the U.S. military service; Shakers and Quakers; professors, teachers, and students in the academies and common schools; officers and members of the organized militia in active service; and such other classes as "idiots, lunatics, paupers, habitual drunkards and persons convicted of infamous crimes."[21]

Although Cortland compared favorably to the other counties in the ratio of exemptions to those enrolled, the local newspaper tainted the motives of all who sought exemptions with the implication that they lacked patriotism and nerve. One article described the "frivolous and ridiculous" excuses used by some seeking medical exemptions: "Some have sore toes, some cannot keep their victuals down, some have a weak back, some are liable to faint at the sight of blood, while the real cause consists in nothing more nor less than downright cowardice."[22]

Another newspaper article, by someone calling himself "a looker on at City Hall," gave a humorous account of four hours' observation of men seeking exemption at the county clerk's office. The following is a sample drawn from a long list:

> Four men claimed exemption because they served their country in the fall of November 1860, by bearing a torch, wearing a cape, yelling hi! hi! and shouting for a free press, free speech and other ridiculous privileges of a similar character.
>
> One man claimed exemption because he was always opposed to the men who carried lanterns, and thought they ought to do the fighting. This man was over forty-five however.
>
> Three desired to be excused because they voted for Lincoln.
>
> One thought he had the right to stay home because he didn't vote for him.[23]

If the threat of the draft provided a stick to prompt volunteer enlistments, generous bounties provided the carrot. Early in the war the Federal government had established a hundred-dollar bounty to be paid to all three-year men at the time of their muster-out from service. On July 19, 1862,

New York added a fifty-dollar bounty for its three-year men (good until September 5), and in late August, Cortland County established local town bounties of various amounts.[24]

The much-maligned bounties seemed to have been scorned by all except those who received them. Burt complained that the bounties started a bidding war among the local communities for recruits. "Worst of all" according to Burt, the bounties contributed to the ending of the period "when patriotism was a motive for enlistment." Historian Ella Lonn laments that the bounties of late 1862 led to the pernicious practice of "bounty jumping," where men joined up to receive a bounty then deserted to enlist in another regiment and receive an additional bounty. Lonn claims that the bounty system contributed to a "noticeably inferior" quality of Northern recruits seen after 1862.[25]

The new bounties also had an adverse effect on the morale of the non-bounty veteran troops in the field and contributed to the Grumbling Time of late 1862. Colonel Hoffman of the 23d (a nonbounty two-year regiment) wrote, "Much merriment is made of the new bounty troops by the old ones. They call them the high-priced soldiers." Fred Burritt charged that "almost every man of Capt. Clark's company, discharged here during the past year for *permanent disability*, has re-enlisted in the Cortland company of the 157th and pocketed the tempting, persuading bounty." True enough, for the record shows that five men of Company H being discharged for health reasons later joined the 157th.[26]

For whatever reason—patriotism, pride, or payment—after only a six-week recruiting drive beginning on or about July 18, 1862, New York reached its July 1 quota of nearly sixty thousand three-year volunteers (forming new infantry regiments numbered 106 to 175) with men to spare to charge against the second sixty-thousand-man militia call. About 470 Cortland County men joined the 157th in Companies C, D, E, H, and K. New York was so successful in raising troops that in late fall the state draft was suspended. Overall during this period, New York furnished 86,097 three-year and 1,660 nine-month troops. Cortlandville led a chorus of relief among the Cortland townships at thus being "relieved of the disgrace of a draft."[27]

Before returning to the Cortland Volunteers camped at Brooke Station, a question remains: Did the Grumbling Time of late 1862 reflect an increasing war weariness produced in part by a transition between the volunteers of 1861, who enlisted for "pure patriotism," and the "mercenary period" identified by the enlistment bounties of 1862? Of benefit, perhaps, might be a comparison of the men of the Cortland Regiment (76th Infantry) raised in the fall of 1861 and of the 157th (a "bounty regiment") formed about a year later.

There is little evidence of a different type or class of soldier emerging in the county between the enlistments of 1861 and 1862. The men of the 76th and the 157th regiments had quite similar personal profiles. The average age continued to be twenty-five years, and about 65 percent of the men from the 157th listed themselves as farmers. The percentage of men married rose from twenty-five in the 76th to thirty-nine in the 157th (67 percent of the married men in the 157th had children). Out of the 460 Cortland men joining the 157th in 1862, only twenty were foreign born, twenty-five had prior service, and only about thirty left the regiment without authority never to return. No evidence is available of any Cortland County men fleeing the county to avoid the draft or any joining up solely to receive the bounty money. The deserters from the 157th do not fit the profile of "bounty jumpers."

Perhaps the "transition" period between the formation of the 76th and 157th regiments is better understood from the standpoint of the changing focus of the war and the effect of that change on the attitudes of both soldiers and civilians. The defeat of McDowell's amateur army at Bull Run followed by the defeat of McClellan's Grand Army before Richmond, along with Union reverses in the West, forced Northerners to abandon their early notions of a limited militia war of reunion and reconciliation. Instead they had to face the prospects of a drawn-out war of unimagined intensity. The names of the dead soldiers that filled the New York City newspapers and the pictures of bloated corpses lying on fields along the Antietam dramatically brought home to New Yorkers the reality of war. As early as the fall of 1861 many civilians began to question where the war was taking the nation and at what additional cost in blood and treasure. Later, Lincoln's Emancipation Proclamation, the threat of a national draft, the Confiscation Acts, Pope's General Orders, and the discrediting of McClellan and his conservative approach to the war added to the impression of the war adrift and of a floundering Lincoln administration not up to the immediate task of victory on the battlefield.

Yet despite the negative cross currents of dissent and doubt, the availability of generous bounties, and the threat of compulsory military service, the greater number of Cortland men who joined the 157th seemed to have done so willingly and with the same depth of commitment to the Union cause as had the earlier volunteers. Historian Bruce Catton falls back on the Civil War–era meaning of the word "patriotism" to explain this. By patriotism he referred not to the "rally-round-the-flag stuff" of modern Fourth of July celebrations but rather to "an unspoken, compelling attitude of mind. You grew up in this country, and enjoyed the life that was possible here; some day when you were grown, your country needed you—and no matter what it asked of you, you stepped up and gave it, and considered yourself lucky to have the chance."[28]

The circumstance of young William Saxton of Cincinnatus exemplifies the motivation of many from the county who joined the 157th. Saxton had spent the summer of 1862 working in the local hay fields while planning a career as a teacher. At the same time he followed in the papers the slow progress of the Union armies and Lincoln's calls for more troops. On August 11 he spent the day cutting hay and thinking hard about the war meeting to be held that evening in the local Presbyterian church. William debated with himself whether to join up:

> I don't think a young man ever went over all the considerations more carefully than I did. . . . I realized that it meant an entire change in my plans for life. It might mean sickness, wounds, loss of limb, and even life itself. It certainly would mean hardships, privations and suffering. But my country was in danger. Did not my country need me more than I needed what I had planned for myself? In fact if my country was not saved, what would my plans amount to anyway? Others had gone, more must go. Was it not my duty now to go also? In the afternoon the matter was settled. I had arrived at a conviction and a conclusion. My country needed me. It was my duty to respond. I would go. When I came to supper that night I told my father my decision and, with tears in his eyes, he said, "God Bless you, William, if you have decided it is your duty to go I shall not say no."[29]

Grumbling aside, Cortland County soldiers and civilians in the fall of 1862 continued to support President Lincoln and the war effort. In November both groups had an opportunity to register their attitudes toward the war in the heated midterm elections. The New York gubernatorial race proved particularly intense. The Democratic candidate, Horatio Seymour, attacked the Lincoln administration for its harsh war measures, the specter of slave emancipation as a war aim, and the recent battlefield reverses. The Republican candidate, former Southern Tier brigade commander James S. Wadsworth, spoke out in favor of abolition and the encouragement of Lincoln in the full prosecution of the war. Although Seymour won the statewide election, Cortland County went for Wadsworth, 3,488 to 1,877. On Election Day, November 4, a straw poll taken of the Cortland Volunteers in camp near Bloomfield, Virginia, indicated all but one man for Wadsworth.[30]

In late 1862 the North once again turned to the Army of the Potomac with hope and the anticipation of an early resolution to the war. "Burnside is nowhere unpopular," wrote Burritt from camp on November 24. Seymour Dexter on December 3 indicated a general eagerness among the soldiers to confront the enemy once again on the battlefield—"not because they love to fight, but because they wish the dreaded inevitable and they think in some measure decisive conflict to be over."[31]

While they waited for the "dreaded inevitable," the men found the Southern Tier camp at Brooke Station a pleasant respite in the campaign. The site provided clear and plentiful water and opportunities to forage for potatoes, turnips, onions, beets, and ripe persimmons to supplement their diet. At the same time, General Doubleday found plenty of work to keep them busy. From dawn to dusk, working parties repaired sections of the railroad and cleared acres of trees to corduroy miles of mud roads and build cities of log huts for the soldiers. Vast pine forests quickly disappeared to feed thousands of campfires, which burned continuously on the hillsides and blanketed the area with a thick fog of acrid smoke that tore at eyes and lungs.[32]

Union commanders set aside Thursday, November 27, as a time for thanksgiving. The day passed in military reviews, speeches, and prayer. General Patrick paid a visit to his old brigade and provided a half-hour "Thanksgiving sermon." Be thankful, he told them, that their homes had not suffered the desolation that they could see around them in Virginia. In the not too distant future they would be going home to their families; prepare now, he enjoined, by resisting the "tide of evil by establishing habits of self control, of sobriety, chastity of speech, etc." The men, as at all similar occasions in the past, listened to Patrick with "exemplary attention." The meeting closed with the men singing the "Star Spangled Banner."[33]

The arrival of the paymaster two days later tested the commitment of the men to walk with the righteous. The pay officer would sit at a table under a tent flap and issue each man in line neat packages of greenbacks. Although some of the money no doubt found its way to games of bluff or to the pockets of the sutlers or outlaw liquor vendors, most of it arrived home to support long-suffering dependent families.

With the change of the season the weather grew colder, and the number of soldiers responding to morning sick call increased. In the 23d, between thirty and fifty out of a total of about 290 men daily reported to sick call, where Dr. Madill issued "good advice, quinine, epsom salts and blue ointment (chiefly the last article)." In a sample three-day period, however, Madill excused only six men from duty. Burritt boasted that time and service had reduced the 23d to a "hardy, dirty, ragged few" who "were never enjoying themselves more, or in better health."[34]

One clear harbinger of action came with the arrival of the first train down the line from Aquia Landing to Potomac Creek. Troops lined the tracks at the first rumbling of the approaching locomotive. "Then the white steam began to roll up in snowy fleeces from behind the trees, and presently the big black monster with his shining harness appeared, slowly sliding up the track, dragging three or four platform cars, loaded with soldiers." All came running down to the tracks to exchange cheers with those riding on the cars. The very sight of the train invigorated the spirits of the men. The familiar military trains had come to symbolize for the Northern soldier the pride and power of the nation that he so willingly served. One man explained, "He sees in it not only plenty of rations, regular mails, and all the other conveniences which facility of communication with the world brings, but he sees also a great step accomplished toward the work that lies before him." By November 28 trains passed almost hourly between Aquia Landing and Falmouth, giving the line the capacity to move 750 tons of freight a day.[35]

By the time Burnside had finally positioned his army to fight, his prospects for success seemed no more promising than the winter storm that struck the area in the first week of December. Temperatures plunged, creeks glazed over, and the ground became covered with several inches of snow. Meanwhile General Lee with about 78,000 troops methodically occupied and fortified a strong eight-mile defensive line following the curve of Spotsylvania Heights behind Fredericksburg. Patrick's brigade had occupied a part of this very ground the summer before, and his men knew its great strengths as a defensive position. At first Burnside tried to outflank the Rebel position by crossing the river twelve miles below Fredericksburg at Skinker's Neck, but Lee checked him by shifting some of his troops to meet the threat. Lacking the skill and imagination of a great commander, Burnside resolved finally to bludgeon his way past Fredericksburg, beginning with a direct assault against Lee's prepared defenses.

Once Burnside's officers became aware of his battle plans, their reaction was overwhelmingly negative. To gain support for his proposals Burnside held at least two conferences with his commanders. He reminded them that he had never sought command and that, despite his admitted deficiencies, he was trying to do his best. "Your duty," he scolded one group, "is not to throw cold water, but to aid me loyally with your advice and hearty service." General Patrick left one strategy meeting at the Lacy House depressed at what he had heard. Knowing better then anyone present the situation the army would face once across the river, he confided in his journal that night, "Oh that my eyes might be spared the sight of such bloodshed—may God in his infinite mercy spare the lives of those who are useful to family and country."[36]

On December 9 Burnside set his plans in motion. He ordered that the men prepare three days' cooked rations and draw sixty rounds of ammunition to be carried in their cartridge boxes and pockets. Generals Sumner and Franklin learned at headquarters that their grand divisions would spearhead the attack. Engineers readied five pontoon bridges (a sixth was added on December 12) for their use at three crossing points on the river. More than 140 guns (including seven large four-and-one-half-inch siege guns) rolled into positions on Stafford Heights to cover and support the river crossings.[37]

Sumner received the most hazardous assignment. His troops had to cross directly in front of Fredericksburg, drive through the town, and then charge across the open plain to assault General Longstreet's defenses on Spotsylvania Heights. Key to Longstreet's position was Marye's Heights, where the Cortland Volunteers had camped the previous summer. Now Confederate cannon crowned the crest, and infantry crowded in behind the stone wall bordering the narrow Telegraph Road below. The position seemed impregnable. Longstreet's artillery chief looked down on the open plain in front of his guns and boasted before the attack that "a chicken could not live on that field when we open on it."[38]

Franklin's troops would cross the Rappahannock two miles below Sumner onto an alluvial plain two and a half miles square, dotted here and there with a few large plantations and flanked by two tributaries of the Rappahannock: Deep Run on the outskirts of Fredericksburg and Massaponax Creek about three and a half miles farther downstream. Approximately two and a half miles back from the river and on a line generally parallel to it, Stonewall Jackson's troops occupied the wooded hills and ridges of Spotsylvania Heights.

Two thoroughfares traversed the open plain between the armies; both ran perpendicular to Franklin's axis of attack. The Richmond, Fredericksburg, and Potomac Railroad emerged from Fredericksburg and closely followed the foothills of the heights until it reached Hamilton's Crossing, a station stop where the Mine Road crossed. Approaching the low ground scoured by the Massaponax, the railroad then turned south, skirting the bald knoll known as Prospect Hill. The second thoroughfare, the Bowling Green Road (locally also called the Old Richmond Stage Road), ran parallel to the railroad at about midpoint on the plain. The road was lined with cedar trees and in many places was "sunken" below banks three or four feet high.[39]

Beginning on December 10 a period of cold nights and warm, sunny days melted much of the snow that remained on the ground. That same day Burnside's forces began moving down to staging areas near the river. When Paul's brigade arrived near Falmouth, the 23d bivouacked in a pinewood not far from their old camp Rufus King. At dark a Union band appeared on the riverbank near the railroad bridge in front of Fredericksburg to play a medley of national airs. The shadowy forms of the enemy pickets beyond the dark river appeared to take no notice until the band struck up "Dixie," whereupon a chorus of friendly cheers and laughter rolled up from both banks of the river.[40]

After midnight Sumner's and Franklin's troops broke camp and advanced to the river crossings, guided by a number of men detailed from Patrick's old brigade who were familiar with the area.[41] In the dark before the dawn on the 11th the troops shivered in their heavy sky-blue overcoats as they crowded by the thousands before the two primary crossing points. At three o'clock army engineers at Franklin's crossing off-loaded the flat-bottomed pontoon boats from their carriers and man-handled them down the bluff to the river's edge. When the first of a string of boats entered the water through the crackling ice, an enemy picket on the opposite bank pulled a burning brand from his campfire and slowly waved it overhead to alert his comrades along the heights that the battle had begun. Knowing they had been discovered, the bridge builders worked quickly to complete the two four-hundred-foot spans by eleven that morning.[42]

The battle opened on December 11 with Sumner's troops attempting to muscle their way into Fredericksburg; Franklin's troops below remained relatively inactive. The men of Paul's brigade sat and watched as the smoke rose above the city from Union artillery fire. As the time slowly passed, the chaplain of the 21st New York could not help but notice the disconcerting sight of a dozen carpenters nearby finishing up a stack of empty coffins. Finally, about sunset, Brig. Gen. Charles Devens's brigade of the Sixth Corps marched across the swaying pontoon bridge behind a tooting brass band to secure the bridgehead. Franklin ordered the rest of his command to follow the next morning.[43]

Colonel Hoffman was to remember the dawn of December 12 as being "still as death." Early welcome rumors circulated through the ranks that the enemy had retreated, abandoning their positions. The men of the 23d anxiously watched as Sixth Corps troops and George D. Bayard's cavalry brigade crossed the bridge and scrambled up the thirty-foot bank to disappear into the fog. By the time their turn came to cross at two that afternoon, the sun had burned off the fog to reveal a view of the plain that took their breath away. Three long lines of soldiers in light-blue coats, 35,000 of them, were formed across the broad open field, with a fourth line behind made up of horse-drawn artillery. "The deployment was the most beautiful sight I have seen yet," wrote General Reynolds's artillery chief, "something really like the movement of troops on the open battlefields of Europe."[44]

Sergeant Crandall of the 23d would recall that the "almost oppressive" silence of the moment did not last. "We were standing at a rest waiting further orders when a column of smoke burst from the hill then a heavy report and the balls come plowing through the ground in front and bounding, fell in the river in rear of us." Other shells exploded overhead, wounding one man of the 23d and just missing Colonel Hoffman. Another round struck a column of cavalry, "emptying several saddles, and the riderless horses were prancing about the field." Thousands of men watched with interest as some of Franklin's artillery rushed forward across this great stage of battle to unlimber and temporarily silence the enemy guns.[45]

By the evening of December 12 Burnside had sent almost a hundred thousand men over the river without critical loss. Franklin's sector remained relatively quiet, but riot reigned in some sections of Fredericksburg. A number of Sumner's troops lost all restraint, both officers and men breaking into and looting abandoned private residences. General Patrick, serving as the army's provost marshal general, spent the day trying to stop the miscreants. At one point he took his riding whip to a cocky soldier attempting to carry away stolen bedding and carpet.[46]

Franklin's men assumed a defensive position for the night in a strong curved line covering the pontoon bridges. The line ran from Deep Run on the right, then along the Bowling Green Road until it bent back to the river between the stately residences of Mr. Thomas Pratt's "Smithfield" and Arthur Bernard's stone mansion, "Mannsfield." Smith's Sixth Corps held the right of the line, Gibbon's and Meade's divisions the left of the line to the river. Doubleday's division (minus Doubleday's old brigade under Col. James Gavin, serving as bridge guard) massed in reserve between the Bowling Green Road and the Bernard house. The 23d, the last in the brigade column of regiments, stacked its two hundred rifles in front of the house on familiar ground where some of them had been posted as guards the previous June.[47]

Franklin established his headquarters in a grove of trees near Mannsfield. About dark Burnside arrived with his staff to meet with Franklin and review his battle plans. He directed Franklin to open the fight early on the 13th with an attack against Jackson's defenses. Sumner would then strike against Longstreet's sector at Fredericksburg a blow that would carry the field and complete the victory.

When Burnside just at dark rode out to inspect Franklin's positions, his soldiers cheered him. Sergeant Crandall would note, "The plain fairly trembled with the sound of human voices." Colonel Hoffman later tried to explain his own enthusiasm on the eve of battle. "I never dreaded going into battle so much as I did crossing that stream," he wrote, "but as soon as across I never was so willing to fight." During the night two opposing pickets taunted each other near the Bowling Green Road. "To-morrow we will drive you into the Rappahannock," the Reb boasted, "or you will drive us into hell."[48]

The blood-red sun rose slowly on the 13th through a gray fog. Commanders tentatively adjusted their battle lines to face the emerging dark ridgeline, still sparkling with Confederate campfires. Around seven the long-awaited final orders arrived from Burnside's headquarters; they instructed Franklin, "Keep your whole command in position for a rapid movement

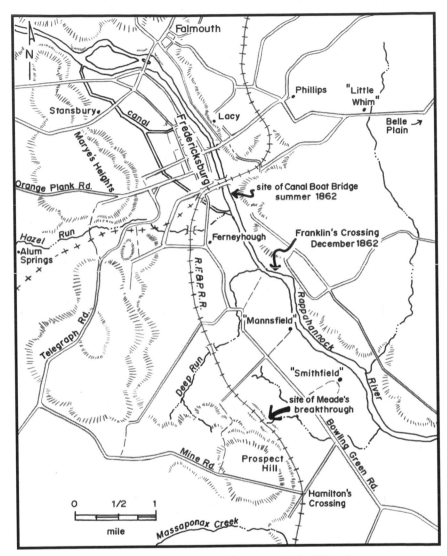

The battlefield of Fredericksburg, December 1862. *(John Heiser)*

down the old Richmond Road, and you will send out at once a division at least to pass below Smithfield, to seize, if possible, the height near Captain Hamilton's, . . . taking care to keep it well supported and its line of retreat open."[49] Far from inspiring a grand effort, the indecisive orders provided the conservative-minded Franklin justification to do relatively little.

Franklin ordered Reynolds's First Corps to lead the attack. Reynolds chose his old division of the Pennsylvania Reserves under George Gordon

Meade to "seize" the heights near Hamilton's Crossing in conformance with Burnside's instructions. Meade moved his small division of 4,500 men seven to eight hundred yards downriver under the cover of fog, across the steep ravine near Smithfield, and then around to align on General Gibbon's left, facing the heights. The troops halted at the Bowling Green Road to remove the hedge fences and bridge the drainage ditches for the passage of artillery.[50]

Doubleday's division followed the Reserves to secure and guard Meade's left flank. His three brigades moved in closed, massed columns across the Smithfield ravine. Paul's brigade under Col. William F. Rogers of the 21st (Doubleday reported Paul in Washington "on account of severe domestic affliction"[51]) lay down in two lines behind a fence near Smithfield, facing downriver. Confederate artillery opened a random cross fire on the New Yorkers, causing a number of casualties. Gerrish's four three-inch rifled guns and Phelps's brigade formed on Rogers's right; Stewart's six twelve-pounder smoothbores along with the Iron Brigade took position on his left.

The extension of Franklin's left flank brought Doubleday's division into contact with Maj. Gen. J. E. B. Stuart's cavalry force guarding Lee's right flank from Hamilton's Crossing to the mouth of the Massaponax. Stuart had under his command two brigades of cavalry, about four thousand sabers, and eighteen cannon under his artillery chief, the twenty-four-year-old Maj. John Pelham. In addition, on a rise of ground south of the Massaponax, artillery officers unlimbered an unusual breech-loading Whitworth field gun imported from England; it could fire a screeching bolt of iron up to three miles.[52]

Doubleday also had to contend with a Rebel force concealed in a wood near the river eight hundred yards to Rogers's left and front. Doubleday's two frontline batteries and the longer-range Union guns across the river directed their fire at these woods to drive them off. Then the 24th Michigan and the 7th Wisconsin of the Iron Brigade, preceded by the 2d U.S. Sharpshooters of Phelps's brigade, advanced to clear the wood and secure Franklin's left.[53]

While Doubleday directed his attention toward his troops skirmishing at the woods, Major Pelham detached one of his twelve-pounder smoothbores and courageously led it forward through the thinning mist to the intersection of the Mine Road and the Richmond Stage Road. Pelham positioned his gun less than four hundred yards off the angle

WHITE DEATH ON A FROZEN HILLSIDE

where Meade's and Doubleday's divisions met, with excellent enfilading lines of fire against both.

Meade's troops had begun to deploy beyond the Bowling Green Road when about ten o'clock they saw the flash of Pelham's gun, instantly followed by the twelve-pound ball tearing down through their ranks. Meade halted his assault while Franklin turned his available guns on Pelham's isolated outpost. After an hour's pounding under shot and shell, the "Gallant Pelham" drew back his gun to near Hamilton's Crossing.[54]

Doubleday now acted to stabilize and secure the positions of his troops. From the river the line of Iron Brigade troops stretched obliquely to the Bowling Green Road. Rogers's men shifted right to extend the Iron Brigade's line along the road near Pelham's former position. Phelps's brigade, now joined by Gavin's, continued the division line to connect with Meade's attacking troops on their right. Rogers sent forward two of his companies, and Phelps sent three companies to occupy the roadbed and protect the division artillery from Rebel skirmishers and sharpshooters.[55]

Rogers's New Yorkers remained inactive in two lines of battle along the road for much of the battle. "All we could do," said one soldier of the 35th, "was to lie as flat as possible while the shells flew over and around us like rain." "Legs, arms and heads flew on all sides of us for a time," Lieutenant Baldwin of the 23d remembered, and "when a man was knocked from the ranks the next took his place with turning a pitying eye to his comrade as he uttered his death shriek." One shell that exploded in front of the 23d sent an iron fragment through the clothes of Capt. Luzern Todd and Lt. William H. Jones before striking Colonel Hoffman full in the chest, knocking him down. Shaken but not seriously wounded, Hoffman remained in command of the regiment throughout the battle.[56]

During the morning's fighting, General Burnside stood at the window of his headquarters, the Alexander K. Phillips house on Stafford Heights, searching desperately through his binoculars for some indication of Franklin's success. High over his head floated the observation balloon *Eagle*, with an unobstructed view of the battlefield.[57] Exhibiting signs of severe anxiety and mental exhaustion, Burnside eventually became so frustrated by Franklin's apparent slow progress that he turned to focus on Sumner's men waiting on the outskirts of Fredericksburg. "Feeling the importance of haste," he later wrote, "I now directed General Sumner to commence his attack."[58] His reversal of previous plans in favor of separate and uncoordinated attacks resulted in one of the worst Northern defeats in the war. For hours, Sumner's brigades surged forward in waves to systematic slaughter before Longstreet's merciless artillery on Marye's Heights.

Franklin, meanwhile, continued his cautious advance toward Lee's right, anchored on Prospect Hill. Twice during the morning Confederate artillery had checked Meade's progress. Pelham first halted Meade's advance, then, as the Pennsylvanians came within eight hundred yards of Prospect Hill, Lt. Col. Reuben Lindsay Walker opened with his fourteen guns dug in along the crest. Meade's troops had to halt near the Bowling Green Road while Franklin's guns pounded Jackson's strong points and attempted to neutralize the Confederate artillery.

Midday passed, the Union artillery fire had spent its fury, and Meade's troops, supported by Gibbon's division, for the third time surged forward with eyes fixed on the distant ridgeline. Jackson's still-defiant artillery opened once more, sending the attackers toward the sparse cover of a point of woods extending out north of the railroad to the right of Prospect Hill. Crossing the railroad track and crashing through the woods over wet and soggy ground, the Pennsylvanians discovered and poured through a six-hundred-yard gap in Jackson's line, only to be thrown back by converging Confederate reserves.

When Meade's defeated troops fled back across the smoky battlefield, followed by the cheering Confederates, Doubleday's troops prepared to receive their attack. Lieutenant Colonel Crane of the 23d, on temporary duty with General Reynolds's staff, rode out among the "flying mob," shouting at them to rally.[59] At one point Rogers hustled his brigade to the right to brace Meade's crumbling line. It soon returned to its former position when the expected Confederate counterattack failed to materialize.

At twilight Jackson's victorious troops probed Franklin's left for weak points preparatory to a general counterstroke. Jackson pushed ten of his batteries forward to duel with the Union guns. Doubleday's men responded quickly to the danger by adjusting their positions—except for the Iron Brigade, which Doubleday found "wandering around" apparently confused and leaderless.[60] The crisis passed as a result of the growing darkness and the effective fire of the Union artillery. Jackson called off any further action that night.

Nightfall did not end the suffering of Doubleday's men. Stuart's skirmishers remained active and deadly to the unwary, and Rebel cannon kept up a harassing fire of canister. Union officers did not allow the men to start any comforting fires, not even to set a match to a pipe bowl that might give away a regiment's position. Throughout the night they had to huddle in the cold, listening to the moans of the wounded and the doleful tolling of the steeple clock of the St. George Episcopal Church in Fredericksburg.[61]

Lee and his lieutenants, on the other hand, could celebrate a great victory. In fact, it all seemed too easy. Standing on a hillside watching the grand spectacle of Franklin's advance in front of Jackson's line, General Lee at one point turned to one of his generals to say, "It is well that war is so terrible—we should grow too fond of it!"[62]

Daylight on December 14 revealed to Franklin's men how terrible this war had truly become. The stark white bodies of dead comrades dotted the hillsides, having been stripped naked by the Rebels "like hogs which had been cleaned," according to one Confederate observer. Colonel Hoffman later referred to the battle simply as "the butchering." Few could doubt that the Army of the Potomac had suffered yet another humiliating defeat. "A feeling of gloom pervaded the army," wrote one of Franklin's soldiers; "in the evening there was a general disposition to sing hymns."[63]

Burnside saw little purpose in further bloodletting at Fredericksburg. On the 15th he ordered the army back across the river to Stafford Heights. At dark Franklin's defeated troops gathered before their bridges and, under softly spoken orders and the cover of a boisterous winter wind, silently slipped back across the river. While Doubleday's troops waited their turn to cross, the men of Paul's brigade received a ration of whiskey to ward off fatigue and lift their spirits. General Paul, having returned from Washington just as the battle ended, led his brigade back over the pontoon bridge at ten o'clock—minus Companies G and B of the 23d, which remained on picket and did not receive the word to cross. Near dawn the orphaned companies appeared on the riverbank bringing up the wounded and stragglers that they had combed from the battlefield. With all across, the engineers swung the bridges to the north bank.[64]

Franklin had committed only about ten thousand of his sixty thousand men to the battle (from Meade's and Gibbon's divisions), and about one-third of that ten thousand were listed as casualties. The 23d had two killed and sixteen wounded. One Southern Tier man claimed, "We did not fire a shot as infantry during the four days we were over the river except as skirmishers."[65]

Once they were safe on the Stafford shore, the soldiers' anger over their defeat intensified. This did not, however, immediately translate into expressions of hatred against their enemies, either soldiers or civilians.[66]

On the 15th, during the lull in the fighting, Lieutenant Baldwin sat with a group of his men "amused" to see a portion of their skirmish line, as casually as you please, advance to chat with their opposites. "Everyone looked up astonished," he observed, to see both sides "engaged in quiet conversation, some trading coffee for whiskey, others discussing the war question." When Doubleday became aware of the situation, he put a stop to it and set the skirmishers to glaring at one another again at a distance.[67]

None were more puzzled by the "friendly" Union behavior toward them than Lee's soldiers. One exasperated Rebel officer talking with a Union soldier during a truce to bury the dead called his attention to the bodies of dead Yankees still lying on the ground and stripped of "every vestige of clothing," indicating a malice on the part of their enemies beyond the practical need for warm clothing. He challenged the Yankee, "Is that not very revolting to you?—don't you think it terrible!" The Rebel concluded by the Yankee's apparent lack of outrage, "You Yankees don't know how to hate—you don't hate us near so much as we hate you. You've yet to learn how to hate."[68]

For the most part, the Union soldiers directed their anger inward toward their own officers and leaders. A man of the 83d New York wrote home on January 1, "If we knew that we were doing some good we would be satisfied, but when we see our companions slaughtered through the ignorance and blunders of officers we have reason to complain." The soldiers felt that they had done their duty, accomplished nothing, and had only the long lists of their dead and wounded comrades to show for it. "They have fallen a sacrifice," spoke Seymour Dexter of the 23d, "but a sacrifice for what? Has it been for our beloved country or has it been to feed the jealousies and pamper the ambition of unprincipled and unqualified leaders?" Another soldier cried out in despair, "Alas, my poor country! It has strong limbs to march, and meet the foe, stout arms to strike heavy blows, brave hearts to dare—but the brains, the brains—have we no brains to use the arms and limbs and eager hearts with cunning? Perhaps Old Abe has some funny story to tell appropriate to the occasion."[69]

Colonel Hoffman saw the burden of the Union defeat resting squarely upon unimaginative generals, hamstrung by the "scientific principles" of warfare taught to them at West Point. Better, thought Hoffman, for Franklin to have massed the bulk of his forces in the dark of night behind his forward skirmishers and then, at first light, rushed upon the enemy infantry lines "like an avalanche" with fixed bayonets. The momentum of such a concerted attack would have carried it forward and quickly uncovered weak points in the enemy position (such as the point of woods in front of Meade), which could have been fully developed and exploited by sheer weight of numbers if nothing else. After Fredericksburg President Lincoln came round to similar thinking. He then sought a different kind of general, one who could "face the arithmetic." By that he meant someone who would aggressively apply the superior numbers and resources of the North on the battlefield, intensifying the war as a consequence, and out of necessity accepting the trade-off of greater losses for greater victories and an earlier end to the war. His search would end in the spring of 1864 with the appointment of the taciturn and determined U. S. Grant as general in chief of the Union armies.[70]

Lincoln's fateful decision placing the incompetent Burnside in command of the Grand Army at a time when the North struggled to find its bearings in rapidly changing conditions brought the military fortunes of the North to their low ebb. When Burnside was finally relieved of his command in late January 1863, desertions from the army had been running at two hundred men a day, and more than eighty thousand men were listed as "absent from causes unknown."[71] It remains one of the most remarkable facts of the war that the Army of the Potomac was to rise from the ashes of Fredericksburg and then from the defeat at Chancellorsville that followed the next May to achieve in July the stellar victory at Gettysburg, which, combined with the victory at Vicksburg, set the country on the path to victory.

The explanation for this accomplishment is illusive. To some significant degree we can credit the character of the Union soldier: his abiding commitment to a reunited nation, the strong battle bonds of comrades united in a common cause, the sense of responsibility and duty, the esprit de corps of the Grand Army formed at Bailey's Cross Roads in 1861, and the strength and resiliency of youth. Even at the darkest hour, on December 14, the men of the 23d refused to lose faith in themselves or their cause. Looking up into the night sky they saw the shimmering bands of red, white, and blue light of an unusual display of the aurora borealis, the "northern lights." Private Maxson was to remember, "As we gazed upon it with delight, we felt that the national emblem had not been dishonored by [any] act of ours, and we worshiped in silence the starry banner."[72]

CHAPTER 10

Home

A fter the Battle of Fredericksburg the regiments of Paul's brigade were assigned to guard and provost duties at critical army supply and support centers, including Falmouth Station, Aquia Landing, and Belle Plain. On December 20, the 23d arrived near Belle Plain to provide protection for the three boat landings along the bay on the south bank of Potomac Creek.[1]

On January 3 news circulated in the brigade that the provost marshal general, Marsena Patrick, had requested the transfer of his old brigade to his command. The order became effective on January 8, 1863. All of the detailed men and the detached Company C were then returned to the 23d, increasing the number in camp to 467 men "present for duty equipped."[2]

Patrick assigned the 20th NYSM and the 21st New York to Aquia Landing, and, after January 10, the 35th took up positions along the railroad between Aquia Landing and Falmouth Station. The 23d separated at Belle Plain to guard the three landings: Companies H, F, K, and C at lower or Pratt's Landing; D, I, and E at Cottage Landing off Pratt's Point, extending out into the bay; and G, A, and B, at the upper (or Belle Plain) Landing.[3]

The thirty-six men of Company H found comfortable winter quarters in sturdy Rebel-built cabins near Pratt's Point in proximity to an abandoned Confederate earthen fort overlooking the entrance to Potomac Creek. The camp had access to good water, plenty of wood for fireplaces, and a panoramic view of the confluence of Potomac Creek and the

Potomac River, often "spotted with the sails of schooners and streaked by the trailing cloud left by the swift passing steamers." Lieutenant Baldwin added to the generally favorable description of the landscape: "Evergreens of red cedar, English Holly and mistletoe in the tops of ancient oaks add enough to make it sublime."[4]

In March 1863 the busy Belle Plain waterfront took on the appearance of a small port city:

At the wharfs the temporary store-houses are filled with barrels of pork, beef, beans, etc. or bales of hay and bags of oats. Thousands of barrels are piled upon the shores, awaiting the endless trains of army wagons to transport them to the interior camps. Much of the labor of unloading and storing goods is done by "contrabands" who seemed happy in their new-born freedom, and worked with a will. They reside in tents near by. . . . They have frequent religious meetings and those who have attended speak of their evident sincerity and truly religious fervor in singing, especially their novel hymns of joy.[5]

Duty for the Southern Tier men continued generally unhurried and untroubled into the spring. Their work schedule consisted of one day of duty at the wharves and two off. Their specific duties included guarding government stores, checking passes of individuals boarding or leaving the ships in the harbor, and seizing contraband goods. Dexter commented in a letter, "A little excitement is now and then raised in the arresting of some disorderly soldier or civilian or in the confiscation of sutler goods." Other notable events for the Cortland Volunteers at Pratt's Landing included the arrival of new uniforms on January 23 and the embarkation of the Ninth Corps beginning on February 7 for Newport News, Virginia.[6]

Rations were adequate and plentiful. A member of the 35th New York wrote from Cottage Landing on December 25:

We draw rations of hard bread, one pound per man per day, or one and a quarter pounds of soft bread; salt pork three quarters of a pound, or fresh beef one pound; beans, rice, coffee, sugar, molasses, vinegar, salt and soap and candles . . . ; and occasionally desiccated potatoes, desiccated vegetables for soup, onions, and split peas. We can also buy from the modest sutler, if we have money or credit, ten potatoes for a quarter of a dollar; five apples for the same price; a pound of butter for sixty cents and a pound of cheese for forty; a dozen small biscuits for fifty cents; a newspaper for ten cents: three 3-cent papers of tobacco for a quarter.[7]

They supplemented their diet by fishing in the bay for shad, sturgeon, eels, perch, and herring. As members of the provost guard they also could receive confiscated foodstuffs.[8]

It soon became evident, however, that with the terrible Union defeat at Fredericksburg still fresh in their memory and their time of mustering-out fast approaching, the men of the brigade fell into a state of disillusionment with military service manifested in lassitude in the performance of their duty. They had had enough of war and could think of little else but going home. Private Maxson wrote, "We have seen too much of bloodshed, and had too many encounters with grim death, to hold any false notions we may have entertained." Captain Clark thought after the Battle of Fredericksburg, "It is all well enough to see two great armies drawn up in line of battle and see them blindly rushing on to death, always provided you are at a respectful safe distance to the rear." He concluded, "After mature deliberation and reflection," that war was "morally wrong"; he preferred "peace 'by a d—d sight!'"[9]

On January 18 Colonel Hoffman acknowledged the "loose" discipline of his troops. He reported that "all seemed to partake of the idea that all that was necessary was to lay around, eat and sleep away 4 or 5 months until their time was out." Army staff officers officially confirmed his fears when they inspected the brigade on February 4 and found the 23d, along with other regiments, deficient in efficiency and discipline. The negative results of the inspection, contained in Special Order No. 18, were published in New York City newspapers.[10]

Hoffman complained to General Patrick on March 7 about the "villainous" inspection reports that brought discredit on his regiment, but he apparently did little to straighten out the situation. For example, he refused to get involved in an ongoing bitter conflict between the men of Company K and their captain, whom they openly accused of cowardice in battle. Adjutant Hayt noticed that by February 7 even Colonel Hoffman seemed to reflect the listless state of the regiment by his "shabby" and careless appearance. In May Hoffman scoffed at talk of his being promoted to a brigadier general, admitting in a letter, "I am above my capacity already." He went on to say, "If I can carry the Regiment through [that] is all I ask."[11]

Hoffman faced many challenges to his authority, especially in regard to the activities of army sutlers. Restricted from using the military railroad from Aquia Landing to transport their goods to Burnside's troops, the sutlers opted to pass through Belle Plain. Before leaving Washington they had to submit inventories to government officials to ensure that their cargoes did not include contraband goods, particularly whiskey. Each sutler then joined with two others to charter a ship for the trip to Belle Plain, where Hoffman's men would check the manifest against the inventory.[12] If all was found in order, the vessel could land its cargo at one of the wharfs, where the sutler could hire wagon transportation for the trip to the camps. Adjutant Hayt noted on January 14, "Sutler stores are being landed in abundance." On January 22 the schooner *Telegraph* arrived, loaded with the stores of sutler O. G. Judd for the 23d as well as for the 14th NYSM and 157th New York Volunteers. Judd listed eighty-five different items in his inventory.[13]

Despite the efforts of Federal authorities to regulate sutler activities, including setting the prices for goods, the system provided plenty of opportunity for abuse. The ability of sutlers to smuggle whiskey to the appreciative soldiers at Belle Plain became a particularly serious problem for authorities. One sutler sent a hundred bottles of whiskey ashore concealed in apple barrels marked "Greenings, Spitsburgh, Gill Flowers, etc." Hayt wrote with disgust on December 25, "The universal rule of celebrating the Saviour's birth by getting drunk was not in many instances deviated from in camp." One man reported on December 27 that whiskey could be easily gotten at Aquia Landing for $2.50 a pint. On January 14 Hayt rode down to the lower landing and confiscated four gallons of whiskey, which he gave to the post hospital for medical use.[14]

Additional difficulties arose from the special arrangements allowed between sutlers and the volunteer officers. Sutlers could act as the officers' personal agents to obtain and deliver items from home, including whiskey.[15] This cozy relationship opened the way to many abuses, as evidenced by the following note written to General Patrick on February 9 and signed, "Privates, Co. H, 23 N.Y.V."

Sir
Capt. M. C. Clark of Co. H, 23rd N.Y. Vols. is in the habit, "when he is an Officer of the Day," of going on board of the Sutler transports lying here in the bay and buying Apples, Cakes, Cidar, milk drink, and

other sutler stores for some Non. Com. officers in his company to sell and he will let no one else buy or land anything and we would like to know if it is right or consistent with good military discipline. If it is not we hope you will see to it immediately.[16]

Things at Belle Plain continued to deteriorate until finally, on February 11, Hoffman, "with blood in his eye, harness all on," rode from headquarters toward the lower landing. That night after Hoffman returned to headquarters, Hayt wrote in his journal, "Look out for breakers." The next day Hoffman sent Major Gregg down to take charge of things, and by the 14th Captains Sumner Barstow (Company C), George H. Powers (E), and Clark (H) were all under arrest. All three soon resigned rather than face charges, citing business or family matters requiring their attention at home. Captain Clark added in his resignation that the reduced number of men in his company did not support an officer of his grade. Hoffman wrote on Clark's application, "This officer has proven himself wholly unreliable. . . . He is a young man of fine ability and is remarkably well connected at home."[17]

Apparently of the three captains only Clark sought later to restore his commission. After a letter-writing campaign to state officials by Clark's influential friends in Cortland, Hoffman wrote to the adjutant general of New York, John T. Sprague, requesting Clark's reappointment as captain, to date the day that his resignation had become effective (18 February). Hoffman claimed that the regrettable events leading to Clark's resignation had stemmed from a "misunderstanding." Clark duly returned to service from his mother's home in Groton, New York.[18]

On March 20, 1863, Army of the Potomac Special Order No. 36 alerted Paul's brigade to prepare for an active campaign under the army's new commander, Major General Hooker. On April 24, however, Hooker received word that his two-year New York regiments were to be mustered out of service in May according to the respective dates upon which the governor had accepted their last companies into state service. Meanwhile, on April 28, the Southern Tier Regiment received orders to join Colonel Rogers and the 21st New York at Aquia Landing. On the evening of April 29 the regiment, "with nine hearty cheers," departed from Belle Plain on the ship *Osceola*.[19]

Aquia Landing, where Aquia Creek flows into the Potomac, marked the terminus of the Richmond, Fredericksburg, and Potomac Railroad. Before the war the most direct journey from Washington to Richmond had included a steamship trip three and a half hours long from Washington's Sixth Street wharf to Aquia Landing and then a five-and-a-half-hour rail trip for the seventy-five miles to Richmond.[20]

The 23d and the 21st regiments were given responsibility for protecting the two landings at Aquia Harbor. The 21st manned twenty-three guard posts, including Beeber's Eating House, and directed construction work by military prisoners either sent from various units of the army or quartered on the prison barge *Walkill* at anchor in the Potomac. The 20th NYSM and the 35th New York were positioned along the railroad from Aquia to Falmouth Station.[21] Two gunboats guarded the harbor while three redoubts, numbered one through three, protected the southern land approaches. The Cortland Volunteers occupied Redoubt Number Two, overlooking the Stafford Court House Road.[22]

In the first week of May the soldiers turned their thoughts from home to the sounds of battle as the forces of Generals Lee and Hooker fought the Battle of Chancellorsville. Drummer Edgcomb wrote in his letter of May 4, "For three days an awful fight has been going on at Fredericksburg—we can hear it very plain and once in a while see a shell burst." Maxson said that "the spirit of the Twenty-third was aroused, and many longed to go and help their noble comrades fight out the battle." Many others no doubt were just as happy to watch from the sidelines. "We know how to pity the boys" doing the fighting, Edgcomb wrote, after standing near the landing and watching a train arrive from Falmouth with a few hundred wounded from the battlefield.[23] The battle turned, like so many others, on the Union commander's shrinking back onto the defensive, after achieving initial success, and consequently losing first the tactical initiative and ultimately the battle.

On May 7 the officers of the brigade gathered in a building at Aquia Landing to surprise General Patrick with a farewell party. Colonel Rogers greeted Patrick when he came through the door and provided a short speech of tribute. The officers then presented Patrick a beautiful silver service that cost $1,200 and weighed altogether seventy-five pounds. Each piece was engraved with names of units of his old brigade and with other insignia of war. Tears welled up in the old general's eyes as he looked upon what he later described as "the most splendid service of silver—massive, rich, elaborate and in excellent taste. . . . I made the best reply to it that I could and our eyes all moistened." He then shook hands all round and departed.[24]

On May 11 the Southern Tier Regiment boarded the mail steamer *John Brooks* to begin its journey home. Arriving at Washington it spent the night in a barracks near the train depot. During the next two days, loaded down with gifts and other small purchases that Hoffman had allowed them to make in Washington, the men continued their journey north in a nineteen-car train pulled by two locomotives. Along the way Hoffman kept up telegraphic communication with Elmira mayor Thomas S. Spaulding, who planned a hero's welcome. The crowds started to gather in Elmira early on the 13th, and the town was "decked in its gayest holiday attire. . . . Numerous flags were flung to the breeze, banners and badges were everywhere present, bustle, activity and preparation characterized the day."[25]

The train had just passed Harrisburg, Pennsylvania, when tragedy struck. Leaving Marysville, many of the men had abandoned the interiors of stuffy cars to ride on their roofs in the open air. When Captain Clark attempted to join some of his men on top of the last car, his head struck the timbers of a bridge under which the train was passing. The blow knocked him from the car onto some rocks, killing him instantly. The train continued an additional mile and a half toward Sunbury before the engineer realized what had happened; he then backed up to recover Clark's mutilated body. Having thereby lost time, he then had to continue in reverse all the way to Marysville in order to let pass a scheduled southbound train. When around noon the anxious Elmira crowd learned the reason for the delay, "a feeling of sympathy ran through the whole community and the thronged streets."[26]

The train resumed its journey in a sudden downpour of rain. At Williamsport, despite the weather and the delays, crowds were on hand to cheer the regiment as the train passed. Sometime after half past six the spires of Elmira came into view, and the soldiers could hear the church bells ringing. From Southport on, enthusiastic spectators lined the tracks and waved from the balconies and windows of houses. The *Advertiser* reported, "From the railroad bridge to the depot one continued vociferous cheer, shouts of welcome and reply went up, which was not restrained until the gallant fellows had left the cars and were drawn up in double lines before the Delavan House." Under "one of the most drenching showers of the season," Mayor Spaulding stepped out on the balcony of the hotel to welcome the regiment home officially.[27]

Spaulding spoke on the reasons for the war and expressed "all honor to the brave hearts who would sacrifice home, friends, the luxuries of wealth, aye, even life, to sustain the government of our country." Hoffman gave a brief speech of thanks for the wonderful reception, after which a procession formed to escort the 23d to its old barracks. The Elmira Cornet Band led, followed by local civic societies, firemen, trustees, citizens, Wisner's Band, the Southern Tiers, and finally a long file of carriages filled with officers of the 12th and 26th New York regiments.[28]

Through the drenching rain the column moved down Main Street, along Water, up Lake, across Church, and up William Street to the barracks. The local paper remarked on the striking effect of "the flashing torches, the varying light and shades, and the steady marching of passing soldiery creating a rapid changing and splendid kaleidoscope, intoned as it was by the booming of cannon, ringing of bells and vociferous cheering, which has scarcely been our fortune to witness before." At the barracks, the local Elmira ladies laid out a "bounteous repast," including a pyramid cake with the inscription "A Welcome to the Brave Southern Tiers."[29]

The Cortland Volunteers, meanwhile, had the sad duty of removing the body of their commander from the train. They had it embalmed and placed for viewing in the new Chemung County Court House, on Lake Street, with an honor guard from the 23d. At half past four on May 14 the men carried Clark's remains to the train depot for the trip home to Cortland. Colonel Hoffman allowed the Cortland Volunteers with their weapons and equipment to escort the body to Cortland for the funeral and burial; they were then to return to Elmira for final mustering-out. Lt. Leonard F. Hathaway of Cuyler and 2d Lt. Archibald N. DeVoe of Elmira, now led the company.[30]

A group of local citizens met the train at Cortland and took Clark's body from the depot to the courthouse, where it lay in state in a small hall "canopied and walled by tastefully wreathed national flags." Bouquets of spring flowers surrounded the body; above Clark's heart lay a cross made from foliage and white flowers. The local paper reported that "from morn till eve came and went sympathizing ones—friends, acquaintances and strangers and the unbroken throng of persons told how universal was the feeling of bereavement." An ad hoc committee of Cortland lawyers met on the morning of the 16th to plan the funeral events and arrange for the pallbearers.[31]

At noon, Hathaway and the forty or so members of the company presented arms on Court Street as the pallbearers removed Clark's coffin from the courthouse and placed it in a waiting hearse. Whitlock's Ithaca Brass Band played the "melting strains of Pleyel's hymn." Only twenty-one men remained from the eighty-six that had stood before the same courthouse two years before to receive the flag that now bore the names of their battles. The procession formed, in order, the Ithaca band, the Cortland Volunteers, the hearse flanked by the six pallbearers, members of the bar, relatives and friends, and finally citizens and others.[32]

The procession turned into Church Street from Court and proceeded to the Universalist Church, where Lieutenant Hathaway had the men stack arms in the field adjacent to the building. The flag-covered coffin was placed before the altar, surrounded by "strewn" white flowers. Clark's sword and belt lay on top of the flag. A silver plate on the lid of the coffin bore the inscription, "Capt. Martin C. Clark, 23rd Reg. N.Y. Vols. Aged 26 years." Hundreds of people sought entrance to the church, but most had to remain outside. The Reverend William H. Fish provided the eulogy.[33]

After the band had played a "solemn air," the procession re-formed outside the church for the walk to Cortland Rural Cemetery, on the slope of Court House Hill. The local paper reported, "Never has our village looked upon so imposing and extensive a pageant. The streets were a river of humanity, all anxious to testify their respect for the brave dead." The soldiers marched with reversed arms behind their flag, which was draped in black. Bringing up the rear came an "immense throng of citizens" who walked silently under the influence of the "solemn and mournful" music of the band.[34]

Entering the cemetery grounds the mourners gathered around at Clark's grave site. After a few remarks by Reverend Fish, the firing of three rounds over the grave, and the playing of "Taps" by a bugler, the crowds dispersed, and the remaining Cortland Volunteers returned to Elmira for mustering-out. The men received their last pay on May 19, and after saying their last good-byes to friends and comrades, they returned the next morning to their families and friends. The Cortland paper castigated Hathaway's "by no means commendable" behavior in allowing the company to disband without a formal homecoming celebration in Cortland.[35]

Of the total ninety-eight men mustered into Federal service in Company H, eleven had died in service: one mortally wounded in battle, Clark in an accident, and the rest from typhoid fever (five), chronic diarrhea (two), pneumonia (one), or "inflammation of the brain and lungs" (one). Eight had been wounded or injured: four in battle, three in accidents, and one intentionally to gain a discharge from service. Of the seventy-nine men who mustered out of the company for one reason or another, forty-three reenlisted in other units. The record indicates that four men had deserted from the company while in Federal service.

After the war Colonel Hoffman settled on a large farm in Horseheads, New York, and served in the state assembly for two terms as a Democrat. He had no children. He died a suicide on August 26, 1883. Lieutenant Colonel Crane went on to serve with the 107th New York, Major Gregg with the 179th New York. Both survived the war. From Company H, Lt. Alvah D. Waters later mustered out of the 10th New York Cavalry as a major and died in Cortland on April 27, 1870. Benjamin Andrews, after discharge from the 157th New York as a captain, took his law practice to Sarasota, Florida. He died around 1870.

Although the Cortland Volunteers had passed into history, the war continued for Cortland County residents. In the spring of 1863 the nation resolved to mobilize all of its resources to bring the war to a rapid and successful conclusion. No war measure was more significant in this regard than the Federal Enrollment Act, or, as it was better known, the Draft Act of 1863. The act established for the first time the primacy of the Federal government in raising large numbers of troops for the national defense. Authority to enroll and draft citizens into Federal service layered down from the provost marshal general's office in the War Department to district provost marshals within the states; the latter were appointed by the president and held the rank of captain. Administratively, Cortland fell within the Western District of New York, under Maj. Alexander S. Diven, and within that the Twenty-third District (conforming to the Twenty-third Congressional District, made up of Cortland and Onondaga counties), under Captain Alonzo Wood. The various Cortland townships made up subdistricts within the Twenty-third, numbered twenty-eight through thirty-five, each with an assigned enrollment officer who reported to a three-man district enrollment board headed by Captain Wood.[36]

The Draft Act of 1863 articulated the principle that all able-bodied male citizens (also aliens intending to become citizens) between the ages of twenty and forty-five had an obligation to perform military service to meet the national emergency. Under this act the provost marshals would create enrollment lists from each district, valid for two years, to be drawn upon if needed under specific troop calls by the president. If a draft of men from a particular district was required, sufficient names would be drawn from the lists to meet the manpower quotas set by the Federal authorities, in proportion to enrollment numbers. Men would be drafted for three years or until the end of the war, whichever came first. When an individual received notification that his name had been drawn, he would present himself—to serve, seek an exemption, hire a substitute, or pay the Federal government a commutation fee of three hundred dollars. Those who tried to evade service after being drafted were identified as deserters, subject to arrest by the provost marshal and military trial.[37]

The first enrollment began on May 25, 1863, with officials going house to house in their respective districts and subdistricts to identify and enroll individuals subject to military service. The first Northern draft followed soon after, starting the first week of July and lasting into August.[38] The famous New York City draft riots resulted in at least a hundred deaths. The process upstate, however, proceeded with relative calm. On August 19 a blindfolded official drew the first name from the Twenty-third District out of a rotating container set up in Syracuse at the courthouse.[39] Two days later, on August 21, officials declared the draft in Cortland County complete, adding with an apparent sigh of relief, "Everything passed off quietly." Of the 2,510 Cortland men enrolled during this time, 657 names were drawn, to fulfill the county quota of 346.[40] Only about ten of the fifty men actually drafted into service from the Twenty-third District during this call were residents of Cortland County.[41] Of the three remaining Federal drafts that would be conducted in the North in response to the 1864 troop calls of March, July, and December, the Twenty-third District had to respond significantly only to the March levy.[42] Nationally, not more than 5.5 percent of all Union soldiers serving during the Civil War did so as state or Federal conscripts.[43]

In fact, Cortland County for the most part avoided the heavy hand of national conscription in the last years of the war. The county benefited from substantial county credits for enlistments (270), substitutes (124), and individual commutation fees (209), as well as from the active county effort through paid agents to find volunteers in other counties and states, recruits who would be credited to Cortland County and receive its generous bounties. In addition, in late 1864 the military committees within the Twenty-third District successfully petitioned the War Department to form a local one-year regiment (the 185th). At the time, a one-year enlistee would receive at minimum the six-hundred-dollar county bounty, the hundred-dollar Federal bounty, and sixteen dollars a month military pay.[44] Two hundred five Cortland men joined the 185th, mostly in Companies E, F, and G.

An interesting profile emerges from the various categories of Cortland men responding to the manpower calls of late 1863 and 1864. The average age of volunteers enlisting was twenty-six; those hiring substitutes, twenty-eight; those paying commutation, thirty; and those joining the 185th, twenty-four. Seventy-three percent of the volunteers were farmers; of those hiring substitutes, 65 percent were farmers; paying commutation, 68 percent; in the 185th, 64 percent. Thirty-six percent of individuals of the volunteer category were married (22 percent of them had children); of those hiring substitutes, 65 percent were married (51 percent with children); paying commutation, 59 percent (32 percent with children); in the 185th, 33 percent (21 percent with children). The figures suggest that the Cortland enlistments in the 185th late in the war represent a new group of young men answering the call to serve. Less than 10 percent had any prior military service. Also, although a number of those acquiring substitutes or paying commutation belonged to the more well-to-do Cortland families, in general the motivations of these groups to avoid service seem to have been related more to family obligations than to taking advantage of the prerogatives of wealth or class.

During the final two years of the war Cortland County suffered greatly in blood and treasure. On July 1, 1863, at Gettysburg, Cortland experienced the bloodiest day in its history. County casualties, primarily in the 76th and 157th regiments, numbered thirty-four killed, ninety-nine wounded, and thirty-four captured. Later, during the opening engagement of the Army of the Potomac's final campaign, which ended at Appomattox, the novice 185th New York charged into an explosion of Confederate fire at the Joseph M. Lewis farm on the Quaker Road, losing eleven Cortland men killed and twenty-seven wounded. By the end of the war the county had suffered 310 service-related deaths out of its 1,500 soldiers and had bond obligations of more than $600,000 to pay for bounty and related expenses.[45]

With an increasing number of its men in uniform, the morale of the county hung on the ebb and flow of military events. Jane Rebecca Randall, associate manager of the Sanitary Commission in the county, reported after the terrible Union defeats at Fredericksburg and Chancellorsville, "There is no *heart* in our people, just now." As a result, she stated, there was little to be done locally "to coerce the movement of the public feelings" to support her soldier relief work. In contrast, on July 13, 1863, after the victories of Gettysburg and Vicksburg, Randall wrote, "We shall commence our earnest effort at once to again wake up our people to more efficient action."[46]

The year 1864 proved a particularly trying time for county residents. Not only did they have to contend with extreme local flooding in the spring and, that autumn, an outbreak of diphtheria that took the lives of many children, but the rolling battles in Virginia gave them little respite from anxiety for their loved ones in service.[47] "When the news came that a great battle was in progress," one woman later remembered in a letter to the Cortland Grand Army of the Republic post, "often I could not sleep but would walk the floor nights, with my knitting in hand thinking of our dear 'boys in blue.' I could seem to see them lying out on the battlefield wounded and dying . . . no wife, no mother and no sister near, and my mother-heart cried out in an agony of grief and of sympathy for them."[48] The dark cloth of mourning was a common sight on the streets of Cortland, and many more families waited with sad longing for news of their soldiers reported missing or unaccounted for. Phebe Tuttle of Freetown, whose seventeen-year-old son had been missing since the Wilderness fight of May 5, 1864, finally in December contacted Federal officials to plead for assistance. "In the deepest solicitude of a mother's heart," she wrote, "I appeal to you to search and see if some trace can be found of my missing soldier boy, in answer to this painful agony I entreat of you to do all in your power. And may God bless you in your effort." Young James C. Tuttle of the 76th New York had most likely died in the fighting, his body consumed by the fires that had swept that battlefield.[49]

On April 3 the long-sought day of victory dawned—word arrived in Cortland confirming that Richmond had fallen to the forces of U. S. Grant. The firing of cannon, the ringing of church bells, and the lighting of bonfires marked the day in Homer.[50] Early on April 10, 1865, an extra printed by the *Gazette and Banner* announced the wonderful news just received by telegraph that Lee had surrendered his army to Grant the day before. Citizens gathered on the Homer green for speeches, while "the cannon began to boom forth its joyous notes, and the bells to ring their merry peals."[51] In Cortland flags flew from public buildings, businesses, private residences, and the windows of the large hotels. The streets filled with happy revelers, including young girls sporting miniature flags in their hats and ladies clothed in "red waists," white aprons, and blue skirts. In midmorning a cannon sounded from Court House Hill, and all the town bells were rung.[52]

In the evening James C. Pomeroy led through the streets of Cortland Village a celebratory procession of citizens who included torch-carrying members of Water-Witch Hose Company and the Excelsior Hook and Ladder Company. The Marathon Brass Band led the crowd as it wound past "brilliantly illuminated" public and private buildings. The procession came to a halt in front of Squires Hall on Main Street, where Horatio Ballard presided over a night of speeches with music provided by the Marathon band and a glee club. "Cheers were given for the Armies of the United States, Generals Grant, Sheridan, Sherman, the Union, the Constitution and the Administration."[53]

On April 15 the country received the terrible news of President Lincoln's assassination. In contrast to the week before, Cortland was thrown into mourning, the people draping the buildings in black and conducting tearful memorial services in the churches. Samuel Babcock of Homer noted that the funeral services at the Baptist church represented "one of the largest gathering[s we] ever had on such an occasion." Samuel, who had lost three sons in the war, wrote, "I trust a heavy hand will rest upon them [Southerners] now they have killed their best friend in killing Mr. Lincoln."[54]

In the weeks that followed, hundreds of Cortland soldiers returned home and attempted to reestablish their civilian lives. Few would dispute that they had been changed by their military service. On the positive side, at minimum they had achieved an emotional maturity and collective outlook that took them far from their boyhood lives and ambitions. While the 23d was still at Belle Plain, Albert Crandall had come to recognize "a difference between Northern refined society and our way of seeing things." In the North, "good clothes make good men, but here the man that does his duty well is a man in spite of his rags and the man that shirks is a nuisance in spite of his paper collar and polished boots."[55] "Should it be my happy lot to survive this rebellion," a soldier in the 76th New York concluded in March 1863, "my friends and companions can only be the manly volunteer."[56] Yet, at the same time, the drunkenness and dissolute behavior they had seen in the service fed fears that they had paid a heavy price for their long separation from home. Had they, as a class of men, succumbed to the debilitating evils of military service, as Congressman Diven, General Patrick, and others had warned that they might?

Many Cortland soldiers found the transition back to civilian life difficult. Levi Loomis of Cincinnatus returned to find that his wife "had taken another man so I was out of the box." He drifted west in 1869 and became, in his words, "a lone Buffalo. . . . The rest of the herd has whipped me about so I have to go off by myself and live alone." Leonard Hathaway of Cuyler eventually acknowledged that his return to civilian life had left him restless. In May 1867 he "took Horace Greeley's advice and went west to grow up with the country." He never married, dying in the old soldiers' home at Bath, New York, in 1909. When John Lane arrived home in Virgil he felt an urgent need to exorcise his pent-up energy by picking up his father's scythe and straight away cutting thirty-five acres of grass.[57]

Most Cortland soldiers, however, successfully integrated themselves back into their home communities, proud of their military service and honored for the sacrifices that they had made in the name of their country. Few would have disagreed with Hosea H. Rockwell when, speaking before the veteran's organization of the 23d in 1885, concluded: "As a rule, we are better citizens for having been soldiers. We learned what citizenship in an undivided union is worth by realizing what it cost. We have out-grown the illusions of youth and have learned that the battle of life is a hard one, with trials, dangers and adversities to meet just as we met them in 1862 in Virginia and Maryland."[58]

In the 1865 New York State census, county officials were asked to answer specific questions as to the influence of the war on their communities. Cortland representatives reported that the war had had a positive effect on many aspects of Cortland life. In some townships wages for laborers had gone up by 70 percent. Prices for farmland had increased, prompting a wave of land speculation that benefited landowners in particular and men of financial means generally. At the same time, officials noted a "humanizing effect" on their communities. The Homer census taker wrote that "the social condition of the people seems to have gradually improved and a higher tone of morality is observable." A representative from the town of Taylor reported that because of the war the people had become better informed, more knowledgeable concerning the principles of government, and "more loyal and wise." From Willett: "Men no longer go about the streets cursing the government under which they live and receive its protection."[59]

The Truxton representative noted his community's pride in its returning soldiers, who, he claimed, were generally "better men physically and morally then when they enlisted for the war." From Cortlandville came the statement that because of the war, "practical sympathies evinced by the most liberal charities have been developed toward the soldier and his family and the *colored race*. An equalizing effect is quite clear. Autocracy is considerably broken and military men from the so called 'lower classes' now lead society, having been elevated by real merit and valor in the great war."[60]

In the postwar North the great number of veterans maintained patriotic fervor in their communities and provided ever-present reminders of those sad but exciting times. Most of the old soldiers did not write memoirs, but a young girl growing up in Onondaga County after the war later recalled, "They told stories of things seen, done, or imagined. They argued strategy and had good and bad words to say for the generals, and on every occasion some of them were ready to deliver orations. No one begrudged them the pride and comfort they found in doing so."[61]

Cortland veterans exerted a strong influence over local politics and social life. They organized regimental associations, Grand Army of the Republic posts, and in 1888 a County Veterans' Association. They were instrumental in erecting the Soldiers' Monument in Cortland (1876–77), and they dominated the impressive annual Memorial Day (Decoration Day) and Old Home Week commemorations. Cortland Memorial Day services late in the century usually began with speeches at the Soldiers' Monument, along Church Street, followed by a parade of veterans and participants to Rural Cemetery in remembrance of the procession that had buried Captain Clark in May 1863. In the cemetery, children decorated the soldiers' graves with flowers; until the number of graves made it impracticable, services included graveside tributes to individuals.[62]

Old Home Week parades featured old, gray-haired veterans in their GAR uniforms proudly marching (or, toward the last, riding in automobiles) down Main Street. The 1908 event mustered almost a hundred veterans; the 23d contingent carried the old company flag for the last time

George Edgcomb leading a 1905 GAR ceremony in Cortland Rural Cemetery. Martin Edgcomb is in the back row, right, holding flag. *(Author's collection)*

before it was laid aside in a glass case.[63] Young boys interspersed in the column carried banners that read, "Such Were the Boys of '61 and '65," and another, "But Our Hearts Are Stout." Demonstrations of skirmishing fire and the discharge of a small cannon along the route lined by thousands of spectators "gave many an idea of what the advance under fire meant."[64]

After the turn of the twentieth century the annual parades lost much of their appeal as fewer and fewer Civil War veterans remained to march down Main Street behind their tattered flags. George W. Edgcomb died June 25, 1920, after serving for ten years as commander of the local GAR Post 98. The last of Cortland's Civil War soldiers, John H. Lane, died on July 17, 1942, at ninety-four.[65]

Today, as we enter the twenty-first century, the communities of Cortland and Homer to a considerable extent retain small-town atmospheres that would be familiar to the veterans. A bit faded, perhaps, from their slow waltz with time, the towns nonetheless reflect a distinct historical character and sense of place. Court House Hill, a focal point of county history, still dominates the Cortland landscape. Along its southern crest reposes the Rural Cemetery, where Cortland's founders and so many of

Cortland's soldiers and prominent historical figures lie buried. Opposite, on the northern crest, sits the Cortland campus of the State University of New York, where students prepare for their futures. The dividing line between the cemetery and the campus comes at the end of a street named Prospect. Cortland County has left future generations of its sons and daughters something to think about.

Epilogue

One of my prized family heirlooms is a 1905 view of the old veterans at the Memorial Day services in Cortland Rural Cemetery. George Edgcomb, officer of the day, proudly stands in his GAR uniform before a color guard of veterans that include his brother Martin. By some magic the photographer has captured an evocative scene. While the spectators in the background appear distracted, caught up in the momentary enjoyment of the event, the veterans stare directly into the camera and beyond to a point we can but imagine. They all appear pensive and serious, some with melancholy expressions on their faces. Are they sadly recalling the images of dead comrades in the shadow of their own dwindling days? Do they again see their young laughing faces around a campfire, or hear their voices in song as a long column of soldiers marches down some dusty, long-forgotten road in far off Virginia? Do they yearn for the clarity of those exciting times, when they reveled in the strength and faith of youth, a singularity of purpose, and the brotherhood of comrades? By precious memory the past and present merge into a single moment.

George and Martin draw deep from the darkening shadows of the past, from beyond memory. A young man, their grandfather, stands in a field near Fort Griswold, his broad shoulders swaying as he swings his scythe to clear away the brush, swaying in a timeless rhythm, like the pendulum of a clock.

Notes

ABBREVIATIONS

DAB Dictionary of American Biography
FSNMP Fredericksburg and Spotsylvania National Military Park
GAR Grand Army of the Republic
MOLLUS Military Order of the Loyal Legion of the United States
NGSNY National Guard State of New York
NYSM New York State Militia
NYSV New York State Volunteers
NYV New York Volunteers
OR *The War of the Rebellion: A Compilation of the Official Records of the Union and Confederate Armies.*
USAMHI U.S. Army Military History Institute
USSC United States Sanitary Commission
USSS United States Sharpshooters

PROLOGUE

1. Alonzo D. Blodgett (1835–1916) was an eyewitness to the event and provided the information for a newspaper article on the subject. Some of his facts were challenged in a subsequent article. Both accounts are found on pages 59 and 60 in volume 20 in the series of twenty-five newspaper scrapbooks kept by Blodgett and preserved by the Cortland County Historical Society.

2. Cortland men served primarily in the following New York regiments: 157th (500), 76th (300), 185th (205), 12th (70), and 23d (60) regiments of infantry; 10th (150) regiment of cavalry; 16th (60) and 9th (50) regiments of heavy artillery; and the 50th (40) and 15th (30) regiments of engineers.

1. THE CITY OF THE SEVEN VALLEYS

1. Bertha Eveleth Blodgett, *Stories of Cortland County,* 2d. ed., rev. Eleanor Dickinson Blodgett (Cortland: Cortland County Historical Society, 1975), 21, 65.

2. In 1838 Cortland village abandoned its courthouse on the hill for a more substantial and accessible brick structure built near the center of town between Church and Main streets. Unidentified newspaper article dated Feb. 22, 1895, "One Hundred Years Old," found in the files of the Cortland County Historical Society, Cortland, New York.

3. Seymour B. Dunn, "The Early Academies of Cortland County," *Cortland County Chronicles* 1 (1970): 57–76. The Cortland revivals of the first half of the nineteenth century were part of what came to be known as the Second Great Awakening. The intensity and frequency of the revivals in New York west of the Catskill Mountains led the area to be known as the "Burned-Over District." See Whitney R. Cross, *The Burned-Over District: The Social and Intellectual History of Enthusiastic Religion in Western New York, 1800–1850* (Ithaca, N.Y.: Cornell Univ. Press, 1950).

4. Curtis D. Johnson, *Islands of Holiness: Rural Religion in Upstate New York, 1790–1860* (Ithaca, N.Y.: Cornell Univ. Press, 1989), 35–36. Johnson uses Cortland County as the focus of his study.

5. H. P. Smith, *History of Cortland County* (Syracuse, N.Y.: D. Mason, 1885), 84; Johnson, *Islands of Holiness,* 34, 38. Johnson found that out of sixty New York counties, Cortland ranked fifty-fifth in manufactured value per capita.

6. Catherine M. Hanchett, "Agitators for Black Equality and Emancipation: Cortland County, 1837–1855," in Louis M. Vanaria, "From Many Roots," *Cortland County Chronicles,* 4 (1986): 87–99; Simeon Bradford, "The Anti–Slavery Society of Cortland County," in *Cortland County Chronicles,* 2 (1984): 241; Cortland County Anti–Slavery Society Records, 1837–1841, Cortland County Historical Society, Cortland, New York. The temperance movement generated the most interest in the county, whiskey being a popular county product for both consumption and market. Johnson notes (115) that the number of distilleries in the county rose from fourteen in 1820 to twenty-two in 1825. By 1832, twenty-six temperance

societies existed in the county, claiming 2,700 members. Society methods relied on "the mildness of persuasion, enforced by all the power of a correct example" to end the "growing evil" intoxicating liquors. The mildness of the sanctions allowed a very pragmatic approach to the issue. The prominent Homer merchant Jedediah Barber, for example, advocated temperance at the same time he sold whiskey in his store. See the Temperance Society, "Report," *Cortland Observer,* Feb. 3, 1832. Henry S. Randall (1811–76) served as a delegate to the National Democratic Convention of 1835. He later served a two-year term as New York secretary of state in the early 1850s. He was a prominent educator, an expert in sheep husbandry, and the author of a highly regarded three-volume biography of Thomas Jefferson. Dumas Malone, ed., *Dictionary of American Biography* (New York: Scribner's, 1935), 15:347–48 [hereafter DAB].

7. Hanchett, *Agitators for Black Equality and Emancipation,* 95–96. Ward was too hard on Cortland. Cortland's attitudes toward blacks were probably no less enlightened than other counties in the region. New York did not totally abolish slavery until 1827. Three times—in 1846, 1860, and 1869—statewide referenda upheld the property qualification for black voters that had been written into the state constitution (the provision was rendered unconstitutional by the Fifteenth Amendment to the U.S. Constitution). A majority of Cortland respondents in each referendum voted in favor of black suffrage (52.5 percent, 60.6 percent, and 62 percent, respectively). For an analysis of this revealing state issue see Phyllis F. Field, *The Politics of Race in New York: The Struggle for Black Suffrage in the Civil War Era* (Ithaca, N.Y.: Cornell Univ. Press, 1982). County voting figures are given in appendix B, 236. The Liberty party, active from 1840 to 1848, stood for the abolition of slavery and racial equality. By 1850, the Liberty party had been absorbed by the more significant Free Soil party. See Milton C. Sernett, *North Star Country: Upstate New York and the Crusade for African American Freedom* (Syracuse, N.Y.: Syracuse Univ. Press, 2002), 112–25.

8. Herbert Barber Howe, *Paris Lived in Homer* (Cortland, N.Y.: Cortland County Historical Society, 1968), 18, 19; Johnson, *Islands of Holiness,* 120; Dunn, "The Early Academies of Cortland County," 71, 75. Minister Keep was further deflated by his horse's having once been sheared by local pranksters (Johnson, 111). He left Homer in 1833 for Ohio, where he served as a trustee of the fledgling Oberlin College.

9. Richard F. Palmer, *Rails through Cortland* (Cortland, N.Y.: Cortland County Historical Society, 1991), 25.

10. Ibid.; H. C. Goodwin, *Pioneer History; or, Cortland County and the Border Wars of New York* (New York: A. B. Burdick, 1859), 302; Irene A. Jennings, "Our Railroad," *Cortland County Chronicles,* 1 (1970):108–109; Blodgett, *Stories of Cortland County,* 242; for the origin of the poem see text and note in James A. Ward, *Railroads and the Character of America, 1820–1887* (Knoxville: Univ. of Tennessee Press, 1986), 30.

11. Goodwin, *Pioneer History,* 291; W. Freeman Galpin, "County History," *Cortland County Chronicles,* 1 (1970): 11; D. Morris Kurtz, "Cortland (Village)," *Cortland County Chronicles,* 1 (1970): 142; Johnson, *Islands of Holiness,* 65, 139,

140; J. H. French, *Historical and Statistical Gazetteer of New York State* (Syracuse, N.Y.: R. P. Smith, 1860), 250–56.

12. Unidentified newspaper account by George Edgcomb, "First War Meeting," in Blodgett scrapbook, 16:253, Cortland County Historical Society. This printed account varies slightly from a handwritten version by Edgcomb, "The First War Meeting," in the files of the Cortland County Historical Society.

13. William Saxton, *A Regiment Remembered: The 157th New York Volunteers* [hereafter NYV] (Cortland, N.Y.: Cortland County Historical Society, 1996), 4; obituary of John H. Lane, the last surviving Cortland Civil War veteran, found in the Grand Army of the Potomac, Post 98, record book, Cortland County Historical Society, Cortland, N.Y.; "Excitement High," *Republican Banner*, May 1, 1861.

14. Abstract of Military Inspections for 1861 in *Annual Report of the Adjutant General of the State of New York* (Albany, N.Y.: C. Van Benthuysen, 1862), 6, 103.

15. Ibid., 6–11, 731.

16. Accounts of the war meeting found in the *Republican Banner*, Apr. 24, 1861, and undated newspaper articles by Abram P. Smith, "Found, a Date," and P. Bacon Davis, "More about That War Meeting," Blodgett scrapbook, 7:42; see also George Edgcomb articles in Blodgett scrapbook, 16:253, and 23:53. Horatio Ballard (1803–1879) served as New York secretary of state during the Civil War and was elected to represent Cortland in the state assembly in 1867.

17. "Union Demonstration in Cortland," *Republican Banner*, Apr. 24, 1861; Edgcomb, "First War Meeting," Blodgett scrapbook, 23:53. The Cortland Free Library today occupies the site of the courthouse. J. C. Pomeroy had served as sheriff and militia brigade inspector with the rank of major. See Pomeroy obituary in the *Cortland Standard and Journal*, Feb. 23, 1875.

18. Smith, "Found, a Date"; "Union Demonstration in Cortland," *Republican Banner*, Apr. 24, 1861.

19. "Union Demonstration," *Republican Banner*, Apr. 24, 1861.

20. Ibid.

21. Ibid. A full list of contributors to the Volunteer Fund, which grew to $1,355, can be found in the Hiram Crandall Papers, Cortland County Historical Society, Cortland, N.Y.

22. "Union Demonstration," *Republican Banner*, Apr. 24, 1861.

23. Smith, "Found, a Date"; Edgcomb, "The First War Meeting."

24. Edgcomb, "First War Meeting," Blodgett scrapbook, 16:253; *Republican Banner* newspaper issues of Apr. 24, 1861, and May 1, 1861.

25. "Cortland Co. Aroused," *Cortland County Republican*, Apr. 25, 1861, Blodgett scrapbook, 2:17; "The Fire Spreading," *Republican Banner*, Apr. 24, 1861; Edgcomb, "First War Meeting," Blodgett scrapbook, 16:253. Squires Hall occupied an upper floor of a building on Main Street opposite the current Cortland Post Office. Willis Babcock letter dated Apr. 23, 1861, to "Dear Brother," found in Babcock family papers, Minnesota Historical Society, St. Paul, Minn. For a sketch of this remarkable family during the Civil War see Edmund Raus, *Where*

Duty Called Them: The Story of the Samuel Babcock Family of Homer, New York, in the Civil War (Daleville, Va.: Schroeder, 2001). Wheadon Hall still stands on the corner of Pine and Main streets in Homer.

26. *Cortland County Republican,* Apr. 25, 1861, and *Cortland Gazette,* May 2, 1861, both found in Blodgett scrapbook, 2:17, 18a, and 19b. By state directive at this time, only thirty-two recruits were needed to form a company and elect officers. The 12th New York Volunteer Regiment should not be confused with the 12th New York Militia Regiment, which mustered into Federal service for three months and then was discharged.

27. "Cortland Volunteers," *Republican Banner,* May 1, 1861; information on Martin Clark in obituary, Blodgett scrapbook, 2:150; the specific date of oath taking and of muster into state service of the Cortland Volunteers is difficult to determine. The *Republican Banner* of May 1 refers to a "muster" that day and identifies the seventy-two officers and men in the company, indicating that an election had taken place. The adjutant of the regiment, in a Feb. 1863 statement found in the muster rolls of the regiment, indicates May 7 as the date the company was "sworn and accepted" into state service. Most likely, May 7 represents the date Clark received his commission. Captain Clark states in a letter dated Jan. 7, 1862, that he received notice May 7 to bring his company to Elmira. Letter, collection of Clark letters in possession of Robert Mudge, Groton, N.Y. [hereafter the Mudge Collection].

28. Seymour Cook, "Early Days in Homer," in *Cortland County Chronicles,* 2:183–203; Frank Place, "A Cortland County Boy in Civil War Times," 250–54.

29. Place, "A Cortland County Boy," 250–51; Cook, "Early Days in Homer," 186.

30. Horatio Ballard, "Reminiscences," in *Cortland County Chronicles,* 2:171; Elizabeth L. Blunt, *When Folks Was Folks* (New York: Cochrane, 1910), 143–46; Blodgett, *Stories of Cortland County,* 209–10; Smith, *History of Cortland County,* 93–95.

31. Daniel O. Clough Civil War pension application file, National Archives, Washington, D.C.

32. Edgcomb, "First War Meeting." The topic of the motivation of soldiers to serve has long occupied Civil War scholars. See the discussion in Reid Mitchell, "Not the General but the soldier," in *Writing the Civil War: The Quest to Understand,* ed. James M. McPherson and William J. Cooper Jr. (Columbia: Univ. of South Carolina Press, 1998), 81–95. Reid finds an "emerging consensus" among scholars that ideology played a key role in sustaining the war effort—a position most ably presented by historians James M. McPherson and Earl J. Hess. See especially McPherson, *What They Fought For: 1861–1865* (Baton Rouge: Louisiana State Univ. Press), and Hess, *Liberty, Virtue, and Progress: Northerners and Their War for the Union* (New York: Fordham Univ. Press, 1997). As I intend to show, Cortland soldiers in general retained their strong commitment to the Union cause and the defense of constitutional freedoms even after they had become disillusioned with war and military service.

33. Clark, letter, Jan. 7,1862, Mudge Collection; "Department of the Volunteers," unidentified newspaper article, Blodgett scrapbook, 2: 22; William P. Maxson [Pound Sterling], *Camp Fires of the Twenty-third: Sketches of the Camp Life, Marches, and Battles of the Twenty-third Regiment, NYV* (New York: Davies and Kent, 1863), i–vi.

34. "Departure of the Volunteers," Blodgett scrapbook, 2:22; reference to neckties found in "Francesca, or Some Memories of the Past Fifty Years," typescript of paper read by Francesca Eudell Edgcomb, Jan. 24, 1900, Cortland County Historical Society, Cortland, N.Y. As a young girl, Eudell witnessed the ceremony at the courthouse. She did not know George Edgcomb at the time, but they would marry in 1872; Maxson, *Camp Fires,* vi.

35. Mighill returned to Massachusetts in 1862 to study for the ministry. He died of illness at age thirty-eight. See biographical sketch in Horatio Ballard, "Some Reminiscences of Cortland, no. 31," Blodgett scrapbook, 3:24; "Departure of the Volunteers," Blodgett scrapbook, 2:22.

36. "Departure of the Volunteers," Blodgett scrapbook, 2:22.

37. Andrews, letter, *Republican Banner,* July 3, 1861.

38. Andrews, letter, *Republican Banner,* May 15, 1861; letter of Sgt. Alvin F. Bailey (Co. H), "Notes from the Army: No. 1," Blodgett scrapbook, 2:24, 25; *Syracuse Daily Journal,* May 10, 1861.

39. Andrews, letter, *Republican Banner,* May 15, 1861; Bailey, letter, "Notes from the Army: No. 1," Blodgett scrapbook, 2:24, 25; *Syracuse Daily Journal,* May 10, 1861.

40. Thomas E. Byrne, "Elmira 1861–1865: Civil War Rendezvous," in *A Civil War Anthology* (Elmira: Chemung County Historical Society, 1993), 1247–52. Most of the units arrived at Elmira as independent companies, the 12th New York Regiment being an exception.

41. Edgcomb, "First War Meeting"; Bailey, letter, "Notes from the Army: No. 1," 25; letters of Andrews in *Republican Banner,* May 15 and 22, 1861.

42. For a discussion of the problems in raising New York troops during this period see A. Howard Meneely, *The War Department, 1861* (New York: Columbia Univ. Press, 1928), 156–66, and Fred Albert Shannon, *The Organization and Administration of the Union Army, 1861–1865* (Cleveland, Ohio: Arthur H. Clark, 1928; repr., Gloucester, Mass.: Peter Smith, 1965), 1:31–38; Capt. Martin Clark, letter, May 18, 1861, unidentified newspaper account, in Blodgett scrapbook, 2:24.

43. Clark, letter, Blodgett scrapbook, 2:24.

44. The two-year regiments were raised under the state militia laws. The companies elected their own commissioned and noncommissioned officers, the company officers elected the regimental field officers, and the field officers elected the state brigadier generals. The governor appointed state major generals. After the Battle of Bull Run, General Orders No. 78 specified that henceforth the governor would appoint the regimental field officers, who would be subject to a military examination before receiving their commissions. Col. Silas W. Burt, *My Memoirs*

*of the Military History of the State of New York during the War for the Union,
1861-65,* ed. State Historian, War of the Rebellion Series Bulletin 1 (Albany: The
Argus Company, 1903), 15, 31, 45.

45. Frederick Phisterer, *New York in the War of the Rebellion, 1861 to 1865,*
5 vols. (Albany, N.Y.: I. B. Lyon, 1912), 3:1994.

46. Saxton, *A Regiment Remembered,* 15-16.

47. Seymour Dexter, Company K, letters and 1861 journal found in the Che-
mung County Historical Society Elmira, N.Y. Reference to Dexter letter dated
June 6, 1861 [hereafter Dexter, Letter, or Dexter, Journal]. Most of the collection
has been edited and published as *Seymour Dexter, Union Army, Journal and Let-
ters of Civil War Service in Company K, 23rd New York Volunteer Regiment of
Elmira, with Illustrations,* ed. Carl A. Morrell (Jefferson, N.C.: McFarland, 1996).
U.S. War Department, *The War of the Rebellion: A Compilation of the Official
Records of the Union and Confederate Armies,* 128 vols. (Washington, D.C.: U.S.
Government Printing Office [GPO], 1880-1901), series 2, vol. 4, 70-74 [hereafter
OR]. The barracks took on the name "Post Barracks" on June 4, 1862. See "Gen-
eral Orders No. 5," *Elmira Weekly Advertiser and Chemung County Republican,*
June 21, 1862.

48. J. Harrison Mills, *Chronicles of the Twenty-first Regiment New York State
Volunteers* (Buffalo, N.Y.: Gies, 1887), 42-43; Henry Clay Scott Diary, 1861-1863,
Company E, 23d New York Volunteers, microfilm, Manuscripts and Archives
Division, New York Public Library [NYPL], entry June 4, 1861 [hereafter Scott,
Diary]; *Hornellsville Weekly Tribune,* June 13, 1861; Andrews, letter, *Republican
Banner,* June 12, 1861.

49. Andrews, letter, *Republican Banner,* June 12, 1861; Bailey, letter, "Notes
from the Army: No. 6," Blodgett scrapbook, 2:29; Andrews, letter, *Republican
Banner,* June 26, 1861. Mascots in other companies included two tame crows and
a duck.

50. C. B. Fairchild, *History of the 27th Regiment N.Y. Vols.* (Binghamton,
N.Y.: Carl and Matthews, 1888), 4.

51. Dexter, letter, June 14, 1861; Andrews, letter, *Republican Banner,* June
26, 1861.

52. *Hornellsville Weekly Tribune,* June 20, 1861.

53. Dexter, letter, May 15, 1861; Bailey, letter, "Notes from the Army: No.
5," Blodgett scrapbook, 2:29; Andrews, letters, *Republican Banner,* June 26 and
July 3, 1861; notice of the attempted rape found in *Elmira Weekly Advertiser and
Chemung County Republican,* July 6, 1861.

54. Maxson, *Camp Fires,* 187; Clarissa Edgcomb, letter, May 30, 1861, author's collection.

55. Service records of individuals mentioned are found in the Civil War military service or pension application files, National Archives, Washington, D.C.;
Wattles situation described in Records of the Provost Marshal General's Office,
record group 110, inventory entry 2159; Bailey, letter, "Notes from the Army:
No. 4," Blodgett scrapbook, 2:28.

56. Andrews, letters, *Republican Banner,* May 29 and July 3, 1861.

57. Andrews, letter of June 22, 1861, *Republican Banner,* June 26, 1861; Clark, letter, June 20, 1861, Mudge Collection; Roger D. Sturcke, "23d New York Volunteer Infantry Regiment," *Military Collector and Historian: Journal of the Company of Military Historians* 25, no. 4 (Winter 1973): 198–200; Camp photographs of the 23d men taken in late summer show many individuals wearing tasseled caps or fezzes similar to those worn by Zouaves. The author believes that these items were not issued but purchased by these individuals to replace their worn-out kepis until they received their new issue of regulation caps in September. Frederick Burritt (Co. H), letter, *Elmira Weekly Advertiser and Chemung County Republican,* Sept. 14, 1861.

58. Sturcke, *Military Collector and Historian,* 200; quote from Andrews, letter, *Republican Banner,* July 3, 1861; *Annual Report of the Adjutant General of the State of New York* for the year 1862, 1041.

59. Report of William Averell, *OR,* series 3, vol. 1, 267; William Woods Averell, *Ten Years in the Saddle: The Memoir of William Woods Averell,* ed. Edward K. Eckert and Nicholas J. Amato (San Rafael, Calif.: Presidio, 1978), 281; Clark, letter, June 20, 1861, Mudge Collection. Apparently the 23d was mustered in by company over a period of days. The inspecting officers directed the muster out of a number of men for medical reasons. Lieutenant Andrews laments in the *Republican Banner* of June 26, 1861, that Pvt. Henry Daines of Company H was rejected for a malformed hand. Andrews comments, "We lost our funny man." The medical inspection of soldiers at the start of the war was typically superficial at best, no doubt reflecting the anticipation of a short war. Henry C. Scott claimed (*Diary,* entry June 22, 1861) that the men simply walked by the mustering officer, who looked for any visible physical defects. Pvt. Willard N. Van Hoesen of the Cortland Volunteers in his pension application file (National Archives, Washington, D.C.) said he did not remember ever being examined by a mustering physician at Elmira. A study of 1,620 men discharged from the Army of the Potomac for medical reasons in Oct. 1861 found that 53 percent of them had been discharged for disabilities that existed before enlistment and could have been uncovered by "any intelligent surgeon." "The Sanitary Commission," *New York Times,* Jan. 9, 1862. Anyone refusing to take the oath was subject to the abuse of comrades. Two members of the 23d "rescued" one such individual belonging to another regiment whom they witnessed being subjected to "kicks, cuffs, jeers, hootings and finally shaving one side of his head, and marching . . . through a gauntlet." "More Drumming-Out Outrages," *Steuben Farmers' Advocate,* May 29, 1861.

60. "Southern Tier Regiment," *Republican Banner,* June 26, 1861; Andrews, letters, *Republican Banner,* June 26 and July 3, 1861; "Got Their Pay," *Elmira Weekly Advertiser and Chemung County Republican,* June 22, 1861; Scott, *Diary,* June 25, 1861.

61. Dexter, *Journal;* Andrews, letter, *Republican Banner,* July 10, 1861; "From 'Our Boys,'" *Steuben Farmers' Advocate,* July 10, 1861. The Brainard House stood at the corner of Water and Baldwin streets.

62. "Departure of the Southern Tier Regiment," *Steuben Farmers' Advocate,* July 10, 1862; Scott, *Diary,* entries July 5 and 6, 1861; Andrews, letter, *Republican Banner,* July 10, 1861. A letter of Sgt. Cyrus Kellogg (Co. D), in *Corning Journal* of July 25, 1861, states that the train had twenty-one cars.

63. Dexter, *Journal;* Andrews, letter, *Republican Banner,* July 10, 1861; Scott, *Diary,* July 5 and 6, 1861.

64. *Hornellsville Weekly Tribune,* July 11, 1861; Scott, *Diary,* July 5 and 6, 1861; Dexter, *Journal.* A reporter for the *Steuben Farmers' Advocate* stated in the July 10, 1861, issue that the crowd lined both sides of the road from Second Street to Water Street, cheering the train as it left the city.

2. BANNERS SOUTH

1. Dexter, *Journal;* Maxson, *Camp Fires,* 12; Lt. Alvah D. Waters, letter, Blodgett scrapbook, 2:31; Sgt. Benjamin Bennitt (Co. A), letter, *Steuben Farmers' Advocate,* July 17, 1861; Sgt. Martin V. Doty (Co. G), letter, *Hornellsville Weekly Tribune,* July 18, 1861.

2. William P. Hogarty, "A 'Medal of Honor,'" in *War Talks in Kansas: A Series of Papers Read before the Kansas Commandery of the Military Order of the Loyal Legion of the United States* [hereafter *War Talks in Kansas: MOLLUS*] (Kansas City: Franklin Hudson, 1906), 352; Andrews, letter, *Republican Banner,* July 10, 1861; Dexter, *Journal;* Maxson, *Camp Fires,* 12–14; Kellogg, letter, *Corning Journal,* July 25, 1861; Sgt. Duane Thompson (Co. K), letter, *Elmira Weekly Advertiser and Chemung County Republican,* July 20, 1861.

3. William Phillips (Co. H), Civil War pension application file, National Archives, Washington, D.C.; Thompson, letter, *Elmira Weekly Advertiser and Chemung County Republican,* July 20, 1861; Waters, letter, Blodgett scrapbook, 2:31; Andrews, letter, *Republican Banner,* July 10, 1861. Surgeon Churchill wrote that the field and staff officers stayed in the National Hotel; *Owego Gazette,* July 25, 1861. U.S. Department of Labor buildings today occupy the site of Trinity Church.

4. John D. Billings, *Hardtack and Coffee* (Boston: George M. Smith, 1887), 112–19; Waters, letter, Blodgett scrapbook, 2:31.

5. Dexter, letter, July 15, 1861; Thompson, letter, *Elmira Weekly Advertiser and Chemung County Republican,* July 20, 1861.

6. Bailey, letter, "Notes from the Army: No. 7," Blodgett scrapbook, 2:33; Andrews, letters, Republican *Banner,* July 10 and 17, 1861.

7. Andrews, letter, *Republican Banner,* July 17, 1861; Dexter, *Journal.* Clark in his July 8 letter referred to the camp area as "Potomac Heights." Cardozo High School today occupies the general area of the camp.

8. Margaret Leech, *Reveille in Washington* (New York: Harper, 1941), 88.

9. William Swinton, *History of the Seventh Regiment, National Guard* (New York: Fields, Osgood, 1870), 168; Andrews, letter, *Republican Banner,*

July 17, 1861; "From Our Own Correspondent," *Hornellsville Weekly Tribune,* July 25, 1861.

10. Dexter, letter, July 8, 1861; Egbert L. Viele, *Hand-Book for Active Service* (New York: D. Van Nostrand, 1861), 58–59; Scott, *Diary,* entry July 9, 1861; Clark, letter, dated "Camp Washington," July 9, 1861, Blodgett scrapbook, 2:32. By July 26, 1861, B. Bennitt (Co. A) states, his company had a total of seventeen tents; Bennitt, letter, *Steuben Farmers' Advocate,* July 31, 1861; Burritt, letter, *Elmira Weekly Advertiser and Chemung County Republican,* July 20, 1861.

11. "From Our Own Correspondent," Hornellsville *Weekly Tribune,* July 25, 1861; Andrews, letter, *Republican Banner,* July 17, 1861; Dexter, *Letter,* July 8, 1861. Mention of Clearwood as tailor found in a letter dated Nov. 19, 1861, by Ira Carpenter (Co. H), found in Carpenter's Civil War pension application file, National Archives, Washington, D.C.

12. Maxson, *Camp Fires,* 188; Scott, *Diary,* July 18, 1861; Edgcomb's Civil War pension application file, National Archives, Washington, D.C. It is estimated that more Civil War soldiers died from diarrhea-type illnesses than were killed outright on the battlefield. Bell Irvin Wiley and Hirst D. Milhollen, *They Who Fought Here* (New York: Bonanza, 1969), 223.

13. *Corning Journal,* July 18, 1861; "Stand of Colors for the 23d Regiment," *Steuben Farmers' Advocate,* July 17, 1861; "Colors for the Southern Tier Regiment," *Elmira Weekly Advertiser and Chemung County Republican,* June 29, 1861.

14. *National Republican* (Washington, D.C.), July 18, 1861; "From Our Own Correspondent," *Hornellsville Weekly Tribune,* July 25, 1861; Maxson, *Camp Fires,* 16–19.

15. Maxson, *Camp Fires,* 16–19.

16. Ibid.

17. Ibid.; *Hornellsville Weekly Tribune,* July 25, 1861.

18. Churchill, letter, *Owego Gazette,* July 25, 1861; Maj. H. H. Rockwell, *Regimental Association of the 23rd Regiment N.Y. Vols.: Third Annual Re-Union, Elmira, N.Y., July 4, 1885* (Elmira: Gazette, 1885), 14; *Hornellsville Weekly Tribune,* July 25, 1861.

19. Scott's comments reported by Dexter in a letter dated July 15, 1861.

20. Andrews, letter, *Republican Banner,* July 17, 1861; *Hornellsville Weekly Tribune,* July 25, 1861.

21. Report of Hoffman dated July 16, 1861, regimental muster rolls and papers, record group 94, National Archives, Washington, D.C.

22. Dexter, *Journal;* letter of Capt. George H. Powers (Co. E), *Waverly Advocate,* Aug. 2, 1861.

23. Powers, letter, *Waverly Advocate,* Aug. 2, 1861; "From Our Own Correspondent," *Hornellsville Weekly Tribune,* Aug. 8, 1861; Dexter, *Journal;* Maxson, *Camp Fires,* 19.

24. Walt Whitman, *Specimen Days* (Boston: David R. Godine, 1971), 12–13.

25. Bruce Catton, *America Goes to War* (Middletown, Conn.: Wesleyan Univ. Press, 1958), 14–27.

26. Meneely, *The War Department, 1861,* 192.

27. McClellan letters of July 30, 1861, and Jan. 31, 1862, in Stephen W. Sears, ed., *The Civil War Papers of George B. McClellan* (New York: Ticknor and Fields, 1989), 71, 163.

28. *National Republican* (Washington, D.C.), July 25, 1861; Sturcke, "23rd New York Volunteer Infantry Regiment," 198.

29. Bennitt, letter, *Steuben Farmers' Advocate,* July 31, 1861; Burritt, letter, *Elmira Weekly Advertiser and Chemung County Republican,* Aug. 3, 1861. An unnamed source from the 23d writes in the *Elmira Weekly Gazette* (paper torn, no date available), "an immense crowd cheered as we passed Willard's [hotel]. Just a short distance below, a man made the remark 'that he hoped half the Regiment would not return.' He was knocked down in a moment by a bystander, but arose to his feet and pitched into his assailant." Microfilm, Chemung County Historical Society, Elmira, N.Y.

30. Bennitt, letter, *Steuben Farmers' Advocate,* July 31, 1861; Andrews, letter, *Republican Banner,* July 17, 1861; Dexter, *Journal.* The camp occupied ground near where the Pentagon stands today.

31. Burritt, letter, *Elmira Weekly Advertiser and Chemung County Republican,* Aug. 3, 1861; Pvt. George F. Dudley (Co. K), letter, *Addison Advertiser,* Sept. 28, 1861.

32. Maxson, *Camp Fires,* 188.

33. Dexter, *Journal.*

34. Francis A. Lord, *They Fought for the Union* (New York: Bonanza, 1960), 141; Private William H. Robinson (Co. K), letter, *Elmira Weekly Advertiser and Chemung County Republican,* Aug. 3, 1861.

35. *OR,* vol. 51, part 1, 434; Lt. Samuel N. Benedict (Co. F), letter, *Elmira Weekly Advertiser and Chemung County Republican,* Aug. 17, 1861; Andrews, letter, *Republican Banner,* Aug. 14, 1861.

36. Benjamin Franklin Cooling III and Walton H. Owen II, *Mr. Lincoln's Forts* (Shippensburg, Pa.: White Mane, 1988), 100; Maxson, *Camp Fires,* 21; Sgt. Lucius W. Bingham (Co. K), letter, *Elmira Weekly Gazette,* Aug. 15, 1861.

37. Dexter, letter, July 24, 1861; Burritt, letter, *Elmira Weekly Advertiser and Chemung County Republican,* Aug. 3, 1861.

38. Andrews, letter, *Republican Banner,* Sept. 4, 1861; Burritt, letter, *Elmira Weekly Advertiser and Chemung County Republican,* Aug. 31, 1861.

39. "From Capt. Todd's Company," *Corning Democrat,* Aug. 29, 1861; Burritt, letter, Aug. 31, 1861, *Elmira Weekly Advertiser and Chemung County Republican.*

40. See "Letter from Fred Burritt" and "Southern Tiers Chopping Wood," *Elmira Weekly Advertiser and Chemung County Republican,* Aug. 17, 1861; "From Capt. Todd's Company," *Corning Democrat,* Aug. 29, 1861. The writer

also mentioned that the Arlington House was "out of repair" with empty rooms and empty gilt picture frames indicating the hasty departure of the owners; *Addison Advertiser,* Sept. 28, 1861.

41. Maxson, *Camp Fires,* 24, 188; Private Cyrus Kellogg (Co. D), letter, *Corning Journal,* Aug. 29, 1861.

42. Maxson, *Camp Fires,* 22; "From Our Own Correspondent," *Hornellsville Weekly Tribune,* Aug. 15, 1861; Burritt, letter, *Elmira Weekly Advertiser and Chemung County Republican,* Aug. 31, 1861; Frederick Stansbury Haydon, *Aeronautics in the Union and Confederate Armies* (Baltimore: Johns Hopkins Press, 1941), 203-204.

43. Burritt, letter, *Elmira Weekly Advertiser and Chemung County Republican,* 31 Aug. 1861. Burritt mentioned retrieval of a fired six-pounder cannon ball embedded in a tree; Dexter, letter, Aug. 18, 1861.

44. Burritt, letter, *Elmira Weekly Advertiser and Chemung County Republican,* Aug. 31, 1861; Edgar Warfield, *Manassas to Appomattox* (McLean, Va.: EPM, 1996), 60; *Hornellsville Weekly Tribune,* Aug. 22, 1861.

45. Hoffman, letter, Sept. 15, 1861, from the typescript collection of Hoffman correspondence in possession of Richard S. Buchanan, Elmira, N.Y. [hereafter Buchanan collection]; "An Interesting Incident," *Richmond Daily Dispatch,* Sept. 9, 1861; "From Our Own Correspondent," *Hornellsville Weekly Tribune,* Sept. 12, 1861; Burritt, letter, *Elmira Weekly Advertiser and Chemung County Republican,* Sept. 14, 1861. The railroad served as the dividing line between opposing pickets. The railroad bed today serves as a bike and walking trail, part of the Washington and Old Dominion Railroad Regional Park. Captain Saunders is most likely Capt. Robert C. Saunders of Company B, 11th Virginia Infantry.

46. Letter of Capt. William W. Dingledey (Co. F), in Maxson, *Camp Fires,* 22. The name "Dutch Wing" refers to the foreign-sounding surnames of some of the officers in these companies.

47. Maxson, *Camp Fires,* 23; Kellogg, letter, *Corning Journal,* Sept. 5, 1861; Burritt, letter, *Elmira Weekly Advertiser and Chemung County Republican,* Sept. 14, 1861; Colby, letter, *Corning Democrat,* Sept. 5, 1861. See also William E. Hughes, ed., *The Civil War Papers of Lt. Colonel Newton T. Colby, New York Infantry* (Jefferson, N.C.: McFarland, 2003), 54-66.

48. Maxson, *Camp Fires,* 23; David Ward (Co. F), letter, *Elmira Weekly Advertiser and Chemung County Republican,* Aug. 31, 1861; *Corning Journal,* Sept. 5, 1861.

49. N. M. Crane and H. H. Rockwell statements from the pamphlet *23rd Regiment N.Y. Vols., Third Annual Reunion,* 1885, 15, 17; *Hornellsville Weekly Tribune,* Sept. 5, 1861; 2d Lt. Lynval A. Davis (Co. F), letter, *Corning Journal,* Sept. 19, 1861. Not everyone was pleased with Crane's behavior under fire. The letter of Ward cited in a previous note opined that Crane's order to retreat was a bit premature.

50. *Hornellsville Weekly Tribune,* Sept. 5, 1861; Bailey, letter, "Notes from the Army: No. 11," Blodgett scrapbook, 2:35.

51. Andrews, letter, *Republican Banner,* Sept. 4, 1861; Burritt, letter, *Elmira Advertiser,* Aug. 31, 1861.

52. Dexter, letter, Aug. 18, 1861. Dexter reported fifty-six cases of Virginia fever in camp; Maxson, *Camp Fires,* 188; Andrews, letter, *Republican Banner,* Sept. 18, 1861.

53. Burritt, letter, *Elmira Weekly Advertiser and Chemung County Republican,* Sept. 21, 1861. Waters subsequently joined Company G of the 10th New York Cavalry as first lieutenant.

54. "From Capt. Todd's Company," *Corning Democrat,* Aug. 29, 1861.

55. Andrews, letter, *Republican Banner,* Aug. 7, 1861; Dexter, letter, Aug. 18, 1861.

56. Edgcomb, letter, Aug. 7, 1861; Clark, letter, Sept. 26, 1861; Andrews, letter, *Republican Banner,* Sept. 18, 1861.

57. Justus Grant Matteson, *Justus in the Civil War,* ed. Ronald G. Matteson, 2d. ed. (n.p.: privately printed, 1995), 8. Justus served in the 10th New York Cavalry; Edgcomb, letters, Aug. 7 and Sept. 5, 1861.

58. Joseph Peek Civil War pension application and military service files, National Archives, Washington, D.C.

59. Robert M. Utley, *Frontiersmen in Blue: The United States Army and the Indian, 1848–1865* (New York: Macmillan, 1967), 29.

60. Clark, letter, n.d., Mudge Collection; Dexter, letter, Oct. 26, 1861; Andrews, letter, Oct. 18, 1861, in Blodgett scrapbook, 2:42.

61. Diary of Ami Osgood, quoted in *Hornellsville Weekly Tribune,* Aug. 8, 1861; Dexter, letter, Oct. 9, 1861; Burritt, letters, *Elmira Weekly Advertiser and Chemung County Republican,* Aug. 17 and 31, 1861. The "precocious warrior" was most likely William H. McKevitt of Truxton, N.Y., one of five McKevitt brothers who served in the Union army.

62. Andrews, letter, *Republican Banner,* July 17, 1861.

63. Andrews, letter, *Republican Banner,* May 22 and July 17, 1861; Dexter, letter, July 15, 1861; Andrews, letter, Oct. 18, 1861, Blodgett scrapbook, 2:42.

64. Clark, letter, May 18, 1861, Blodgett scrapbook, 2:24; Andrews, letter, Oct. 18, 1861, Blodgett scrapbook, 2:42.

65. Burritt, letter, *Elmira Weekly Advertiser and Chemung County Republican,* Aug. 17, 1861; Kellogg, letter, *Corning Journal,* Aug. 29, 1861; Waters, letter, Blodgett scrapbook, 2:31.

66. "From the Southern Tiers," *Elmira Weekly Gazette,* Aug. 22, 1861. Little is known of the women mentioned. It is possible that Mrs. Morse stayed in Elmira with the sick and did not travel with the regiment to Virginia.

67. *OR,* series 3, vol. 1, 729; sutler records pertaining to Judd are in record group 393, preliminary inventory, vol. 1, entry 4075, National Archives, Washington, D.C.; *General Regulations for the Military Forces of the State of New York,* prepared by a board of officers (Albany: Adjutant General's Office, 1858), 18. See also Francis A. Lord, *Civil War Sutlers and Their Wares* (New York: Thomas Yoseloff, 1969). New York State regulations specified that the sutlers could not sell

any "spiritous [sic] liquor, cards or gaming materials." An investigation by the Sanitary Commission in the fall of 1861 found a lack of control and supervision over regimental sutlers by the officers and evidence of "corrupt bargains" being struck by some officers to bring contraband goods to camp; "The Sanitary Commission," *New York Times,* Jan. 9, 1862. As the war progressed the activities of Sutlers came under greater scrutiny and regulation by the War Department.

68. *OR,* vol. 51, part 1, 473; Crane received all letters in his tent. His assistant then carried them to Washington for mailing, returning with the regiment's mail, which Crane then separated into piles and distributed to the appropriate company officers. *Steuben Courier,* July 24, 1861.

69. Burritt, letter, *Elmira Weekly Advertiser and Chemung County Republican,* Aug. 31, 1861; Hornellsville *Weekly Tribune,* Aug. 8, 1861; Edgcomb, letter, Aug. 7, 1861; "From Rev. E. F. Crane," *Elmira Weekly Advertiser and Chemung County Republican,* Sept. 21, 1861; Dexter, letter, Sept. 15, 1861.

70. Edgcomb, letter, Sept. 5, 1861, author's collection; Hugh J. Baldwin, letter, Dec. 1861, typescript collection of letters found in Chemung County Historical Society, Elmira, N.Y.; Judd, letter, Aug. 5, 1861.

71. Waters, letter, dated July 14, 1861, in Blodgett scrapbook, 2:31; Clark, letter, Sept. 26, 1861, Mudge Collection. Thirteen recruits for the 23d enlisted Sept. 27 and 28 to serve the unexpired two-year term of enlistment. Bailey's efforts at recruitment after September netted only four men from Onondaga County: Hamilton and Lucien Squires, Alfred Tuttle, and Henry White. Green quote from his Civil War pension application file, National Archives, Washington, D.C.

72. Andrews, letter, *Republican Banner,* Aug. 21, 1861.

73. "Breckinridge Conspirators in Conclave!" *Republican Banner,* Sept. 4, 1861; "A Secessionist Obliged to Retract," *Republican Banner,* Sept. 18, 1861; Andrews, letter, *Republican Banner,* Sept. 18, 1861.

74. Kohler obituary found in *Cortland Democrat,* Nov. 9, 1877.

75. "Cortlandville Contribution of Hospital Stores," *Republican Banner,* Aug. 14, 1861; Mrs. Henry S. Randall, letters, Oct. 18, 1861 and Apr. 4, 1862, boxes 654 and 655, United States Sanitary Commission [hereafter USSC] Records, Manuscript and Archives Division, NYPL.

76. Mrs. Randall, letter, Nov. 24, 1861, box 654, USSC Collection, NYPL.

77. Blodgett scrapbook, 2:121; Mrs. Randall, letter, Nov. 26, 1862; box 655, USSC Collection, NYPL; breakdown of the number of packages sent from each community found in book 666, USSC Collection. Randall claimed that Cortlandville's total official contributions for the sick and wounded from the beginning of the war until 1864 amounted to almost nine thousand dollars; *Syracuse Journal,* Dec. 3, 1864.

78. Andrews, letter, *Republican Banner,* Aug. 7, 1861; Burritt, letter, *Elmira Weekly Advertiser and Chemung County Republican,* Aug. 17, 1861.

79. Matteson, *Justus in the Civil War,* 3; letter of Polly Underwood to Ogden Underwood (109th New York) dated Oct. 29, 1863, "Underwood Family Records" archive box, Cortland County Historical Society, Cortland, N.Y.; Bailey, letter, *Cortland Gazette and Banner,* Dec. 12, 1861.

80. Clark, letter, July 8, 1861, Mudge Collection; Matteson, 8; Dexter, letter, July 24, 1861.

3. A HUNDRED CIRCLING CAMPS

1. Clark, letter, July 8, 1861, Mudge Collection; Matteson, 8; Dexter, letter, July 24, 1861.

2. David L. Thompson, "With Burnside at Antietam," in *Battles and Leaders of the Civil War,* ed. Robert Underwood Johnson and Clarence Clough Buel, 4 vols. (New York: Century, 1887), 2:660.

3. Burt, *My Memoirs of the Military History of the State of New York,* 31.

4. Burt, *Memoirs,* 46, 56; Lincoln's authorization to convene military review boards found in General Orders No. 49 from the War Department, dated Aug. 3, 1861, and approved July 22, 1861. Shannon, *The Organization and Administration of the Union Army,* 1:186–88.

5. William Thompson Lusk, *War Letters* (New York: privately printed, 1911), 247–48.

6. Ideas for this paragraph drawn from two of Bruce Catton's speeches, "The Citizen Soldier," and "Making Hard War," published in Catton, *America Goes to War,* 48–86. Characterization of the Northern soldier follows description on page 71.

7. *OR,* vol. 51, part 1, 434; Sears, *The Civil War Papers of George B. McClellan,* 76.

8. "Extract of a Letter from One of the Southern Tier Regiment," dated Aug. 14, found in Aug. 22, 1861, *Elmira Weekly Gazette.*

9. "From Our Volunteers," *Hornellsville Weekly Tribune,* Sept. 12, 1861.

10. *OR,* vol. 51, part 1, 455; William Howard Russell, *My Diary North and South,* ed. Eugene H. Berwanger (New York: Knopf, 1988), 301–302; Andrews, letter, *Republican Banner,* Sept. 4, 1861; Burritt, letter, *Elmira Weekly Advertiser and Chemung County Republican,* Sept. 7, 1861.

11. Andrews, letter, *Republican Banner,* Aug. 14, 1861.

12. "The Grand Review," *New York Times,* Nov. 23, 1861.

13. Jacob D. Cox, *Military Reminiscences of the Civil War,* 2 vols. (New York: Scribner's, 1900), 1:243.

14. "Letter from Bould Soger," *Buffalo Morning Express,* July 31, 1862.

15. Letter of Capt. Sidney J. Mendell (35th N.Y.), *Jefferson County News,* Sept. 19, 1861; "The Ulster Guard on the Rappahannock," *Kingston Argus,* May 14, 1862.

16. Dexter, letter, Sept. 22, 1861; McDowell, DAB, 12:29–30; Edward G. Longacre, "Fortune's Fool," *Civil War Times Illustrated* 18, no. 2 (May 1979): 20–31.

17. William Starr Myers, *A Study in Personality: General George Brinton McClellan* (New York: D. Appleton-Century, 1934), 250; Averell, *Ten Years in the Saddle,* 284, 289; John C. Tidball, journal, West Point Archives, West Point, N.Y., 229a; typescript found in the files of Manassas National Battlefield Park; John

Pope, *The Military Memoirs of General John Pope,* ed. Peter Cozzens and Robert I. Girardi (Chapel Hill: Univ. of North Carolina Press, 1998), 214.

18. James Harrison Wilson, *Under the Old Flag,* 2 vols. (New York: D. Appleton, 1912), 1:66.

19. All quotes from Tidball, *Journal,* 225–30.

20. Burritt, letter, *Elmira Weekly Advertiser and Chemung County Republican,* Sept. 14, 1861; letter of David Hovencamp (Co. I), Sept. 22, 1861, *Havanna Journal,* Oct. 5, 1861.

21. Rockwell, letter, *Elmira Weekly Gazette,* Aug. 15, 1861; Dudley, letter, *The Addison Advertiser,* Sept. 28, 1861; Burritt, letter, *Elmira Weekly Advertiser and Chemung County Republican,* Sept. 21, 1861. Rockwell's suggestions on what new recruits should bring with them into service are interesting enough to quote at length: "For clothing, *Take just what the State provides,* and no more, unless it be a pair of overalls, to wear in cooking and to keep your pants clean. Bring a fine and a course comb, tooth brush, needles and thread, scissors, buttons, pins, etc. For writing materials, get a memorandum book of the largest size, one that will hold a bunch of note paper, and a good pencil. Pens are out of style here. If you like fishing, bring a sea-weed line and some small hooks. Three or four pockets, or bags, holding about a quart each, would be good to hold rations of coffee, rice, beans, etc. A small table knife, one that will keep sharp enough to cut raw beef and pork; fork and spoon, with a pair of small towels, a silk and a linen pocket handkerchiefs [*sic*], and a piece of sponge will complete your outfit."

22. Dexter, letter, Oct. 2, 1861; letter from the 35th N.Y. in "Notes from the Camp and Field," *Rochester Daily Democrat and American,* Oct. 9, 1861; Burritt, letter, *Elmira Weekly Advertiser and Chemung County Republican,* Oct. 12, 1861; "Army Correspondence," *Hornellsville Weekly Tribune,* Oct. 17, 1861.

23. Burritt, letter, *Elmira Weekly Advertiser and Chemung County Republican,* Oct. 12, 1861; Dexter letter of Oct. 2, 1861, and *Journal.*

24. Mills, *Chronicles of the Twenty-first Regiment, NYSV,* 118, 120; *Hornellsville Weekly Tribune,* Oct. 17, 1861.

25. *Hornellsville Weekly Tribune,* Oct. 17, 1861; John Bryson, *History of the 30th NYSV,* Manuscript Division, New York State Library, Albany, N.Y., 20.

26. Charles H. Banes, *History of the Philadelphia Brigade* (Philadelphia: J. B. Lippincott, 1876), 20–22.

27. Dexter, letter, Oct. 2, 1861; Cooling and Owen, *Mr. Lincoln's Forts,* 110.

28. George B. McClellan, *McClellan's Own Story,* ed. William C. Prime (New York: Charles L. Webster, 1887), 96; *OR,* vol. 5, 15; U.S. Congress, *Report of the Joint Committee on the Conduct of the War,* 3 parts (Washington, D.C.: Government Printing Office, 1863; 5 vols., 1865), part 1, 131 [hereafter *CCW*].

29. Theodore B. Gates, *The Ulster Guard* (New York: Benj. H. Tyrrel, 1879), 153.

30. Ibid., 162; Maxson, *Camp Fires,* 28–29; *OR,* vol. 5, 438.

31. Louise Hall Tharp, "The Song That Wrote Itself," *American Heritage* 8, no. 1 (Dec. 1956): 13; Willard A. and Porter W. Heaps, *The Singing Sixties* (Norman: Univ. of Oklahoma Press, 1960), 53–54; Rufus R. Dawes, *Service with the*

Sixth Wisconsin Volunteers, ed. and intro. Alan T. Nolan (Ann Arbor, Mich.: Cushing-Malloy, 1962), 28–29. For a newspaper description of the Nov. 18 review, see "Our Washington Correspondence," *New York Times,* Nov. 24, 1861.

32. George B. McClellan, *McClellan's Own Story,* 97–98; Sears, *Papers of George B. McClellan,* 137.

33. Orders of Nov. 12 and 18, 1861, in record group 393, preliminary inventory, vol. 2, control no. 234, National Archives, Washington, D.C.

34. "The Grand Review," *New York Times,* Nov. 24, 1861.

35. *Buffalo Morning Express,* Nov. 26, 1861; Burritt, letter, *Elmira Weekly Advertiser and Chemung County Republican,* Dec. 7, 1861.

36. Edwin W. Stone, *Rhode Island in the Rebellion* (Providence, R.I.: Knowles, Anthony, 1864), 5; George Lewis, *The History of Battery E, First Regiment Rhode Island Light Artillery* (Providence, R.I.: Snow and Farnham, 1892), 22; *New York Tribune,* Nov. 21, 1861; Robert McAllister, *The Civil War Letters of General Robert McAllister,* ed. James I. Robertson Jr. (New Brunswick, N. J.: Rutgers Univ. Press, 1965), 97. The use of cavalry as guards from "The Grand Review," *New York Times,* Nov. 24, 1861. Washington entrepreneurs charged civilians an inflated rate of six dollars for a buggy and twelve dollars for a hack. See "The Grand Review, of 70,000 Troops," *Cortland County Republican,* Nov. 28, 1861; "Particulars of the Grand Review," *Philadelphia Inquirer,* Nov. 21, 1861.

37. Stone, *Rhode Island in the Rebellion,* 5. Lewis Bailey came from upstate New York and was related to the famous circus family of James A. Bailey. See Nan Netherton et al., *Fairfax County Virginia: A History* (n.p.: Fairfax County Board of Supervisors, 1978), 254.

38. "The Grand Review," *New York Times,* Nov. 24, 1861.

39. *Buffalo Morning Express,* Nov. 26, 1861.

40. Stone, *Rhode Island in the Rebellion,* 4; "The Grand Review: A Magnificent Display," *New York Tribune,* Nov. 21, 1861; Lewis, *Battery E,* 22.

41. Jas. H. Stevenson, *"Boots and Saddles": A History of the First Volunteer Cavalry of the War Known as the New York (Lincoln) Cavalry* (Harrisburg, Pa.: Patriot, 1879), 64; "The Grand Review," *New York Times,* Nov. 23, 1861; H. Seymour Hall, "Experience in the Peninsular and Antietam Campaigns," in *War Talks in Kansas, MOLLUS,* 163.

42. "The Grand Review," *New York Times,* Nov. 24, 1861.

43. Ibid., Nov. 23, 1861; Bennitt, letter, *Steuben Farmers' Advocate,* Dec. 2, 1861.

44. "The Grand Review," *New York Times,* Nov. 23, 1861; Dawes, *Service,* 30. McDowell was "picked up by Generals McClellan and McCall, and soon mounted." See "Particulars of the Grand Review," *Philadelphia Inquirer,* Nov. 21, 1861.

45. "The Grand Review," *New York Times,* Nov. 24, 1861; Averell, *Ten Years in the Saddle,* 347.

46. Stevenson, *Boots and Saddles,* 65. Even after the terrible Union defeat at Fredericksburg a soldier from the 76th New York ("Cortland Regiment?") could

proudly tell his parents, in Mar. 1863, "I will ask no greater honor that to have it said of me that I once belonged to the Army of the Potomac." Sgt. Maj. Thomas Martin, letter, Blodgett scrapbook, 6:98.

47. Dexter, letter, Nov. 27, 1861, and Dexter, *Journal;* "The Grand Review," *New York Times,* Nov. 24, 1861.

48. Sears, *The Civil War Papers of George B. McClellan,* 72, 164.

49. Ibid., 59, 128. Letter from McClellan to Samuel L. M. Barlow stated: "Help me dodge the nigger—we want nothing to do with him. I am fighting to preserve the integrity of the Union and the power of the Govt. on no other issue." McClellan added, "The Presdt . . . is really sound on the nigger question"; Roy P. Basler, ed., *The Collected Works of Abraham Lincoln,* 9 vols. (New Brunswick, N.J.: Rutgers Univ. Press, 1953), 5:49.

50. Dexter, *Journal,* and letter, Dec. 15, 1861; letter of J. J. Loveless (Co. C), *Owego Gazette,* Feb. 13, 1862; Bennitt, letter, *Steuben Farmers' Advocate,* Dec. 18, 1861; Bailey, letter, *Cortland Gazette and Banner,* Dec. 26, 1861; letter of Lt. Florence Sullivan (Co. K), *Elmira Daily Advertiser,* Jan. 11, 1862.

51. Carpenter, letter, Civil War pension application file, National Archives, Washington, D.C.

52. Dexter, *Journal;* Sullivan, letter, *Elmira Daily Advertiser,* Jan. 11, 1862; "Army Correspondence," *Hornellsville Weekly Tribune,* Jan. 2, 1862; Clark, letter, Jan. 7, 1862, Mudge Collection; Edgcomb, letter, Dec. 27, 1861, author's collection.

53. Burritt, letter, *Elmira Weekly Advertiser and Chemung County Republican,* Dec. 21, 1861; Enos B. Vail, *Reminiscences of a Boy in the Civil War* (n.p.: privately printed, 1915), 43; Adjutant W. W. Hayt, letter, *Corning Journal,* Jan. 16, 1862; Maxson, *Camp Fires,* 189; Surgeon Churchill, letter, *Owego Gazette,* Jan. 2, 1862. The three other men of the Cortland Volunteers who died of camp fever were William Decker (Dec. 16), Adelbert Taylor (Dec. 29), and Frederick Tiffany (Dec. 12).

54. Squires, letter, dated Nov. 7. Typescript from the collection of Sylvia Shoebridge, town historian of Pompey, N.Y.; Bailey, letter, *Cortland Gazette and Banner,* Dec. 12, 1861. "Members of the New York Twenty-third in Hospital," *New York Times,* Dec. 17, 1861, stated that forty-one men were in the Falls Church hospital at that time, "most of them suffering from typhoid fever." The reporter added that "each company of this regiment has a fund to be used in defraying the expenses of sending home their dead comrades."

55. Letters of Gilbert and Hayt, *Corning Journal,* Jan. 2 and 16, 1861; Surgeon Churchill, letter, *Elmira Weekly Gazette,* Dec. 26, 1861; Edgcomb, letter, dated Dec. 12, 1861, author's collection. Churchill apparently was not uniformly popular in the regiment. In the Aug. 15, 1861, issue of the *Elmira Weekly Gazette,* Commissary Sgt. L. W. Bigham (Co. K) noted that Churchill was ill in Washington and added, "we do not miss him much . . . as Dr. Madill has been the working man from the start."

56. Maxson, *Camp Fires*, 28; Bennitt, letter, *Steuben Farmers' Advocate*, Oct. 2, 1861.

57. Viele, *Hand-Book for Active Service*, 11, 12; Burritt, letters, *Elmira Daily Advertiser*, Feb. 24 and 28, 1862; Bennitt, letters, *Steuben Farmers' Advocate*, Feb. 5 and Mar. 5, 1862.

58. Bennitt, letter, Feb. 5, 1862; Chauncey Judd, letter, Jan. 31, 1862, Civil War pension application file, National Archives, Washington, D.C.; muster rolls of the 23d New York, National Archives, Washington, D.C., roll Dec. 31–Feb. 28, 1862.

59. Burritt, letter, *Elmira Daily Advertiser*, Feb. 24, 1862.

60. Dexter, letter, Jan. 19, 1862; *Waverly Advocate*, Jan. 31, 1862; Crane, letter, excerpts, *Corning Journal*, Jan. 16, 1862.

61. Dexter, letters of Oct. 9, 1861, and Dec. 15, 1861. Pvt. Henry Scott (Co. E) mentions cutting logs for a church in his diary entry for Feb. 15 (microfilm, NYPL). Edgcomb, letter, Jan. 20, 1862, author's collection; trading pens (or "pins") reference from the Scott, *Diary*, Jan. 27, 1862. Charles Hathaway (Co. G) writes home on Jan. 10, 1862: "Send some of that itch ointment for they have lots of lice in this country" (pension application file, National Archives, Washington, D.C.).

62. Charles A. Cuffel, *History of Durell's Battery in the Civil War* (Philadelphia: Craig Finley, 1903), 26; C. V. Tevis and D. R. Marquis, comps., *The History of the Fighting Fourteenth* (New York: Brooklyn Eagle, 1911), 244; Burritt, letter, *Elmira Daily Advertiser*, Feb. 28, 1862; Mills, *Chronicles*, 145.

63. Dexter, letter, Dec. 25, 1861; Edgcomb, letters, Jan. 19 and Feb. 6, 1862, author's collection.

64. Augustus Buell, *The Cannoneer* (Washington, D.C.: National Tribune, 1890), 18–19; Hogarty, "A Medal of Honor," in *War Talks in Kansas: MOLLUS*, 353.

65. Burritt, letter, *Elmira Daily Advertiser*, Feb. 24, 1862. For information on Fergus Moore see his compiled service record, microfilm, National Archives, Washington, D.C. Burritt added, "The volunteers to be returned to their regiments when their services on the waters were no longer needed."

66. Muster returns for Feb. 1862, 23d New York, record group 94, National Archives, Washington, D.C.; Burritt, letters, *Elmira Daily Advertiser*, Jan. 10 and Feb. 24, 1862; Maxson, *Camp Fires*, vi; Colby, *Civil War Papers*, 74.

4. MCCLELLAN MAKES HIS MOVE

1. CCW, part 1 (1863), 426.

2. Burritt, letter, Mar. 9, 1862, quoted in Maxson, *Camp Fires*, 32; William Wisner Hayt, *All Over the Sacred Soil: The Journal of Adjutant William Wisner Hayt* (Mar. 9, 1862–Feb. 13, 1863), entry Mar. 9, 1862, from typescript of original journal in possession of David W. Hayt, Los Angeles, Calif. [hereafter Hayt, *Journal*]. Used by permission.

3. Gregg, letter to "My Dear Thurston," Mar. 9, 1862, manuscript collection 16361 (three Gregg letters), New York State Library, Albany.

4. Bennitt, letter, *Steuben Farmers' Advocate,* Mar. 19, 1862; Mills, *Chronicles,* 146–47; General Orders No. 26 issued by Colonel Hoffman's headquarters directing the march are found in Burritt correspondence, *Elmira Weekly Advertiser and Chemung County Republican,* Mar. 8, 1862. The figure of four wagons per regiment seems low by Civil War standards. For more on this issue see Erna Risch, *Quartermaster Support of the Army: A History of the Corps, 1775–1939* (Washington, D.C.: Center of Military History, U.S. Army, 1989), 422–23; Billings, *Hardtack and Coffee,* 350–57. There is no information on the number of ambulances, if any, assigned to the 23d at this time.

5. Mills, *Chronicles,* 147; Burritt, letter, *Elmira Daily Advertiser,* Mar. 15, 1862.

6. McDowell's march directive found in General Orders No. 22, dated Mar. 13, 1862, record group 393, preliminary inventory, vol. 2, control no. 234, entry 3713, National Archives, Washington, D.C. See also instructions given by Brig. Gen. George L. Hartsuff of McDowell's corps, May 11, 1862, in Charles E. Davis Jr., *Three Years in the Army: The Story of the Thirteenth Massachusetts Volunteers* (Boston: Estes and Lauriat, 1894), 59.

7. John A. Martin, "Reminiscences," in *War Talks in Kansas: MOLLUS,* 366–67.

8. Davis, *Thirteenth Massachusetts Volunteers,* 92–93.

9. Martin, "Reminiscences," 367.

10. Ibid.

11. Mills, *Chronicles,* 147; Burritt, *Elmira Daily Advertiser,* Mar. 15, 1862.

12. Tevis, *Fighting Fourteenth,* 31; "The Advance upon Fredericksburg," *New York Herald,* Apr. 22, 1862; *Buffalo Express,* Mar. 20, 1862.

13. CCW, part 1 (1863), 243, 247.

14. The Bull Run battlefield soon took on the aura of America's first Civil War National Park. Georgia troops erected a monument on Henry Hill in Sept. 1861 to honor their fallen leader Francis S. Bartow. Once the area came under Union occupation, an excursion train began operation from Washington to Manassas Junction, and a stage left three times per week from a point near Willard's Hotel for guided tours of the battle sites. ("Fare for the round trip, $10. Refreshments furnished. Passes required.") Found battle relics could fetch ten dollars for a carved pipe bowl and eight dollars for a bowie knife. Robert E. L. Krick, "The Civil War's First Monument," *Blue and Gray Magazine,* Apr. 1991; Leech, *Reveille in Washington,* 163–64; "The Trophies of Manassas," *Philadelphia Inquirer,* Mar. 19, 1862.

15. Vail, *Reminiscences,* 40–41; Henry Greenleaf Pearson, *James S. Wadsworth of Geneseo* (New York: Scribner's, 1913), 89; Hayt, *Journal,* Mar. 13, 1862; Bennitt, letter, *Steuben Farmers' Advocate,* Mar. 19, 1862; Burritt, letter, *Elmira Daily Advertiser,* Mar. 19, 1862; Mills, *Chronicles,* 150.

16. Rufus King, DAB, 10: 400; *OR,* vol. 51, part 1, p. 62.

17. Mills, *Chronicles,* 150–51; Maxson, *Camp Fires,* 38; Burritt, letter, *Elmira Daily Advertiser,* Mar. 31, 1862. Burritt identified the stream as Hunting Creek.

18. George B. McClellan, *Report on the Organization and Campaigns of the Army of the Potomac* (New York: Sheldon, 1864), 152.

19. Lewis, *The History of Battery E, First Regiment Rhode Island Light Artillery,* 34; Regis de Trobriand, *Four Years with the Army of the Potomac* (Boston: Ticknor, 1889), 159–60; Elisha Hunt Rhodes, *All for the Union: A History of the 2d Rhode Island Volunteer Infantry,* ed. Robert Hunt Rhodes (Lincoln, R.I.: Andrew Mowbray, 1985), 61; Gilbert Adams Hays, *Under the Red Patch: Story of the Sixty Third Regiment* (Pittsburgh: Regimental Association, 1908), 60.

20. De Trobriand, *Four Years,* 160; James A. Wright, *No More Gallant a Deed,* ed. Steven J. Keillor (St. Paul: Minnesota Historical Society, 2001), 109; Charles B. Haydon, *For Country, Cause and Leader: The Civil War Journal of Charles B. Haydon,* ed. Stephen W. Sears (New York: Ticknor and Fields, 1993), 207.

21. Hays, *Under the Red Patch,* 60–61; Rhodes, *All for the Union,* 61; Alexander Hays, *Life and Letters of Alexander Hays,* ed. George Thornton Fleming (Pittsburgh: privately printed, 1919), 199. Over the next month this scene was repeated division by division. In all, about four hundred steamers, schooners, and barges ferried 121,500 men, 14,592 animals, 1,150 wagons, 44 artillery batteries, and 74 ambulances, along with mountains of supplies, to the lower peninsula of Virginia. McClellan, *McClellan's Own Story,* 238.

22. Clark, letter, Mar. 29, 1862, Mudge Collection. Clark's irritation might have stemmed in part from charges brought against him on Mar. 20 by Col. Theodore B. Gates of the 20th New York State Militia [hereafter NYSM], for "disobedience of orders." Although Gen. R. King approved the case for trial, apparently it went no further, and the charges were dropped. See record group 393, preliminary inventory, vol. 2, entry 3690, dated Apr. 1, 1862, National Archives, Washington, D.C.; Theodore B. Gates, *The Civil War Diaries of Col. Theodore B. Gates, 20th New York State Militia,* ed. Seward R. Osborne (Hightstown, N.J.: Longstreet House, 1991), 13; Edgcomb, letters, Mar. 17 and 30, 1862, author's collection.

23. Marsena R. Patrick, DAB, 14: 296.

24. Journal of Marsena Patrick, Manuscript Division, Library of Congress, Washington, D.C., journal entries of Mar. 21 and 25, 1862. An edited version of this wonderfully revealing journal has been published by David S. Sparks as *Inside Lincoln's Army* (New York: Thomas Yoseloff, 1964). Subsequent Patrick quotations are from the original journal.

25. Burt, *Memoirs,* 78.

26. Gates, *Ulster Guard,* 191; Sparks, *Inside Lincoln's Army,* 15.

27. Albert D. Shaw, *A Full Report of the First Re-Union and Banquet,* published in book form as *History of the Thirty-fifth New York Vols.* (Watertown, N.Y.: Times, 1888), 25; Colby, *Civil War Papers,* 109; Patrick, DAB, 14:297; Gates, *The Ulster Guard,* 191–92; Vail, *Reminiscences,* 59.

28. OR, vol. 12, part 3, 43.

29. Ibid.

30. Report of Rufus King, dated Apr. 5 and 6, 1862, record group 393, preliminary inventory, vol. 2, control no. 230, entry 3580, National Archives, Washington, D.C.; Burritt, letter, *Elmira Advertiser,* Apr. 15, 1862; Patrick, *Journal,* Apr. 6, 1862; *Edward Dicey's Spectator of America,* ed. Herbert Mitgang (Chicago: Quadrangle, 1971), 153. According to Lieutenant Andrews the locals pronounced the name "Ma-nass-ah"; Andrews, letter, Apr. 10, 1862, in Blodgett scrapbook, 2:84.

31. Andrews, Letter, Apr. 10, 862, Blodgett scrapbook, 2:84; King's Division, General Orders No. 36, Apr. 6, 1862, record group 393, preliminary inventory, vol. 2, control no. 234, entry 3712, National Archives, Washington, D.C.

32. Maxson, *Camp Fires,* 41; Vail, *Reminiscences,* 61; for a discussion of McDowell's problems with receiving supplies see *OR,* vol. 51, part 1, 569–70. King was told to expect forage and rations to be waiting for him when he arrived at Bristoe. Instead he found only 128,000 pounds of bacon. King's report dated Apr. 6, 1862, record group 393, preliminary inventory, vol. 2, control no. 230, entry 3580, National Archives, Washington, D.C.

33. Baldwin, letter, Apr. 7, 1862.

34. *OR,* vol. 12, part 3, 54–55.

35. Maxson, *Camp Fires,* 42; Patrick, *Journal,* Apr. 12, 1862; Burritt, letter, *Elmira Advertiser,* Apr. 19, 1862.

36. Patrick, *Journal,* Apr. 13, 1862; Hayt, *Journal,* Apr. 13, 1862.

37. Mills, *Chronicles,* 158–59.

38. Two excellent sources are available for the activities of McDowell's headquarters during this period: Headquarters, *Journal of Events,* Mar. 10, 1862, to June 22, 1862, in *OR,* vol. 51, part 1, 61–79; and the diary of Maj. Joseph C. Willard, aide de camp to McDowell, covering the period Apr. 3, 1862, to Sept. 4, 1862, in Willard Family Papers, Manuscript Division, Library of Congress, Washington, D.C. La Mountain's balloon arrived at Catlett's on Apr. 17, 1862.

39. *CCW,* part 1 (1863), 267; record group 393, preliminary inventory, vol. 2, control no. 2130, entry 3580, National Archives, Washington, D.C.

40. *OR,* vol. 12, part 1, 434.

41. Testimony of Gen. Irvin McDowell, *CCW,* part 1 (1863), 262–63; *OR,* vol. 12, part 1, 93.

42. *OR,* vol. 51, part 1, 68, and vol. 12, part 3, 80–81.

43. Official reports of Augur, Bayard, and Kilpatrick, *OR,* vol. 12, part 1, 428–39, and part 3, 80; Tevis, *Fighting Fourteenth,* 32; Willard Glazier, *Three Years in the Federal Cavalry* (New York: R. H. Ferguson, 1871), 58; "The Advance upon Fredericksburg," *New York Herald,* Apr. 22, 1862.

44. *OR,* vol. 12, part 1, 428–39; Robert K. Krick, *9th Virginia Cavalry* (Lynchburg, Va.: H. E. Howard, 1982), 4. The Confederate force consisted of the 9th Virginia Cavalry and the 40th Virginia Infantry.

45. James W. Hunnicutt, *The Conspiracy Unveiled: The South Sacrificed, or the Horrors of Secession* (Philadelphia: J. B. Lippincott, 1863), 317–18; "The Advance upon Fredericksburg," *New York Herald,* Apr. 22, 1862; Wyman S. White,

The Civil War Diary of Wyman S. White, ed. Russell C. White (Baltimore: Butternut and Blue, 1993), 59.

46. White, *Diary,* 60–61; Charles McCool Snyder, *Oswego County: New York in the Civil War,* Oswego County Historical Society, 1962, 24.

47. "Army Correspondence," *Hornellsville Weekly Tribune,* May 1, 1862; Patrick, *Journal,* Apr. 16, 1862; *OR,* vol. 51, part 1, 68. The abstemious commander was not at his headquarters at the time. McDowell returned from Washington early on the 16th. Before reaching Catlett's, his train struck a drunken soldier lying on the rails. The train stopped to discover that the man had been thrown into a ditch by the impact but was unharmed. "The Advance upon Fredericksburg," *New York Herald,* Apr. 22, 1862.

48. Gates, *Ulster Guard,* 208; "The Advance from Washington," *New York Times,* Apr. 26, 1862, indicates Quisenberry owned 1,130 acres of land. According to soldier accounts, Quisenberry was a "true Union man," incarcerated at one time in Richmond for his pro-Union beliefs. See *Hornellsville Weekly Tribune* cited above, plus Burritt, letter, *Elmira Daily Advertiser* of Apr. 29, 1862.

49. Mills, *Chronicles,* 161.

50. Patrick, *Journal,* Apr. 20, 1862; Mills, *Chronicles,* 159–61; Geo. C. Smithe, *Glimpses: Of Places, and People, and Things* (Ypsilanti, Mich.: Ypsilantian, 1887), 16; Albert Rogers Crandall (Co. D), letter, Apr. 20, 1862, Papers of Albert Crandall, no. 2628, Division of Rare and Manuscript Collections, Cornell University, Ithaca, N.Y.

51. Dexter, letter, Apr. 22, 1862; Maxson, *Camp Fires,* 44.

52. Hoffman, letter, Apr. 22, 1862, Buchanan Collection. Major Gregg in the *Owego Gazette,* Oct. 30, 1862, called Hoffman one of the "Ultra-democrats" in his politics. Hoffman's comments about Gregg could be a reference to Gregg's statements quoted in Mar. 27, 1862, *Corning Journal* directing slaves to travel by the North Star "if they preferred freedom to slavery"; Crandall, letter, Apr. 20, 1862; Mills, *Chronicles,* 160.

53. "Army Correspondence," *Hornellsville Weekly Tribune,* May 8, 1862; Maxson, *Camp Fires,* 43; Mills, *Chronicles,* 161; Burritt, letter, *Elmira Daily Advertiser,* Apr. 29, 1862.

54. Hayt, letter, dated Apr. 23 in *Corning Journal,* May 8, 1862; Burritt, letter, *Elmira Daily Advertiser,* Apr. 29, 1862; Mills, *Chronicles,* 161–62.

55. Patrick, *Journal,* Apr. 20, 1862; *Wellsboro (Pa.) Agitator,* May 7, 1862. Another soldier wrote in the May 8, 1862, *Hornellsville Weekly Tribune* that Patrick "seems trying to enforce all the severe discipline which is supposed to be found among regulars. Many of his orders seem onerous to a volunteer corps, and to speak mild, bitter are the anathemas uttered against him at times." Lt. Newton T. Colby wrote on May 1, 1862, "Everybody—both officers and men—dislike him exceedingly"; Colby, *Civil War Papers,* 116.

56. Hayt, *Journal,* Apr. 18, 1862; there were two Briggs families living in the area. Evidence indicates that Patrick's main column took the Spotted Tavern Road (modern Route 612) to Hartwood Church, which makes the Stony Hill

property his most likely headquarters. See Jerrilynn Eby, *They Called Stafford Home* (Bowie, Md.: Heritage, 1997), 345–57.

57. Cuffel, *Durell's Battery*, 35; "Army Correspondence," *Hornellsville Weekly Tribune*, May 8, 1862; Bennitt, letter, *Steuben Farmers' Advocate*, Apr. 30, 1862.

58. Patrick, *Journal*, Apr. 20, 1862.

59. E. M. Woodward, *History of the Third Pennsylvania Reserve* (Trenton, N.J.: MacCrellish and Quigley, 1883), 71; Mills, *Chronicles*, 165; *New York Herald*, Apr. 22, 1862; Noel G. Harrison, *Fredericksburg Civil War Sites: Dec. 1862–Apr. 1865*, 2 vols. (Lynchburg, Va.: H. E. Howard, 1995), 167. A newspaper reporter described the Phillips house as having all the modern conveniences, including indoor plumbing: "It has hot and cold water throughout, bathrooms, speaking tubes, frescoed ceilings, gas fixtures"; "Gen. McDowell's Column," *New York Times*, Apr. 30, 1862. A fire destroyed the house on Feb. 14, 1863.

60. Mills, *Chronicles*, 167–68. Apparently not all Fredericksburg citizens remained unmoved by the patriotic concert. Resident Betty Herndon Maury wrote that when she heard a Union band playing "Yankee Doodle" and the "Star Spangled Banner," she "could not realize that they were *enemies* and invaders. The old tunes brought back recollections of the old love for them. It was a sad and painful feeling!" Betty Herndon Maury, *The Confederate Diary of Betty Herndon Maury*, ed. Alice Maury Parmelee (Washington, D.C.: privately printed, 1938), 69. It is unclear whether Maury was referring to the Union Cornet Band concert described above. Maury said she heard the concert on Sunday evening Apr. 20. Mills thought the concert occurred on the 19th but was not sure.

5. FREDERICKSBURG

1. Description of the physical features of Fredericksburg in *New York Times*, Apr. 22, 1862. See also "Sketch of Fredericksburg and Vicinity," *New York Herald* Apr. 22, 1862, 3, 10, and S. E. Chandler, "In the Thick of It," *National Tribune*, Oct. 17, 1895.

2. Ervin L. Jordan Jr., *Black Confederates and Afro-Yankees in Civil War Virginia* (Charlottesville: Univ. Press of Virginia, 1995), 12.

3. G. W. Redway, *Fredericksburg: A Study in War* (London: George Allen and Unwin, l906), 72.

4. By 1862 roads, Fredericksburg was fifty-six miles from Washington and sixty-two miles from Richmond. *New York Times*, Apr. 22, 1862.

5. Maury, *Confederate Diary*, 67.

6. John Washington, "Memorys of the Past," manuscript memoir, undated, Library of Congress. Typescript in files of Fredericksburg and Spotsylvania National Military Park [hereafter FSNMP]. See chapter 8, for Apr. 18, 1862.

7. The Union delegation crossed the river in two leaky boats under a flag of truce. The group included Lieutenant Wood of King's staff, Lt. Joseph B. Campbell (4th U.S. Artillery), and Maj. Alfred N. Duffié (2d N.Y. Cavalry). "From McDowell's Advance," *New York Daily Tribune*, Apr. 22, 1862; "Latest From

McDowell's Advance," *Owego Gazette,* Apr. 24, 1862; "The Advance upon Fredericksburg," *New York Herald,* Apr. 22, 1862.

8. The committee included the mayor, William A. Settle, and J. Gordon Wallace, Thomas B. Barton, William F. Broaddus, and John L. Marye Jr.; *New York Times,* Apr. 26, 1862. The location of Augur's headquarters, where the surrender most likely took place, remains a mystery. Augur probably had a headquarters tent set up near "Belmont," the home of Joseph Burwell Ficklen. We know that the pro-Union Ficklen invited Augur into his home and on Apr. 18 served a meal to his staff. "The Advance upon Fredericksburg," *New York Herald,* Apr. 22, 1862.

9. *OR,* vol. 12, part 1, 437.

10. This road (Route 218) is better known as the White Oak Road. In the section of road mentioned, from Patrick's camp to the Chatham Bridge into town, both names are appropriate.

11. Patrick, *Journal,* Apr. 23, 1862; King's Division, General Orders No. 45, Apr. 24, 1862, National Archives, record group 393, preliminary inventory, vol. 2, control no. 234, entry 3712; *OR,* vol. 12, part 3, 124, 134. The three railroad bridges crossed Accakeek and Potomac creeks, as well as the Rappahannock River.

12. *OR,* vol. 51, part 1, 72, 583, and vol. 12, part 3, 109; Herman Haupt, *Reminiscences of General Herman Haupt* (Milwaukee, Wis.: Wright and Joys, 1901), 45–47; Patrick, *Journal,* May 3, 1862. Road distances from Burritt, *Elmira Advertiser,* May 3, 1862. Two locomotives were landed and placed on the tracks by May 2, 1862; "Camp 23d. Regiment," *Hornellsville Weekly Tribune,* May 8, 1862.

13. Patrick, *Journal,* Apr. 21 and 30, 1862.

14. Mills, *Chronicles,* 169.

15. Maxson, *Camp Fires,* 45; Mills, *Chronicles,* 170; Burritt, *Elmira Advertiser,* May 3, 1862.

16. Letter of Newton T. Colby, "Letters from the Army," *Corning Journal,* May 8, 1862; "The Advance upon Fredericksburg," *New York Herald,* Apr. 22, 1862; Woodward, *History of the Third Pennsylvania Reserve,* 71.

17. "The Showmen," *Philadelphia Inquirer,* May 23, 1862.

18. Burritt, letter, *Elmira Advertiser,* May 3, 1862.

19. Maxson, *Camp Fires,* 44; Edgcomb, letter, May 26, 1862; "Letter of Capt. Todd," *Corning Journal,* May 22, 1862; Lt. Willoughby Babcock, letter, June 30, 1861, found in Willoughby M. Babcock Jr., *Selections from the Letters and Diaries of Brevet-Brigadier General Willoughby Babcock of the Seventy-fifth NYV,* War of the Rebellion Series, Bulletin 2 (n.p.: University of the State of New York, 1922), 100; Crandall, letter, dated May 23, 1862, Albert Crandall Papers, Cornell University.

20. Letter of Dr. Seymour Churchill, *Owego Gazette,* Mar. 6, 1862; Andrews, letter, Nov. 7, 1861, Blodgett scrapbook, 2:44.

21. "Letter from Capt. Todd," *Corning Journal,* May 22, 1862.

22. Tevis, *The Fighting Fourteenth,* 252; "Major Gregg of the Twenty-third," *Corning Journal,* Mar. 27, 1862.

23. Dawes, *Service with the Sixth Wisconsin Volunteers,* 41; report of Maj. H. E. Davis Jr., acting provost marshal, May 5, 1862, record group 393, preliminary

inventory, vol. 2, control no. 230, entry 3580, National Archives, Washington, D.C. The abusive slave owner was named Green; Maury, *Confederate Diary*, 75.

24. Vail, *Reminiscences*, 63; General Orders No. 10, Headquarters, Department of the Rappahannock, May 10, 1862, found in record group 393, preliminary inventory, control no. 230, entry 3589, National Archives, Washington, D.C. The badges, issued by the quartermaster, were "made to designate them in gangs of tens and hundreds"; *New York Tribune*, May 2, 1862. "From the 26th Regiment, NYV," Rochester *Union and Advertiser*, May 19, 1862; "Letter from Bennitt," *Steuben Farmers' Advocate*, May 7, 1862 (letter of May 2, 1862).

25. *Hornellsville Weekly Tribune*, May 8, 1862; Leo W. and John I. Faller, *Dear Folks at Home*, ed. Milton E. Flower (Carlisle, Pa.: Cumberland County Historical Society, 1963), 70–71; Burritt, letter, *Elmira Daily Advertiser*, Apr. 29, 1862; Mills, *Chronicles*, 167.

26. "From the 26th Regiment NYV," Rochester *Daily Union and Advertiser*, May 19, 1862.

27. *New York Herald*, May 9, 1862, July 15, 1862, and July 25, 1862. Betty Maury in her diary entry of June 22 (page 82) noted, "We hear that there is great want and suffering among those in Washington. Many are shipped direct for Haiti from here."

28. *OR*, vol. 12, part 3, 134–35; Jane Howison Beale, *The Journal of Jane Howison Beale of Fredericksburg, Virginia, 1850–1862* (Fredericksburg, Va.: Historic Fredericksburg Foundation, 1984), 43, entry of May 14, 1862; Maury, *Confederate Diary*, 70, 75, entries of Apr. 25 and May 16, 1862.

29. Henry R. Pyne, *Ride to War: The History of the First New Jersey Cavalry*, ed. Earl Schenck Miers (New Brunswick, N.J.: Rutgers Univ. Press, 1961), 17–21; "Department of the Rappahannock," *New York Times*, Apr. 29, 1862. According to King's letter of Apr. 25, 1862, in record group 393, part 2, entry 3580, National Archives, Washington, D.C., all but the canal boats and the ferryboat were to return downriver the next day. The "old double-ender" ferryboat served during the summer as a lighter at the Fredericksburg wharf; Burritt, letter, *Elmira Advertiser*, May 3, 1862. One gunboat was the *Island Belle*; Mills, *Chronicles*, 168.

30. Patrick, *Journal*, Apr. 29, 1862; Daniel O. Clough, "The First to Enter Fredericksburg," *National Tribune*, Dec. 21, 1905; James R. Putnam, "Occupying Fredericksburg," *National Tribune*, Sept. 21, 1905; *OR*, vol. 12, part 3, 115; "The Ulster Guard on the Rappahannock," Kinston, *Argus*, May 14, 1862. Hayt, *Journal*, May 3, 1862, gives the figure of seventeen or eighteen boats supporting the bridge.

31. *OR*, vol. 12, part 3, 105, 114, 117, 125. A reporter for the *New York Times* stated that on Apr. 25 two Morrison brothers and a man named Armstrong complained to King that Rebel pickets would visit Fredericksburg nightly and harass Union men. The Morrisons claimed that five family members had been arrested or forced south. They offered to point out prominent Rebels for arresting and holding as hostages for the return of their relatives. "Department of the Rappahannock," *New York Times*, Apr. 28 and May 1, 1862. King wrote to McDowell on Apr. 26 that "small cavalry pickets have come into the town, during the last two

nights, harassing and arresting several Union men and carrying them off south, for no other offence than their fidelity to the Union. They ask protection at my hands." Found in record group 393, preliminary inventory, vol. 2, control no. 230, entry 3580, National Archives, Washington, D.C. Actually, four men were arrested by Confederate authorities around this time and sent to Richmond: Charles Williams, Moses Morrison, Thomas Morrison, and Peter Couse. The Morrisons were arrested when neighbors reported their "disloyal sentiments." See Lucille Griffith, "Fredericksburg's Political Hostages," *Virginia Magazine of History and Biography* 72, no. 4 (Oct. 1964): 395–98.

32. Beale, *Journal,* 41.

33. Clough, "The First to Enter Fredericksburg"; Patrick, *Journal,* May 2, 1862; *OR,* vol. 12, part 3, 126. Fredericksburg historian Noel Harrison locates the bridge as striking the Fredericksburg shore about forty yards downstream from the foot of Berkeley Street ("Rocky Lane"). He states that at least twelve boats went into making the bridge; Harrison, *Fredericksburg Civil War Sites,* 97.

34. Patrick, *Journal,* May 2, 1862; *Owego Gazette,* May 15, 1862.

35. "Letter From Capt. Todd," *Corning Journal,* May 22, 1862; Hunnicutt; *The Conspiracy Unveiled,* 320–21; Bennitt, letter, *Steuben Farmers' Advocate,* May 14, 1862; Maury, *Confederate Diary,* 72–73. Captain Clark in a letter of May 3, 1862, Mudge Collection, claimed that a company of the 2d New York cavalry crossed into Fredericksburg with Todd's company.

36. "Our Rappahannock Letter," *Philadelphia Inquirer,* May 16, 1862; Haupt, *Reminiscences,* 47; reference to rubber pontoon boats in *OR,* vol. 12, part 3, 383. The boats had rubber cylinders that had to be inflated by hand bellows. For a history of this type of pontoon boat see Mike Woshner, *India-Rubber and Gutta-Percha in the Civil War Era* (Alexandria, Va.: O'Donnell, 1999), 131–40; and *OR,* vol. 51, part 1, 72.

37. Cuffel, *Durrell's Battery,* 37; *Christian Banner* 1, no. 2, "Second Edition," May 20, 1862.

38. "Department of the Rappahannock," *New York Times,* May 10, 1862; *OR,* vol. 51, part 1, 72; "Letter from Capt. Clark," *Cortland Gazette and Banner,* May 15, 1862.

39. Patrick, *Journal,* May 3, 1862; Gates, *The Civil War Diaries of Col. Theodore B. Gates, 20th New York State Militia,* 18–19; Bennitt, letter, *Steuben Farmers' Advocate,* May 14, 1862.

40. Patrick, *Journal,* May 6 and 7, 1862.

41. Dexter, letter, May 13, 1862; "Army Correspondence," *Hornellsville Weekly Tribune,* May 22, 1862; description of tobacco factory in Harrison, *Fredericksburg Civil War Sites,* 76–78; Burritt, letter, *Elmira Daily Advertiser,* May 19, 1862; Maxson, *Camp Fires,* 46. Colonel Gates, thus relieved of his duties in Fredericksburg, returned to his camp in Stafford County; see Gates, *Diaries,* 19, entry of May 7, 1862. Gates writes that he returned to Fredericksburg as a "sort of Provost Marshal" on the 8th and apparently continued in that capacity until May 20. Prussia Street is present-day Lafayette Boulevard.

42. Patrick, *Journal,* May 13, 1862. The Plank Road picket line was extended

to the Toll Gate on May 13, was subsequently withdrawn, and was reestablished on May 20; Gates, *Diaries*, 20.

43. Burritt, letter, *Elmira Daily Advertiser*, May 19, 1862; George C. Sumner, *Battery D, First Rhode Island Light Artillery, in the Civil War, 1861–1865* (Providence, R.I.: Rhode Island Printing, 1897), 9; Bennitt, letter, *Steuben Farmers' Advocate*, May 14, 1862. The regimental book records of the 2d New York Cavalry, record group 94, National Archives, Washington, D.C., indicate that Company L came across the river on the 8th as a bodyguard to Patrick. Company D reported to Patrick on the 9th , and Major Duffié reported to Patrick with Companies A and B early on the 11th.

44. Patrick, *Journal*, entries of May 7–10, l862; "Rebel Barbarity," *Philadelphia Inquirer*, May 9, 1862. Also, on May 20 two members of the 14th "Brooklyn" Regiment were reported to have been shot at their guard posts by two men "disguised as farmers"; "Department of the Rappahannock," *New York Times*, May 25, 1862. Patrick had his troops round up a mother and daughter by the name of Smuck on May 10 for, according to Burritt, "signaling the enemy from a house on the borders"; Burritt, letter, *Elmira Daily Advertiser*, May 19, 1862.

45. Smithe, *Glimpses*, 18; Maury, *Confederate Diary*, 74; Mills, *Chronicles*, 174; Patrick, *Journal*, May 10, 1862. The 35th camped just south of the mill pond; "War Correspondence," *Jefferson County News*, May 22, 1862.

46. *OR*, vol. 12, part 3, 195–96; Franklin Sawyer, *A Military History of the 8th Regiment Ohio Vol. Inf'y* (Cleveland: Fairbanks, 1881), 48. For a breakdown of regiments within the Department and division number totals, see *OR*, vol. 12, part 3, 309–12.

47. Gates, *The Ulster Guard*, 225. At least ten men were captured from the 13th South Carolina Infantry of (Brig. Gen. Maxcy) Gregg's Brigade, Anderson's Division. See also "From Gen. McDowell's Army," *New York Times*, May 19, 1862; the *Times* reporter said that twelve privates and one lieutenant captured were dressed in dark gray uniforms with palmetto-tree badges on their hats.

48. Patrick, *Journal*, May 12, 1862.

49. Smithe, *Glimpses*, 18–19; Maxson, *Camp Fires*, 47.

50. Patrick, *Journal*, May 12, 1862; Burritt, letters, *Elmira Daily Advertiser*, May 19 and 27, 1862; Maxson, *Camp Fires*, 47; "From Gen. McDowell's Army," *New York Times*, May 19, 1862.

51. *OR*, vol. 51, part 1, 73; Patrick, *Journal*, May 12, 1862; Burritt, letter, *Elmira Daily Advertiser*, May 19, 1862; Maury, *Confederate Diary*, 74.

52. *OR*, vol. 12, part 3, 170–71; Burritt, letter, *Elmira Advertiser*, May 27, 1862.

53. Burritt, letter, *Elmira Daily Advertiser*, May 19, 1862. The Fredericksburg National Cemetery currently lies on a portion of the campsite occupied by the Cortland Volunteers.

54. "Letter from Capt. Clark," *Cortland Gazette and Banner*, May 15, 1862.

55. "Peculiar Effect of the Virginian Climate," *New York Times*, May 21, 1862.

56. Burritt, letter, *Elmira Daily Advertiser*, May 13, 1862; Clark, letter, May 3,

1862, Mudge Collection; Edgcomb, letters of May 18 and June 22 and 29, 1862, author's collection. Andrew's resignation elevated Leonard F. Hathaway to lieutenant, Archibald N. DeVoe to second lieutenant, and Frederick Burritt to sergeant major—all to date as of May 7, 1862.

57. Cuffel, *Durell's Battery*, 39.

58. Ibid., 37–38; Hunnicutt, *The Conspiracy Unveiled*, 303; Maxson, *Camp Fires*, 46.

59. "Army Correspondence," *Hornellsville Weekly Tribune*, May 22, 1862; "Letter from Capt. Clark," *Cortland Gazette and Banner*, May 15, 1862.

60. *OR*, vol. 12, part 1, 53; record group 393, preliminary inventory, vol. 2, control no. 230, entry 3712, National Archives, Washington, D.C.

61. *OR*, vol. 12, part 1, 52.

62. "Letter from Capt. Todd," *Corning Journal*, May 22, 1862; Vail, *Reminiscences*, 66–67; Judd letter of May 1, 1862, Civil War pension application file, National Archives, Washington, D.C.; Haupt, *Reminiscences*, 49; Smithe, *Glimpses*, 22–23; *Christian Banner* 1, no. 3, dated May 27, 1862.

63. Letter of Sidney J. Mendell, *Jefferson County News*, May 29, 1862.

64. Clark, letter, *Cortland Gazette and Banner*, May 15, 1862, Burritt, letter, *Elmira Weekly Advertiser and Chemung County Republican*, May 31, 1862.

65. Burritt, letter, *Elmira Daily Advertiser*, May 19, 1862; George F. Noyes, *The Bivouac and the Battle-Field; or, Campaign Sketches in Virginia and Maryland* (New York: Harper, 1863), 48.

66. Burritt, letter, *Elmira Daily Advertiser*, May 13, 1862; Mills, *Chronicles*, 178; Maxson, *Camp Fires*, 46; "Letter from Capt. Todd," *Corning Journal*, May 22, 1862. Maury, *Confederate Diary*, 75–76, adds that flags were "tacked on to the trees, stuck in the soldiers' guns, and even tied to the horns of their oxen"; Charles F. Hobson and Arnold Shankman, "Colonel of the Bucktails: Civil War Letters of Charles Frederick Taylor," letter, May 4, 1862, in *Pennsylvania Magazine of History and Biography* 97, no. 3 (July 1973): 346. Lizzie Maxwell Alsop, journal Wynne Family Papers, Virginia Historical Society, typescript in library of FSNMP, 4.

67. Burritt, letter, *Elmira Daily Advertiser*, May 19, 1862; Judd, letter, May 13, 1862, Civil War pension application files, National Archives; "Gen. McDowell's Operations," *Daily Pittsburgh Gazette and Commercial Journal*, May 9, 1862; Blodgett scrapbook, 2:101; letter from Conrad Hanks, May 12, 1862, Conrad C. Hanks Papers, Special Collections, Duke University Library; Maxson, *Camp Fires*, 46; George C. Sumner, "Recollections of Service in Battery D, First Rhode Island Light Artillery," *Soldiers' and Sailors' Historical Society of Rhode Island*, Personal Narratives, fourth series, no. 11 (Providence, R.I.: Historical Society of Rhode Island, 1891), 18–19.

68. *Corning Journal*, May 22, 1862; Maury, *Confederate Diary*, 74; "From Gen. McDowell's Division," *New York Tribune*, May 26, 1862.

69. John S. Applegate, *Reminiscences and Letters of George Arrowsmith of New Jersey* (Red Bank, N.J.: John H. Cook, 1893), 129, 136. On June 18, 1862, a former chaplain of the 13th New York wrote to McDowell charging Hunt and

his partners with keeping what amounted to a house of prostitution at the Shakespeare; E. M. Remington, letter, record group 393, preliminary inventory, vol. 2, entry 3580, National Archives, Washington, D.C.; Gates, *Diaries*, entry of May 16, 1862, 19; Burritt, letter, *Elmira Daily Advertiser*, May 27, 1862; Beale, *Journal*, 55.

70. Patrick, *Journal*, May 18, 1862; Gates, *Ulster Guard*, 227. Apparently Worthington got only as far as Patrick's headquarters; see Gates, *Diaries*, 20, entry May 18, 1862. The service conducted by Reverend Alfred M. Randolph at St. George's Episcopal Church seems to be the one most commented upon. For a description by a participant see Mendell, letter, *Jefferson County News*, May 29, 1862. Mills, *Chronicles*, 178–80; Dawes, *Service*, 44. The captain's full name was William Nicholas Worthington. The message he carried concerned the family of Fauquier County resident Robert E. Scott, murdered on May 3; "The Department of the Rappahannock," *New York Times*, May 20, 1862.

71. *OR*, vol. 12, part 3, 214, and part 1, 97, 281; *CCW*, vol. 1 (1863), 267–68.

72. *Christian Banner* 1, no. 13 (July 14, 1862); Mills, *Chronicles*, 175; Beale, *Journal*, 41, entry of May 7, 1862.

73. *OR*, vol. 12, part 3, 207, and part 1, 78, 281; Cuffel, *Durell's Battery*, 40; Haupt, *Reminiscences*, 46, 49; Burritt, letter, *Elmira Daily Advertiser*, May 27, 1862; "Affairs at Fredericksburg," *New York Herald*, May 22, 1862. After the railroad was completed, most of McDowell's supplies arrived by rail or steamship, thus diminishing the importance of Belle Plain as a supply base; "From McDowell's Army," *New York Tribune*, May 22, 1862.

74. *OR*, vol. 12, part 3, 211, 218; "Affairs at Fredericksburg," *New York Herald*, May 22, 1862; Harrison, *Fredericksburg Civil War Sites*, 124; E. M. Woodward, *Our Campaigns; or the Marches, Bivouacs, Battles, Incidents of Camp Life and History of Our Regiment during Its Three Years Term of Service* (Philadelphia: Collins, 1865), 100. For the particulars of the bridge construction see S. E. Chandler, "In the Thick of It," *National Tribune*, Oct. 17, 1895, and "Our Fredericksburg Letter," *Philadelphia Inquirer*, May 27, 1862.

75. Burritt, letter, *Elmira Daily Advertiser*, May 27, 1862; Mendell, letter, *Jefferson County News*, May 29, 1862; "Our Fredericksburg Letter," *Jefferson County News*; Gates, *Ulster Guard*, 228; *OR*, vol. 12, part 1, 78, 282.

76. The bands were from the 9th, 14th, and 26th New York regiments and the 90th Pennsylvania. *OR*, vol. 51, part 1, 75; Rodgers Family Papers, Library of Congress, series 1, box 5, letter of Col. John N. Macomb, May 23, 1862.

77. "Presidential Visit to Fredericksburg," *National Intelligencer*, May 27, 1862; Haupt, *Reminiscences*, 47–49.

78. *OR*, vol. 51, part 1, 75; Davis, *Three Years in the Army*, 69; Woodward, *History of the Third Pennsylvania Reserve*, 72; Cuffel, *Durell's Battery*, 40; Samual L. Gillespie, *A History of Company A, First Ohio Cavalry* (Washington Court House: Press of Ohio State Register, 1898), 84.

79. "Presidential Visit to Fredericksburg"; Hunnicutt, *The Conspiracy Unveiled*, 343–44; Mendell, letter, *Jefferson County News*, May 29, 1862. Mendell confirms that Lincoln visited the camp of the 35th. The 21st had moved its camp

on May 22 to an elevated site near the "reservoir" along the Plank Road, closer to town; Patrick, *Journal,* May 23, 1862. Letter of Macomb, May 23, 1862, Rodgers Family Papers, Library of Congress; Mills, *Chronicles,* 180, 184; Sawyer, *A Military History of the 8th Regiment Ohio Vol. Inf'y,* 49; Haupt, *Reminiscences,* 50.

6. The Summer of Forlorn Hopes

1. John White Geary, *A Politician Goes to War: The Civil War Letters of John White Geary,* ed. William Alan Blair (University Park: Pennsylvania State Univ. Press, 1995), 44. The three gaps through the mountains referred to are: Ashby's Gap leading down the Little River Turnpike (Route 50) toward Washington, D.C.; Manassas Gap to Gainesville (Route 55); and Chester Gap to Warrenton (Route 211).

2. *OR,* vol. 12, part 3, 219–20, and part 1, 282–83.

3. *OR,* vol. 12, part 3, 220.

4. Patrick, *Journal,* May 25, 1862. Bayard's brigade of about two thousand men was formed by an order from McDowell dated May 25. It consisted of the 1st New Jersey and 1st Pennsylvania cavalry regiments, four companies (264 men) of the 13th Pennsylvania Reserve Infantry, the "Bucktails," and four mountain howitzers; see Hobson and Shankman, "Colonel of the Bucktails," *Pennsylvania Magazine of History and Biography* 97, no. 3 (July 1973): 335, 347; *OR,* vol. 51, part 1, 639, and vol. 12, part 3, 284. Apparently some of Shields's men went by train from Catlett's to Manassas Junction; *OR,* vol. 12, part 3, 248; Frederic Denison, *Sabres and Spurs: The First Regiment Rhode Island Cavalry* (Central Falls, R.I.: E. L. Freeman, 1876), 79. From Manassas Junction to Front Royal the troops marched along the line of the Manassas Gap Railroad and parallel roadways. The Manassas Gap Railroad at this time was not operational beyond Thoroughfare Gap in the Bull Run Mountains. Late on June 8, 1862, after work on the Bull Run Railroad Bridge was completed, trains could travel from Alexandria to Front Royal; *OR,* vol. 51, part 1, 664.

5. Patrick, *Journal,* May 25, 1862; Burritt, letter, *Elmira Daily Advertiser,* June 17, 1862; Maxson, *Camp Fires,* 48; *OR,* vol. 51, part 1, 76.

6. *Christian Banner* 1, nos. 3 and 4, May 27 and 31, respectively, for newspaper accounts; Noyes, *The Bivouac and the Battle-Field,* 34. One of Marsh's legs was found on the roof of another building. Maxson, in his book, *Camp Fires,* 48, reports, "His remains were collected and buried"; the reporter for the *Hornellsville Weekly Tribune* (June 5, 1862) attributed the accident to Marsh's carelessness in handling a live shell. The munitions magazine was of Confederate origin, as noted in a report of acting Provost Marshal Maj. H. E. Davis Jr., May 5, 1862, record group 393, preliminary inventory, vol. 2, control no. 230, entry 3850, National Archives, Washington, D.C.

7. Patrick, *Journal,* May 23, 1862; Alsop, *Diary,* 3. Alsop said the locals referred to the general as "Doubledevil."

8. Gen. Abner Doubleday, journal, U.S. Army General's Reports of Civil War Service, 1864–1888, record group 94, microfilm no. 1098, National Archives [hereafter Doubleday, *Journal*], entries of 23 May 23 and 25, 1862. Doubleday on May 26 claimed that Reynolds stopped issuing passes to fugitive blacks attempting to cross the river. The *Christian Banner* reported in the June 7 issue (vol. 1, no. 5) that former slaves were not given a pass to cross unless they had written authorization from their masters. Doubleday would later command a brigade of three regiments (76th and 95th N.Y. and 56th Pa.) attached to King's division.

9. Woodward, *Our Campaigns*, 99.

10. Burritt, *Elmira Daily Advertiser*, June 17, 1862; *Hornellsville Weekly Tribune*, June 5, 1862.

11. Mills, *Chronicles*, 185.

12. A reporter traveling with Bayard said that they rode to within fifteen miles of the fighting. "From General M'Dowell's Army," *Philadelphia Inquirer*, June 5, 1862.

13. *OR*, vol. 12, part 3, 243, 266, 269, 270, 276. Shields wrote to McDowell on May 27, 1862, that Geary's retreat had amounted to "a disgraceful panic"; ibid., 256.

14. *OR*, vol. 12, part 3, 265, 270, 274, 276.

15. Patrick, *Journal*, May 29, 1862; *Hornellsville Weekly Tribune*, June 19, 1862. For information on the still-standing Gordon house and family see Harrison, *Fredericksburg Civil War Sites*, 59.

16. *OR*, vol. 12, part 1, 694, and part 3, 290.

17. Robert G. Tanner, *Stonewall in the Valley* (Garden City, N.Y.: Doubleday, 1976), 277.

18. *OR*, vol. 12, part 3, 283, 291, and vol. 51, part 1, 76. McDowell officially relieved Ord from command on 8 June 1862; *OR*, vol.12, part 3, 355. McDowell directed Bayard to maintain his horses by having the troopers walk their mounts for one half-hour out of every two hours of travel; *OR*, vol. 51, part 1, 643.

19. *OR*, vol. 12, part 3, 295.

20. Patrick spells the name "Irwin." *Journal*, May 30, 1862; for a sketch of the family see Eby, *They Called Stafford Home*, 351–56; Mills, *Chronicles*, 188.

21. Davis, *Three Years in the Army*, 76; Haupt, *Reminiscences*, 60; *OR*, vol. 12, part 3, 314.

22. *OR*, vol. 12, part 3, 300; Patrick, *Journal*, May 31 and June 1, 1862; Burritt, letter, *Elmira Daily Advertiser*, June 17, 1862.

23. Mills, *Chronicles*, 191–92; Mendell, letter, *Jefferson County News*, June 12, 1862; William B. Greene, *Letters from a Sharpshooter*, trans. William H. Hastings (Belleville, Wis.: Hastings, 1993), 118. At the time of the crash Greene was amusing his comrades by drawing a mustache on a sleeping comrade with a burned cork. Greene was violently thrown against the side of the car but got out unhurt; Capt. C. A. Stevens, *Berdan's United States Sharpshooters in the Army of the Potomac, 1861–1865* (St. Paul, Minn.: Price-McGill, 1892), 163.

24. Patrick, *Journal*, June 1, 1862; Haymarket description from Cuffel, *Durell's Battery*, 44.

25. *OR*, vol. 12, part 3, 318.

26. *OR*, vol. 12, part 3, 326–67; Patrick, *Journal*, June 2, 1862; Burritt, letter, *Elmira Daily Advertiser*, June 17, 1862. Charles Green, a merchant in Georgia and a farmer in Greenwich, was a British citizen and flew a British flag over his property; see Earle P. Barron, *Ewell's March Home: The Civil War and Early Times in and around Greenwich, Virginia* (Kearney, Neb.: Morris, 1999), 27.

27. Burritt, letter, *Elmira Daily Advertiser*, June 17, 1862; Maxson, *Camp Fires*, 49.

28. Muster roll, 23d NYV, record group 94, National Archives, Washington, D.C.

29. Haupt, *Reminiscences*, 63; Patrick, *Journal*, June 4, 1862.

30. Woodward, *Our Campaigns*, 102; *OR*, vol. 12, part 3, 343.

31. *OR*, vol. 12, part 3, 354, and part 1, 96–97.

32. *OR*, vol. 12, part 3, 343, 351; Patrick, *Journal*, June 6, 1862. While at Warrenton King established his headquarters in the Warren Green Hotel; see Washington, "Memorys of the Past," typescript, FSNMP. Washington served at the time as King's mess servant.

33. Patrick, *Journal*, June 7, 1862; *Hornellsville Weekly Tribune*, June 26, 1862; Burritt, letter, *Elmira Daily Advertiser*, June 17, 1862; Douglas S. Freeman, *R. E. Lee: A Biography*, 4 vols. (New York: Scribner's, 1934), 1:30.

34. Patrick, *Journal*, June 10, 11, and 18, 1862; Maxson, *Camp Fires*, 50; Burritt, letter, *Elmira Daily Advertiser*, June 17, 1862.

35. Burritt, letter, *Elmira Daily Advertiser*, July 12, 1862; Maxson, *Camp Fires*, 50.

36. Smithe, "The Mail-Bag in Camp," *Glimpses*, 21; Maxson, *Camp Fires*, 51, 61; Burritt, letter, *Elmira Daily Advertiser*, July 12, 1862.

37. *OR*, vol. 51, part 1, 78–79. McDowell, a teetotaler, expressed gratification at learning that even when unconscious his medical officer had been unable to part his clenched teeth to give him brandy; Haupt, *Reminiscences*, 63. Willard, *Diary*, entry of June 18, 1862; George Washington Partridge Jr., *Letters from the Iron Brigade*, ed. Hugh L. Whitehouse (Indianapolis, Ind.: Guild, 1994), 36.

38. *OR*, vol. 12, part 3, 363–64, 427, 432–34.

39. Doubleday, *Journal*, June 10 and 15, 1862. Lacy served as a volunteer aide on the staff of Confederate Maj. Gen. Gustavus W. Smith. The *New York Herald* of June 16, 1862 ("From Gen. McDowell's Division"), reported that Federal authorities captured Lacy by following the track of his wife, whom they had suspected was traveling to see him. A notice in the June 14, 1862 *Christian Banner* (vol. 1, no. 7), in addition to describing Lacy's capture, lists the activities of the provost guard for a two-day period. Along with the arrest of Lacy, sixteen soldiers were arrested for being out after curfew, one citizen for "carrying letters to the enemy," and one soldier for being disorderly and "dressed in female dress";

Patrick, *Journal,* June 15, 1862. Burritt, *Elmira Daily Advertiser,* July 12, 1862; "Father Patrick" quote in King's letter of June 17, National Archives, record group 393, preliminary inventory, vol. 2, entry 3583.

40. *OR,* vol. 12, part 3, 435. For Pope's statement in regard to his strategic plans see p. 454; Pope wrote in his memoirs, "I was expected to go down to or toward Richmond and seize and hold the bear by the tail, whilst McClellan beat out its brains"; Cozzens and Girardi, eds., *The Military Memoirs of General John Pope,* 121.

41. *OR,* vol. 12, part 3, 433, 448; Cuffel, *Durell's Battery,* 50. Cuffel writes that on July 16 eight gunboats were near the railroad bridge.

42. Patrick, *Journal,* June 27, 1862; Mills, *Chronicles,* 196; Gates, *Diaries,* 24; Dexter, letter, July 4, 1862; Vail, *Reminiscences,* 66.

43. Patrick, *Journal,* June 27, 1862; Mendell, letter, *Jefferson County News,* July 10, 1862; Edgcomb, letter, June 29, 1862, author's collection.

44. Maxson, *Camp Fires,* 53; book records, 20th NYSM, record group 94, National Archives, Washington, D.C., camp schedule dated June 30, 1862; *Christian Banner* 1, no. 9, June 24, 1862; "Camp Rufus King," *Cazenovia Republican,* July 30, 1862; drawing of seine fishing at Falmouth in Harrison, *Fredericksburg Civil War Sites,* 172. Soldiers fished in the Rappahannock for shad, herring, bullheads, and suckers; Colby, *Civil War Papers,* 121.

45. Burritt, letter, *Elmira Daily Advertiser,* July 12, 1862; Clark, letter, July 1, 1862, Clark family collection.

46. Burritt, letter, *Weekly Advertiser and Chemung County Republican,* July 12, 1862; "Letter from Sergeant Kellogg," *Corning Journal,* July 10, 1862; Mills, *Chronicles,* 199; Dexter, letter, July 4, 1862.

47. Burritt, letter, *Weekly Advertiser and Chemung County Republican,* July 12, 1862; "Letter from Sergeant Kellogg," *Corning Journal,* July 10, 1862; Mills, *Chronicles,* 199; Dexter, letter, July 4, 1862.

48. Dawes, *Service,* 51. The famous mule race apparently had a ten-dollar purse for both the fastest and slowest entries; see letter of Henry C. Marsh in Craig L. Dunn, *Iron Men, Iron Will* (Indianapolis, Ind.: Guild, 1995), 53; Cuffel, *Durrell's Battery,* 47–48; Vail, *Reminiscences,* 66–68. The captor of the pig received the animal as a prize.

49. "The Ulster Guard on the Rappahannock," *Kingston Argus,* July 16, 1862; Maxson, *Camp Fires,* 54–57; On July 11 another sword was presented to Major Gregg by the line officers; Hayt, *Journal,* entry of July 11, 1862.

50. *Hornellsville Weekly Tribune,* July 17, 1862; Edward P. Tobie, *History of the First Maine Cavalry* (Boston: Emery and Hughes, 1887), 73; mention of gunboats being illuminated in letter of William L. Johnson, Battery B, 4th U.S. Artillery, July 9, 1862, collection of Jim Woodworth, available at www.batteryb.com; Cuffel, Durell's *Battery,* 48; Dexter, letter, July 4, 1862; Patrick, *Journal,* July 4–5, 1862. For an account of the Chatham speeches see "Our Fredericksburg Correspondence," *New York Herald,* July 10, 1862. Also the Virgil W. Mattoon letters, manuscript collection, Connecticut Historical Society, typescript, FSNMP, letter 60, July 7, 1862.

51. *Steuben Farmers' Advocate*, July 16, 1862; Mills, *Chronicles*, 201.

52. Maury, *Confederate Diary*, 82; *Christian Banner* 1, nos. 7 (June 14, 1862), 8 (June 18, 1862), and 11 (July 2, 1862); Hunnicutt, *The Conspiracy Unveiled*, 368.

53. Patrick, *Journal*, July 22, 1862.

54. Maury, *Confederate Diary*, 82; Burrett, letter, *Elmira Weekly Advertiser and Chemung County Republican*, July 12, 1862; *Christian Banner* 1, no. 13 (July 14, 1862); Samuel J. B. V. Gilpin, 3d Indiana cavalry, *Diary*, Aug. 1861–Oct. 1864 (5 vols.), entry of July 24, 1862, Manuscript Division, Library of Congress, Washington, D.C.

55. Burritt, letter, *Elmira Weekly Advertiser and Chemung County Republican*, July 12, 1862; Mills, *Chronicles*, 165; Judd, letter, May 13, 1862, Civil War pension application file, National Archives, Washington, D.C.; Dodd account in pension application file for Charles Barnes, 23d New York Infantry, National Archives; Noyes, *Bivouac and the Battle-Field*, 34.

56. Patrick, *Journal*, entries of July 6, 7, 14, 15, 19, and 20, 1862; Mills, *Chronicles*, 196.

57. Peter Cozzens, *General John Pope: A Life for the Nation* (Urbana: Univ. of Illinois Press, 2000), 76.

58. *CCW*, part 1(1863), 276–79; *OR*, vol. 12, part 3, 474; Pope's "War means desolation" letter quoted in Wallace J. Schutz and Walter N. Trenerry, *Abandoned by Lincoln: A Military Biography of General John Pope* (Urbana: Univ. of Illinois Press, 1990), 177.

59. For the full text of Pope's orders see *OR*, vol. 12, part 2 (orders 5, 6, 7, 11), 50–52; part 3 (order 13), 509.

60. "Our Military Position," *New York Times*, July 27, 1862; Davis, *Three Years in the Army*, 90; Patrick, *Journal*, July 18, 1862; Dexter, letter, Aug. 9, 1862; Burritt, letter, *Elmira Daily Advertiser*, Aug. 2, 1862; Gregg, letter, *Elmira Daily Advertiser*, July 5, 1862.

61. Patrick, *Journal*, entries July 18 and 20, 1862; Sears, *The Civil War Papers of George B. McClellan*, 387–88.

62. Patrick, *Journal*, July 21, 1862; Patrick wrote that Pope's orders have "demoralized the Army and Satan has been let loose." Cuffel, *Durell's Battery*, 51; *Christian Banner* account found in Hunnicutt, *The Conspiracy Unveiled*, 418; "From Gen. Pope's Army," *New York Tribune*, July 28, 1862.

63. The charges against Mansfield were determined to be unfounded, and he was returned to duty with his regiment. See note in George H. Otis, *The Second Wisconsin Infantry*, ed. and intro. Alan D. Gaff (Dayton, Ohio: Morningside Bookshop, 1984), 146–47. Doubleday took credit for the tit-for-tat hostage crisis; Doubleday, *Journal*, July 23, 1862. McDowell, according to Patrick, considered Doubleday a spiteful troublemaker and "the cause of more evil to him than any one else, having made the matter of his guarding rebel property a test of his loyalty"; Patrick, *Journal*, July 12, 1862; and see *OR*, ser. 2, vol. 4, 274. For the particulars on the Fredericksburg hostage issue and the names of both Union and Confederate hostages, see Webb Garrison, *Civil War Hostages: Hostage Taking*

in the Civil War (Shippensburg, Pa.: White Mane, 2000), 54–60; Patrick, *Journal,* July 22, 1862; S. J. Quinn, *The History of the City of Fredericksburg, Virginia* (Richmond, Va.: Hermitage, 1908), 76–81; Griffith, "Fredericksburg's Political Hostages." The last of the Fredericksburg hostages were released on Sept. 24, 1862. Young Lizzie Maxwell Alsop, niece of Thomas Barton, one of the first Confederate hostages, claimed that the original four men had been lured from their homes to Union headquarters for arrest under the pretext that they would be providing information in support of Mansfield; Alsop, *Diary,* 20.

64. *OR,* vol. 12, part 3, 450, 466–68; Willard, *Diary,* entry of July 17, 1862.

65. *OR,* vol. 12, part 3, 915.

66. *OR,* vol. 12, part 3, 450–51, 454, 479, 484, 499, 502–503; Angus James Johnston II, *Virginia Railroads in the Civil War* (Chapel Hill: Univ. of North Carolina Press, 1961), 73; Glazier, *Three Years in the Federal Cavalry,* 72–80. Hearing of the "success" of one raid, Patrick harrumphed, "My belief is they stole more horses than they captured"; Patrick, *Journal,* July 23, 1862.

67. *OR,* vol. 12, part 3, 503; John Gibbon, *Personal Recollections of the Civil War* (New York: Putnam, 1928), 41; Burritt, letter, *Elmira Weekly Advertiser and Chemung County Republican,* Aug. 9, 1862; letter of Martin V. Doty, *Hornellsville Weekly Tribune,* Aug. 7, 1862.

68. Maxson, *Camp Fires,* 59–60; Doty, letter, *Hornellsville Weekly Tribune,* Aug. 7, 1862; Burritt, letter, *Elmira Advertiser,* Aug. 9, 1862; Hoffman, letter, July 28, 1862, Buchanan collection.

69. Doty, letter, *Hornellsville Weekly Tribune,* Aug. 7, 1862; Maxson, *Camp Fires,* 59–60.

70. Burritt, letter, *Elmira Weekly Advertiser and Chemung County Republican,* Aug. 9, 1862. Burritt claimed 401 men present from the 23d.

71. Otis, *The Second Wisconsin Infantry,* 53; Maxson, *Camp Fires,* 61–62; Burritt, *Elmira Weekly Advertiser and Chemung County Republican,* Aug. 9, 1862; Doty, letter, *Hornellsville Weekly Tribune,* Aug. 7, 1862; "From the Camp," *Cazenovia Republican,* Aug. 6, 1862; Scott, *Diary,* July 27, 1862. For an explanation of the regulation concerning uniforms see Risch, *Quartermaster Support of the Army,* 445.

72. Patrick, *Journal,* entries July 25–28 and 30, 1862. Patrick found the acting provost marshal of Fredericksburg, Captain Scott, "completely under 'Secesh' influences"; Mills, *Chronicles,* 203; Gates, *The Ulster Guard,* 233; Samuel J. B. V. Gilpin, *Diary,* entry for July 31, 1862, Manuscript Division, Library of Congress.

73. The 217-ton *Anacostia* had a complement of sixty-seven men and mounted two nine-inch smoothbore guns. Paul H. Silverstone, *Warships of the Civil War Navies* (Annapolis, Md.: Naval Institute, 1989), 103.

74. "From the Camp," *Cazenovia Republican,* Aug. 6, 1862; Burritt, *Elmira Weekly Advertiser,* Aug. 9, 1862. The suspension bridge, opened for wagon traffic on July 18, reflected the genius of the engineer in charge, Lt. Washington Augustus Roebling. His father, John, had designed the famous Niagara Railway suspension bridge and developed the use of wire rope to replace chain bridge cable in the

construction of suspension bridges. The Chatham Bridge, built mostly in the first three weeks of July, was 1,028 feet in length and consisted of thirteen piers and fourteen spans ranging in length from seventy-five to eighty-five feet, with two large wire ropes on each side. Roebling would go on after the war to build the famous Brooklyn Bridge. See Washington Augustus Roebling, ed. Earl Schenck Miers, *Wash Roebling's War* (Newark, Del.: Spiral, 1961); measurements of the bridge in *Christian Banner* 1, no. 13 (July 14, 1862).

75. Patrick, Journal, entries July 25 and 29 and Aug. 1, 2, 4, and 9, 1862; "War Correspondence," *Hornellsville Weekly Tribune*, Aug. 14, 1862; *New York Herald*, Aug. 9, 1862; Burritt, letter, *Elmira Weekly Advertiser and Chemung County Republican*, Aug. 16, 1862.

76. "From the Camp," *Cazenovia Republican*, Aug. 13, 1862; Hayt, *Journal*, Aug. 8, 1862. Taylor and Dickinson were detained for suspected support of and active association with the enemy; Alsop, *Diary*, 22. Burritt wrote that when one of the "high strung" gentlemen was taken out of his bed the young ladies attached to the household "attempted most ludicrous sensations by screaming, fainting, etc., which amused our sleepy men very much"; Prentiss letter, *Hornellsville Weekly Tribune*, Aug. 7, 1862, plus "War Correspondence" in Aug. 14, 1862, issue. It is difficult to know how many Fredericksburg civilians, if any, were actually sent outside the Union lines for refusing to take the oath of allegiance to the United States. A correspondent for the *Hornellsville Weekly Tribune* (Aug. 14) writing on Aug. 7 claimed that the order "has already procured passes for several to Richmond." Halleck, on Aug. 6, warned Pope that the forced removal of citizens from their homes to beyond his lines "should be the exception, not the general rule." *OR*, vol. 12, part 3, 540. The *Christian Banner* (vol. 1, no. 17) of Aug. 13, 1862, noted that as of yet no Fredericksburg citizens had been called upon to take the oath.

77. Gilpin, *Diary*, July 29, 1862; Patrick, *Journal*, Aug. 5, 1862; Burritt, letter, *Elmira Daily Advertiser*, Aug. 16, 1862.

78. "Arrival of Gen. Pope at Warrenton," *New York Tribune*, July 31, 1862. At Warrenton, Pope made his headquarters at the Fauquier Female Institute, run by a noted educator from upstate New York, Dr. Joel Smith Bacon (1802–69).

79. *OR*, vol. 11, part 1, 80–81.

80. Cecil D. Eby Jr., ed., *A Virginia Yankee in the Civil War: The Diaries of David Hunter Strother* (Chapel Hill: Univ. of North Carolina Press, 1961), 73; Cozzens and Girardi, *The Military Memoirs of General John Pope*, 121.

81. Cozzens and Girardi, *Military Memoirs of General John Pope*, 118.

82. *OR*, vol. 12, part 3, 529, 550–51, 554; Gibbon, *Recollections*, 41; Hayt, Aug. 5, 1862.

83. Patrick, *Journal*, Aug. 9, 1862; Hayt, *Journal*, Aug. 8–9, 1862.

84. "Letter From Bould Soger," *Buffalo Morning Express*, July 31, 1862.

85. Mills, *Chronicles*, 202–203; *Cazenovia Republican*, Aug. 6, 1862.

7. PINCHED BELLIES AND A HELL OF A FIGHT.

1. Tevis, *Fighting Fourteenth*, 36.

2. Maxson, *Camp Fires*, 69–70; Hayt, *Journal*, Aug. 12, 1862.

3. Patrick, *Journal*, Aug. 13 and 14, 1862.

4. Edward J. Stackpole, *From Cedar Mountain to Antietam, August–September 1862* (Harrisburg, Pa.; Stackpole, 1959), appendix, table 2. Unit numbers for this campaign taken from this table unless otherwise noted. Sergeant Major Burritt of the 23d wrote on Aug. 17 that the regiment had that day 707 men and 37 officers present and absent. Excluding detached men, extra-duty men (teamsters, ambulance drivers, hospital attendants, etc.), and about seventy in general hospitals, "We can then turn out in ten minutes about 530 cool men"; Burritt, letter, *Elmira Weekly Advertiser and Chemung County Republican*, Aug. 30, 1862. Burritt, in the issue of Aug. 16, 1862, added that the regiment, down to fighting trim, carried no more than 150 knapsacks. The rest probably traveled as light as possible, with any personal possessions and extra clothing rolled in a blanket and slung over the shoulder.

5. Mills, *Chronicles*, 216.

6. Full text of General Orders No. 19 in *OR*, vol. 12, part 3, 573; Patrick, *Journal*, Aug. 15 and 16, 1862; Mills, *Chronicles*, 217.

7. Stackpole, *From Cedar Mountain to Antietam*, 80. Pope claimed on Aug. 20 that he had an effective force of forty-five thousand men ready to march, not including cavalry. For the corps breakdown, see *OR*, vol. 12, part 3, 603.

8. *OR*, vol. 12, part 3, 598.

9. Noyes, *The Bivouac and the Battle-Field*, 81, 99–101.

10. Mills, *Chronicles*, 222; Noyes, *The Bivouac and the Battle-Field*, 81.

11. James S. Lyon, *War Sketches: From Cedar Mountain to Bull Run* (Buffalo: Yung, Lockwood, 1882), 13.

12. S. E. Chandler, "In the Thick of It," *National Tribune*, Oct. 24, 1895.

13. Mills, *Chronicles*, 223; "From the 23d Regiment," *Corning Journal*, Sept. 11, 1862.

14. Patrick, *Journal*, Aug. 20, 1862; W. H. Proctor, 2nd USSS, manuscript reminiscence, copy in Manassas National Battlefield Park library; George Kimball, "With Pope at Bull Run," in *Stories of Our Soldiers*, 2 vols. (Boston: Journal, 1893), 2:89; Denison, *Sabres and Spurs: The First Regiment Rhode Island Cavalry*, 131.

15. Maxson, *Camp Fires*, 64; Noyes, *The Bivouac and the Battle-Field*, 86; Eby, *The Diaries of David Hunter Strother*, 84; David L. Hamer, *One Man's War*, typescript, Manassas National Battlefield Park library, 3; "From the Camp," *Cazenovia Republican*, Sept. 3, 1862.

16. Washington A. Roebling, Journal (extracts), Porter Papers, Manuscript Division, Library of Congress, Washington, D.C., microfilm reel 2, 896 [hereafter Porter Papers (a set of thirty-one reels of microfilmed documents primarily related to the military career of Porter)]. McDowell's hat was the subject of much derision and comment by his men, in whose eyes it seemed worthy of the great Don

Quixote. Variously described as an inverted Japanese washbowl or a canoe wrong side up, it was apparently similar in design to a modern pith helmet. For comments on the issue of McDowell's hat, see John J. Hennessy, *Return to Bull Run: The Campaign and Battle of Second Manassas* (New York: Simon and Schuster, 1993), 7 and note; Patrick, *Journal*, Aug. 24, 1862.

17. Crane's report in Maxson, *Camp Fires*, 65–66. Pvt. Darius Lindsey of the Cortland Volunteers was one of four men in the regiment wounded that day. He later claimed in his pension application that he had been hit in the leg while guarding a battery. An eyewitness, however, wrote the pension bureau that Lindsey was crawling through bushes on picket when a comrade accidentally shot him; Lindsey's pension application file, National Archives, Washington, D.C.

18. Kimball, "With Pope at Bull Run," 89.

19. See Pope's report of military operations in *OR*, vol. 12, part 2, 30–31.

20. Sumner, *Battery D, First Rhode Island Light Artillery*, 13; Eby, *The Diaries of David Hunter Strother*, 86.

21. Mills, *Chronicles*, 218.

22. Patrick, *Journal*, Aug. 24 and 25, 1862.

23. Freeman, *R. E. Lee: A Biography*, 2:301.

24. Perceval Reniers, *The Springs of Virginia* (Chapel Hill: Univ. of North Carolina Press, 1941), 155–61; William Burns Jones, "This Picturesque Spot; Fauquier White Sulphur Springs" (master's thesis, spring semester, 1993, George Mason University, Fairfax, Virginia, copy in Fauquier County Public Library, Warrenton, Virginia); Chandler, "In the Thick of It," *National Tribune*, Oct. 24, 1895; George Alfred Townsend, *Rustics in Rebellion* (Chapel Hill: Univ. of North Carolina Press, 1950), 207; John D. Billings, *The History of the Tenth Massachusetts Battery* (Boston: Hall and Whiting, 1881), 80–82.

25. Mills, *Chronicles*, 240; Report of Col. John Beardsley, 9th New York Cavalry, *OR*, vol. 12, part 2, 271. Beardsley stated that he did not know which side fired the artillery rounds that destroyed the hotel; George H. Gordon, *History of the Campaign of the Army of Virginia, under John Pope, from Cedar Mountain to Alexandria, 1862* (Boston: Houghton, Osgood, 1880), 103.

26. Patrick, *Journal*, Aug. 26, 1862; "From Virginia," *Rochester Union and Advertiser*, Sept. 11, 1862; *Buffalo Courier*, Sept. 6, 1862; Mills, *Chronicles*, 241.

27. Extract from the after-action report of Lieutenant Colonel Crane in Maxson, *Camp Fires*, 72–73; *Cazenovia Republican*, Oct. 29, 1862.

28. A correspondent for the *Buffalo Courier* newspaper wrote on Aug. 26 that the woman was a half-witted laundress of the 29th New York Infantry, Sigel's corps, who had been left sick at Warrenton and was trying to escape her situation. *Buffalo Courier*, Sept. 6, 1862. On the fate of the woman, Patrick says only, "She came in"; *Journal*, Aug. 26, 1862.

29. Pope estimated his army's available strength at this time to be about 55,000 men ready to fight; *OR*, vol. 12, part 2, 34. Historian John Hennessy estimates the army at 66,000; Hennessy, *Return to Bull Run*, 118.

30. *OR*, vol. 12, part 2, 70–72.

31. Washington A. Roebling, journal, Porter Papers, microfilm reel 2, 898.

32. Patrick, *Journal*, Aug. 27, 1862; testimony of Marsena Patrick, U.S. Congress, Senate, Executive Document 37, *Proceedings and Report of the Board of Army Officers in the Case of Fitz John Porter*, 4 parts (Washington, D.C.: GPO, 1879) [hereafter Porter Trial], part 2, 223–27; Mills, *Chronicles*, 245.

33. *OR*, vol. 12, part 2, 72, 360.

34. Sigel, letter, Porter Papers, microfilm reel 5, 2240.

35. The Brawner family rented the farm from Augusta Douglass; account of McDowell's hat from Washington A. Roebling's notes, W. H. Paine Diary, NYPL. Paine was a topographical engineer serving under Pope. For the Second Manassas campaign section of Paine's diary, he indicates, he used Roebling's notes verbatim. See also Roebling's account in Porter Papers, microfilm reel 2, 899.

36. Paine Diary; *OR*, vol. 12, part 2, 336, 393, 397. Monroe Hill, used by McDowell and his officers as a command post, is today called Stuart's Hill. Gen. Robert E. Lee occupied the same ground for similar purposes on Aug. 29–30. At the time of the Civil War, the generals could look to the east from the hill and see the heights of Centreville about seven miles distant.

37. The relevant orders halting King's column found in *OR*, vol. 12, part 3, 717, and part 2, 74.

38. Mills, *Chronicles*, 247.

39. *OR*, vol. 12, part 1, 191–96, and part 2, 360: Gibbon, *Personal Recollections of the Civil War*, 51. Since Gibbon was the lowest-ranking brigade commander, his brigade was out of place in the column. Had he been behind Doubleday, as the proper order of march would dictate, the Brawner Farm battle might have developed quite differently.

40. Testimony of Marsena Patrick, Porter Trial, part 2, 224.

41. J. Albert Monroe, "Reminiscences of the War of the Rebellion of 1861–5," *Soldiers' and Sailors' Historical Society of Rhode Island*, no. 11, second series, 1881, 28; Philip Cheek and Mair Pointon, *History of the Sauk County Riflemen* (Madison, Wis.: Democrat, 1909), 38; Noyes, *The Bivouac and the Battle-Field*, 115.

42. E. K. Parker, "Second Bull Run," *National Tribune*, July 14, 1892.

43. Hamer, "One Man's War," 8.

44. John Bryson, *History of the 30th NYV*, 48; John A. Judson, letter, Jan. 9, 1882, Porter Papers, microfilm reel 12, 5437.

45. Noyes, *The Bivouac and the Battle-Field*, 115–16; Abram P. Smith, *History of the Seventy-sixth Regiment, NYV* (Syracuse, N.Y.: Truair, Smith, and Miles, 1867), 117.

46. Mills, *Chronicles*, 248; Patrick, *Journal*, Aug. 28, 1862. See also Patrick's letter of June 4, 1878, to Porter in Porter Papers, microfilm reel 2, 673; Maxson, *Camp Fires*, 75.

47. *OR*, vol. 12, part 2, 381; testimony of John Gibbon, Porter Trial, part 2, 289. Patrick wrote that he had had to help "save" Gibbon, who had "sailed in, without any authority, or plan of action, so far as I can learn, and brought on a fight"; Patrick, letter, Porter Papers, microfilm reel 4, 1734.

48. Doubleday, *Journal,* Aug. 28, 1862.

49. Patrick, *Journal,* Aug. 28, 1862.

50. Noyes, *The Bivouac and the Battle-Field,* 121; Gibbon, *Personal Recollections,* 55–57; testimony of Patrick, Porter Trial, part 2, 225; Patrick letter to Charles King, dated Nov. 6, 1882, Porter Papers, microfilm reel 13, 6062 and following; King account in Charles King, "Gainesville, 1862," in *War Papers, Being Papers Read before the Commandery of the State Of Wisconsin: MOLLUS,* 3:259–83; Doubleday, *Journal,* Aug. 28, 1862; *OR,* vol. 12, part 1, 208, and part 3, 717–18. For a conflicting account of this important conference see James H. Stine, *History of the Army of the Potomac* (Philadelphia: J. B. Rodgers, 1892), 136–37.

51. Mills, *Chronicles,* 251; Patrick, *Journal,* Aug. 29, 1862.

52. Testimony of Patrick, Porter Trial, part 2, 227; Willard, *Diary,* entry Aug. 29, 1862; Washington Roebling, letter, Porter Papers, microfilm reel 6, 2861.

53. Mills, *Chronicles,* 251, 254.

54. Testimony of Patrick, Porter Trial, part 2, 228; Charles M. Pyne, letter, Porter Papers, microfilm reel 3, 1489.

55. John A. Judson, letter, dated May 9, 1878, Porter Papers, microfilm reel 6, 2770; Doubleday, *Journal,* Aug. 29, 1862.

56. David Hunter Strother, "Personal Recollections of the War by a Virginian," *Harper's New Monthly Magazine* 35 (Nov. 1867): 717.

57. Patrick, letter, Porter Papers, microfilm reel 2, 674; Mills, *Chronicles,* 259.

58. Maxson, *Camp Fires,* 78; Henry C. Meyer, *Civil War Experiences* (New York: privately printed, 1911), 14.

59. Mills, *Chronicles,* 259.

60. Ibid., 259–60; *Cazenovia Republican,* Nov. 12, 1862. Fire from the 23d killed three and wounded four in the 35th.

61. Testimony of Patrick, Porter Trial, part 2, 231; Patrick, *Journal,* Aug. 29, 1862; Strother, "Recollections," *Harper's New Monthly Magazine* 35 (Nov. 1867): 717. Bouvier suffered a lung wound. He was initially taken to the Dogan House for treatment; he did not return to active service until Nov. 1862.

62. James Longstreet, *From Manassas to Appomattox* (Philadelphia: J. B. Lippincott, 1896), 186; *The Wartime Papers of R. E. Lee,* ed. Clifford Dowdey (New York: Bramhall House, 1961), 266–67.

63. Eby, *Strother Diaries,* 95; testimony of Patrick, Porter Trial, part 2, 233.

64. *OR,* vol. 12, part 2, 361.

65. Gates, *The Ulster Guard,* 275; Mills, *Chronicles,* 263.

66. Newspaper article by Edgcomb, no date, found in the Edgcomb family scrapbook, Cortland County Historical Society, Cortland, New York.

67. Numbers for Porter's Fifth Corps from Hennessy, *Return to Bull Run,* manuscript copy in the library of Manassas National Battlefield Park, 543. Estimate of five thousand based on the field return of King's division on Sept. 1 (*OR,* vol. 12, part 3, 795). Mills, *Chronicles,* 263; Hamer, "One Man's War," 24, 26.

68. *OR,* vol. 12, part 2, 376.

69. "Battles of the Thirty-fifth," no. 6, *Cazenovia Republican,* Nov. 19, 1862.

Hatch was quoted as saying, "Have every gun of this division posted on that eminence to cover our retreat."

70. William W. Blackford, *War Years with Jeb Stuart* (New York: Scribner's, 1945), 131.

71. Hamer, "One Man's War," 25.

72. Ibid., 27; Theron W. Haight, "Gainesville, Groveton, and Bull Run," in *War Papers Being Papers Read before the Commandery of the State of Wisconsin: MOLLUS*, 2:369.

73. Mills, *Chronicles*, 264–65; Patrick, *Journal*, Aug. 29, 1862.

74. Letter J. C. H. (83d Pa.), *Erie Weekly Gazette*, Sept. 18, 1862; Mills, *Chronicles*, 265–66.

75. Testimony of Stephen M. Weld, Porter Trial, part 2, 295.

76. Ibid. See also testimony of Fisher A. Baker, 247–48; Haight, "Gainesville, Groveton, and Bull Run," 370.

77. Extract of Crane's after-action report of the battle in Maxson, *Camp Fires*, 84–88. Civil War pension application file for Lorenzo Sykes, National Archives, Washington, D.C.; *Cazenovia Republican*, Nov. 19, 1862.

78. Maxson, *Camp Fires*, 86; John M. Gould, *History of the First-Tenth-Twenty-ninth Maine Regiment* (Portland, Maine: Stephen Berry, 1871), 211. Gould says McDowell was shouting, "or squealing rather, for his voice was like a woman's"; *OR*, vol. 12, part 2, 358.

79. Newspaper article, no date, Edgcomb family scrapbook, Cortland County Historical Society, Cortland, New York. George's brother Sgt. Martin Edgcomb of the 76th New York Regiment was captured on Aug. 29, paroled on the field (probably at the Stone House), and sent to Camp Chase, near Columbus, Ohio. He did not return to his regiment until after Gettysburg.

80. Sawyer, *A Military History of the 8th Regiment Ohio, Vol. Inf'y*, 65; Maxson, *Camp Fires*, 87; *OR*, vol. 12, part 2, 44.

81. *Cazenovia Republican*, Nov. 26, 1862; Patrick, *Journal*, Sept. 1, 1862.

82. David L. Smith, letter, Porter Papers, microfilm reel 11, 5120.

83. "News From Fredericksburg," *New York Times*, Aug. 31, 1862. The Woolen Mill was a two-story brick building on Princess Anne Street near the Fredericksburg canal. It served as a Union hospital beginning in late June. Fredericksburg *Christian Banner* 1, no. 9 (June 24, 1862).

84. "From Fredericksburg," *New York Times*, Sept. 7, 1862; Gilpin, *Diary*, entry of Sept. 2, claims that about three thousand blacks were sent north from Aquia at this time.

85. *OR*, vol. 12, part 3, 774.

86. "The Evacuation of Fredericksburg," *New York Herald*, Sept. 2, 1862; Gilpin, *Diary*, entry of Aug. 31, 1862.

87. *OR*, vol. 12, part 2, 254–62; *Elmira Advertiser*, Sept. 5, 1862; Maxson, *Camp Fires*, 85.

88. Cox, *Military Reminiscences of the Civil War*, vol. 1, 245; Eby, *Strother Diaries*, 100.

89. Cox, *Military Reminiscences of the Civil War*, 245.

8. BATTLE AUTUMN

1. Stephen W. Sears, *Landscape Turned Red* (New Haven, Conn.: Ticknor and Fields, 1983), 69. Dr. Joseph L. Harsh, *Taken at the Flood* (Kent, Ohio: Kent State Univ. Press, 1999), 171, asserts that by mid–campaign Lee commanded an army of seventy thousand men "present for duty." Due to casualties at South Mountain, Sept. 14, 1862, as well as to sickness and straggling, Lee reported a strength of less than forty thousand on Sept. 17, during the Battle of Antietam; Lee's report of the battle, *OR,* vol. 19, part 1, 151. For a discussion of Confederate numbers, see Harsh, *Sounding the Shallows* (Kent, Ohio: Kent State Univ. Press, 2000), 138–40.

2. Sears, *Landscape Turned Red,* 102. Sears believes McClellan had an "effective strength" of about 71,500 on the day of the Antietam battle (p. 173).

3. *Diary of Gideon Welles,* 3 vols. (Boston: Houghton Mifflin, 1911), vol. 1 (1861–Mar. 30, 1864): 114–15.

4. Lee spoke of McClellan to one of his officers during the campaign: "He is an able general but a very cautious one." John G. Walker, "Jackson's Capture of Harper's Ferry," in *Battles and Leaders,* 2:606.

5. King marched forty-five miles in six days, passing through Leesboro (Wheaton, in Maryland), Brookeville, Lisbon, and New Market, to the Monocacy River; Mills, *Chronicles,* 278. Noyes, *Bivouac and the Battle-Field,* 164; Gates, *Ulster Guard,* 520–21.

6. McClellan, letter, Sept. 12, 1862. Sears, *The Civil War Papers of George B. McClellan,* 449–50; Patrick, *Journal,* Sept. 13, 1862.

7. Eby, Strother, *Diaries,* 105.

8. Ezra A. Carman, "The Maryland Campaign of September 1862," Carman Papers, Manuscript Division, Library of Congress, Washington, D.C., 3–4; Gibbon, *Personal Recollections of the Civil War,* 73.

9. *OR,* vol. 19, part 2, 196.

10. Burritt, letter, *Elmira Weekly Advertiser and Chemung Republican,* Oct. 4, 1862; the number of men in the brigade from *Corning Journal,* Sept. 11, 1862.

11. Noyes, *The Bivouac and the Battle-Field,* 165.

12. Gibbon, *Personal Recollections of the Civil War,* 75.

13. *OR,* vol. 19, part 1, 214.

14. Woodward, *History of the Third Pennsylvania Reserve,* 176.

15. Mills, *Chronicles,* 280.

16. Burritt, letter, *Elmira Weekly Advertiser and Chemung County Republican,* Oct. 18, 1862; Patrick, *Journal,* Sept. 14, 1862; Maxson, *Camp Fires,* 193. Hoffman's after-action report at pp. 98–100. Company C of the 23d was serving with Hatch's headquarters.

17. George W. Smalley, *Anglo-American Memories* (London: Duckworth, 1911), 125.

18. Ibid., 124; McClellan letter, June 2, 1862, in Sears, *The Civil War Papers of George B. McClellan,* 287–88.

19. Patrick, *Journal,* Sept. 14, 1862.

20. "From the 23d Regiment," *Corning Journal*, Oct. 2, 1862; Maxson, *Camp Fires*, 99.

21. Maxson, *Camp Fires*, 100; Noyes, *The Bivouac and the Battle-Field*, 174; Patrick, *Journal*, Sept. 14, 1862. Lieutenant Bennitt of the 23d noted in a letter to the *Steuben Farmers' Advocate* published Oct. 1, 1862, that during the fight at Turner's Gap (he calls it Frog Gap) Col. John B. Strange of the 19th Virginia Infantry was killed "within three rods of our lines."

22. *OR*, vol. 19, part 1, 184–87.

23. W. N. Pickerill, "The Battle of Quebec School-House," *Middletown Valley Register*, Apr. 8, 1898. Pickerill belonged to the 3d Indiana Cavalry.

24. Noyes, *The Bivouac and the Battle-Field*, 181, 184.

25. William Foster Biddle, "Recollections of McClellan," in *United Service*, n.s., 11 (May 1894): 462.

26. Lee initially had in position ten to twelve thousand men, of infantry and artillery. William Allan, *The Army of Northern Virginia in 1862* (Boston: Houghton, Mifflin, 1892), 366.

27. W. H. Morgan, *Personal Reminiscences of the War of 1861–5* (Lynchburg, Va.: J. P. Bell, 1911), 141.

28. Sears, *Landscape Turned Red*, 174. The Confederates netted in the surrender of Harpers Ferry eleven thousand prisoners, twelve thousand stand of arms, and seventy pieces of artillery, as well as harness and horses, a large number of wagons, and commissary, quartermaster's, and ordnance stores; *OR*, vol. 19, part 1, 981.

29. Walter H. Hebert, *Fighting Joe Hooker* (Indianapolis: Bobbs-Merrill, 1944), 141; *OR*, vol. 19, part 2, 349.

30. Miles C. Huyette, *The Maryland Campaign and the Battle of Antietam* (Buffalo, N.Y.: 1915), 27–28: William Thomas Poague, *Gunner with Stonewall*, ed. Monroe F. Cockrell (Jackson, Tenn.: McCowat-Mercer, 1957), 45; George W. Smalley, "The Contest in Maryland," *New York Daily Tribune*, Sept. 20, 1862.

31. William Brooke Rawle, et al., *History of the Third Pennsylvania Cavalry, Sixtieth Regiment Pennsylvania Volunteers, in the American Civil War, 1861–1865* (Philadelphia: Franklin, 1905), 124; Benjamin F. Cook, *History of the Twelfth Massachusetts Volunteers* (Boston: Twelfth Regiment Association, 1882), 71.

32. Smalley, "The Contest in Maryland." The reporter Smalley traveled with Hooker's headquarters and so, it would seem, was in a good position to comment on the commander's thinking. Smalley states erroneously, however, that two-thirds of the corps had "broken" at Second Manassas when under McDowell.

33. Thomas L. Livermore, *Days and Events, 1860–1866* (Boston: Houghton Mifflin, 1920), 129–30.

34. Carman, "The Maryland Campaign of Sept. 1862," 23.

35. Patrick, Report, *OR*, vol. 19, part 1, 243–45

36. The 20th numbered only 135 men. Book records and muster rolls of the 20th NYSM, record group 94, National Archives, Washington, D.C.; Doubleday, *Journal*, Sept. 17, 1862; *OR*, vol. 19, part 1, 244.

37. Dawes, *Service*, 90.

38. Carman, "The Maryland Campaign of Sept. 1862," 31.

39. Dawes, *Service*, 91.

40. Strother, "Recollections," *Harper's New Monthly Magazine* 36 (Feb. 1868): 282.

41. Carman, "The Maryland Campaign of Sept. 1862," 58; Buell, *The Cannoneer*, 39; Rufus R. Dawes, letter, Mar. 4, 1898, "Antietam Studies," record group 94, National Archives, Washington, D.C.

42. *OR*, vol. 19, part 1, 218; Temple story from Doubleday, *Journal*, original in possession of Harpers Ferry Center, National Park Service, Harpers Ferry, West Virginia.

43. Carman, "The Maryland Campaign of Sept. 1862," 56.

44. Hoffman report found in Maxson, *Camp Fires*, 100–102; Bennett, letter, *Steuben Farmers' Advocate*, Oct. 1, 1862.

45. The number of men in the 23d at the rock ledge is an estimate. Colonel Hoffman states in his after-action report that he had nine companies at South Mountain, numbering 202 officers and men. At Antietam he says that he had altogether 238 officers and men. Maxson, *Camp Fires*, 102.

46. John W. Boileau (Co. A, 23d), letter, "Antietam Studies," record group 94, National Archives, Washington, D.C.

47. J. R. Putman, "Patrick's Brigade: Its Share in the Stormy Scenes on the Right at Antietam," *National Tribune*, Apr. 30, 1908. Putnam belonged to Company I, 23d New York.

48. Nagle, Theodore M., *Reminiscences of the Civil War* (Erie, Pa.: Dispatch, 1923), 41; Benedict R. Maryniak, "Famous Long Ago," *Civil War Courier* 11, no. 6 (Aug. 1995); Carman, "The Maryland Campaign of Sept. 1862," 60–61; Patrick, *Journal*, Sept. 17, 1862.

49. Putnam, *National Tribune*, Apr. 30, 1908; Lieutenant Bennitt claimed that the 23d had captured thirteen Confederates at the fence. *Steuben Farmers' Advocate*, Oct. 1, 1862.

50. Mills, *Chronicles*, 292.

51. Company A lost two killed and seven wounded that day, and Company G two killed and nine wounded. Bennitt, letter, *Steuben Farmers' Advocate*, Oct. 8, 1862.

52. Smalley, "The Contest in Maryland," and *Anglo–American Memories*, 130; Rawle, *History of the Third Pennsylvania Cavalry*, 127.

53. Putnam, *National Tribune*, Apr. 30, 1908.

54. Maxson, *Camp Fires*, 102; Lt. Benjamin Bennitt quotes Howard as saying, "That is the way for a regiment to fall back"; Bennitt, letter, *Steuben Farmers' Advocate*, Oct. 8, 1862. Maxson, *Camp Fires*, vii, has Doubleday subsequently remarking that "the Twenty-third is decidedly the coolest regiment on the field that I have." Bennitt, in the same letter quoted above, suggests that the incident shows the regiment's growing respect for Patrick: "I like Gen. Patrick and he seems to like his Brigade, and does not seem at all ambitious to swell the list of killed and wounded therein. When he moves us on the battle-field or off again, he is sure to

seek the friendly shelter of some intervening woods or hill as soon as possible to protect us from the enemy's fire. The men have confidence in his command and there is no faltering or panic amongst them."

55. *OR*, vol. 19, part 1, 189–91. Campbell is buried in the Antietam National Cemetery; Edgcomb, letter, Sept. 26, 1862, author's collection.

56. The Richmond papers acknowledged that after the Battle of Sharpsburg and the issuance of the Emancipation Proclamation the prospects for intervention by Great Britain and France had "dissolved like a snow-wreath." "News From Richmond," *New York Times*, Nov. 12, 1862.

57. John Prentiss (Company G), letter, *Hornellsville Weekly Tribune*, Aug. 7, 1862; Polly Underwood, letter, Underwood Family Records, Cortland County Historical Society, Cortland, New York. Historians James M. McPherson and Earl J. Hess have suggested that late in the war the North increasingly came to see black freedom as a moral imperative and war aim; see McPherson, *For Cause and Comrades: Why Men Fought in the Civil War* (New York: Oxford Univ. Press, 1997), 128–30, and Hess, *Liberty, Virtue, and Progress*, 97–102. While I believe general support can be found among the Cortland community for the Emancipation Proclamation as a war measure, racial prejudice and concern for the status of free blacks limited their perspective as to its broader meanings.

58. Maryniak, "The Famous Long Ago," 47.

59. Patrick, *Journal*, Sept. 19, 1862.

60. "Visit to the Battlefield," *Rochester Union and Advertiser*, Sept. 24, 1862; Patrick, *Journal*, Sept. 20, 1862; Clifton Johnson, *Battleground Adventures* (Boston: Houghton Mifflin, 1915), 103. One Saturday in early October Patrick tried to improve morale by marching the men down to the Potomac to bathe and boil their filthy and vermin-infested clothing. He then allowed them the remainder of the day to themselves; Maxson, *Camp Fires*, 104.

61. Burritt, letter, *Elmira Advertiser*, Oct. 4, 1862; Vail, *Reminiscences*, 87; Patrick, *Journal*, Sept. 21 and 22, 1862.

62. *Elmira Advertiser*, Oct. 18, 1862; full text of Patrick's final order to his brigade found in Gates, *The Ulster Guard*, 338.

63. Camp Barnett was named for Capt. James R. Barnett of the 35th, killed in the battle.

64. Clark, letter, Sept. 28, 1862, Mudge Collection. The soldier who received his Red Badge of Courage must be either L. C. Ball, E. Campbell, or J. Stebbins (wounded at Antietam) or R. O'Donnell, H. Peek, or J. Walton (wounded at Second Manassas).

65. Charles S. Wainwright, *A Diary of Battle*, ed. Allan Nevins (New York: Harcourt, Brace, 1962), 119; Noyes, *The Bivouac and the Battle-Field*, 267–68.

66. George Ticknor Curtis, *McClellan's Last Service to the Republic* (New York: D. Appleton, 1886), 120.

67. Ibid., 82; letter of Robert E. Jameson, Nov. 16, 1862, Bruce Catton, Research Notes, 153, Manuscript Division, Library of Congress; Alfred Bellard,

Gone for a Soldier: The Civil War Memoirs of Private Alfred Bellard, ed. David Herbert Donald (Boston: Little, Brown, 1975), 170.

9. WHITE DEATH ON A FROZEN HILLSIDE

1. Burnside testified before Congress on Dec. 19, 1862, that he had "over and over again" told Lincoln and Secretary of War Stanton that he "was not competent to command such a large army as this." *CCW,* part 1 (1863), 650.

2. McClellan, in a letter dated Nov. 7, reported, "Poor Burn feels dreadfully, almost crazy—I am sorry for him." Sears, *The Civil War Papers of George B. McClellan,* 520. Description of events in Warrenton during this period in the *New York Times,* Nov. 12, 13, and 14, 1862; Oliver O. Howard, *Autobiography of Oliver Otis Howard* (New York: Baker and Taylor, 1907), 1:314.

3. *New York Times,* Nov. 14, 1862; "Still on the Advance," *Philadelphia Inquirer,* Nov. 14, 1862.

4. *OR,* vol. 19, part 2, 553, 579.

5. Maj. Gen. Lafayette McLaw's Division of Longstreet's First Corps arrived at Fredericksburg on Nov. 20. *OR,* vol. 21, 584.

6. Fred Burritt of the 23d described the "village" of Fayettesville as consisting of "one very old house, formerly used as a store and post office . . . [and now] occupied by Brig. Gen. Doubleday." *Elmira Advertiser,* Nov. 22, 1862.

7. Hoffman, letter, Nov. 27, 1862, Buchanan Collection; Burritt, letters, *Elmira Advertiser* of Nov. 22 and Dec. 6, 1862; *Names and Records of All the Members Who Served in the First N.H. Battery of Light Artillery* (Manchester, N.H.: Budget Job, 1891), 23.

8. Patrick, *Journal,* Nov. 22, 1862; full text of the demands against the town found in *OR,* vol. 21, 783.

9. Gabriel René Paul (1813–86), a professional soldier who had grown up in St. Louis, Missouri, had little to do with New York or New York troops until his appointment to the command of the brigade. He would spend only a brief time with the brigade (Oct. 14, 1862–Mar. 4, 1863) and had little influence over it.

10. Burritt, letters, *Elmira Weekly Advertiser and Chemung County Republican,* Dec. 6 and 13, 1862.

11. Crandall, letter, Nov. 28, 1862. Crandall adds, "Pope never was a favorite because he risked the reputation of the army upon a campaign planned for his own aggrandizement at the dictation of Northern sentiment."

12. Baldwin, letter, Oct. 11, 1862, Chemung County Historical Society; Burritt, letter, *Elmira Weekly Advertiser and Chemung County Republican,* Dec. 13, 1862. A study of the chaplains in King's Division in the summer of 1862 concluded that "but two in the whole number are worthy of the title and pay of the position." After describing the chaplains' failings, the writer pleaded, "Let means be adopted at the earliest possible date to rid our Army of these pests"; *Christian Banner* 1,

no. 17 (Aug. 13, 1862). Burritt's comments could have been directed toward Chaplain James DeBois of the 23d, who replaced the popular Ezra F. Crane after Crane resigned in Jan. 1862. Before the war DeBois deserted his wife to travel to the California gold fields to seek his fortune; see DeBois Civil War pension application file, National Archives, Washington, D.C.

13. Baldwin, letter, Nov. 12, 1862; Hoffman, letter, Nov. 27, 1862, Buchanan Collection; Burritt, letter, *Elmira Weekly Advertiser and Chemung County Republican*, Dec. 6, 1862.

14. Burt, *My Memoirs*, 93–95; *Annual Report of the Adjutant General of the State of New York, for the Year 1862*, 10.

15. *Annual Report*, 11; Harris H. Beecher, *Record of the 114th Regiment, NYSV* (Norwich, N.Y.: J. F. Hubbard Jr., 1866), 17–22.

16. Beecher, *Record of the 114th*, 17–22; Applegate, *Reminiscences and Letters of George Arrowsmith*, 166–69; for a list of Cortland recruiters see recruiting advertisement, *Cortland Gazette and Banner*, Aug. 28, 1862.

17. Burt, *My Memoirs*, 120–23; Shannon, *The Organization and Administration of the Union Army*, vol. 1, 280; "Regulations for the Enrollment and Draft of the Militia," *New York Herald*, Aug. 15, 1862; "Concerning Drafting, Again," *New York Times*, Aug. 6, 1862.

18. Burt, 123; *OR*, series 3, vol. 2, 370. The state enrollment was intended to facilitate a possible state draft to fill the 128 newly designated National Guard units or to create a ready reserve to meet any public emergency or new military call-up. See *Annual Report of the Adjutant General of the State of New York, for 1862*, 30–31, and Burt, 80–81, 91–92, 119. The new National Guard regiments would conform geographically to the state assembly districts.

19. "Concerning Drafting, Again," *New York Times*, Aug. 6, 1862; for township quotas see "Apportionment of the Draft," *Cortland Gazette and Banner*, Sept. 18, 1862; the four hundred figure from *Gazette and Banner*, Aug. 28, 1862; Burt, 124; *Annual Report of the Adjutant General of the State of New York, for 1862*, 40.

20. *Cortland Gazette and Banner*, Aug. 14 and 28, 1862.

21. *Annual Report of the Adjutant General of the State of New York* (1862), 35. This source provides the enrollment figures for all New York counties. For a breakdown of enrollment figures in the Cortland townships see p. 1130. About one thousand county residents applied for medical exemptions, and, as indicated, 654 were approved. Dr. George W. Bradford, the examining surgeon for Cortland County, gives a full accounting of medical exemptions in his report, Hiram Crandall Papers, Cortland County Historical Society, Cortland New York. For a full list of the nonmedical categories of exemptions see "Who Are Exempt, and Who Are Not," *New York Times*, Aug. 15, 1862 and Burt, 125.

22. Newspaper article, no date, Blodgett scrapbook, 2:104.

23. "Grounds of Exemption," *Cortland Gazette and Banner*, Aug. 28, 1862.

24. "The Town Meetings," *Cortland Gazette and Banner*, Aug. 28, 1862, indicates that "nearly every town" in the county held a town meeting on raising money for bounties. Cuyler, for example, approved a fifty-dollar bounty.

25. Burt, 126; Ella Lonn, *Desertion during the Civil War* (Gloucester, Mass.: American Historical Association, 1928; repr., Lincoln: Univ. of Nebraska Press, 1998), 138–39.

26. Hoffman, letter, Nov. 27, 1862, Buchanan Collection; Burritt, letter, *Elmira Advertiser*, Nov. 22, 1862. The five men were B. B. Andrews, Stephen Clearwood, Norman Francis, Cornelius Lansing, and Dennis O'Donahue.

27. New York was able to meet its quota after a determination by the War Department in May 1863 that one surplus three-year man enlisting under the first call would be equal to four nine-months men in meeting the second call. *Adjutant General of the State of New York for 1863*, 12–14; "Our Quota Full," *Cortland Gazette and Banner*, Oct. 2, 1862.

28. Catton, *America Goes to War*, 69.

29. Saxton, *A Regiment Remembered*, 13. In Mar. 1863 a man in the 76th New York explained to his parents his need to serve: "Should I remain at home at times like the present and find *security* only in the blood of others, I would be a coward indeed"; Thomas Martin, letter, Mar. 14, 1863, Blodgett scrapbook, 6:98.

30. Allan Nevins, *The War for the Union*, 4 vols. (New York: Scribner's, 1959–71), 2:302–5; "The State Election," *New York Times*, Nov. 21, 1862; the straw poll results are given in Burritt, letter, *Elmira Advertiser*, Nov. 22, 1862. The regiment as a whole gave 356 votes for Wadsworth and 25 for Seymour. No doubt fond memories of their beloved former leader had something to do with the lopsidedness of the vote. The *Hornellsville Weekly Tribune* of Nov. 13, 1862, reported, "Of 349 enlisted men present, but 24 expressed themselves for Seymour. Among 29 line officers, but 8 endorse the Democratic candidate, while among the field and staff officers, all but a single vote are for James S. Wadsworth." In the 1864 presidential election, out of 6,043 county votes cast, 3,980 were in support of Lincoln; "Our County," *Cortland County Republican*, Dec. 8, 1864.

31. Burritt, letter, *Elmira Advertiser*, Dec. 6, 1862; Dexter, letter, Dec. 3, 1862.

32. Dexter, letter, Dec. 3, 1862; Smithe, *Glimpses*, 29.

33. Patrick, *Journal*, Nov. 27, 1862; Maxson, *Camp Fires*, 113; Mills, *Chronicles*, 321; "From the Twenty-third," *Steuben Courier*, Dec. 10, 1862.

34. *Elmira Weekly Advertiser and Republican*, Dec. 6, 1862.

35. *OR*, vol. 21, 798; "Our War Correspondence," *Cazanovia Republican*, Dec. 17, 1862; *CCW*, part 1 (1863), 687. Some of the men took to playfully knocking boxes of rations from the slow-moving trains, using long poles. Authorities soon put a stop to it by posting guards along the tracks. See Arthur A. Kent, ed., *Three Years with Company K* (London: Associated Univ. Presses, 1976), 141.

36. Howard, *Autobiography*, 1:321; Patrick, *Journal*, Dec. 10, 1862.

37. *OR*, vol. 21, 63; *CCW*, part 1, 656.

38. James Longstreet, "The Battle of Fredericksburg," in *Battles and Leaders*, 3:79.

39. Lt. Col. G. F. R. Henderson, *The Campaign of Fredericksburg, Nov.–Dec., 1862*, 3d ed. (London: Gale and Polden, 1891), 44.

40. Maxson, *Camp Fires*, 114; Lafayette McLaws, "The Confederate Left at Fredericksburg," in *Battles and Leaders*, 3:86.

41. Patrick, *Journal,* Dec. 11, 1862.

42. *OR,* vol. 21, 168; Gilbert Thompson, *The Engineer Battalion in the Civil War* (Washington, D.C.: Press of the Engineer School, 1910), 26.

43. Mills, *Chronicles,* 325; William Farrar Smith, "Franklin's 'Left Grand Division,'" in *Battles and Leaders,* 3:131; Report of Charles Devens Jr., *OR,* vol. 21, 536.

44. Hoffman's report of the battle and letter dated Dec. 31, 1862, found in Maxson, *Camp Fires,* 117–25. Three brigades of Doubleday's division crossed on the upper of Franklin's two bridges. The Iron Brigade and the division artillery used the lower bridge; Doubleday, *Journal,* Dec. 12, 1862; Wainwright, *A Diary of Battle,* 138.

45. Crandall, letter, Jan. 3, 1863, Albert Crandall Papers, Cornell University, Ithaca, New York.

46. Patrick, *Journal,* Dec. 14, 1862.

47. Smithfield stands today as headquarters of the Fredericksburg Country Club. Bernard remained at his home, "Mannsfield," when it was taken over by Union officers before the battle. His outspoken objections to the Yankee presence led to his forced removal across the Rappahannock. His house burned in Apr. 1863 as a result of the carelessness of Confederate soldiers and was never rebuilt; see Harrison, *Fredericksburg Civil War Sites,* 2:76–80; Maxson, *Camp Fires,* 118. Gavin's brigade remained behind as bridge guard and did not join the division until sometime the next morning; the figure of two hundred muskets comes from Baldwin, letter, Dec. 17, 1862. Colonel Hoffman claimed in his report that the 23d crossed the river with 276 enlisted men, with Company C detached.

48. Crandall, letter, Jan. 3, 1863, Albert Crandall Papers, Cornell University; Hoffman, letter, published in Maxson, *Camp Fires,* 123–24.

49. *OR,* vol. 21, 71. For a full discussion of this important order and its implications, see William Marvel, *Burnside* (Chapel Hill: Univ. of North Carolina Press, 1991), 180–84.

50. General Meade's detailed description of his movements in *CCW,* part 1(1863), 691, 695.

51. Doubleday's Report, *OR,* vol. 21, 461. Quote on 465.

52. Henderson, *The Campaign of Fredericksburg,* 67.

53. Doubleday, Report, 462.

54. Pelham sent out a second gun to assist the first, but it was quickly disabled by enemy fire and was withdrawn.

55. *OR,* vol. 21, 462.

56. "Our War Correspondence," *Cazenovia Republican,* Jan. 7, 1863; Baldwin, letter, Dec. 17, 1862; Crandall, letter, Jan. 3, 1863; Burritt, letter, under the heading "Col. Hoffman is bomb proof," *Elmira Weekly Advertiser and Chemung County Republican,* Dec. 27, 1862.

57. Haupt, *Reminiscences,* 177; Col. William W. Teall, " . . . Ringside Seat at Fredericksburg," *Civil War Times Illustrated* 4, no. 2 (May 1965): 27; Marvel, *Burnside,* 205.

58. *OR,* vol. 21, 94.

59. Maxson, *Camp Fires*, 116.

60. Doubleday, *Journal*, Dec. 13, 1862.

61. Clock reference from "Our Special Army Correspondence," *New York Times*, Dec. 15, 1862.

62. Freeman, *R. E. Lee*, 2:462.

63. William H. Runge, ed., *Four Years in the Confederate Artillery: The Diary of Private Henry Robinson Berkeley* (Chapel Hill: Univ. of North Carolina Press for the Virginia Historical Society, 1961), 39; Maxson, *Camp Fires*, 122; Mason Whiting Tyler, *Recollections of the Civil War* (New York: Putnam's, 1912), 66.

64. Vail, *Reminiscences*, 100; Maxson, *Camp Fires*, 119; Burritt, letter, *Elmira Weekly Advertiser and Chemung County Republican*, Dec. 27, 1862.

65. *OR*, vol. 21, 138–40. Burritt identifies the dead and their wounds in his letter dated Dec. 18 to the *Elmira Weekly Advertiser and Chemung Republican*, appearing in the issue of Dec. 27, 1862. There were no casualties in Company H. Burritt also mentions a man in Company E being captured and paroled; quote from Bennitt, letter, Steuben *Farmers' Advocate*, Jan. 7, 1863.

66. This is not to imply that Northern soldiers did not over time harden in their attitude toward Southerners. Sgt. Maj. Thomas Martin of the 76th New York, for example, wrote to his parents in Mar. 1863: "I am daily growing more rabid as I think of the rebellion and the noble slain. I have long since forgotten to call the rebel states wayward sisters." His watchword then became "Traitors, die"; Blodgett scrapbook, 6:98.

67. Baldwin, letter, Dec. 17, 1862, Chemung County Historical Society.

68. Oliver Christian Bosbyshell, *The 48th in the War: Being a Narrative of the Campaigns of the 48th Regiment, Infantry, Pennsylvania Veteran Volunteers* (Philadelphia: Avil, 1895), 100.

69. George A. Hussey, *History of the Ninth Regiment NYSM-NGSNY (Eighty-third N.Y. Volunteers)*, ed. William Todd (New York: J. S. Ogilvie, 1889), 233; Dexter, letter, Dec. 25, 1862; Lusk, *War Letters of William Thompson Lusk*, 244–45.

70. Hoffman, letter, found in Maxson, *Camp Fires*, 120–25. Lincoln's "face the arithmetic" statement recorded by his secretary, William O. Stoddard, who had been born and raised in Homer, New York. Full Stoddard reference: "No general yet found can face the arithmetic, but the end of the war will be at hand when he shall be discovered." William O. Stoddard, *Inside the White House in War Times*, ed. Michael Burlingame (Lincoln: Univ. of Nebraska Press, 2000), 101.

71. William Swinton, *Campaigns of the Army of the Potomac* (New York: Scribner's, 1882), 262.

72. Letter of Maxson dated Dec. 21, 1862, in Maxson, *Camp Fires*, 114–17.

10. HOME

1. Hayt, *Journal*, Dec. 20, 1862.

2. Ibid., Jan. 3 and 8, 1863. In his journal Hayt termed the early rumor of their transfer "Good news"; Gates, *Diaries*, 58. Consolidated Morning Report,

muster rolls, 23d New York, record group 94, National Archives, Washington, D.C.; Patrick stated, concerning his request for the brigade, "It was absolutely indispensable that I should have troops around me on whom I could rely"; Gates, *The Ulster Guard,* 194.

3. Hayt, *Journal,* Jan. 10, 1863. The point of land mentioned is more accurately named Waugh's Point.

4. Muster roll, Jan. 1, 1863; letter of A. P. Smith, *Homer Republican,* Mar. 12, 1863; Dexter, letter, Dec. 25, 1862; Baldwin, letter, Dec. 27, 1862.

5. *Corning Journal,* Mar. 26, 1863.

6. Dexter, letter, Feb. 15, 1863; Hayt, *Journal,* Jan. 23 and Feb. 7, 1863.

7. Smithe, *Glimpses,* 37–38.

8. Maxson, *Camp Fires,* 127.

9. Ibid., vii; Clark, letter, Dec. 28, 1862, Mudge Collection.

10. Hoffman, letter, Jan. 18, 1863, Buchanan Collection. For the particulars of Special Order [S.O.] No. 18 see "From the Army of the Potomac," *New York Times,* Mar. 6, 1863.

11. Patrick, *Journal,* Mar. 7, 1863; Hoffman, letter, May 8, 1863; Dexter, letters, Oct. 12 and Nov. 7, 1862. Dexter mentions that Company K men had an intense dislike for their captain and that some would "frequently taunt him with being a coward to his face"; Hayt, *Journal,* Feb. 7, 1863. Hayt writes that he had been "many times mortified" by the colonel's appearance.

12. Lord, *Civil War Sutlers and Their Wares,* 74.

13. Hayt, *Journal,* Jan. 14 and 22, 1863; particulars on the schooner *Telegraph* from record group 393, preliminary inventory, vol. 1, entry 4075. Judd's products included: ten thousand "segars," two thousand pounds of cheese, ten cases of tomato catsup, five cases of canned peaches, ten boxes of oranges, twenty-five pounds of licorice, gumdrops, a hundred pounds of sausage, and stocks of tinplates and cups, combs, gloves, boots, tooth brushes, military hats, writing materials, pocket diaries, soap, candle sticks, and briar and clay smoking pipes.

14. Hayt, *Journal,* Dec. 25, 1862, and Jan. 14 and Feb. 7, 1863; Dexter, letter, Feb. 15, 1863; Smithe, *Glimpses,* 38.

15. Lord, *Civil War Sutlers and Their Wares,* 46.

16. Letter from privates found in regimental records, 23d New York, National Archives, Washington, D.C.

17. Hayt, *Journal,* Feb. 11 and 12, 1863; compiled service records for Clark in National Archives, Washington, D.C.

18. Horatio Ballard letter of Mar. 2, 1863, to Gen. John T. Sprague; Samuel G. Hathaway Jr., letter of Feb. 25, 1863, to Governor Horatio Seymour, and Hoffman's letter of Feb. 25, 1863, to General Sprague; all in series 0462, Correspondence and Petitions, 1821–1896, box 60, folder 3, New York Archives and Records Administration, Albany, New York.

19. S. O. No. 36 found in record group 393, preliminary inventory, vol. 2, control no. 57, entry 1357, National Archives, Washington, D.C. For instructions to Hooker on muster out of New York regiments see record group 393, book records, vol. 2, control no. 57, under date Apr. 24, 1863. Maxson, *Camp Fires,*

128. Edgcomb mentions sailing on the ship *Osceola* in his letter of May 4, 1862, author's collection.

20. Mary Alice Wills, *The Confederate Blockade of Washington, D.C., 1861–1862* (Parsons, W.Va.: McClain, 1975), 5–6.

21. The camp of the 21st was located about one mile from the landing. Mills, *Chronicles*, 338, record group 393, preliminary inventory, vol. 2, entry 1357. A description of the "Eating Saloon," where one could get a meal for from one to two dollars, in *Corning Journal*, Mar. 26, 1863.

22. *Corning Journal*, Mar. 26, 1863. Redoubt Number Two remains today in a good state of preservation.

23. Edgcomb, letter, May 4, 1863; Maxson, *Camp Fires*, 129.

24. Patrick, *Journal*, May 7, 1863; Maxson, *Camp Fires*, 129; "Honors to a New York Officer," *Elmira Weekly Gazette*, May 12, 1863. Patrick went on to become provost marshal general of all the armies operating against Richmond. He served as commander of the District of Henrico (Richmond) until relieved on the suggestion of U. S. Grant, who feared that Patrick's "kindness of heart [toward civilians] may interfere with the proper government of the city." Patrick resigned June 12, 1865, and returned to Geneva and then Manlius, New York, where he pursued his interest in agriculture. After the death of his wife, he became governor of the Soldier's Home of Dayton, Ohio. He died on July 27, 1888; *OR*, vol. 46, part 3, 1244.

25. Maxson, *Camp Fires*, 130; "Reception of the Southern Tiers," *Elmira Weekly Gazette*, May 19, 1863.

26. Maxson, *Camp Fires*, 131. James C. Carmichael writes in a biographical sketch of Clark that he had climbed to the roof of the car to inform his men of the expected reception at Elmira; Blodgett scrapbook, 4:28. Edgcomb, who was on the train at the time, indicated that Clark, like the others, was after fresh air. Edgcomb, account, "The First War Meeting," Blodgett scrapbook, 16:254; "Arrival of the Southern Tiers," *Elmira Advertiser*, May 14, 1863; "Funeral of the Late Captain Clark," Blodgett scrapbook, 2:150.

27. Maxson, *Camp Fires*, 131; "Arrival," *Elmira Advertiser*, May 14, 1863. The Delavan House stood on the corner at Railroad Avenue and Clinton Street.

28. Maxson, *Camp Fires*, 132; "Arrival," *Elmira Advertiser*, May 14, 1863.

29. "Arrival," *Elmira Advertiser*, May 14, 1863; "Reception of the Southern Tiers," *Elmira Weekly Gazette*, May 19, 1863.

30. "Death of Captain Clark," *Elmira Weekly Gazette*, May 9, 1863; *Hornellsville Weekly Tribune*, May 21, 1863. Both the Hornellsville paper and the *Elmira Advertiser* of May 14, 1863, indicate that Clark had a fiancée. "Local Matters," *Rochester Union and Advertiser*, May 14, 1863, had it that she stood in the crowd as the train arrived and, realizing what had happened, "was overwhelmed with grief and was borne away by sorrowing friends." The author has found no evidence of a fiancée in Clark's correspondence to his friend Powers Mudge.

31. Blodgett, scrapbook, 2:150. Benjamin B. Andrews served as secretary of the funeral committee. The pallbearers were Hiram Crandall, F. D. Wright, J. S. Barber, Arthur Holmes, George B. Jones, and S. R. Hunter.

32. Blodgett, scrapbook, 2:150; Edgcomb, "The First War Meeting," Blodgett scrapbook, 16:253. The event marked probably the only time in the history of Cortland County that the citizens saw an active unit of United States troops marching on their streets under arms and fully equipped for service.

33. "Funeral of the Late Captain Clark," Blodgett scrapbook, 2:150.

34. Ibid., 151.

35. Blodgett scrapbook, 2:150, also "Mustered Out," 2:153.

36. Marvin A. Kreidberg and Merton G. Henry, *History of Military Mobilization in the United States Army, 1775–1945*, Pamphlet 20–212 (Washington, D.C.: Department of the Army, Nov. 1955), 104–105; Phisterer, *New York in the War of the Rebellion*, 1:43; *OR*, series 3, vol. 5, 895.

37. Those exempted included the physically or mentally unfit, those convicted of a felony, certain government officials, and individuals with specific categories of dependents; prior state or Federal service did not exclude one from the draft. Congress later amended the Draft Act: commutation release from service would apply only to a single draft call; African-American citizens were specifically subject to enrollment and compulsory service; substitutes could be obtained only from those groups not normally subject to the draft (those aged eighteen or nineteen, for example); and exemption from the draft for a substitute would only last as long as the substitute remained in service. On July 4, 1864, the commutation provisions of the act were eliminated altogether except in the case of conscientious objectors. The cost of a substitute went up accordingly. A woman wrote from McGrawville on Mar. 28, 1864, that the local going rate for a substitute was a thousand dollars. Kreidberg and Henry, *Military Mobilization*, 105–107, 112; Shannon, *The Organization and Administration of the Union Army*, 2:33, 182; Matteson, *Justus*, 46.

38. Kreidberg and Henry, *Military Mobilization*, 106.

39. Dwight H. Bruce, *Onondaga's Centennial* (n.p.: Boston History, 1896), 1:249. Greenfield Gaylord from Camillus, Onondaga County, was the first name drawn from the 23d District.

40. "List of Drafted Men," *Syracuse Standard*, Aug. 22, 1863. The 2,510 figure includes only Class I enrollees (all age twenty to thirty-five, and all unmarried persons between thirty-five and forty-five). See also record group 110, inventory entry 2146, National Archives, Washington, D.C. for the accounting dated Dec. 15, 1863, which shows 2,505 Class I enrolled with a quota of 346; and *OR*, series 3, vol. 3, 718. Authorities intentionally drew twice the needed number of names, to allow for anticipated service exemptions.

41. For the breakdown of the 1863 Federal draft in the 23d District, see *Annual Report of the Adjutant General of the State of New York*, for 1863, 639.

42. Murdock, *Patriotism Limited*, 209.

43. James W. Geary, *We Need Men: The Union Draft in the Civil War* (DeKalb: Northern Illinois Univ. Press, 1991), 78.

44. Notice, "Volunteer in the New Regiment," *Cortland Gazette and Banner*, Aug. 25, 1864. Men could enlist in the regiment for one, two, or three years.

45. Cost of bounty program from Smith, *History of Cortland County*, 119.

46. Mrs. Henry S. Randall, letters, June 5, 1863, and July 13, 1863, box 676, USSC Records, Manuscript and Archives Division, NYPL.

47. Matteson, *Justus*, 45, 46, 60, 68.

48. Postwar letter of Helena J. Bryant to the Cortland Grand Army of the Republic Grover Post 98 [hereafter GAR]. Post 98 record book, Cortland County Historical Society, Cortland, New York, 317.

49. Civil War service record and pension application file, James C. Tuttle, National Archives, Washington, D.C. See also notation in the Freetown section of the 1865 state census book, Cortland County Clerk's office, County Courthouse, Cortland, New York.

50. Matteson, *Justus*, 86.

51. *Cortland County Republican,* Apr. 13, 1865. Original single issue, Cortland County Historical Society.

52. "The Jubilee," undated newspaper account, Blodgett, scrapbook, 2:221.

53. Ibid.

54. Matteson, *Justus*, 89, 93; Maria W. Bishop, "Early Days and Ways," *Cortland County Chronicles*, 1:86; Samuel Babcock, letter to "My Dear Daught," collection of Babcock family papers in possession of Michael Babcock, Lynchburg, Virginia.

55. Crandall, letter, Mar. 30, 1863.

56. Thomas Martin, letter, Mar. 14, 1863, Blodgett scrapbook, 6:98.

57. Information on individuals from Civil War service records and pension application forms in the National Archives in Washington, D.C. Lane account from his obituary, GAR Post 98 record book, Cortland County Historical Society, 369.

58. Rockwell, *Third Annual Re-Union,* 15–16.

59. Cortland County census book for 1865, Cortland County Court House.

60. Ibid.

61. Anne Gertrude Sneller, *A Vanished World* (Syracuse, N.Y.: Syracuse Univ. Press, 1994), 29.

62. "Company H marched 65 Years Ago," newspaper article, May 28, 1926, Stillwell Papers, 316, Cortland County Historical Society; "Decoration Day," (1869), Blodgett scrapbook, 2:305.

63. Although the flag has disappeared, the white silk banner that was attached to the staff is preserved by the Cortland County Historical Society, Cortland, New York.

64. "The Veterans' Parade," newspaper account, Aug. 6, 1908, found in files of Cortland County Historical Society.

65. See obituaries for Edgcomb and Lane in GAR Post 98 record book, Cortland County Historical Society.

Bibliography

ARCHIVES

Alsop, Lizzie Maxwell. Journal. Wynne Family Papers. Virginia Historical Society, Richmond, Va.

Babcock Family Papers, Minnesota Historical Society, St. Paul, Minn.

Baldwin, Hugh J. Letters. Chemung County Historical Society, Elmira, N.Y.

Bryson, John. "History of the 30th New York State Volunteers." New York State Archives, Albany, N.Y.

Carman, Ezra Ayers. "The Maryland Campaign of September 1862." Carman Papers. Library of Congress, Washington, D.C.

Catton, Bruce. (E. B. Long) Research Notes for Bruce Catton's Centennial History of the Civil War, made available by Doubleday and Company. Library of Congress, Washington, D.C.

Clark, Martin C. Letters. Collection of Robert C. Mudge, Groton, N.Y.

Cortland County Anti-Slavery Records, 1837–1841. Cortland County Historical Society, Cortland, N.Y.

Crandall, Albert Rogers. Papers. Division of Rare and Manuscript Collection, Cornell University Library, Ithaca, N.Y.

Crandall, Hiram. Papers. Cortland County Historical Society, Cortland, N.Y.

Dexter, Seymour. Journal and letters. Chemung County Historical Society, Elmira, N.Y.

Doubleday, Abner. Journal. U.S. Army General's Reports of Civil War Service, 1864–1888. Record Group 94, microfilm 1098, National Archives, Washington, D.C.

Edgcomb, Francesca Eudell. "Francesca, or Some Memories of the Past Fifty Years." Typescript of paper read by Francesca Edgcomb Jan. 24, 1900. Cortland County Historical Society.

Edgcomb, George W. Letters and Papers. Author's Collection.

Edgcomb, George. "The First War Meeting," unpublished manuscript found in files of Cortland County Historical Society, Cortland, N.Y.

Gilpin, Samuel J. B. V. Diary, Aug. 1861–Oct. 1864. 5 vols. Library of Congress, Washington, D.C.

Grand Army of the Republic. Post 98 record book. Cortland County Historical Society, Cortland, N.Y.

Gregg, William M. Letters. New York State Library, Albany, N.Y.

Hamer, David L. "One Man's War." Typescript. Manassas National Battlefield Park Library, Manassas, Va.

Hanks, Conrad C. Conrad C. Hanks Papers. Duke University, Durham, N.C.

Hayt, William W. *All Over the Sacred Soil: The Journal of Adjutant William Wisner Hayt*. Typescript journal compiled by David W. Hayt, Los Angeles, Calif.

Hoffman, Henry C. Letters (typescripts) in the collection of Richard S. Buchanan, Elmira, N.Y.

Jones, William Burns. "This Picturesque Spot: Fauquier White Sulphur Springs." Master's thesis, George Mason University, spring 1993.

Patrick, Marsena R. Journal. Library of Congress, Washington, D.C.

Porter, Fitz John. Fitz John Porter Papers. Library of Congress, Washington, D.C.

Proctor, W. H. Reminiscences. Typescript. Manassas National Battlefield Park Library, Manassas, Va.

Randall, Mrs. Henry S. Letters. United States Sanitary Commission Records, Manuscripts and Archives Division, New York Public Library, Astor, Lenox and Tilden Foundations, New York, N.Y.

Rodgers Family Papers. Library of Congress, Washington, D.C.

Scott, Henry Clay. Diary, 1861–1863. Manuscripts and Archives Division, New York Public Library, Astor, Lenox and Tilden Foundations, New York, N.Y.

Tidball, John C. Journal. West Point Archives, West Point, N.Y.

Underwood, Polly. Letters. Underwood Family Records. Cortland County Historical Society, Cortland, N.Y.

U.S. Army Continental Commands 1821–1920, record group 393, "Successions of Commands." National Archives, Washington, D.C.

Washington, John. "Memorys of the Past." Undated memoir. Library of Congress, Washington, D.C.

Willard, Joseph C. Diary. Willard Family Papers. Library of Congress, Washington, D.C.

Wynne, Elizabeth Maxwell (Alsop). Diary. Virginia Historical Society, Richmond, Va.

PUBLISHED SOURCES

Books and Articles

Allan, William. *The Army of Northern Virginia in 1862.* Intro. John C. Ropes. Boston: Houghton Mifflin, 1892.

Annual Report of the Adjutant General of the State of New York [for 1861]. Albany: C. Van Benthuysen, 1862 (also published as Assembly Document 25, 1862).

Annual Report of the Adjutant General of the State of New York [for 1862]. Albany: Comstock and Cassidy, 1863 (also published as Assembly Document 49, 1863).

Annual Report of the Adjutant General of the State of New York [for 1863]. 2 vols. Albany: Comstock and Cassidy, 1864 (also published as Assembly Document 80, 1864).

Applegate, John S. *Reminiscences and Letters of George Arrowsmith of New Jersey.* Red Bank, N.J.: John H. Cook, 1893.

Averell, William Woods. *Ten Years in the Saddle: The Memoir of William Woods Averell.* Ed. Edward K. Eckert and Nicholas J. Amato. San Rafael, Calif.: Presidio, 1978.

Babcock, Willoughby, Jr. *Selections from the Letters and Diaries of Brevet Brigadier General Willoughby Babcock of the Seventy-fifth New York Volunteers.* War of the Rebellion Series, Bulletin 2. N.p.: University of the State of New York, 1922.

Ballard, Horatio. "Reminiscences." *Cortland County Chronicles* 2 (1984): 166–72.

Banes, Charles H. *History of the Philadelphia Brigade.* Philadelphia: J. B. Lippincott, 1876.

Barron, Earle P. *Ewell's March Home: The Civil War and Early Times in and around Greenwich, Virginia.* Kearney, Neb.: Morris, 1999.

Basler, Roy P., ed. *The Collected Works of Abraham Lincoln.* 9 vols. New Brunswick, N.J.: Rutgers Univ. Press, 1953.

Beale, Jane Howison. *The Journal of Jane Howison Beale of Fredericksburg, Virginia, 1850–1862.* Fredericksburg: Historic Fredericksburg Foundation, 1981.

Beecher, Dr. Harris H. *Record of the 114th Regiment, NYSV* Norwich, N.Y.: J. F. Hubbard Jr., 1866.

Bellard, Alfred. *Gone for a soldier: The Civil War Memoirs of Private Alfred Bellard.* Ed. David Herbert Donald. Boston: Little, Brown, 1975.

Biddle, William Foster. "Recollections of McClellan." United Service, n.s., 11 (May 1894): 460–69.

Billings, John D. *Hardtack and Coffee.* Boston: George M. Smith, 1887.

———. *The History of the Tenth Massachusetts Battery.* Boston: Hall and Whiting, 1881.

Bishop, Maria W. "Early Days and Ways." *Cortland County Chronicles* 1 (1970): 83–102.

Blackford, William W. *War Years with Jeb Stuart.* New York: Scribner's, 1945.

Blodgett, Bertha Eveleth. *Stories of Cortland County.* 2d. ed. Ed. Eleanor Dickinson. Cortland, N.Y.: Cortland County Historical Society, 1975.

Blunt, Elizabeth L. *When Folks Was Folks.* New York: Cochrane, 1910.

Bosbyshell, Oliver Christian. *The 28th in the War: Being a Narrative of the Campaign of the 48th Regiment, Infantry, Pennsylvania Veteran Volunteers.* Philadelphia: Avil, 1895.

Bradford, Simeon. "The Anti-Slavery Society of Cortland County." *Cortland County Chronicles* 2, second printing, publication 7 (1984): 240–46.

Bruce, Dwight H. *Onondaga's Centennial.* N.p.: Boston History, 1896.

Buell, Augustus. *The Cannoneer.* Washington, D.C.: National Tribune, 1890.

Burt, Silas W. *My Memoirs of the Military History of the State of New York during the War for the Union, 1861–65.* War of the Rebellion Series. Bulletin 1. Albany, N.Y.: The Argus Company, 1903.

Byrne, Thomas E. "Elmira, 1861–1865: Civil War Rendezvous." In *A Civil War Anthology,* publication of the Chemung County Historical Society (Aug. 1985, repr. 1993), 1247–52.

Catton, Bruce. *America Goes to War.* Middletown, Conn.: Wesleyan University Press, 1958.

Chandler, S. E. "In the Thick of It." *National Tribune,* Oct. 17, 1895, and Oct. 24, 1895.

Cheek, Philip, and Mair Pointon. *History of the Sauk County Riflemen.* Madison, Wis.: Democrat, 1909.

Clough, Daniel O. "The First to Enter Fredericksburg." *National Tribune,* Dec. 21, 1905.

Colby, Newton T. *The Civil War Papers of Lt. Colonel Newton T. Colby, New York Infantry.* Ed. William E. Hughes. Jefferson, N.C.: McFarland, 2003.

Cook, Benjamin F. *History of the Twelfth Massachusetts Volunteers.* Boston: Twelfth Regiment Association, 1882.

Cook, Seymour. "Early Days in Homer." *Cortland County Chronicles* 2 (1984): 183–203.

Cooling, Benjamin Franklin, III, and Walton H. Owen II. *Mr. Lincoln's Forts.* Shippensburg, Pa.: White Mane, 1988.

Cox, Jacob D. *Military Reminiscences of the Civil War.* 2 vols. New York: Scribner's, 1900.

Cozzens, Peter. *General John Pope: A Life for the Nation.* Urbana: Univ. of Illinois Press, 2000.

Cross, Whitney R. *The Burned-Over District: The Social and Intellectual History of Enthusiastic Religion in Western New York.* Ithaca, N.Y.: Cornell Univ. Press, 1950.

Cuffel, Charles A. *History of Durell's Battery in the Civil War.* Philadelphia: Craig Finley, 1903.

Curtis, George Ticknor. *McClellan's Last Service to the Republic.* New York: D. Appleton, 1886.

Davis, Charles E., Jr. *Three Years in the Army: The Story of the Thirteenth Massachusetts Volunteers.* Boston: Estes and Lauriat, 1894.

Dawes, Rufus R. *Service with the Sixth Wisconsin Volunteers.* Ed. and intro. Alan T. Nolan. Ann Arbor, Mich.: Cushing-Malloy, 1962.

Denison, Rev. Frederic. *Sabres and Spurs: The First Regiment Rhode Island Cavalry.* Central Falls, R.I.: E. L. Freeman, 1876.

De Trobriand, Regis. *Four Years with the Army of the Potomac.* Boston: Ticknor, 1889.

Dexter, Seymour. *Seymour Dexter, Union Army, Journal and Letters of Civil War Service in Company K, 23rd New York Volunteer Regiment of Elmira, with Illustrations.* Ed. Carl A. Morrell. Jefferson, N.C.: McFarland, 1996.

Diary of Gideon Welles. Intro. John T. Morse Jr. Boston: Houghton Mifflin, 1911.

Dowdey, Clifford, ed. *The Wartime Papers of R. E. Lee.* New York: Bramhall House, 1961.

Dunn, Craig L. *Iron Men, Iron Will.* Indianapolis, Ind.: Guild, 1995.

Dunn, Seymour B. "The Early Academies of Cortland County." *Cortland County Chronicles* 1 (1970): 57–76.

Eby, Cecil D., Jr., ed. *A Virginia Yankee in the Civil War: The Diaries of David Hunter Strother.* Chapel Hill: Univ. of North Carolina Press, 1961.

Eby, Jerrilynn. *They Called Stafford Home.* Bowie, Md.: Heritage, 1977.

Fairchild, C. B. *History of the 27th Regiment N.Y. Vols.* Binghamton, N.Y.: Carl and Matthews, 1888.

Faller, Leo W., and John I. Faller. *Dear Folks at Home.* Ed. Milton E. Flower. Carlisle, Pa.: Cumberland County Historical Society, 1963.

Field, Phyllis F. *The Politics of Race in New York: The Struggle for Black Suffrage in the Civil War Era.* Ithaca, N.Y.: Cornell Univ. Press, 1982.

Freeman, Douglas S. *R. E. Lee: A Biography.* 4 vols. New York: Scribner's, 1934–35.

French, J. H. *Historical and Statistical Gazetteer of New York State.* Syracuse, N.Y.: R. P. Smith, 1860.

Galpin, W. Freeman. "County History." *Cortland County Chronicles* 1 (1970): 5–11.

Garrison, Webb. *Civil War Hostages: Hostage Taking in the Civil War.* Shippensburg, Pa.: White Mane, 2000.

Gates, Theodore B. *The Civil War Diaries of Col. Theodore B. Gates, 20th New York State Militia.* Ed. Seward R. Osborne. Hightstown, N.J.: Longstreet, 1991.

——. *The Ulster Guard.* New York: Benj. H. Tyrrel, 1879.

Geary, James W. *We Need Men: The Union Draft in the Civil War.* DeKalb: Northern Illinois Univ. Press, 1991.

Geary, John White. *A Politician Goes to War: The Civil War Letters of John White Geary.* Ed. by William Alan Blair. University Park: Pennsylvania State Univ. Press, 1995.

General Regulations for the Military Forces of the State of New York. Albany: Adjutant General's Office, 1858.

Gibbon, John. *Personal Recollections of the Civil War*. New York: Putnam's, 1928.

Gillespie, Samual L. *A History of Company A, First Ohio Cavalry*. Washington Court House, Ohio: Ohio State Register, 1898.

Glazier, Willard. *Three Years in the Federal Cavalry*. New York: R. H. Ferguson, 1871.

Goodwin, H. C. *Pioneer History; or Cortland County and the Border Wars of New York*. New York: A. B. Burdick, 1859.

Gordon, George H. *History of the Campaign of the Army of Virginia, under John Pope, from Cedar Mountain to Alexandria, 1862*. Boston: Houghton, Osgood, 1880.

Gould, John M. *History of the First—Tenth—Twenty-ninth Maine Regiment*. Portland, Maine: Stephen Berry, 1871.

Greene, William B. *Letters from a Sharpshooter*. Trans. William H. Hastings. Belleville, Wis.: Hastings, 1993.

Griffith, Lucille. "Fredericksburg's Political Hostages." *Virginia Magazine of History and Biography* 72, no. 4 (Oct. 1964): 395–429.

Haight, Theron W. "Gainesville, Groveton, and Bull Run." In *War Papers Read before the Commandery of the State of Wisconsin, Military Order of the Loyal Legion of the United States* 2 (Milwaukee, Wis.: 1896): 357–72.

Hall, H. Seymour. "Experience in the Peninsular and Antietam Campaigns." In *War Talks in Kansas: A Series of Papers Read before the Kansas Commandery of the Military Order of the Loyal Legion of the United States* (Kansas City: Press of the Franklin Hudson Publishing Company, 1906): 161–84.

Hanchett, Catherine M. "Agitators for Black Equality and Emancipation: Cortland County, 1837–1885." In Louis M. Vanaria, ed., *Cortland County Chronicles* 4 (1986): 87–99.

Harrison, Noel G. *Fredericksburg Civil War Sites, Apr. 1861–Nov. 1862*. Lynchburg, Va.: H. E. Howard, 1995.

——. *Fredericksburg Civil War Sites, Dec. 1862–Apr. 1865*. Vol. 2. Lynchburg, Va.: H. E. Howard, 1995.

Haupt, Herman. *Reminiscences of General Herman Haupt*. Milwaukee, Wis.: Wright and Joys, 1901.

Haydon, Charles B. *For Country, Cause and Leader: The Civil War Journal of Charles B. Haydon*. Ed. Stephen W. Sears. New York: Ticknor and Fields, 1993.

Haydon, Stansbury. *Aeronautics in the Union and Confederate Armies*. Baltimore: Johns Hopkins Univ. Press, 1941.

Hays, Alexander. *Life and Letters of Alexander Hays*. Pittsburgh: privately printed, 1919.

Hays, Gilbert Adams. *Under the Red Patch: Story of the Sixty Third Regiment*. Pittsburgh: Regimental Association, 1908.

Heaps, Willard A., and Porter W. Heaps. *The Singing Sixties*. Norman: Univ. of Oklahoma Press, 1960.

Hebert, Walter H. *Fighting Joe Hooker*. Indianapolis: Bobbs-Merrill, 1944.

Hennessy, John J. *Return to Bull Run: The Campaign and Battle of Second Manassas*. New York: Simon and Schuster, 1993.

Henderson, G. F. R. *The Campaign of Fredericksburg, Nov.–Dec., 1862*. London: Gale and Polden, 1891.

Hess, Earl J. *Liberty, Virtue, and Progress: Northerners and Their War for the Union*. 2d ed. New York: Fordham Univ. Press, 1997.

——. *The Union Soldier in Battle: Enduring the Ordeal of Combat*. Lawrence: Univ. Press of Kansas, 1997.

Hobson, Charles F., and Arnold Shankman. "Colonel of the Bucktails: Civil War Letters of Charles Frederick Taylor." *Pennsylvania Magazine of History and Biography* 47, no. 3 (July 1973): 333–61.

Hogarty, W. P. "A Medal of Honor." In *War Talks in Kansas: A Series of Papers Read before the Kansas Commandery of the Military Order of the Loyal Legion of the United States* (Kansas City: Press of the Franklin Hudson Publishing Company, 1906): 352–60.

Howard, Oliver O. *Autobiography of Oliver Otis Howard, Major General*. 2 vols. New York: Baker and Taylor, 1907.

Howe, Herbert Barber. *Paris Lived in Homer*. Cortland, N.Y.: Cortland County Historical Society, 1968.

Hunnicutt, James W. *The Conspiracy Unveiled: The South Sacrificed, or the Horrors of Secession*. Philadelphia: J. B. Lippincott, 1863.

Huyette, Miles C. *The Maryland Campaign and the Battle of Antietam*. Buffalo, N.Y.: 1915.

Hussey, George A. *History of the Ninth Regiment NYSM-NGSNY (Eighty-third N.Y. Volunteers)*. Ed. William Todd. New York: J. S. Ogilvie, 1889.

Jennings, Irene A. "Our Railroad (The Syracuse and Binghamton)." *Cortland County Chronicles* 1 (1970): 104–109.

Johnson, Clifton. *Battleground Adventures*. Boston: Houghton Mifflin, 1915.

Johnson, Curtis D. *Islands of Holiness: Rural Religion in Upstate New York, 1790–1860*. Ithaca, N.Y.: Cornell Univ. Press, 1989.

Johnston, Angus James II. *Virginia Railroads in the Civil War*. Chapel Hill: Univ. of North Carolina Press, 1961.

Jordan, Ervin L., Jr. *Black Confederates and Afro-Yankees in Civil War Virginia*. Charlottesville: Univ. Press of Virginia, 1995.

Kent, Arthur A., ed. *Three Years with Company K*. London: Associated Univ. Presses, 1976.

Kimball, George. "With Pope at Bull Run." In *Stories of Our Soldiers: War Reminiscences, Collected from the Series Written Especially for the Boston Journal* 2 (1893): 85–93.

King, Charles. "Gainesville, 1862." In *War Papers, Read before the Commandery of the State of Wisconsin, Military Order of the Loyal Legion of the United States* 3 (Milwaukee: 1896): 258–83.

Kreidberg, Marvin A., and Merton G. Henry. *History of Military Mobilization in the United States Army, 1775–1945.* Pamphlet 20–212. Washington, D.C.: Department of the Army, November 1955.

Krick, Robert E. L. "The Civil War's First Monument." *Blue and Gray Magazine* (Apr. 1991): 32–34.

Krick, Robert K. *9th Virginia Cavalry.* Lynchburg, Va.: H. E. Howard, 1982.

Kurtz, D. Morris. "Cortland (Village): Its Rise and Progress—The Past and Present." *Cortland County Chronicles* 1 (1970): 128–50.

Leech, Margaret. *Reveille in Washington.* New York: Harper, 1941.

Lewis, George. *The History of Battery E, First Regiment Rhode Island Light Artillery.* Providence, R.I.: Snow and Farnham, 1892.

Livermore, Thomas L. *Days and Events 1860–1866.* Boston: Houghton Mifflin, 1920.

Longacre, Edward G. "Fortune's Fool," *Civil War Times Illustrated* 18, no. 2 (May 1979): 20–31.

Longstreet, James. "The Battle of Fredericksburg." In Johnson and Buel, eds., *Battles and Leaders,* 3:70–85.

——. *From Manassas to Appomattox.* Philadelphia: J. B. Lippincott, 1896.

Lonn, Ella. *Desertion during the Civil War.* Gloucester, Mass.: American Historical Association, 1928. Reprint; Lincoln: Univ. of Nebraska Press, 1998.

Lord, Francis A. *They Fought for the Union.* New York: Bonanza, 1960.

——. *Civil War Sutlers and Their Wares.* New York: Thomas Yoseloff, 1969.

Lusk, William Thompson. *War Letters.* New York: privately printed, 1911.

Lyon, James S. *War Sketches: From Cedar Mountain to Bull Run; Consisting of Personal and Historical Incidents of the Campaign under Major General Pope, in the Summer of 1862; by a Staff Officer.* Buffalo: Young, Lockwood, 1882.

Martin, John A. "Reminiscences." In *War Talks in Kansas: A Series of Papers Read before the Kansas Commandery of the Military Order of the Loyal Legion of the United States* (Kansas City: Press of the Franklin Hudson Publishing Company, 1906): 366–70.

Marvel, William. *Burnside.* Chapel Hill: Univ. of North Carolina Press, 1991.

Matteson, Justus Grant. *Justus in the Civil War.* 2d ed. Ed. Ronald G. Matteson. N.p.: privately printed, 1995.

Maury, Betty Herndon. *The Confederate Diary of Betty Herndon Maury.* Ed. Alice Maury Parmelee. Washington: privately printed, 1938.

Maxson, William P. [Pound Sterling]. *Camp Fires of the Twenty-Third: Sketches of the Camp Life, Marches, and Battles of the Twenty-third Regiment, NYV.* New York: Davies and Kent, 1863.

McAllister, Robert. *The Civil War Letters of General Robert McAllister.* Ed. James I. Robertson Jr. New Brunswick, N.J.: Rutgers Univ. Press, 1965.

McClellan, George B. *McClellan's Own Story.* Ed. William C. Prime. New York: Charles L. Webster, 1887.

————. *Report on the Organization and Campaigns of the Army of the Potomac.* New York: Sheldon, 1864.

McLaws, Lafayette. "The Confederate Left at Fredericksburg." In Johnson and Buel, eds., *Battles and Leaders*, 3:86–94.

McPherson, James M. *What They Fought For: 1861–1865.* Baton Rouge: Louisiana State Univ. Press, 1994.

————. *For Cause and Comrades: Why Men Fought in the Civil War.* New York: Oxford Univ. Press, 1997.

————, and William J. Cooper Jr., eds. *Writing the Civil War: The Quest to Understand.* Columbia: Univ. of South Carolina Press, 1998.

Meneely, A. Howard. *The War Department, 1861.* New York: Columbia Univ. Press, 1928.

Meyer, Henry C. *Civil War Experiences.* New York: privately printed, 1911.

Mills, J. Harrison. *Chronicles of the Twenty-first Regiment New York State Volunteers.* Buffalo, N.Y.: Gies, 1887.

Mitchell, Reid. *Civil War Soldiers.* New York: Penguin, 1997.

————. *The Vacant Chair: The Northern Soldier Leaves Home.* New York: Oxford Univ. Press, 1993.

Monroe, J. Albert. *Reminiscences of the War of the Rebellion of 1861–5.* Soldiers' and Sailors' Historical Society of Rhode Island. Second Series, no. 11, 1881.

Morgan, W. H. *Personal Reminiscences of the War of 1861–5.* Lynchburg, Va.: J. P. Bell, 1911.

Murdock, Eugene Converse. *Patriotism Limited, 1862–1865. The Civil War Draft and the Bounty System.* Kent, Ohio: Kent State Univ. Press, 1967.

Mushkat, Jerome. *The Reconstruction of the New York Democracy, 1861–1871.* East Brunswick, N.J.: Associated Univ. Presses, 1981.

Myers, William Starr. *A Study in Personality: General George Brinton McClellan.* New York: D. Appleton-Century, 1934.

Nagle, Theodore M. *Reminiscences of the Civil War.* Erie, Pa.: Dispatch, 1923.

Names and Records of All the Members Who Served in the First N.H. Battery of Light Artillery (Manchester, N.H.: Budget Job, 1891).

Netherton, Nan., et al. *Fairfax County: A History.* N.p.: Fairfax County Board of Supervisors, 1978.

Nevins, Allan. *The War for the Union.* 4 vols. New York: Scribner's, 1959–71.

Noyes, George F. *The Bivouac and the Battle-Field; or, Campaign Sketches in Virginia and Maryland.* New York: Harper, 1863.

Otis, George H. *The Second Wisconsin Infantry.* Ed. and intro. Alan D. Gaff. Dayton, Ohio: Morningside Bookshop, 1984.

Palmer, Richard F. *Rails through Cortland.* Cortland, N.Y.: Cortland County Historical Society, 1991.

Parker, E. K. "Second Bull Run." *National Tribune,* July 14, 1892.

Partridge, George Washington, Jr. *Letters from the Iron Brigade.* Ed. Hugh L. Whitehouse. Indianapolis, Ind.: Guild, 1994.

Patrick, Marsena R. *Inside Lincoln's Army: The Diary of Marsena Rudolph Patrick, Provost Marshal General, Army of the Potomac.* Ed. David S. Sparks. New York: Thomas Yoseloff, 1964.

Pearson, Henry Greenleaf. *James S. Wadsworth of Geneseo.* New York: Scribner's, 1913.

Phisterer, Frederick. *New York in the War of the Rebellion, 1861 to 1865.* 5 vols. Albany, N.Y.: I. B. Lyon, 1912.

Place, Frank. "A Cortland County Boy in Civil War Times." *Cortland County Chronicles* 2 (1984): 250–54.

Poague, William Thomas. *Gunner with Stonewall.* Ed. Monroe F. Cockrell. Jackson, Tenn.: McCowat-Mercer, 1957.

Pope, John. *The Military Memoirs of General John Pope.* Ed. Peter Cozzens and Robert I. Girardi. Chapel Hill: Univ. of North Carolina Press, 1998.

Putnam, James R. "Occupying Fredericksburg." *National Tribune,* Sept. 21, 1905.

———. "Patrick's Brigade: Its Share in the Stormy Scenes on the Right at Antietam." *National Tribune,* Apr. 30, 1908.

Pyne, Henry R. *Ride to War: The History of the First New Jersey Cavalry.* Ed. Earl Schenck Miers. New Brunswick, N.J.: Rutgers University Press, 1961.

Quinn, S. J. *The History of the City of Fredericksburg, Virginia.* Richmond: Hermitage Press, 1908.

Ratner, Lorman. *Powder Keg: Northern Opposition to the Antislavery Movement, 1831–1840.* New York: Basic, 1968.

Raus, Edmund. *Where Duty Called Them. The Story of the Samuel Babcock Family of Homer, New York, in the Civil War.* Daleville, Va.: Schroeder, 2001.

Rawle, William Brooke, et al. *History of the Third Pennsylvania Cavalry, Sixtieth Regiment Pennsylvania Volunteers, in the American Civil War, 1861–1865.* Philadelphia: Franklin, 1905.

Redway, G. W. *Fredericksburg: A Study in War.* London: George Allen and Unwin, 1906.

Reniers, Perceval. *The Springs of Virginia.* Chapel Hill: Univ. of North Carolina Press, 1941.

Rhodes, Elisha Hunt. *All for the Union: A History of the 2nd Rhode Island Volunteer Infantry.* Ed. Robert Hunt Rhodes. Lincoln, R.I.: Andrew Mowbray, 1985.

Risch, Erna. *Quartermaster Support of the Army: A History of the Corps, 1775–1939.* Washington, D.C.: Center of Military History, 1989.

Roebling, Washington Augustus. *Wash Roebling's War.* Ed. Earl Schenck Miers. Newark, Del.: Spiral, 1961.

Rockwell, H. H. *Regimental Association of the 23rd Regiment, N.Y. Vols.: Third Annual Re-Union, Elmira, N.Y., July 4, 1885.* Elmira: Gazette, 1885.

Runge, William H., ed. *Four Years in the Confederate Artillery: The Diary of Private Henry Robinson Berkeley.* Chapel Hill: Univ. of North Carolina Press for the Virginia Historical Society, 1961.

Russell, William Howard. *My Diary North and South*, Ed. Eugene H. Berwanger. New York: Knopf, 1988.

Saxton, William. *A Regiment Remembered: The 157th New York Volunteers.* Cortland, N.Y.: Cortland County Historical Society, 1996.

Sawyer, Franklin. *A Military History of the 8th Regiment Ohio Vol. Inf'y.* Cleveland, Ohio: Fairbanks, 1881.

Schutz, Wallace J., and Walter N. Trenerry. *Abandoned by Lincoln: A Military Biography of General John Pope.* Urbana: Univ. of Illinois Press, 1990.

Sears, Stephen W., ed. *The Civil War Papers of George B. McClellan.* New York: Ticknor and Fields, 1989.

———. *Landscape Turned Red.* New Haven, Conn.: Ticknor and Fields, 1983.

Sernett, Milton C. *North Star Country: Upstate New York and the Crusade for African American Freedom.* Syracuse, N.Y.: Syracuse Univ. Press, 2002.

Shannon, Fred Albert. *The Organization and Administration of the Union Army, 1861–1865.* 2 vols. Cleveland, Ohio: Arthur H. Clark, 1928. Reprint; Gloucester, Mass.: Peter Smith, 1965.

Shaw, Albert. *A Full Report of the First Re-Union and Banquet.* Published in book form as *History of the Thirty-fifth New York Vols.* Watertown, N.Y.: Times, 1888.

Silverstone, Paul H. *Warships of the Civil War Navies.* Annapolis, Md.: Naval Institute, 1989.

Smalley, George W. *Anglo-American Memories.* London: Duckworth, 1911.

Smith, Abram P. *History of the Seventy-sixth Regiment, New York Volunteers.* Syracuse, N.Y.: Truair, Smith, and Miles, 1867.

Smith, H. P. *History of Cortland County.* Syracuse, N.Y.: D. Mason, 1885.

Smith, William Farrar. "Franklin's 'Left Grand Division.'" In Johnson and Buel, eds., *Battles and Leaders,* 3:128–38.

Smithe, Geo. C. *Glimpses: Of Places, and People, and Things.* Ypsilanti, Mich.: Ypsilantian, 1887.

Sneller, Anne Gertrude. *A Vanished World.* Syracuse, N.Y.: Syracuse Univ. Press, 1994.

Snyder, Charles McCool. *Oswego County, New York in the Civil War.* Oswego: Oswego County Historical Society, 1962.

Stackpole, Edward J. *From Cedar Mountain to Antietam, August–September, 1862.* Harrisburg, Pa.: Stackpole, 1959.

Stevens, C. A. *Berdan's United States Sharpshooters in the Army of the Potomac, 1861–1865.* St. Paul, Minn.: Price-McGill, 1892.

Stevenson, Jas. H. *"Boots and Saddles," a History of the First Volunteer Cavalry of the War Known as the New York (Lincoln) Cavalry.* Harrisburg, Pa.: Patriot, 1879.

Stine, James H. *History of the Army of the Potomac.* Philadelphia: J. B. Rodgers, 1892.

Stoddard, William O. *Inside the White House in War Times.* Ed. Michael Burlingame. Lincoln: Univ. of Nebraska Press, 2000.

Stone, Edwin W. *Rhode Island in the Rebellion*. Providence, R.I.: Knowles, Anthony, 1864.

Strother, David Hunter. "Personal Recollections of the War by a Virginian." *Harper's New Monthly Magazine* 35 (Nov. 1867): 704–27.

Sturcke, Roger D. "23rd New York Volunteer Infantry Regiment." *Military Collector and Historian: Journal of the Company of Military Historians* 25, no. 4 (Winter 1973): 198–200.

Sumner, George C. *Battery D, First Rhode Island Light Artillery, in the Civil War, 1861–1865*. Providence, R.I.: Rhode Island, 1897.

——. *Recollections of Service in Battery D., First Rhode Island Light Artillery*. Soldiers' and Sailors' Historical Society of Rhode Island, Personal Narratives, Fourth Series, no. 11. Providence, R.I.: Published by the Society, 1891.

Swinton, William. *History of the Seventh Regiment, National Guard*. New York: Fields, Osgood, 1870.

——. *Campaigns of the Army of the Potomac*. New York: Scribner's, 1882.

Tanner, Robert G. *Stonewall in the Valley*. Garden City, N.Y.: Doubleday, 1976.

Taylor, Eva. *A History of the Park Church*. Rev. ed. N.p.: privately printed, 1946. Reprinted 1981.

Teall, William W. "Ringside Seat at Fredericksburg." *Civil War Times Illustrated* 4, no. 2 (May 1965): 18–34.

Tevis, C. V., and D. R. Marquis, comps. *The History of the Fighting Fourteenth*. New York: Brooklyn Eagle, 1911.

Tharp, Louise Hall. "The Song That Wrote Itself." *American Heritage* 8, no. 1 (Dec. 1956): 11–13, 100–101.

Thompson, David L. "With Burnside at Antietam." In Johnson and Buel, eds., *Battles and Leaders*, 2:660–62.

Thompson, Gilbert. *The Engineer Battalion in the Civil War*. Washington, D.C.: Engineer School, 1910.

Tobie, Edward P. *History of the First Maine Cavalry*. Boston: Emery and Hughes, 1887.

Townsend, George Alfred. *Rustics in Rebellion*. Chapel Hill: Univ. of North Carolina Press, 1950.

Tyler, Mason Whiting. *Recollections of the Civil War*. New York: Putnam's, 1912.

U.S. Congress. *Report of the Joint Committee on the Conduct of the War*. 3 parts. 5 vols. Washington, D.C.: Government Printing Office [GPO], 1863.

——. *Senate Executive Document 37: The Proceedings and Report of the Board of Army Officers in the Case of Fitz John Porter*. 4 parts. Washington, D.C.: GPO, 1879.

U.S. War Department. *The War of the Rebellion: A Compilation of the Official Records of the Union and Confederate Armies*. 128 vols. Washington, D.C.: GPO, 1880–1901.

Utley, Robert M. *Frontiersmen in Blue: The United States Army and the Indian, 1848–1865*. New York: Macmillan, 1967.

Vail, Enos B. *Reminiscences of a Boy in the Civil War.* N.p.: privately printed, 1915.

Viele, Egbert L. *Hand-Book for Active Service.* New York: D. Van Nostrand, 1861.

Wainwright, Charles S. *A Diary of Battle.* Ed. Allan Nevins. New York: Harcourt, Brace, 1962.

Ward, James A. *Railroads and the Character of America, 1820–1887.* Knoxville: Univ. of Tennessee Press, 1986.

Warfield, Edgar. *Manassas to Appomattox.* McLean, Va.: EPM, 1996.

White, Wyman S. *The Civil War Diary of Wyman S. White.* Ed. Russell C. White. Baltimore: Butternut and Blue, 1993.

Whitman, Walt. *Specimen Days.* Boston: David R. Godine, 1971.

Wiley, Bell Irvin, and Hirst D. Milhollen. *They Who Fought Here.* New York: Bonanza, 1969.

Wills, Mary Alice. *The Confederate Blockade of Washington, D.C., 1861–1862.* Parsons, W.Va.: McClain, 1975.

Wilson, James Harrison. *Under the Old Flag.* 2 vols. New York: D. Appleton, 1912.

Woodward, E. M. *History of the Third Pennsylvania Reserve.* Trenton, N.J.: MacCrellish and Quigley, 1883.

———. *Our Campaigns; or the Marches, Bivouacs, Battles, Incidents of Camp Life and History of Our Regiment during Its Three Years Term of Service.* Philadelphia: Collins, 1865.

Wright, James A. *No More Gallant a Deed.* Ed. Steven J. Keillor. St. Paul: Minnesota Historical Society Press, 2001.

Newspapers

Addison Advertiser
Agitator (Wellsboro, Pa.)
Buffalo Morning Express
Cazenovia Republican
Christian Banner (Fredericksburg, Va.)
Civil War Courier
Corning Journal
Cortland County Republican
Cortland Gazette and Banner
Cortland Observer
Cortland Republican Banner
Daily National Intelligencer (Washington, D.C.)
Elmira Daily Advertiser
Elmira Weekly Advertiser and Chemung County Republican
Elmira Weekly Gazette
Erie Weekly Gazette (Pa.)

Hornellsville Weekly Tribune
Jefferson County News
Kingston Argus
National Tribune (Washington, D.C.)
New York Herald
New York Times
New York Tribune
Owego Gazette
Philadelphia Inquirer
Rochester Daily Democrat and American
Rochester Daily Union and Advertiser
Steuben Farmers' Advocate
Syracuse Daily Journal
Syracuse Daily Standard
Waverly Advocate

Index